**Cambridge Studies in Social and Emotional Development**



# Comparisons in Human Development

# Comparisons in Human Development

## Understanding Time and Context

Edited by

JONATHAN TUDGE
*University of North Carolina at Greensboro*

MICHAEL J. SHANAHAN
*Pennsylvania State University*

JAAN VALSINER
*University of North Carolina at Chapel Hill*

Published by the Press Syndicate of the University of Cambridge
The Pitt Building, Trumpington Street, Cambridge CB2 1RP
40 West 20th Street, New York, NY 10011-4211, USA
10 Stamford Road, Oakleigh, Melbourne 3166, Australia



First published 1997

Printed in the United States of America

*Library of Congress Cataloging-in-Publication Data*

Comparisons in human development: understanding time and context / edited by Jonathan Tudge, Michael J. Shanahan, Jaan Valsiner.
p. cm. – (Cambridge studies in social and emotional development)

Includes bibliographical references.

ISBN 0-521-48202-X (hc)

1. Developmental psychology. 2. Developmental psychology – Cross-cultural studies. 3. Developmental psychology – Longitudinal studies. I. Tudge, Jonathan. II. Shanahan, Michael J. III. Valsiner, Jaan. IV. Series.
BF713.5C66 1997
155 – dc20

96-12287
CIP

A catalog record for this book is available from the British Library.

ISBN 0-521-48202-X hardback

# Contents

# Contributors

**Angela Branco**
Institute of Psychology
University of Brasilia
70910.900 Brasilia
Brasil

**Patricia A. Clubb**
Department of Psychology
CB 3270 Davie Hall
University of North Carolina
Chapel Hill, NC 27599

**William A. Corsaro**
Department of Sociology
Ballantine Hall 744
University of Indiana
Bloomington, IN 47405-6628

**Agnes E. Dodds**
Center for the Study of Higher Education
University of Melbourne
Parkville, VIC 3052
Australia

**Glen H. Elder, Jr.**
Carolina Population Center
CB 8120, University Square East
University of North Carolina
Chapel Hill, NC 27599

**Gilbert Gottlieb**
Center for Developmental Science
University of North Carolina
Chapel Hill, NC 27599-8115

**Jacquelyn T. Gray**
EduTech Institute
Georgia Institute of Technology
Atlanta, GA 30332-0280

**Diane M. Hogan**
The Children's Centre
University of Dublin, Trinity College
Dublin 2
Ireland

**Dorothy C. Holland**
Department of Anthropology
CB 3115, 301 Alumni Building
University of North Carolina
Chapel Hill, NC 27599

**Hideo Kojima**
School of Education
Nagoya University
Chijusa-Ku
Nagoya 464-01
Japan

**Beth Kurtz-Costes**
Department of Psychology
CB 3270 Davie Hall
University of North Carolina
Chapel Hill, NC 27599

**Jeanette A. Lawrence**
Department of Psychology
University of Melbourne
Parkville, VIC 3052
Australia

**Rona McCall**
Department of Psychology
CB 3270 Davie Hall
University of North Carolina
Chapel Hill, NC 27599

**Debra Mekos**
Department of Maternal and Child Health
Johns Hopkins University
624 N. Broadway
Baltimore, MD 21205

**Sarah E. Putnam**
Department of Human Development and Family Studies
155 Stone Building
University of North Carolina
Greensboro, NC 27412-5001

**Wolfgang Schneider**
Department of Psychology
University of Würzburg
Wittelsbacherplatz 1
D-8700 Würzburg
97074 Germany

**Michael J. Shanahan**
Department of Human Development and Family Studies
Pennsylvania State University
110 Henderson Building South
University Park, PA 16802

**Debra G. Skinner**
Frank Porter Graham Child Development Center
CB 8180
University of North Carolina
Chapel Hill, NC 27599-8180

**Jonathan Tudge**
Department of Human Development and Family Studies
155 Stone Building
University of North Carolina
Greensboro, NC 27412-5001

**Jaan Valsiner**
Department of Psychology
CB 3270 Davie Hall
University of North Carolina
Chapel Hill, NC 27599

**Lucien T. Winegar**
Department of Psychology
Randolph-Macon College
Ashland, VA 23005

**Paul A. Winterhoff**
Department of Human Environmental Sciences
Meredith College
3800 Hillsborough St.
Raleigh, NC 27607

**James Youniss**
Life Cycle Institute
Catholic University of America
Washington, DC 20064

# Comparisons in Human Development: To Begin a Conversation

*Jonathan Tudge, Michael J. Shanahan, and Jaan Valsiner*

## Studying Comparisons and Development

Comparisons are perhaps the fundamental heuristic tool with which developmentalists generate knowledge. Since the sine qua non of developmental phenomena is the passing of time, developmental knowledge will always involve comparisons across time points. However, given the multiple time frames that often characterize this change, temporal comparisons can be complex. How do patterns of change over ontogenetic time relate to patterns of change over historical time, and how do both relate to microgenetic processes of change? Moreover, many developmentalists adhere to context-sensitive models of development, which imply comparisons through both time and place. What makes for an appropriate comparison group, particularly if groups are chosen from different ages, historical periods, or cultures? And so we begin with the basic premise that comparisons are fundamental but complex tools for understanding development.

Given their foundational role and the multitude of issues that complicate their use, comparisons have been surprisingly absent from developmental discourse. The purpose of this volume is to initiate discussions about how comparisons are and should be used to produce knowledge about development. We choose to focus on their conceptualization, although comparisons lie at the heart of methodological issues as well. These latter issues include historically based (Porter, 1986) and statistical (Rubin, 1974) debates about inference, as well as advanced treatments of methods appropriate for the analysis of change and context (Bryk & Raudenbush, 1991; Collins & Horn, 1991).

Of course, the distinction between methods and concepts is

permeable. As Gigerenzer (1991) has forcefully argued, the ubiquitous analysis of variance strategy has enabled and constrained the concepts that psychology uses. This is equally true of the concepts that we use to study development. Thus, conceptual concerns about comparisons frequently are influenced by methodological orientations. For example, should individuals unique within groups be thought of as a source of "error variance" or "outliers" and dropped from analyses? Or are they worthy of explanation? These are the types of questions that the authors of this volume address.

The contributors to the volume have all been or are currently associated with the Carolina Consortium on Human Development, an interdisciplinary group of scholars drawn primarily from the University of North Carolina at Chapel Hill, Duke University, and the University of North Carolina at Greensboro. Its members – including scholars from departments of psychology, sociology, anthropology, education, psychiatry, and human development and family studies – have been involved in weekly seminar meetings since 1987. This volume grew out of the seminar series that took place in the spring of 1993.

Members of the Consortium have come to share some basic perspectives about developmental science; the study of development must be concerned with processes that operate over time and that are inextricably regulated by their physical, biological, social, and cultural contexts. Development is thus understood in systemic terms, with multidirectional influences that cross levels of analysis, including the cellular, the individual, the family, the ecological, the cultural, and the historical. Two questions need to be raised. First, given the richness of this perspective, how are we, as scholars interested in development, to deal effectively with issues of comparisons? Second, how are we, as authors, to ensure that our views are not simply parochial, reflecting our particular orientation? The volume as a whole reflects our answer to the first question. And to balance what might otherwise be a series of parochial statements, we have asked a number of scholars to serve as commentators. Their task is to locate our efforts in a broader context of developmental science. As is true of the Consortium itself, the commentators come from a variety of disciplinary (sociology, psychology, and education) and societal (the United States, Japan, Brazil, and Australia) backgrounds.

## *Comparisons in a Multilevel Framework*

The systemic approach to development is evident in all of the chapters, although it is addressed most explicitly by Winegar, by Shanahan, Valsiner, and Gottlieb, and by Tudge, Gray, and Hogan, who argue for an approach to developmental science that emphasizes the interrelations between different levels of a system. Each of these chapters is set at the metatheoretical and theoretical levels, but the necessity of seeing development in systemic terms is as evident in the more paradigmatic and empirical chapters – for example, those by Holland and Skinner on Tij dances in Nepal, by Kurtz-Costes, McCall, and Schneider on cultural and sociopolitical changes in Germany, and by Shanahan and Elder on historical change and individual adaptation in the United States.

A systemic approach, as Shanahan, Valsiner and Gottlieb, point out, requires that comparisons cross traditionally isolated levels of analysis. This is exemplified by Mekos and Clubb in their call for combining quantitative and qualitative analyses and by Shanahan and Elder, who argue that comparisons crossing historical, structural, family, and individual levels are necessary to make sense of trajectories across the life course. Such multilevel analyses require stepping beyond the confines of any one discipline, a position illustrated by Tudge and Putnam as they draw from sociology, psychology, and cultural anthropology to discuss ways in which children acquire culture.

## *Processes of Development and the Comparisons They Imply*

Many of the authors provide data that deal explicitly with change over time, whether considered at the level of history, ontogeny, microgenesis, or a combination thereof. Three chapters are clearly set in historical time, with a focus on development in times of war or economic hardship (Shanahan & Elder), on the process of sociopolitical change in Germany following reunification (Kurtz-Costes et al.), and at the end of one-party rule in Nepal (Holland & Skinner). Mekos and Clubb point to the advantages of taking both an ontogenetic and microgenetic approach to development, and Winterhoff discusses the course of friendship formation over the course of the first year of formal school. Tudge and Putnam discuss process at the most microgenetic level, identifying mechanisms by which social class is related to children's self-directedness.

## Organization of the Volume

The volume is organized into four parts. The first includes essays on the theory of comparisons. The second focuses on methodology and methods, as viewed from the perspectives of life course study (Shanahan & Elder), developmental psychology (Mekos & Clubb), and cross-cultural psychology (Kurtz-Costes et al.). The third part offers empirical examples of comparative strategies, dealing with development of women in a rural community in Nepal (Holland & Skinner), the development of friendship relations in school in the United States (Winterhoff), and engagement in lessons among U.S. preschoolers (Tudge & Putnam). The fourth consists of commentaries on earlier chapters.

### *Part One: Metatheoretical Approaches to Developmental Comparisons*

Part One includes three essays on the metatheory of comparisons in developmental science. Winegar's chapter argues for an integrative approach to "research," which encompasses metatheory, theory, methodology, and methods. He argues that all scientists (social as well as natural) must state their theoretical assumptions, the ways in which their theory of choice fits the phenomena under study, and the appropriateness of their methods. Comparative strategies should take place at all levels of the research enterprise, although common practice devotes most resources to comparisons at the levels of method and data.

In her commentary, Jeanette Lawrence (Chapter 10) goes one step beyond Winegar, placing the latter's concerns in contemporary sociocultural context. She points to the pressures that currently serve to shape our field in ways that run counter to Winegar's goal. According to her analysis, scholars (particularly, though by no means exclusively, those entering the field) concern themselves primarily with methods and data, rather than with securing coherent linkages between metatheory, theory, methods, and data. The "social dimensions of . . . science," particularly in North American universities, include demands for productivity and grantsmanship if tenure is to be attained, and these demands are not easily met by the type of multilevel research for which Winegar has made a cogent argument.

The chapter by Shanahan, Valsiner and Gottlieb takes a metatheoretical approach to focus on conceptual commonalities among psychobiologists, psychologists, and sociologists studying development. As such, their effort represents comparative work at the level of metatheory. From their perspective, a multidisciplinary developmental science is most likely to advance if it crosses the boundaries of traditionally isolated disciplines. The authors suggest that five propositions are common to developmental science in dealing with structure, time, change, and development, and they use these propositions to illustrate similarities in the perspectives of developmentally oriented psychobiologists, psychologists, and sociologists. The benefits that derive from this approach are acknowledged by Lawrence and Dodds in their commentary (Chapter 11), but they add a novel balance to calls for interdisciplinary research by identifying its potential drawbacks.

The chapter by Tudge, Gray, and Hogan focuses on two theories that have been labeled *ecological*, a comparative effort at the level of theory. Gibson's and Bronfenbrenner's frameworks are first placed in the broader context of the development of ecological perspectives in the field of psychology. As Tudge and his coauthors point out, these perspectives, while not new in psychology, have never been a part of the mainstream, dominated by the behaviorist tradition and its most recent information-processing reincarnation. Much of this chapter is devoted to an explication of each theory to show that despite striking differences on the surface, the two theories have much in common.

Branco argues in her commentary (Chapter 12) that the differences between them are more important than the fact that both are based on the ecological position. However, just as is true of many minority positions (e.g., a political fringe group), differences in ideology that may be deemed insignificant by those from different ideological perspectives are viewed as critical by proponents. Despite obvious differences in analytical focus, both Gibson and Bronfenbrenner have played a major role in the struggle to make mainstream psychology more open to transactional, dialectical, or interactional links between developing individuals and the environments that surround them.

*Part Two: Paradigmatic Statements*

The next three chapters, by Shanahan and Elder, by Mekos and Clubb, and by Kurtz-Kostes, McCall, and Schneider, focus on comparisons in three different fields within developmental science – sociology, developmental psychology, and cross-cultural psychology. The authors discuss how comparisons have been used in these disciplines, and outline the strengths and limitations of these strategies.

As developmentally oriented sociologists, Shanahan and Elder deal with the relations between broad historical changes and the ways in which individuals adapt to those changes. They argue that a comparative strategy well-suited to the study of such adaptations is a "nested comparisons" approach. Linking the nested comparisons strategy with quasi-experimental research designs, they indicate how such comparisons allow researchers to explain and understand the complex relations between historical events (such as World War II and the Great Depression) and individual functioning. They draw attention to historical events, family dynamics, and individual characteristics and show that this interweaving of comparisons is necessary to make sense of life-course trajectories.

In his commentary, Hideo Kojima (Chapter 13) notes the importance of *not* treating individuals who do not fit the typical pattern as "outliers" but, rather, seeing their situation as an explicable phenomenon and tracing the particular trajectories that led to outlier status. While Kojima applauds this analytic strategy, he also offers alternative ways of thinking about historical change and individual development.

The approach used by Mekos and Clubb is in many ways similar to that of Shanahan and Elder, although it focuses on comparisons in developmental psychology. The central thesis of these authors is that while comparisons are necessary, the types of comparisons typically employed by developmental psychologists (based on such factors as race, gender, or age group) are what Bronfenbrenner (1988) terms "social address models." As such, they are incapable of elucidating the mechanisms that explain group differences.

However, Mekos and Clubb argue that group comparisons should not be eschewed. First, membership in a group (whether defined by gender, age, or developmental status) often serves to constrain and enable developmental pathways; groups are relevant to the structuring of developmental pathways. Second, group comparisons are starting points, as one begins to lay bare critical developmental processes. In particular, Mekos and Clubb demonstrate the effectiveness of combining group comparisons with development over time and, like Shanahan and Elder, the gains of combining quantitative and qualitative comparative strategies.

Kurtz-Costes, McCall, and Schneider are interested in cross-cultural issues and their relevance for adjustments to a new culture, or acculturation. Like Mekos and Clubb, they focus both on the difficulties associated with making comparisons and on ways of conducting research that address these problems. Comparisons lie at the heart of cross-cultural study, and yet, as the authors point out, far too many cultural comparisons are prone to one of five theoretical or methodological problems: the use of "culture" as a "social address"; ethnocentrism; the use of research materials and the selection of samples that are not adequately comparable; and an insufficent concern for both similarities and differences across cultural groups. Kurtz-Costes and her colleagues use their analysis of these comparative problems to highlight research in the area of acculturation, to discuss a model of acculturation, and to introduce a longitudinal study of acculturation in Germany.

As Corsaro points out in his commentary (Chapter 14), the longitudinal study by Kurtz-Costes and colleagues of children and their parents from four different groups in East and West Germany will allow them to set the processes of acculturation in a grounded historical context. Corsaro notes that large-scale quantitative longitudinal studies of acculturation are surprisingly rare. However, despite their level of sophistication, these studies need to be augmented with qualitative ethnographic work in order to understand precisely what is happening to immigrants.

## *Part Three: Comparisons at the Level of Data*

The chapters in Part Three move from discussions of the potential pitfalls of comparative research and focus primarily on specific comparative studies. Chapter 7 by Holland and Skinner provides an account of women's identity in the process of formation and expression in songs sung at the Tij festival in rural Nepal. The strength of this chapter can be found in the authors' study of historical events (the decline of the one-party system in Nepal) in conjunction with individual development. Holland and Skinner also examine how different trajectories of development are linked both to individual characteristics and to sociocultural changes.

This point is discussed by Kojima (Chapter 13), who extends this comparative framework to historical change in Japan. Kojima uses the expression "Songs change with the times, and the times change with songs" to illustrate the ways in which popular songs often reflect prevailing social conditions while also allowing the possibility that what is being sung about may foreshadow, or even effect, change.

Youniss, in his commentary (Chapter 15), reflects on the approach to identity taken by Holland and Skinner – an approach linking individual, social, historical, and cultural forces that is quite at variance with the individualistic, stage-related stance taken by most child psychologists. Like Kojima, Youniss draws connections with historical processes of change, with particular reference to the history of women in the United States a century or more ago. He also sets Holland and Skinner's work in the context of recent work in self, narratives, and political change.

Winterhoff's chapter is concerned with children's friendships, including cross-cultural and within-group comparisons and the heterogeneity of developmental pathways. At the conceptual level he deals with friendships among young children in both agrarian and technocratic societies, examining the ways in which settings, possible partners, and adult conceptions of friendship help determine the development of friendship. Winterhoff provides data from 5- and 6-year-olds in two kindergarten classes to illustrate his more general points.

As Corsaro points out in his commentary (Chapter 14), the strength of Winterhoff's longitudinal analysis lies in its ability to show the "developmental fluidity" of friendships and how they are supported or constrained by the setting (teachers and classrooms). Drawing a contrast with traditional research in developmental psychology, with its use of positivist methodology and emphasis on outcomes, Corsaro highlights Winterhoff's interpretive design and concern with process.

The chapter by Tudge and Putnam draws on psychology, sociology, and cultural anthropology. The authors argue, like other contributors to this volume (particularly Shanahan, Valsiner, & Gottlieb), that understanding developmental phenomena involves comparisons across levels of analysis. They focus on aspects of the developing child (gender and the extent to which the children initiate activities), the processes of interaction with partners in their activities, and aspects of the context (children from different social classes, at home and in day care). Their data deal with the different types of lessons that children become involved in, both under their own instigation and from other people.

Corsaro, in his commentary (Chapter 14), draws attention to the way in which these data support the work of the sociologist Melvin Kohn and his colleagues (1977; Kohn & Slomszynski, 1990). Whereas Kohn showed that parents' child-rearing beliefs are partly a function of their position in the social stratification system, Tudge and Putnam demonstrate that parents and children behave in ways quite consistent with these beliefs. As Youniss points out (Chapter 15), approaches to child rearing need to focus more on the ways in which children participate in communication and interaction patterns in coming to acquire culture – and, in the process, simultaneously construct (or "reproduce" in Corsaro's terms) culture.

## Conclusion

We subtitle this introductory chapter "To Begin a Conversation" to convey our belief that discussion of the issues raised in this volume is essential if we are to increase our understanding of developmental processes. Models of development have become increasingly complex, in recognition of the systemic and time-dependent nature of development (Bronfenbrenner, 1989; Gottlieb, in press; Lerner, 1991). Discussions of, and collaborative conceptualization and research on, the nature of development have to take place between historians, cultural anthropologists, sociologists, psychologists, biologists, and scholars located in departments of education and human and family development (e.g., Elder, Modell, & Parke, 1993). Integration that cuts across disciplinary boundaries is essential in the process of coming to a better understanding of development.

Similarly, as Winegar argues in his chapter, integration across all levels of "research" from metatheory to data analysis is also essential if we are to avoid the conceptual and methodological traps to which our field has been prone. This integration also requires discussions between those primarily involved in metatheoretical and theoretical issues and those interested more in methodological and statistical approaches.

The study of comparisons lies at the heart of such discussions. How can we choose appropriate comparison groups when faced with variations of culture, context, temperament, and biology that are developing simultaneously over historical, ontogenetic, and microgenetic time? Each of the following chapters raises questions about these issues. We hope that they contribute to a conversation about comparative strategies in the emerging field of developmental science.

## References

Bronfenbrenner, U. (1988). Interacting systems in human development. Research paradigms: Present and future. In N. Bolger, A. Caspi, G. Bowney, & M. Moorehouse (Eds.), *Persons in context: Developmental processes* (pp. 25–49). Cambridge University Press.

(1989). Ecological systems theory. In R. Vasta (Ed.), *Annals of child development* (Vol. 6, pp. 187–249). Greenwich, CT: JAI Press.

Bryk, A., & Raudenbush, S. (1991). *Hierarchical linear models: Applications and data analysis*. Newbury Park CA: Sage.

Collins, L. M., & Horn, J. L. (Eds.). (1991). *Best methods for the analysis of change*. Washington, DC: American Psychological Association.

Elder, G. H., Jr., Modell, J., & Parke, R. D. (1993). *Children in time and place: Developmental and historical insights*. Cambridge University Press.

Gigerenzer, G. (1991). From tools to theories: A heuristic discovery in cognitive science. *Psychological Review*, *98*, 254–267.

Gottlieb, G. (in press). Contemporary theory in developmental psychobiology. In B. Cairns & G. H. Elder Jr. (Eds.), *Developmental science*. Cambridge University Press.

Kohn, M. L. (1977). *Class and conformity: A study in values* (2nd ed.). Chicago: University of Chicago Press.

Kohn, M. L., & Slomszynski, K. M. (1990). *Social structure and self-direction: A comparative analysis of the United States and Poland*. Oxford: Basil Blackwell.

Lerner, R. M. (1991). Changing organism–context relations as the basic process of development: A developmental contextual perspective. *Developmental Psychology*, *27*, 27–32.

Porter, T. M. (1986). *The rise of statistical thinking: 1820–1990*. Princeton, NJ: Princeton University Press.

Rubin, D. B. (1974). Estimating causal effects of treatments in randomized and nonrandomized studies, *Journal of Educational Psychology*, *66*, 688–701.

# PART ONE

# Metatheoretical Approaches to Developmental Comparisons

# 1 Developmental Research and Comparative Perspectives: Applications to Developmental Science

*Lucien T. Winegar*

The goal of this volume is to report recent work in an emerging discipline that refers to itself as *developmental science.* It is the position of most practitioners identifying themselves with this discipline that development must be conceptualized as processes of structural or organizational change, particularly such change as leads to emergence of novelty. Development so defined is not limited to a process that occurs only for human individuals; many other entities can be considered as undergoing development. Based on these fundamental assumptions, this volume devotes its attention to the more specific consideration of the role and value of comparative perspectives in developmental science.

This chapter contributes to this goal by providing a metatheoretical framework for thinking about scientific practice that may prove useful for developmental science generally and its consideration of comparative perspectives specifically. Although much of the content of this chapter concerns areas that traditionally have been considered the purview of philosophy, particularly philosophy of science, I write it as a person trained in human development. My perspective is related to my general acceptance of co-constructive metatheory, particularly as it is expressed in cultural-historical or sociogenetic theories of development. The primary purpose of my presentation and discussion of this particular framework is to contribute to making whatever metatheoretical positions are adopted

I would like to thank Renée J. Cardone for her constructive, "postmodern" comments on several drafts of this chapter and for her general support and encouragement during its preparation. I also thank the organizers and participants of the Carolina Consortium on Human Development for their provision of a forum for the discussion of ideas such as those presented in this chapter, and the editors of this volume for their comments on an earlier draft.

by developmental scientists the result of conscious, reflective processes, the outcome of which are acknowledged clearly. It is my position that any scientific practice will be more successful if its practitioners direct at least some of their energy toward the explicit consideration of metatheory, rather than letting such assumptions remain solely implicit as the unreflective consequences of particular practices. Arguing for the acceptance by developmental science of the specific metatheory discussed here is only a secondary goal of this chapter. Even if the specific framework presented here is rejected, this chapter will have realized its primary goal if proposing this particular perspective generates active consideration of the metatheoretical assumptions of developmental science.

This chapter has two sections. The first presents an overview of the metatheoretical framework and discusses the general value of this framework using the case of developmental science as a specific illustration. The second section applies this framework specifically to applications of comparative perspectives within developmental science. This section concludes by anticipating some of the practical implications for developmental science of adopting the framework as previously described and indicates at which points of integration the process of developmental research seems most likely to encounter conceptual or practical difficulties. By the nature of this discussion, this last section also functions as the conclusion of this chapter.

## Return to Research

### *Definition of Research*

Currently in most scientific disciplines, the term *research* is applied in a quite restricted sense.[1] In both the formal and informal conversations of scientists, *research* usually is used synonymously with the term *empirical investigation*. So, for example, when practitioners of the physical, natural, or social sciences are asked about their research, they tend to respond in terms of the data collection activity most recently completed or currently underway. This tendency to consider research as empirical investigation seems built in even at the earliest stages of the socialization process of budding scientists; undergraduate students (and I expect even elementary school students) in the sciences use the term *research* to mean empirical investigation. Most undergraduate and graduate courses in research methods, at least as currently taught in North America, serve to reinforce this usage. Although such courses often pay lip service to a "research" cycle that includes mention of theory and, in some courses, metatheory, the majority of the training and education in these courses is directed toward various procedures for data collection and analysis.

The prevalent application of the term *research* to refer almost exclusively to empirical investigation might be taken by some to be a trivial observation. This usage could be seen as an inadvertent underextention of the term, as merely social convention, or as meaningless. Such interpretations of the established usage of the term *research* in our scientific discourse serve to underscore how prevalent and automatic is this particular application of the term. In so doing, these interpretations themselves provide further evidence for a claim that the way we talk about and refer to science and its activity has important implications for the way in which scientific practice actually is conducted.

This alternative position claims that the language we use to describe and reference an activity has important implications for the way we conduct this activity. In the specific case of science, some support for this position can be found by examining the way in which *research* is used in other disciplines. In the humanities, particularly philosophy and literature, the term *research* is used to refer to a scholarly activity more comprehensively construed. Empirical investigation, the gathering of information from the world, is an important part of this activity. However, in these disciplines, the gathering of information from the world is viewed as only a small part, and often the least intellectual part, of research. Making sense of this gathered information, integrating it into a larger conceptual picture, and considering the implications of such sense making and integration are all seen as integral parts of research. Scholars in these disciplines view and refer to their work as research, but they do not apply this term solely or even primarily to data collection.

What can we learn by comparing our activity with that of our colleagues in other disciplines? At a minimum we can recognize that it is possible to construe research in ways other than the one currently applied in our own science. Taking this one step further, we might consider whether our own science would benefit from an intentionally broadened conception of the term *research.*

I suggest, then, that developmental science and other scientific practices would benefit from the term *research* not being applied as if it represented only empirical investigation. Research, in our language and professional activity, could then include not only work that gathers, analyzes, and interprets information from the world; it would be extended to include explicitly work that considers the nature of the phenomena of interest and the nature of theories appropriate for an understanding of such phenomena. Research also would include work that attempts to provide more adequate description of and explanation for phenomena, particularly explanatory work that can be translated into investigative opportunities. Research, then, would refer to work that supports the construction of information-gathering procedures, particularly the construction of these procedures through the explicit consideration of relations between description/explanation and phenomena.

To summarize, the term *research* can be reconceptualized to include work addressing questions at any level of scientific practice that may be relevant to successful scientific practice. Altering the way in which we use language to refer to our scientific practice acknowledges that there are relevant questions to be addressed at each level, and that addressing all of these questions is a valued, integral part of our scientific practice. Thus, it need not be the case that scientific work of one kind is preferred or rewarded more than work of another, even if this preference in indicated by nuance in our linguistic conventions.

## *Levels of Research*

As a starting point, I suggest that the levels of research in need of our attention might include metatheory, theory, methodology, method, data, and phenomenon. Each level of research serves a particular, primary function and has its own mode of discourse, as well as its own conventional rules of practice. One summary of the function, mode of discourse, and rules of practice of each level of research is presented in Table 1.1.

**Metatheory.** Metatheory is theory about theory. Metatheoretical work considers explicitly the nature of phenomena of interest, and this consideration leads to decisions about what theories may be appropriate for further understanding of that phenomena. These decisions provide guiding assumptions that direct further work

Table 1.1. *Levels of Research*

| Level of Research | Function | Mode of Discourse | Rules of Practice |
|---|---|---|---|
| Metatheory | Provide organizing principles for work at all levels | Language of nature of phenomenon and so nature of theories for understanding such a phenomenon<br>Usually stated as beliefs, assumptions, guiding principles | Aesthetics |
| Theory | Provide explanations for phenomenon that, through methodology, should translate as investigative opportunities | Language of descriptive and explanatory concepts and their relations<br>Usually stated as constructs and their relations | Internal consistency |
| Methodology | Provide for construction of method through explicit consideration of relations between theory and phenomenon | Language of theory–phenomenon relations | Elegance and faithfulness of articulation between theory and phenomenon |
| Method | Provide for collection of data | Language of procedure | Validity |
| Data | Provide representation of phenomenon | Language of observation<br>Often stated as recording and measurement | Reliability |
| Phenomenon | Provide object of study | Language of presumed reality<br>May be stated as veridicality | Domain-relevant common sense |

toward some varieties of theories and away from other varieties.[2] For example, if development is the phenomenon of interest then metatheoretical decisions about the nature of this phenomenon will result in some categories of theories being viewed as more likely to explain development than other theories. Thus, if development is defined as a process of structural change (a metatheoretical decision), then theories that are directed at structural reorganization (e.g., Piaget's theory of cognitive development, Vygotsky's theory of internalization of higher mental functions) may be included in the varieties of theory that might account for reorganization. Conversely, theories that are not directed at structural reorganization, but rather account for change by processes resembling accretion (e.g., Skinner's theory of verbal behavior) or by processes of unfolding (e.g., Chomsky's theory of language maturation), may not be included. As illustrated by this example, one outcome of metatheoretical work is the classification of some theories as possible candidates for successful description or explanation of phenomena of interest. This category of theories would include those that are similar along metatheoretically defined relevant dimensions (e.g., that include consideration of structural reorganization). Either as the result of this enterprise or as part of a separate undertaking, another outcome of metatheoretical work is the classification of some theories as unlikely candidates for successful description or explanation. This classification includes theories that are at variance with the metatheoretically defined relevant dimension (e.g., that do not include consideration of structural reorganization) and so are classified as less likely candidates for application to the phenomena.

Thus, one function of metatheory is to provide fundamental assumptions and organizing principles that canalize work at the theoretical level. Metatheory can best fulfill this function if its guiding assumptions are made explicit. (See Shanahan, Gottlieb, & Valsiner, Chapter 2, this volume, for an example of making metatheory explicit.) All too often, empirical investigation is conducted without explicit consideration of the metatheoretical assumptions that guide it. Such is the case in many psychological studies for which data are collected that indicate a number of differences between groups of different ages or genders, and yet little or no consideration is given to the processes by which these differences arise or to the meaning of these differences for the members of these groups or those around them. Although such practice may lead to the generation of a substantial amount of data, the implications of these data are difficult to ascertain without a grounded reference to the basic principles guiding its collection. (However, see Mekos & Clubb, Chapter 5, this volume, for an apparently alternative perspective.) Metatheory can be implied by particular decisions at other levels of research, but inferring metatheory in this manner may be more susceptible to post hoc salvaging and the loss of coherence that this entails. Thus, investigators are compelled to explain the differences between groups that they may find, but, in not having integrated such explanation into their investigation from the beginning, these explanations are often speculative and may endure only until the next study.

The mode of discourse of metatheory is the language of the nature of phenomena. This discourse may include specifically the language of the nature of theories appropriate for understanding such phenomena. This is most often expressed in the language of beliefs, assumptions, and basic principles. Although many believe that metatheory functions according to rules of practice of philosophy, I suggest that judgments of the soundness of metatheory most often are made by the application of aesthetics. That is, we accept metatheoretical assumptions because they "fit" with who we are as researchers and persons. A variety of influences and their combination may contribute to whether particular metatheoretical assumptions are judged as being a good fit. Such judgments may arise from fundamental beliefs (e.g., a preference for individualism vs. collectivism), from a person's or discipline's worldview (e.g., preference for contextualism vs. mechanism), or from a researcher's or practice's standards of intellectual comportment (e.g., preference for parsimony or consistency). The variety of possible influences on judgments of metatheory provides additional strength to the argument that regardless of the bases for judgments of its appropriateness, metatheory is best if explicit.

**Theory.** Theory is coherent description and explanation that translates as investigative opportunities through the application of methodology. One's choice of theory is constrained, and thus empowered, by metatheoretical decisions about what categories of theory are most appropriate given the phenomena of interest and the relevant questions about these phenomena. Theoretical work attempts to provide adequate description and explanation of phenomena through iterative processes of accouting for empirical data. As one level of operation in this process, theory functions to provide explanations for data – data we believe to be reflective of phenomena of interest.

The language of theory is concepts, including descriptive and explanatory constructs and relations between them. (See Tudge, Gray, & Hogan, Chapter 3, this volume, for an example of the language of theory.) Although theory need not be oriented toward prediction, it must function as more than a black box or magical phrase. That is, interpretive description and explanation are not achieved by simple reference to a theoretical construct or even by reference to relations between theoretical constructs; those constructs themselves need adequate description and development. For example, explanation of children's development is not achieved simply through application of the term *internalization* unless this application makes use of adequate description of the process of internalization. Although an elaborated version of this description need not accompany each application of the term, the availability of such description makes it possible for this term to carry descriptive or explanatory value.

The rule of practice most often applied to theory is that of internal consistency. Thus, theory can be judged by rules of coherence applied to both the components of theory and the theory as a whole. Nonetheless, theory can often tolerate some degree of inconsistency, particularly if the inconsistency is perceived as minor and so the descriptive or explanatory power of the theory is judged as surviving.

**Methodology.** The next level of research to be considered is methodology. Like the term *research*, the term *methodology* often is used currently in a limited sense such that both *methodology* and *method* are applied to data collection procedures. Occasionally, the term *methodology* is reserved for reference to a set of data collection procedures that are thought of as related along some dimension. In such cases, *methodology* functions as a collective term for methods.

Historically, however, the practice of collecting data as part of a particular study was considered to be a separate activity from the construction of method more generally. Reflecting this distinction, these two activities were referred to as method and methodology, respectively (Danziger, 1988). For example, the observational procedures used to collect data in a study of children's peer relations in preschool (exemplified in Winterhoff, Chapter 8, this volume) would be referred to as method. In contrast, considering what categories of data collection procedures (or what categories of observational procedures) would be most effective for the study of children's peer relations would be referred to as methodology. This latter activity would include a consideration of the nature of the phenomena (e.g., children's peer relations) and a consideration of the categories of theory appropriate for description of this phenomenon (e.g., theories focusing on individual traits versus those focusing on interactional patterns), in order to delimit the categories of data collection procedures that seem appropriate for the further study of the phenomena of interest.

Although presented here as a separate level of research, the preceding description suggests that methodology alternatively may be thought of as a particular application of metatheory. That is, methodology operates within metatheoretical assumptions about both the phenomenon of interest and the nature of theories appropriate to the study of such a phenomenon. This enables the construction of method that potentially is useful under particular metatheoretical assumptions. Whether considered as an application of metatheory or as a separate level of research, methodology is a necessary and often underemphasized component of research practice. Just as returning to a broader definition of research may have benefit for our current enterprise, so too the return to a different definition of methodology may realize similar benefits.

According to this broad definition, methodology is the construction of empirical investigation procedures utilizing explicit consideration of relations between theory and phenomenon. Thus, methodology simultaneously constructs direct connections between theory and method, on the one hand, and connections between method and phenomenon, on the other. Methodology functions to enable the construction and development of particular investigative methods by considering relations between theory and phenomenon. Given this function of methodology, it follows that data can be connected to phenomena only through an application of metatheoretically constrained theory to methodology. The language of methodology is that of theory–phenomenon relations and includes the implication of these relations for methods of empirical investigation. Rules of practice of methodology include faithfulness of articulation between theory and phenomenon and elegance in translating theory–phenomenon relations into a particular investigative method.

**Method.** Although discussed earlier in comparison to methodology, a brief, separate consideration of the function, mode of discourse, and rules of practice of method is in order. Method is the investigative procedures of particular empirical investigations. Method functions to provide for collection of data. The quality of the work done at the methodological level strictly limits the degree to which data are linked to theory and are representative of the phenomena of interest. The mode of discourse of method is the language of procedure, and its rules of practice include those of validity. Thus, method provides procedures directed toward gathering relevant observations with the goal of articulating these observations with appropriate theory.

**Data.** Data are one representation of the phenomenon of interest. Just as the map is not the territory, data are not the phenomena. However, some understanding of the possible relationships between the two is necessary if research is to proceed. Data represent phenomena of interest, and they contribute to our understanding only insofar as they provide adequate representation given particular research questions. Thus, the quality of data is dependent on the quality of work done at both a methodological and a method level.

The mode of discourse of data is the language of recording and classification. For qualitative studies, classification often is viewed as a necessary first step toward explanation. In these cases, it may be claimed that the language of data moves beyond categorization to interpretive description that, itself, functions as explanation. In quantitative approaches, classification usually is accomplished by the application of numbers and is viewed as a necessary first step toward statistical analysis. In these cases the language of data may become the language of measurement.

Prior to *data reduction*, the rules of practice applied to data seem most related to rules of observation, particularly those of representativeness or reliability. The rules of practice applied to qualitative studies may include adequate consideration of context. In quantitative studies, precision may be an additional rule of practice. After data reduction, at least in quantitative studies, the rules of practice of data may shift to rules of statistics. Here again, careful methodological work is essential to ensure that accurate representation of phenomena is maintained even though data are subjected to statistical manipulation.

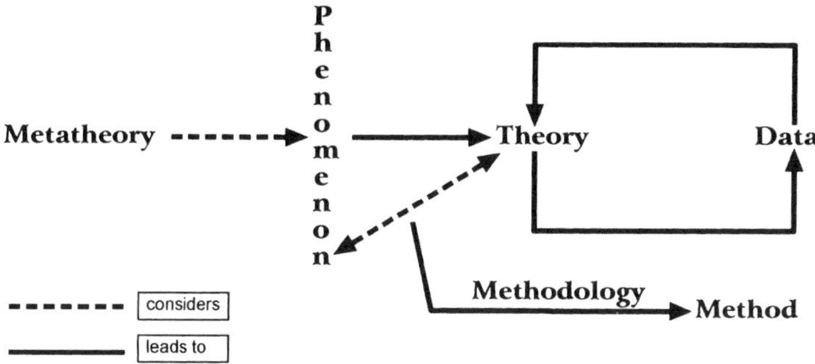


**Figure 1.1.** Relationships between levels of research.

**Phenomenon.** Finally, phenomena are the targets of study. In our research, as in our daily lives, we do not have direct assess to phenomena; we have access only to our representations of phenomena. One's choice of, or preference for, some versus other possible representations is dependent on assumptions about the nature of the phenomena and decisions about how the phenomena are best represented. In research, such assumptions and decisions follow from work at the metatheoretical and methodological levels, respectively. For research, the function of phenomena is to provide objects of study. The mode of discourse of phenomena is the language of presumed reality, although such reality is constructed within metatheoretical constraints. The rules of practice at the level of phenomena might be characterized as domain-relevant common sense, although what is considered common sense and domain relevant is, again, constructed within metatheoretical constraints.

One relationship between levels of research is represented in Figure 1.1. The portion of the figure representing theory–data relations depicts the traditional research cycle. The portion of the figure representing method–data relations depicts the usual, current referent of *research.* According to the currently proposed approach, each of these sections is but a part of a more comprehensive practice of research, as illustrated by the complete figure.

## *Problems of Autonomy and Fusion*

The differences between these levels suggest that a scientist's ability to function with expertise at one level may not translate necessarily into functioning with expertise at another level. Differences between levels also suggest that work at one level may not be able to be taken directly as work at another level unless necessary translation is accomplished successfully.

Given their different functions, modes of discourse, and rules of practice, work in each of these levels of research can and does proceed with some degree of autonomy from the other levels. However, work at one level that is conducted with too high a degree of autonomy may result in this work being isolated from work at other levels, and thus, being irrelevant or, at least, of diminished usefulness. Such a high degree of autonomy might be reflected, for example, in claims by researchers that particular metatheoretical approaches have not yielded adequate investigative procedures, or that all the data collected do not shed further theoretical understanding on the phenomena of interest. Insofar as these claims reflect a lack of articulation or translation between levels of research, they illustrate problems of autonomy.

However, integration between levels of research that is accomplished by inappropriate method or to an extreme degree can result in a fusion between levels such that work at one level is taken as work at another level. As two examples of inappropriate or extreme fusion of research levels, generalizations from data may be presented as if they constitute theory, or more concrete statements of metatheory may be presented as if they constitute theory. A claim that all currently available theories are either higher-level data or lower-level metatheory might reflect this condition. As with problems of autonomy, the problem of fusion also reduces the efficiency of research, although under these latter circumstances the cause may be less clear; because work at one level is perceived as and considered to be work at another level, there may be no apparent reason why research is not proceeding. Nonetheless, understanding of the phenomenon remains less than adequate.

The current state of developmental psychology can be interpreted as reflecting both problems of autonomy and problems of fusion. On the one hand, our metatheory and theory seem to have become more adequate for conceptualizing the phenomena of interest. Elaborations of co-constructive or cultural-historical metatheory or theory seem to many to be more heuristic than many previous approaches for our understanding of processes of human development. However, the emergence of these approaches has left some unsure of how to investigate phenomena from these stances without violating basic metatheoretical or theoretical assumptions that these perspectives entail. To the degree that this is the case, there exists a lack of articulation between metatheory/theory and methodology/method. Thus, the current state of developmental psychology may be viewed as reflecting an autonomy of research levels in which work at one level does not speak directly to work at another level.

On the other hand, empirical investigation currently enjoys such a high status in our discipline that it is the sole activity usually referred to by the term *research*. In yet another linguistic convention reflecting our beliefs about our scientific practices, it has become customary to end empirical articles with some version of the phrase *further research is necessary*. One implication of these statements appears to be that empirical investigation (work at the levels of methods and data) can be expected to function as work at other levels (theory and/or phenomena). However, insofar as levels of research differ in fundamental ways, this can never be the case. Thus, the current state of developmental psychology also may be viewed as reflecting a fusion of research levels in which work at one level is taken as work at other levels.

Given the potential problems of autonomy and fusion, it seems possible that research may proceed more effectively if explicit consideration is given to work at all levels and, most significantly, to work that attempts to integrate across levels. One source that may direct us toward consideration of all levels of research and toward integration across levels might be found in research questions.

### *Questions in Research*

As a general principle of operation, research proceeds most effectively when it is undertaken at all levels and considers integration across levels. Nonetheless, at a particular time in a research program, work at one level may be more necessary for immediate progress than work at other levels. That is, work at all levels is not equally valuable at all times in the development of a research program. For example, as suggested earlier, after a discipline has undergone a reconceptualization of its metatheory or theory, work at the level of methodology may be most immediately necessary to enable subsequent empirical investigation.

The circumstance of one or another level of research being more necessary for progress at a particular time may result in attention being given to this level, perhaps almost to the exclusion of attention to work at other levels. However, this circumstance is not in all ways the same as one level of research being valued as the primary activity of a discipline, as was suggested about the current status of empirical investigation in developmental psychology. These two circumstances differ from each other in an important way. In the latter circumstance it is not clear why a particular level of research enjoys its preferred status. In the case of the current, apparently preferred status of empirical investigation in developmental psychology, perhaps its current status is related to notions of the presumed rationality of science that seem to some to be better reflected in the "objective" activity of data collection rather than in the more subjective activity of constructing theory or methodology. Whatever the reason for this status, it does not seem to be based on an explicit decision that additional data is what is needed at this time to advance the understanding of the discipline.

In contrast, the amount of attention given to any level of research at a particular time is based ideally on explicit consideration of what level of research is most necessary for further progress given the current circumstances of the discipline. This decision follows from careful accounting of the history of the discipline, giving particular attention to recent developments that suggest avenues for further pursuit. Such decisions take into account the past and the present and look forward to the future. I refer to this collection of information that guides decisions about levels of research as the *questions* of research. Thus, the choice of a particular level of research at which to work at a given time is not determined a priori. Rather, such choices are best made through a direct consideration of the particular questions being asked at a given stage of research.

So, given its history, what are the questions of developmental science at the present time? One source for these questions is the definition of development that has been adopted by developmental science: Development is the process of structural (organizational) change,[3] particularly change that leads to emergence of novelty. Each major part of this definition provides a starting point for revealing the most fundamental questions of developmental science.

**Questions of Process.** If development is to be defined as a process, then the research questions of developmental science must include those that attempt to clarify, elaborate, describe, or explain what is the meaning and implication of construing development in this way. Developmental scientists must ask the following metatheoretical questions: What does it mean to say that development is a process? What are the implications of construing development as process, as opposed to construing it in some other manner – for example as age-related change? Other metatheoretical questions related to process include those that consider categories of influence, for example, What are the categories of other phenomena that contribute to or conceivably influence development?

As metatheoretical questions, these queries are about the nature of the phenomenon of interest, development. Answers to them guide theory development: What is the possible range of theories that include these other, relevant phenomena and, so, might describe or explain development as process? What are the defining features of theory that follow from the definition of development as process? What do such theories suggest about possible relations between particular outcomes of development under particular circumstances and the processes related to these outcomes? These questions are about the nature of theory that can be applied to development construed as process. Answers to these questions direct us toward the goal of providing guidelines for the construction of methodology that adheres to the metatheoretical framework as reflected in particular answers to these theoretical questions. The most general methodological question is, what methods of investigation are capable of providing data that enable understanding of developmental processes?

**Questions of Organization.** Defining development as organizational change also requires that the research questions of developmental science include those directed toward the meaning and implication of construing development in this way. At the level of metatheory, developmental scientists must ask: What is meant by organizational change? What are the implications of construing development as organizational change as opposed to construing it in some other manner – for example, as associationistic or accretion models in which development is considered to be more of the same? What are the processes by which organizational change might occur?

Again, because these questions are about the nature of the development, answers to them guide theory development: What is the range of theories that might describe or explain organizational change? What do such theories suggest about possible relations between structural elements and their organization? These questions are about theory that can be applied to development construed as organizational change. Again, answers to these theoretical questions can provide guidelines for the construction of methodology that articulates with the adopted metatheoretical framework. This leads to the methodological question, what methods of investigation are capable of providing data that enable understanding of organizational change?

**Questions of Novelty.** As a final example of the questions of developmental science, defining development as emergence of novelty requires that research questions include those about the meaning and implication of this construal of development. These include metatheoretical questions: What does it mean to say that something is novel? What are the implications of placing emphasis on novelty as opposed to some other outcome – for example, continuity? What might be the processes by which and circumstances under which novelty can emerge? Once again, these questions about the nature of development can be used to guide theory construction: What is the possible range of theories that might describe or explain emergence of novelty? What do such theories suggest about possible relations between the novel condition and the preceding condition out of which it emerged? Finally, answers to these questions can once again guide construction of metatheoretically relevant methodology: What methods of investigation are capable of providing data that enable understanding of emergence of novelty?

Only by actively considering these questions and by beginning to provide currently relevant answers to them can we proceed to empirical investigation that might be of value. Usually, the targets or conclusions of empirical investigation are presented as the questions of a discipline. However, our ability to provide useful answers to these empirical questions hinges largely on our success at providing answers to our discipline's more fundamental questions at all levels of research.

## Developmental Science and Comparative Perspectives

Given the argument that research should be driven by questions, we can now utilize the questions of developmental science outlined in the preceding section to evaluate the potential value for developmental science in considering comparative perspectives. In keeping with the general theme of this volume, it is important to remember that given the questions of interest to developmental science, comparative perspectives of potential value include more than cross-species comparisons. This implication follows directly from metatheoretical assumptions of developmental science and, particularly, its definition of development. Other comparative perspectives of potential value include cross-cultural, cross-historical, and cross-population (i.e., "typical" compared with "atypical"). I will briefly consider three of these perspectives and their potential value in turn. (See Mekos & Clubb, Chapter 5, this volume, for more specific discussion of several comparative perspectives.) I want to be clear that what I present here are general overviews of these perspectives written by an interested outsider. I recognize the cost of oversimplification that my presentation entails, but I believe that it has value for current purposes nonetheless.

### *Cross-species Comparison*

Metatheory and theory of evolution guide much research with nonhuman species. Certainly, at least in its broadest construal, evolutionary metatheory and theory is about process. However, the processes proposed by theories of evolution are not usually ones of organizational change, at least not organizational change across all levels of the phenomenon of interest. Emergence of novelty also may be part of an evolution-based comparative approach. Again, this novelty is not usually presented as emerging from reorganization, at least not reorganization at an individual level. Usually, the process of evolution is described as one by which relative proportions of populations (or other evolutionarily relevant categories, e.g., demes) change through mechanisms of variation and selection. What novelty does arise from this process is considered to be an emergent property of such redistribution. This is not organizational change at the level of individuals and may not be organizational change at the population level, at least by some definitions of organizational change. Moreover, the variation and selection model of evolution may not be compatible with a constructivist model, which often is adopted by developmental science.

There are other evolutionary models that may be more relevant to the questions of developmental science. As one example, Lewontin

(1983) argues that it is not the case that "the life and death and reproduction of an organism are a consequence of the way in which a living being is acted upon by an autonomous environment. Natural selection is not a consequence of how well the organism 'solves' a set of fixed 'problems' posed by the environment" (p. 68). Rather, he continues, "The environment and the organism co-determine each other in an active way" (p. 68). Thus, he questions the prevailing assumption that organisms are only the *object* of evolution and suggests that we also must consider organisms as the *subject* of evolution. This model, which is by some interpretations a constructivist model of evolution, may hold more promise for developmental science than more traditional variation and selection models.

### *Cross-cultural Comparison*

Anthropology, perhaps particularly cultural anthropology, considers process. This process often is conceptualized as organizational change, and the possibility of emergence of novelty is clearly acknowledged. Moreover, anthropology includes consideration of many of the same categories of influence that could be of interest to developmental science. Anthropologists operating from an ecological perspective include in their categories of influences factors such as the physical environment's effect on a biological organism.

Perhaps the influence of most interest to anthropology, and thus more fully elaborated, is one that traditionally has been of less interest to psychology – sociocultural influences. As developmental science includes sociocultural influences in the categories it is willing to consider, the contribution of anthropology may prove particularly valuable. (See Holland & Skinner, Chapter 7, this volume, for an anthropological perspective that contains developmental considerations, and Tudge & Putnam, Chapter 9, this volume, for a related viewpoint.)

### *Cross-historical Comparison*

For a large part of this century, and partially continuing to the present time, history, like science, operated under many of the assumptions of logical positivism. Insofar as this tradition continues, developmental science may learn little about process from contemporary metatheory and theory of history. However, some metatheory and theory of history may be of value to developmental science. In some of the philosophy of history espoused in the early part of this century, history is clearly viewed as process. For example, Collingwood (1939) claims that history "is concerned not with events but with processes. Processes are things which do not begin and end but turn into one another" (pp. 98–99). It is less clear whether this process is properly construed as organizational change. The question of novelty depends on which perspective of historical change one adopts. From one perspective, historical change is viewed as a repetition in some fundamental way of similar events that have occurred previously. From another perspective, similar events are viewed as having some resemblance to events occurring previously, but the influence of previous events on later events is acknowledged clearly. The phrase "History repeats itself" summarizes the first of these perspectives; "History rhymes" summarizes the second. The former is not developmental; the latter clearly is.

### *Cautions in the Use of Comparative Perspectives*

With these overviews in mind, I suggest three cautions that might be kept in mind whenever developmental science looks to comparative perspectives. First, we must be aware that comparative perspectives are not homogeneous. This is true both across perspectives (e.g., cross-species and cross-cultural comparisons) and within perspectives (e.g., animal models and other cross-species comparisons). Even from the perspective of an interested outsider, some of the differences are visible. This suggests that all of a perspective may not be of value to developmental science, but rather that some aspect of some level of research may have such potential.

Second, it is important to be aware that even when a perspective seems to be talking the same language as developmental science, it may not be. As one example, the theory of evolution applied in much cross-species research may utilize the language of process of structural change. As noted earlier, what is meant and understood by process of structural change may not be applicable to developmental science.

Third, we should expect that translations must be undertaken if the work of comparative perspectives is to be of value to developmental science. To the extent that the orienting questions of particular comparative perspectives differ from parallel questions in developmental science, the theory and methodology of these perspectives cannot be transported directly into developmental science. This caution may be most important when considering the application of methods and data from comparative perspectives to developmental science. Although such application may have some value, given differences between these perspectives in research activity at all levels it is unreasonable to expect that data drawn from other perspectives will address the questions of developmental science directly.

In summary, it does not seem advisable to expect that one can simply reach into a perspective and pull out something that, in its current form, will be of value to another perpsective. Careful, knowledgeable work is necessary here.

## Conclusion: Practical Implications and Alternative Practices

I see some practical implications of this framework and of the possible contributions of comparative perspectives discussed subsequently in two areas. First, this framework and discussion have implications for our current educational practices. I have claimed that work at all levels of research is valuable to a discipline. I further have suggested that a discipline may need to have the flexibility to apply its resources to different levels of research given particular demands at any one time. It follows from both of these claims that the education of practitioners in our discipline must include training at all levels of research. Even while fluency in methods and data may be the dominant currency in our discipline currently, we sacrifice the value of potential flexibility by devoting the majority of our education efforts in only these two directions. As for comparative perspectives, if they are judged relevant to our research questions, we can include a reasonable introduction to their history and research in our educational efforts.

A second category of practical implications applies to our professional practice. Again, given a need for research at all levels, our discipline must engage in practices that explicitly value work at all levels of research. At a minimum this requires giving full consideration to research at all levels in our funding and personnel decisions. Again, if comparative perspectives contribute to our own discipline, we must also value and recognize collaborative research and other professional interaction with practitioners of these disciplines. Finally, we must value the ability to teach others about all levels of research, about the history of our discipline, and about the research of other developmental disciplines. This is the ultimate recognition by our discipline of the process of development.

## Notes

1. An earlier presentation of levels of research, definitions of research and methodology, and problems of autonomy and fusion can be found in Winegar and Valsiner (1992).
2. It is quite common for beliefs usually considered to be outside of scientific practice to exert influence on metatheoretical decisions. Specifically, cultural or societal preferences translated through personal beliefs can create a bias for some metatheoretical positions and against others. Although perhaps not properly considered part of scientific practice, these beliefs and their influence also require our attention. This issue is considered again in the final section of this chapter.
3. Personally, I prefer the term *organization* over the term *structure*. This preference is based on the connotation of stasis that often is attributed to structure and to the possible philosophical connection between structure and structuralism. I use organization from here on, although I do not believe my doing so places me at metatheoretical odds with the majority of developmental scientists.

## References

Collingwood, R. G. (1939). *An autobiography*. Oxford University Press.

Danziger, K. (1988). On theory and method in psychology. In W. J. Baker, L. P. Moss, H. V. Rappard, & H. J. Stam (Eds.), *Recent trends in theoretical psychology* (pp. 87–93). New York: Springer.

Lewontin, R. C. (1983). The organism as the subject and object of evolution. *Scientia*, *118*, 65–82.

Winegar, L. T., & Valsiner, J. (1992). Contextualizing context: Analysis of metadata and some further elaborations. In L. T. Winegar & J. Valsiner (Eds.), *Children's development within social context: Vol. 2. Research and methodology* (pp. 249–266). Hillsdale, NJ: Erlbaum.

# 2 Developmental Concepts across Disciplines

*Michael J. Shanahan, Jaan Valsiner, and Gilbert Gottlieb*

Psychobiologists, psychologists, and sociologists often differ markedly in the method and substance of their developmental research. Yet fundamental similarities bridge these orientations in the form of concepts applicable to multiple levels of analysis. Many of these concepts were identified by Gottlieb (1991a), generalizing from research on the interplay between genes and experience in the canalization of behavior: "The principal ideas concern the epigenetic characterization of individual development as an emergent, coactional, hierarchical system" (p. 7). In this chapter, we consider the transposability of these ideas to the psychology and sociology of human development. As such, our effort represents a cross-disciplinary comparison of developmental concepts, in keeping with Winegar's (Chapter 1, this volume) argument for research at all levels of scientific practice.

We begin by locating our comparisons in the metatheory of developmental studies. We then propose a series of "heuristic definitions" (Werner, 1957), statements not empirically testable in themselves but "valuable to developmental psychologists in leading to a determination of the actual range of applicability of developmental concepts" (p. 126). The heuristic definitions provide a basis for multi- and interdisciplinary communication. They can also be used to assess theoretical coverage – the specific ways in which a model addresses basic developmental issues. By example, the heuristic definitions

We would like to acknowledge the importance of the weekly meetings of the Carolina Consortium on Human Development in stimulating our thoughts on the nature of developmental theory. These meetings provided a framework in which the authors – a sociologist, a culturally oriented psychologist, and a biologically oriented psychologist – learned to speak with each other; this chapter attempts to share some of this common language.

are used to assess Fischer's theory of cognitive development and Sullivan's interpersonal theory of psychiatry.

## Metatheoretical Strategies in Developmental Studies

Metatheory covers a broad range of reflexive strategies to examine one's discipline. Ritzer (1988) classifies metatheoretical studies along social–intellectual and external–internal dimensions. The social–intellectual dimension differentiates social (e.g., zeitgeist influences) from substantive aspects of theories. The external–internal dimension distinguishes between phenomena located outside of or within a discipline.

Thus, social-external metatheory examines how social forces outside a discipline influence its substance. This influence can take place at the level of theory formulation; for example, Youniss (1992) observes how G. Stanley Hall, "steeped in the American ethos," formulated a developmental psychology consistent with the liberal, Christian reform movements of the late nineteenth century. Social influences also take place in the process of turning phenomena into data (Winegar & Valsiner, 1992). For example, Shif designed sentence completion tasks in accordance with socially accepted values of early Soviet Russia (e.g., "There are still workers who believe in god, although . . ."; see van der Veer and Valsiner, 1991). More generally, the emergence of quantitative methods intersected with socially based interests (e.g., Porter, 1986), including the consolidation and monitoring capacity of modern nation-states (e.g., Giddens, 1985; Patriarca, 1994).

Social-internal metatheory focuses on communal aspects of theory within a discipline and is exemplified by Kuhn (1970) and Lakatos (1978), who view theoretical change as part social movement; some of their ideas have been applied to developmental science (Horowitz, 1987). Social-internal metatheory also identifies schools of thought and networks of scholars. For example, Freud broadened the appeal of his psychoanalytic theory by maintaining relationships with Wilhelm Fliess and Carl Jung (Gay, 1988). The life histories of scholars also inform their research, especially in the human sciences. Numerous developmentalists (e.g., Baldwin, Preyer, Cooley, Piaget, and Skinner) formulated some of their theories based on experiences with their own children.

Intellectual-external metatheory concerns how various disciplines influence each other. For example, Herbert Spencer, committed to "the ubiquity of fundamental processes," applied biological concepts like evolution to sociological aggregates by analogy (Andreski, 1971). However, analogical transfer between disciplines has had both positive (Crick, 1988) and questionable (Gigerenzer, 1991) effects on specific disciplines. For example, Gigerenzer argues that with psychology's uncritical adoption of statistical methods, cognitive theories amount to metaphors of statistical methods (Gigerenzer & Murray, 1987; see also, Edelman, 1992).

The intellectual-internal category – dealing with the substance of theories – includes several distinct approaches (e.g., the history of a discipline, the reexamination of various theories or theorists). Most metatheoretical efforts in human development concern the representation of theories and theorists (e.g., on Piaget: Flavell, 1963; Furth, 1981; and on Vygotsky: Cole, 1978; Wertsch, 1985). However, intellectual-internal metatheory also includes the development of theoretical tools. Such tools can include the identification of a theory's assumptions or scope conditions, strategies for dealing with theoretical problems generic to the field (e.g., internalization, Lawrence & Valsiner, 1993; or transitions, van Geert, 1988a), or the underlying structure of a group of theories.

Theoretical structure – what Kalberg (1983) calls the "architectonics of theory" – has been studied from several vantage points. One strategy has been to assume parallelism – that the same genetic logic (i.e., principles describing the origins of phenomena) applies to all time frames and levels of analysis within a system. For example, Hobhouse (1927/1969) delineated six ways of acting (e.g., trial and error) that he argued were characteristic of mental activity in both phylogeny and ontogeny. Indeed, Baldwin (1906) established the field of genetic epistemology based on his interest in the parallels between mental life in phylogeny and ethnogeny (i.e., social development; see Cairns, 1992; Langer, 1970).

A second form of architectonic metatheory can be found in van Geert's (1987, 1988b) graph approach. He argues that developmental theories have a common "grammar," which includes rules for state, sequence, and transition descriptions; this idea is extended by applying graph theory to these grammars (in much the same way that sentences can be diagrammed) to generate structural representations of developmental theories. Our chapter represents an intellectual-

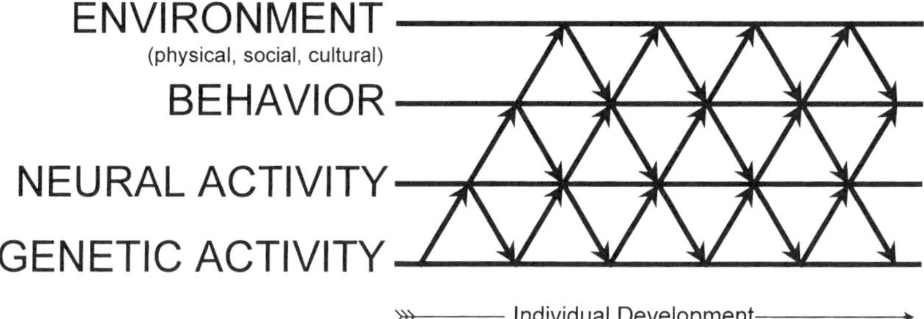


**Figure 2.1.** A simplified scheme of the developmental systems view showing a hierarchy of four mutually interacting components in which there are "top-down" as well as "bottom-up" bidirectional influences. (From Gottlieb, 1992; reprinted with permission.)

external metatheoretical effort that traces the principles of probabilistic epigenesis through psychology and sociology.

## Cross-disciplinary Concepts in Human Development

We begin with Gottlieb's (1991a) psychobiological principles of human development, then examine in a cursory manner parallel concepts found in psychology and sociology. Our purpose is not to imply that these heuristic definitions are characteristic or necessary components of all developmental approaches, but rather to demonstrate their potential transposability through the three disciplines.

**Structure: Development Occurs in Systems That Are Structured Both Hierarchically and Horizontally, and Relationships within These Systems Are Bidirectional.** This proposition requires a clear conceptualization of structure (the vertical and horizontal differentiation of the system within which development occurs) and a provision for bidirectional influences, as illustrated in Figure 2.1

*Structure.* Pattee's (1973) concept of "control devices" in developing systems defines structure in the broadest sense: "a time-dependent constraint which alters the path of selected degrees of freedom of the system it controls in a regular but variable way" (p. 42). In addition to Pattee's focus on constraint, others have noted the enabling function of structure (i.e., structures define the framework in which action that is not fully determined occurs; see, e.g., Giddens, 1979).

Biological approaches focus on the genetic, physiological, and anatomical properties of an organism, but also include the structural and functional contributions of experience. As Gottlieb (1991a, 1992) notes, many psychologists interested in the structuring nature of human biology still subscribe to Waddington's (1971) purely genetic notion of canalization, which does not take into account canalizing influences at all levels of Figure 2.1, including organism–environment coactions. Normally occurring experience, in concert with genetic and neural activity, can canalize behavioral and psychological development (Gottlieb, 1991b). Thus, a contemporary biological approach views the physical properties of biology and experience (i.e., organism–environment coactions) as enabling and constraining factors.

The fundamental place of structure can also be found in more psychological and sociological approaches to development. Nonbehaviorial psychology defines structure in terms of mental life. For Werner (1957), mental structure is indicated by the operations an organism is capable of performing; similarly, Piaget (1970) conceptualizes structure as operations that can be represented by logical rules. Freud's (1933/1937) notion of structure begins with psychic agencies, but symbols are frequently discussed in terms of structure (e.g., Fine, 1979; Shapiro, 1991). Two historical sources inform these psychological approaches to structure. First, one of embryology's major legacies to developmental psychology is the notion of the somatic structure of the developing organism. Second, the conceptualization of structure by the Gestalt theorists (Smith, 1988) and other structuralist traditions in psychology (e.g., Ganzheitspsychologie; see Sander & Volkelt, 1962; or the natural philosophy of Piaget, 1970) has been most influential.

Sociology has likewise formulated various approaches to structure. Common to many of these, however, is an emphasis on nonrandom (i.e., repetitive in time and/or place) relationships between socially based elements (Smelser, 1988). For example, situational imperatives define the behavioral requirements or structural characteristics of an environment and are associated conceptually with individual functioning (House & Mortimer, 1990). In this tradition, Kohn and Schooler (1983) link specific working conditions with both occupational and parental socialization values. Coleman's (1988) conceptualization of social capital represents another approach to social structure and is defined in explicitly developmental terms: the relational ties with other people that facilitate development. Coleman has studied the creation of human capital (typically an economic approach to human development), especially with respect to intergenerational relationships (Coleman, 1988) and the ability of public ties to compensate for a lack of family ties (Coleman, 1991).

Thus, the concept of structure is pervasive throughout psychobiology, psychology, and sociology. Although its specific usage can differ through levels of analysis, the common theme is that structure constrains and enables the processes and outcomes of development.

*Hierarchical and Horizontal Differentiation.* The metaphor of a multilayered system recognizes vertical and horizontal differentiation, which has been well represented in numerous conceptual models of development: biological (Weiss, 1959; Wright, 1968), ecological (Bronfenbrenner, 1979), transactional (Sameroff, 1983), contextual (Lerner & Kaufman, 1985), interactive (Magnusson, 1988), individual-socioecological (Valsiner, 1987), and probabilistic epigenetic (Gottlieb, 1970).

Vertical differentiation has been a prominent theme (Weiss, 1959; Wright, 1968) in biological approaches to human development. The organismic hierarchy proceeds from the lowest level, that of intranuclear phenomena such as the genome or DNA, and extends upward through the nucleus in cytoplasm, the cell, tissue, organs, the organism, and its environment, comprising other organisms and the ecosystem as defined in physical terms. Biological approaches frequently detail horizontal differentiation, as well. For example, during the embryonic period a cell's interactions with neighboring cells and its location in the major axes of the body influence the cell's ultimate differentiation. Each of the cells of the body contains the same total genetic complement in its nucleus, so horizontal and vertical influences must necessarily be involved to account for qualitative differences in developmental outcomes (i.e., cell differentiation).

A similar use of vertical and horizontal differentiation processes can be found in psychology. For example, Werner's (1957) orthogenetic principle entails both horizontal (articulation) and vertical (hierarchical integration) notions. Piaget's recognition of horizontal and vertical decalage in cognitive development constitutes a variation on this theme.

In terms of vertical differentiation, sociologists have recognized institutions (e.g., the educational system), formal organizations (a specific school), small groups (classroom), dyads (teacher–student), and the socially based, reflexive mind. Horizontal differentiation at the institutional level might involve connections between the educational system and the workplace; at the level of small groups, between the peer clique and family; and within groups, between individuals.

The sociological concern for vertical differentiation is well articulated in Dannefer's (1984) argument against "life-span reductionism," whereby social structure is reduced to immediate context and usually inferred from characteristics of the individual. From this perspective, contextual studies of development need to measure properties of individuals and contexts, but they also need to consider the situated nature of contexts within the broader society. For example, work trajectories can be studied in terms of the constellation of work roles in different organizations and industries (Baron & Bielby, 1980). A more provocative example relating broader and circumscribed social structures can be found in Giddens (1991, 1992), who contrasts the social organization of premodern and modern societies and considers implications for institutions, the family, intimate relationships, and the life course.

Thus, each discipline shows the pattern of differentiating its subject matter in both horizontal and vertical terms.

*Bidirectionality.* Bidirectional influences take place both between and within levels. As documented by Gottlieb (1970, 1991a, 1991b), vertical bidirectionality as applied to genetic activity has not always been recognized in psychology or even biology; Waddington's (1971) unidirectional understanding of genetic canalization has been the predominant approach for many years and is still promoted in some quarters (Fishbein, 1976; Kovach & Wilson, 1988; Lumsden & Wilson, 1980; Parker & Gibson, 1979; Scarr-Salapatek, 1976). While the influence of environmental factors on genetic expression is still being clarified, there is considerable evidence to document that genetic activity is responsive to the developing organism's external environment (Gottlieb, 1992). For example, Ho (1984) induced a second set of wings on fruit flies by exposing them to ether during a certain period of embryonic development; the ether altered the cytoplasm of the cells and thus the protein produced by the DNA–RNA–cytoplasm coaction. This particular influence also continues to operate transgenerationally, as do the effects of many drugs and other substances (Campbell & Perkins, 1988). There are now many examples of external sensory and internal neural events that both excite and inhibit gene expression (e.g., Anokhin, Mileusnic, Shamakina, & Rose, 1991; Calamandrei & Keverne, 1994; Rustak, Robertson, Wisden, & Hunt, 1990).

At the psychological level, bidirectionality has been prominent in many dynamic accounts of person–environment relationships. J. M. Baldwin's (1906) "circular reaction" (and its later elaboration by Piaget), Vygotsky's (van der Veer & Valsiner, 1991) emphasis on the person's interactions with his or her cultural-historical worlds, and William Stern's (1938) personology of person–Umwelt relatedness are all examples of bidirectionality in psychology.

Within sociology, the concept of reflexivity, using the standpoint of others to view oneself as an object, captures horizontal bidirectionality. From this perspective, the development of the self depends on the individual experiencing him- or herself as an object that is viewed by others (Mead, 1934; Sullivan, 1953). Bidirectionality is captured in this reflexive process, as the actor's identity is constituted in the continual interplay between actor as subject and actor as object. Horizontal bidirectionality at higher levels of aggregation is found in Bronfenbrenner's (1979) conceptualization of the mesosystem, the interconnections between developmental settings, like the workplace and educational system (see Tudge, Gray, & Hogan, Chapter 3, this volume).

Vertical bidirectionality has proved more difficult to conceptualize, with sociologists traditionally emphasizing the determinative role of macrostructures on individuals and not the reverse, as would be required by bidirectionality (Hinde, 1990). Yet individuals and groups can cause changes in society and culture. Riley and her colleagues (Riley, Foner, & Waring, 1988) have been developing the "aging and society paradigm," which posits that different cohorts experience different patterns of aging because of social changes, but also that cohorts can influence social arrangements. For instance, numerous factors may have led a greater number of individuals to early retirement, but those who retired early and enjoyed greater longevity have had a profound influence on the modern system of Social Security.

More recently, some conceptual models have emphasized that broader social structures represent the aggregate of interaction patterns among individuals. In this sense, the "micro–macro" problem is recast from a concern for individual effects on the macrostructural order to how the macro is constituted in microsettings (Collins, 1988; Giddens, 1976). This theme is especially prominent in Corsaro's (1992) interpretive reproductive framework of development, which emphasizes how individuals appropriate and re-create the social order in everyday interactions.

Although examples of bidirectionality can be found across disciplines, unidirectional thinking is still quite common. It is only recently that biologists have found the macro to micro causal flow empirically justified, and this top-down influence has not yet taken hold in psychology as a whole. Sociologists have had difficulties with the micro to macro causal flow, although Riley's work is an excellent, developmentally sensitive exception.

**Temporality: Developmental Analysis Is Necessarily Historical; Explanations of Present States of Affairs Necessarily Involve Earlier Events.** Within biology and psychology, interest in time had been limited to a concern for development as "temporal accretions," or critical periods (Turkewitz & Devenney, 1993). Among the classical theorists, Werner stands out for his relative lack of interest in stages as defined by chronological age. As Langer's (1970) excellent survey observes, Werner moved away from "a temporal formulation that would only fit the growth trends of individual life cycles, and a movement toward an ever more logical and abstract formal characterization of progressive, arrested, and regressive development" (p. 745). This perspective rejects connections among chronological time, developmental stage, and the orthogenetic principle. Rather, development is seen as increasing differentiation and centralization or hierarchic integration (Werner, 1957).

More contemporary efforts reflect an interest in time operating at various levels within the system. Cairns (1993) observes that specific time frames attend to different levels of analysis: phylogenetic issues are typically studied in geologic time, ontogeny within the life span, and microgenetic processes in episodes, with interplay between these levels possible. For example, Fuller (1967) formulated the notion of the emergence response, whereby presumed genetic differences (i.e., breed differences in dogs) appear more salient early in adaptive sequences and diminish with time. The interplay between time frames is well illustrated in studies by Cairns and his colleagues

(Cairns, Gariépy, & Hood, 1990; Cairns, MacCombie, & Hood, 1983), showing that genetic (selective breeding for high and low aggression), developmental (prepubertal, early, and late maturers), and experiential (especially social) factors coact to determine levels of interanimal attack. A concern for temporal interplay between levels is also found in Turkewitz and Devenny's (1993) suggestion that development follows from heterochrony, which occurs when two or more elements at different levels in a system experience differential rates of change.

Sociologists in the life course and aging tradition also recognize various time frames and their interplay (Elder & Caspi, 1990; Riley et al., 1988). Historical time references broad social changes within a society; social time refers to age-graded roles, expectations, and opportunities that define the life course; and personal time characterizes the specific pattern of trajectories and transitions that describe the course of an individual's development.

The interplay between these distinctions are numerous and potentially complex. Elder's research emphasizes the relations among historical, social, and personal time. For example, among older individuals, entry into the military during World War II disrupted established career patterns. On the other hand, early entrants were afforded a social moratorium from age-graded roles and were able to begin careers in the postwar economic boom (Elder, 1986, 1987). Trajectories in social time are often interrelated, as well. Numerous studies (e.g., Hogan & Astone, 1986) document interconnections between the timing of education, marriage, employment, and childbearing transitions.

Sociologists have also studied heterochronic phenomena, although not labeled as such. This tradition traces back to sociology's early interest in the individual in times of rapid social change as found, for example, in Durkheim's (1951) discussion of anomie. One example of socially based heterochrony involves disjunctions between social time and personal time, *off-time* events. From this perspective, off-time transitions are changes that occur before or after the customary time (Neugarten, Moore, & Lowe, 1965). While very little is known about the normative basis of timing expectations or the social-psychological mechanisms surrounding their "enforcement" (for a notable exception, see Kalicki, 1994), studies have linked a wide range of unfavorable outcomes with off-time transitions. For example, Glick and Norton (1977) show how off-time marriages are more likely to end in divorce; of course, social time norms for marriage may be changing in historical time, which suggests birth cohort differences in the definition of off-time marriage.

Thus, each discipline utilizes different time scales and has developed concepts that reflect an interest in the interplay between time frames.

**Change: Change Originates with Tension and Its Exact Manifestation Is Probabilistic and Epigenetic.** Tension is created by any force that disrupts homeostasis. The disruption of homeostasis and subsequent adjustment processes represent change. According to this definition, all development does not necessarily involve change in the sense of the induction or production of qualitative novelties, since existing adaptive capacity may be enhanced simply by maintenance efforts. Critical issues include the classification of tensors, the identification of processes of disruption, and an understanding of the resultant transformation with respect to the prior structural and functional attributes of the organism.

*Tension.* Since at least the early nineteenth century, biologists have recognized that environmental assaults on the organism lead to internal, adaptive efforts; for example, the French physiologist Claude Bernard argued that an organism's independence from the environment depended on the complexity of its internal, adaptive capacity (Johnson, Kamilaris, Chrousos, & Gold, 1992). The contemporary biological approach has sought to specify the central and peripheral reactions that preserve homeostasis (Chrousos & Gold, 1992). This emphasis has resulted in a detailed understanding of the biochemical processes by which homeostasis is achieved, all of which involve redirection of energy (e.g., the inhibition of growth and reproductive systems, or altered cardiovascular tone and increased respiratory rate). The phenomenon of DNA repair – whereby DNA make enzymes to repair tissue damage or defects (Mazzarello, Poloni, Spadari, & Focher, 1992) – exemplifies a homeostatic-maintaining process at the genetic level.

The central role of tension can be found among psychologists and sociologists interested in development, as well. Concern for tension is implicit in the concept of equilibrium, which is pervasive in psychology. Indeed, as Langer (1969) notes, psychological theories of development almost unanimously make provisions for the concept of equilibration, the major exception being behaviorist models. For example, psychoanalytic approaches emphasize tensions between the id, ego, and superego (Silberman, 1981). Piaget (1971) adopted the equilibration terminology as an explanatory principle in development, following traditions in the social and biological sciences that can be traced to Herbert Spencer (Bailey, 1984). Janet (1926) placed tension at the center of his action-oriented theory of psychological functioning, although he was not influenced by the concept of equilibrium. From this perspective, tension refers to a synthesizing element in mental life and behavior (Sjövall, 1967).

Organismic theorists – such as Vygotsky, Baldwin, and Werner – view equilibration as the synthesis resulting from the dialectical nature of development (Kahlbaugh, 1993). From this perspective, tension is found in the clash between thesis and antithesis, the tendency toward conservation and plasticity. For Vygotsky, this tension was found in the connection between self and the sociohistorical context: Development proceeds from qualitative changes in the social situation that require an expansion of one's activities. In Werner, this tension was found between "the global and specific orientations [as they] develop in opposition to each other and are synthesized into a more inclusive position" (Kahlbaugh, 1993, p. 83). Werner (1957) postulated that the organism becomes more equilibrated with increased differentiation, centralization, and hierarchical integration.

Sociological concerns for socially based tensions and individual identity trace to the beginnings of sociology as a discipline (Mazlish, 1989) and are prominent in contemporary life course studies. W. I. Thomas's model of control cycles has been useful in linking social disruptions with individual lives (Elder & Caspi, 1990). This model depicts how change disrupts equilibrium within the household and the subsequent coordinated efforts of family members toward reequilibration. Research on the relationships among economic stress, family functioning, and individual adaptation illustrates this point nicely (e.g., see Moen, Kain, & Elder, 1983). More recently, an interdisciplinary study group (Elder, Modell, & Parke, 1993) has identified a series of social changes thought to influence child development: the rise of television and telecommunications, postwar affluence and widening economic inequality, state-initiated policies in times of crisis (the Great Depression, wars), social change in women's lives, and ideological changes in child rearing. Such changes frequently pose challenges to the family. The sociological focus is on how such tensions modify social institutions, organizations, the family, and its members.

Thus, the relationship between tension and subsequent adaptive change is central to the disciplines of biology, psychology, and sociology.

*Probabilistic Epigenesis.* Developmental approaches need to allow for a range of responses to tension, such that adaptive structures and functions are probable and potentially novel. The probable nature of epigenetic development is rooted in the reciprocal coactions taking place within complex systems, as shown in Figure 2.1.

Since the overthrow of biological preformation in favor of epigenesis in the nineteenth century, it has been recognized that development takes place sequentially and is therefore an emergent phenomenon. And since the advent of experimental embryology in the late nineteenth century, it is an accepted fact that cellular and organismic development occurs as a consequence of coactions at all levels from the genes to the developing organism itself (review in Gottlieb, in press). With the gradual realization that influences in developmental systems are fully bidirectional and that genes do not, in and of themselves, produce finished (i.e., mature) traits, the predetermined concept of epigenesis has receded from all but a few viewpoints in biology and psychology. Epigenesis is now defined as increased complexity of organization: the emergence of new structural and functional properties and competencies as a consequence of horizontal and vertical coactions among the system's parts, including organism–environment coactions (Gottlieb, 1991a).

The emergent nature of development is well represented in the concept of equifinality. The embryologist Hans Driesch (1929) defined equifinality as "starting from one and the same initial state and leading to one and the same end, but using very different means, following very different ways in the different individuals of one and the same species, taken from the same locality, or even colony" (p. 114). Organisms of the same species can start at the same place and end at the same place by traversing different pathways. In developmental psychobiology, equifinality has been demonstrated experimentally in the research of Banker and Lickliter (1993), Lickliter and Hellewell (1992), and Miller, Hicinbotham, and Blaich (1990).

Probabilistic epigenesis is in accord with Baldwin's (1906) understanding of developmental phenomena: Anything that is completely predictable could not be developmental. The stochastic nature of developmental phenomena ultimately derives from the range of responses at any given level. Thus, responses to tension can vary within levels; and given that responses to stress occur in highly related sets of behaviors (i.e., they are organized), there will be variability in the overall patterns between levels. London's (1949) argument for the "behavioral spectrum" exemplifies the concern for a range of responses. From this perspective, developmental phenomena cannot be represented so as to imply subsequent derivations, though they can suggest classes of outcomes. This notion is captured well by Fischer's theory of cognition, as he adopts the principles of adaptive resonance theory to explain the generation of multiple cognitive forms in ontogeny (Fischer, Bullock, Rotenberg, & Raya, 1993).

Within sociology, there has been much appreciation for variability in social processes and how people respond to social contingencies. For example, Durkheim (1951) recognizes the multiple, socially based pathways (altruism, fatalism, egoism, and anomie) to suicide; an appreciation for equifinality also runs through much of Weber and Simmel's work. As Wallace (1988) notes, equifinality can be found in sociological concepts like structural flexibility, functional alternatives, and structural substitutability; these concepts recognize that specific outcomes are more likely in open, hierarchical systems when they can be reached through multiple pathways.

Probabilistic epigenesis is also found in the life course, which places great emphasis on human agency, the capability of individuals to do things (Giddens, 1984). In the life course tradition, the concept of loose coupling (i.e., variability among individuals in the same cohort) reflects in part agency. Giddens (1991) notes that a defining characteristic of modernity is the availability of options in life, which makes the concept of human agency meaningful. Indeed, demographic studies document substantial diversity in people's lives at times of life course transitions (Hogan, 1981; Rindfuss, Swicegood, & Rosenfeld, 1987). The aging and society paradigm of Riley and her colleagues (1988) views age stratification as a critical counterpoint to biological determinism and psychological ontogenesis in the study of human aging, emphasizing the socially based sources of cohort diversity and individual plasticity.

In the symbolic interactionist tradition, variability of response is emphasized in the negotiated order, the processes by which individuals continually locate shared meaning while interacting. For example, Denzin (1977) argues that the developmental emergence of self reflects the continual negotiation of lines of action into workable patterns, as between infant and caregiver, child and peers.

Thus, the hallmarks of probabilistic epigenesis – bidirectionality and indeterminacy – are widely utilized in the disciplines of biology, psychology, and sociology.

**Patterns of Change: The Levels of the System Are Coactional, with Functionally Coordinated Changes Occurring Throughout.** Although unidirectional, additive causal thinking pervades developmental studies, this proposition is meant to establish a coactional perspective: an emphasis on highly interrelated elements, the coordination of which represent patterns of adaptation (Gottlieb, 1991a, 1992). From this perspective, developmental explanations attend to how various structures and functions within a system change in a coordinated fashion to adapt to a disruption in homeostasis and to maintain or restore balance. This focus shifts inquiry from notions of unidirectional (micro to macro or macro to micro) causality to the intermeshing of elements within a system.

Cairns, McGuire, and Gariépy (1993) persuasively argue for studying behavior as a system of "correlated constraints," functionally coordinated elements that regularly co-occur. As Cairns and his colleagues explain, this approach traces to von Bertalanffy's seminal argument for holism and was advanced by T. C. Schneirla, who proposed that biological, maturational, and experiential forces "coalesce" in development. The argument ultimately rests on evolutionary principles: in phylogeny and ontogeny "there should be mutual accommodation of behavioral propensities and the social and physical requirements of adaptation" (Cairns et al., 1993, p. 110).

This idea has been supported in animal research. In this tradition, Gariépy (1994), reviewing findings on aggressive behavior in mice, observes:

> It would be rather surprising if a *strong network of correlations* would not exist between the various components leading to an action. For instance, mechanisms controlling the perceived intensity of stimulations, the subsequent motivation to attack or flee, and the eventual initiation of an action, should be expected to *operate*

> *jointly in support of the effective organization* of one or the other strategy. (p. 268; emphasis added)

Simple (i.e., unidirectional and additive) causal models, both conceptual and statistical, have played a major role in psychology and sociology, despite trenchant criticisms (e.g., Abbott, 1988; Berk, 1988). Yet a concern for coalesced elements can be found. In psychoanalytic theory, Spitz (1965) argued that development proceeds along multiple lines, which integrate to varying degrees to produce organization and reorganization of the self. The lines of development are actively associated, but in complex and changing ways.

In sociology, Weber's emphasis on structural affinities, complex patterns of association between the material and normative bases of society, represents an early argument for less causally based analyses of change. The life course concept of "linked lives" represents a more contemporary sociological idea reflecting a concern for coaction. For example, a family system is composed of individual trajectories of development that may be mutually accommodating, creating a pattern of organization and adaptation. One also sees a retreat from narrowly conceived causal analyses in some studies of chronic poverty and individual functioning. The pervasive, complex social patterns that define chronic poverty suggest a shift away from isolating the unique effects of specific variables, toward an appreciation for impoverished conditions as a system of influences. For example, Kruttschnitt, McLeod, and Dornfeld (1994) suggest that family violence is both a consequence of and constitutive force in economic deprivation and violence generally.

Simple causal thinking, involving assumptions of unidirectionality and additivity, pervade developmental research. Nonetheless, efforts to understand how elements coordinate in complex ways can be found across the disciplines. The notion of coaction stresses the activity of multiple influences from various levels rather than an identification of one or two major causes of development, as, for example, one finds in simplistic approaches to behavioral genetics (genes + environment = phenotype). From the developmental point of view, the separation of genes and environment as independent causes is invalid (Wahlsten & Gottlieb, in press).

**Development: Intellectual and Social Criteria Distinguish the Types of Change That Developmentalists Study.** This proposition acknowledges that developmental models are fundamentally concerned with change and that change which constitutes development is constructed. This construction reflects both intellectual and social criteria, which need to be recognized. Studies of intellectual factors that influence the types of change studied by developmentalists represent exercises in intellectual history. The intellectual history of developmental studies is useful to the refinement and appraisal of theories, especially when framed in terms of competing models and their empirical support (e.g., Gottlieb, 1970, on predetermined vs. probabilistic prenatal behavior). However, very little attention has been devoted to social influences on the types of change studied by developmentalists, particularly how social forces frame research efforts in contemporary developmental studies (cf. Best, 1990, for a socially based approach to social problems).

The disciplines continually construct an intellectual heritage that itself constrains and enables the types of change that are studied. The role of social forces in this process is often only implicit.

## The Assessment of Theoretical Coverage: Two Case Studies

We now turn to applications of the heuristic definitions to specific theoretical models of development. Kurt Fischer's theory of cognitive development is noteworthy in cognitive science for its fundamental concern with developmental process. Fischer charted out his theory in a programmatic article over a decade ago (Fischer, 1980) and has returned to it for further elabortation and application since that time (Bidell & Fischer, 1992; Fischer & Bullock, 1984; Fischer & Farrar, 1987; Fischer & Kenny, 1986; Fischer et al., 1993).

Harry Stack Sullivan's theory presents a unique case study as a truly interdisciplinary approach to human development. It is not incidental that the first chapter to his *Interpersonal Theory of Psychiatry* is entitled "The Developmental Approach," since he is concerned foremost with temporally intrinsic adaptation. Further, his theoretical system is remarkable for its commitment to an interdisciplinary formulation; Sullivan (1953) stated that psychiatry "seeks to study the biologically and culturally conditioned, but *sui generis*, interpersonal processes occurring in interpersonal situations" (p. 20). In studying how Sullivan realized this purpose, we survey the confluence of the medical science, Freudian psychology, social psychology, anthropology, semiotics, and physics of his time.

### *Fischer's Skill Development Theory*

The concept of skill entails a transaction between organism and environment. To paraphrase Fischer's own brief overview: Skills develop step by step through 10 hierarchical levels divided into three tiers. The tiers specify skills of different types: sensorimotor skills, representational skills, and abstract skills. The levels specify skills of gradually increasing complexity, with a skill at one level built directly on skills from the preceding level. Each level is characterized by a structure, which indicates the kinds of behaviors that the person can control at that level. Skills at each level are constructed by a person acting on the environment. Individuals combine and differentiate skills from one level to form skills at the next higher level. This movement occurs in many microdevelopmental steps specified by a series of transformation rules. Fischer emphasizes that skills develop through levels, not stages: Development is relatively continuous and gradual, and the person is never at the same level for all skills.

The development of skills must be induced by the environment, and only the skills induced most consistently will typically be at the highest level of which the individual is capable. Unevenness of development is considered the rule. The level of skills that is strongly induced by the environment is limited, however, by the highest level of which the person is capable. As the individual develops, the highest level increases, and so he or she can be induced to extend these skills to a new, higher level (Fischer, 1980, pp. 479–480).

**Structure: Development Occurs in Systems That Are Structured Both Hierarchically and Horizontally, and Relationships within These Systems May Be Bidirectional.** Fischer's theoretical model addresses issues of structuration explicitly. His hierarchical system of tiers (sensorimotor, representational, and abstract), which organize 10 levels of skill development, constitutes the vertical structure. At the same time, the context dependency of the child's actions at each level (organized by task domains, and with social assistance by others) provides for the horizontal structure. Fischer recognizes bidirectionality in the relationship of the person and the context, as that relationship exists within the hierarchical organization of levels (Fischer et al., 1993). Fischer defines exactly the structures at that relationship level, as well as transformation rules that organize the move between levels, and from one task domain to another. In general, the ontogeny of the cognitive system is regulated by some upper limit on capacities, which increases through childhood.

**Temporality: Developmental Analysis Is Necessarily Historical; Explanations of Present States of Affairs Necessarily Involve Earlier Events.** Fischer's emphasis on the dynamics of person–context transactions in skill construction recognizes temporality, especially in its microgenetic version. His description of levels also recognizes temporality in the ontogenetic domain.

**Change: Change Originates with Tension and Its Exact Manifestation Is Probabilistic and Epigenetic.** With respect to tension, Fischer's theory remains uncertain. On the one hand, it is possible to view the five transformation rules as set into action by tension introduced in an encounter with the environment (comparable to Piaget's emphasis that contradictions challenge development). Yet Fischer did not specifically emphasize that point in his earlier theory. Alternatively, his formal descriptions of transformations can be understood in computational (algorithmic) terms: Given previous conditions (of skills) and a new input, the cognitive system harmoniously "computes" a transformation either within a level or between levels, without tensions in the computation process. Later, with the incorporation of adaptive resonance networks into his model, Fischer recognized the appearance of "surprises" in the course of change (Fischer et al., 1993). Yet the computability of such surprises remains unaltered (only the nature of the computational network has become more complex). Specific forms of transaction between the developing person and the environment are not made explicit in Fischer's theory; hence, the adaptational focus remains largely a "black box"-type explanation of how the intricate complexity of the skill hierarchy is being transformed within the possibilities for multilinear development.

If the role of tension is somewhat unclear, Fischer's theoretical treatment does exhibit the defining features of epigenesis: the emergent increase in complexity of organization based on coactions within and among different levels of analysis. It is also interesting that similar to many other cognitive theories, Fischer de facto allows for the deterministic (inborn) unfolding mechanism of maximum capacity (highest level of capability) to drive ontogenetic process. The emphasis on "induction by the environment" (of specific skills) works as a mechanism within those limits and explains the experience-linked unevenness of cognitive development. That unevenness is recognized in the form of *developmental range* (i.e., the range of developmental levels an individual can exhibit while solving a given task in a variety of contexts; see Biddell & Fischer, 1992, p. 24), as well as in the recognition of the *multilinearity of development* (the "web of constructive generalizations" as depicted in Bidell & Fischer, 1992, Figure 1.B). From the very outset of the formulation of skill theory, Fischer (1980) has been a clear proponent of the latter:

> Skill theory predicts that individuals will frequently follow different paths of development and that these differences will take at least two forms. First, different individuals will develop in different skill domains. One person will develop basket-making skills but not reading skills. . . .
>
> Second, different individuals will follow different developmental paths in the same skill domain. . . . The developmental transformation rules predict a large number of different possible paths in any single domain. (p. 513)

Fischer's strong emphasis on the *reality of unevenness* in cognitive development (which, in Piaget's terms, has been labeled – but not explained – by the term *décalage*) leads skill theory to the possibility of concentrating on the processes of development. Fischer's empirical basis comes from Piaget-type experimental tasks, yet in much of his theoretical explanation he emphasizes "prediction of developmental sequences."

**Patterns of Change: The Levels of the System Are Coactional, with Functionally Coordinated Changes Occurring Throughout.** Fischer's theory fits this proposition in terms of his emphasis on cognitive profile: A child may at the same time be at different levels in different skill domains, and the mapping of schemes as well as transformation rules indicate the specific ways (as in interrelated changes) in which the profile of levels at a given time can change. The five transformation rules posited by Fischer are intercoordination, compounding, focusing, substitution, and differentiation.

*Intercoordination* specifies how the person combines skills to develop from level to level. Fischer (1980) likens it to the chemical combining of atoms into molecules:

> The child has two well-formed skills, *a* and *b*, at a specific Level L. The two skills are functioning separately from each other until some object or event in the environment induces the child to relate the two skills to each other. When the intercoordination is complete, the two skills, *a* and *b*, from Level L have been transformed into a new skill, *d*, at Level L + 1, which includes them. (p. 498)

Obviously, intercoordination entails emergence of new skills (at a higher level), while subsuming the previous skills into a new whole. In contrast, the transformation rule of *compounding* is limited to the given level; previously unlinked skills are combined into a new one within the same level ($a + b = c$). Likewise, *focusing* entails the moment-to-moment shifting of attention between skills the child has already established (Fischer, 1980, pp. 500–501). The function of transfer is covered by Fischer through the transformation rule of *substitution*:

> A skill at Level L is mastered with one task, and then the person attempts to transfer it to a second, similar task. The rule applies when all components but one in the first task are identical with those in the second task and when that one different component can be generalized to the second task.

A notable moment in Fischer's notion of substitution is the intercoordination of two opposing tendencies in the history of transfer of training – those of "identical elements" (E. L. Thorndike) and "higher-level generalization" (the Gestalt perspective of G. Katona). Yet the recognition of generalization as the crucial moment in transfer verifies that Fischer's transformation rule of substitution fits with the notion of correlated changes in a developing system.

Finally, Fischer considers *differentiation* as a transformation rule. Here he directly borrows from Heinz Werner's general theoretical emphasis, considering differentiation and integration of skills from level to level as complementary, consistent with the idea of correlated changes.

**Development: Intellectual and Social Criteria Distinguish the Types of Change That Developmentalists Study.** Fischer's skill theory is itself an adaptation to the social world of developmental psychologists in North America in the past few decades. On the one hand, it has behaviorist elements (e.g., continuity with operant learning theory, emphasis on the notion of control and prediction) and, on the other hand, a Piagetian empirical emphasis (utilizing Piagetian experimental probes to explicate the skills) without borrowing Piaget's developmental theory of equilibration. Fischer's theory (in its 1980 version) reflects the ongoing disputes by U.S. psychologists – Piagetian versus information-processing views on cognition, empirical arguments about cross-sectional and longitudinal designs (see Fischer, 1980, pp. 511–512), and maintaining behavior, thought, and language as equal contributors (to otherwise hierarchical theory).

Coordinating the "voices" in North American psychology, Fischer carefully distances himself from all of his predecessors, while retaining the major theoretical ideas of each, and synthesizing these into his own theory. The general focus of the theory can be seen to remain continuous with Piaget's structuralist-transformational orientation (which distinguishes Fischer from other North American cognitivists), yet the theory provides for substantial novelty of ideas by making the unevenness of development and its multilinearity of pathways (equifinality) the core phenomenon to be explained, rather than an outlier phenomenon to be dismissed.

Following our metatheoretical criteria, Fischer's skill theory remains vague in some of the basic propositions, while demonstrating a clear fit with others (structure and temporality). The areas of vagueness can be traced in part to Fischer's identification of his theory as *cognitive*, which includes nondevelopmental components. The label can act to shift the developmental focus of cognitive studies, replacing the study of processes with the study of outcomes, ordered as comparisons between ontogenetic age groups. This transformation is well illustrated by the attention paid to Piaget's description of the content of stages, to the neglect of efforts to explain the process of equilibration (entailing assimilation and accommodation in mutually complementary processes). Fischer's theory inherits this tension between description of outcomes and explanation of processes.

### *Harry Stack Sullivan's Interpersonal Theory of Psychiatry*

While Sullivan continually advances conceptual distinctions and nuances, his basic approach to development includes the following ideas: A person's pattern of living is derived from consensually validated learning that takes place in interpersonal exchange. This pattern reflects the individual's effort to satisfy needs (e.g., hunger, sex, intimacy) with minimal anxiety. Culture defines and conditions each person's efforts to satisfy his or her needs when interacting with others. Consensual validation occurs when parties syntactically communicate (i.e., share a common meaning of the situation). Situations can, however, disintegrate when anxiety prevents syntactic communication and needs are not satisfied. Psychiatry is the study of how anxiety disrupts syntactic communication in the satisfaction of needs, a study that necessarily takes place in interpersonal fields and includes the "tensional history" of the individual.

**Structure: Development Occurs in Systems That Are Structured Both Hierarchically and Horizontally, and Relationships within These Systems May Be Bidirectional.** As a physician, Sullivan had a clear appreciation for the anatomical and physiological levels of human existence, as evidenced in his concepts of zones of interaction and receptor–effector organ complexes (e.g., the mouth), "end stations" where the human's physiochemical world engages in communal existence. On the other hand, he also includes less physically based conceptions of structure, with semiotic tools (such as personifications, language, signs, and symbols) being paramount. For Sullivan, all semiotic tools are organizers of experience. For example, in his treatment of language, he follows Sapir closely: Language is the reduction of experience to familiar forms. Thus, in early experience, infants have primitive understandings, or personifications, of a good-mother and bad-mother. With the acquisition of language, various mothers are fused into the category *mother*, leading Sullivan to the striking observation that "language is the fusion of personifications."

Perhaps Sullivan's most interesting approach to structure can be found in the concept of the dynamism, an enduring pattern of energy transformation. Here he is influenced by the physicist's emphasis on energy as "the ultimate reality" (1953, p. 102) and cites Whitehead, who argued that an entity is a process and so not describable in terms of static morphology. Sullivan's system clearly takes morphology seriously, but the advantage of the dynamism concept is its appreciation of nonphysical structurings, as in the self-system of in patterns of interactions that characterize interpersonal fields.

Given his interests, Sullivan differentiates his developmental system more elaborately at lower levels of aggregation. He recognizes biological differentiation in detailed discussions of the zones of interaction, and he recognizes mental differentiation in his treatment of personifications and the self-system. The former is morphological structure; the latter are dynamisms. One form of bidirectionality is found in the interplay between the social system and the self-system. Cultural prescriptions condition the self-system, defining one's orientation to living – how needs can be satisfied in a socially acceptable way and the self's security maintained. These cultural prescriptions are instantiated in the interpersonal field, where anxiety gradients created by relative degrees of discomfort prompt the self-system to anxiety-reducing or -inducing behaviors. However, acculturated persons train others as well, so that individuals are acculturated and are acculturating. Thus, the bidirectional connection between culture and the self is rooted in the bidirectional, Meadian social psychology that Sullivan fully adopted.

However, vertical bidirectionality remains elusive. Cultural understandings in the form of norms and values are frequently implicit in Sullivan, although he neglects their systematic consideration. He shares with Freud and socialization theorists of his time an understanding of culture as a superstructure that imposes on the individual. For example, he quotes Ruth Benedict (1934, pp. 2–3): "By the time he [the newborn] can talk, he is the little creature of his culture, and by the time he is grown and able to take part in its activities, its habits are his habits, its beliefs are his beliefs, its impossibilities are his impossibilities." Thus, the macro–micro relationship is essentially top-down, not unlike many efforts in contemporary sociology.

**Temporality: Developmental Analysis Is Necessarily Historical; Explanations of Present States of Affairs Necessarily Involve Earlier Events.** In most respects, Sullivan takes a fairly standard position on time as a phase theorist, postulating ontogenetically based periods through early life; these phases are considered heuristic and appear to be based on clinical experiences that indicate sensitive periods of adaptation. For example, adolescence begins with sexual interest in someone of the opposite sex and ends as one develops stable patterns that satisfy lust. To Sullivan, such a definition is useful because these criteria identify developmental vulnerabilities.

Sullivan also employs several time-sensitive concepts, including regression and arrested development. His treatment of regression is standard, and while the concept of arrested development is not in itself noteworthy, its application in the interpersonal field deserves attention as an example of heterochrony. Arrested development is a statistical deviation from the course of events, the failure to formulate a patterned and socially acceptable way of satisfying a need in a time frame that roughly corresponds to this same patterning by one's peers. Since needs are serially emergent and satisfied in interpersonal relationships, arrested development threatens the typical process whereby age-mates satisfy their needs interdependently. With arrested development, the group's composition now includes individuals with different salient needs.

For Sullivan, the problem of arrested development is not the individual's delay per se, but rather that the interpersonal field now includes developmentally advanced individuals who may not be helpful in the resolution of needs. The temporal interplay of importance is found in the interpersonal field. Sullivan offers powerful examples of how juveniles, preadolescents, and adolescents experiencing developmental arrest can leave the child developmentally stranded in the interpersonal field. It is not merely the timing of one's development, but the orchestration of developmental timings within the interpersonal field.

Sullivan (1953) is straightforward on future orientations: he rejects the Freudian notion of instincts and refocuses on how ontogenetically based needs define human motivation. His stance on the importance of personal history is reasonably subject to a strong interpretation. Concerning earliest experience he states that gross patterns describing the infant's relationship with parents constitute "utterly buried but quite firm foundations on which a great deal more is superimposed or built" (p. 6). Thus, patterns of past relationships, as they are "colored" by the zones of interaction, become patterns within the self-system.

**Change: Change Originates with Tension and Its Exact Manifestation Is Probabilistic and Epigenetic.** Tension is the central concept of Sullivan's theory; indeed, he describes the interpersonal theory as a "tensional history" of the child. Given its centrality, tension is elaborated in several ways, including the classification of tensors, the process by which tensions manifest themselves and possible outcomes. First, tensors are classified as needs or anxiety. Needs result from biological disequilibrium, and in early development, the satisfaction of needs is the engine that drives the newborn's communal nature, acquisition of semiotic tools, and the emergence of foresight: In satisfying needs through the mothering one, the infant is immediately confronted with the inherent sociality of existence and with the gradual realization that certain patterns of energy transformations lead to the satisfaction of needs. Needs give rise to interpersonal relationships, which may be conjunctive or disjunctive, depending on whether a given interaction in fact satisfies a need.

In marked contrast to needs, anxiety is a nonspecific feeling – described as dread, awe, horror, or loathing – that results from disturbances in significant others in the interpersonal field. Whereas the satisfaction of needs leads to the reestablishment of biological equilibrium, the relaxation of anxiety leads to a sense of psychological security. In early development, Sullivan argued that the "me" differentiates into a good-me, bad-me, and not-me, all of which are personifications made up from prior experiences. Good-me contains integrating experiences that led to satisfactions and is most often the "I" of conversations. Bad-me is the personification of disintegrating experiences, when anxiety was induced in the child because of disturbances in the mother. Eventually, a secondary dynamism, the self-system, emerges to organize present experience so as to avoid the self's experiencing of anxiety. The self-system escapes experience incompatible with its current organization and functional activity by promoting insensitivity to experience. Sullivan considers many strategies typically used to censor experience of bad-me connotations (e.g., selective inattention, by which individuals fail to take note of specific details in the field). Unfortunately, such inattention can lead to understandings of the field that cannot be consensually validated by others, the beginning of mental disorder.

On the other hand, anxiety is the basis for all cultural learning and hence the maintenance of cultural systems. (The relationship between anxiety and the maintenance of cultural systems represents an example of how microinteractions reproduce larger social structures; cf. Corsaro, 1992.) Less intense anxiety acts as a signal to alert individuals of inhibitions; in fact, the anxiety gradient (i.e., changes in anxiety as a function of the situation) is used by the individual to discriminate between inhibited and socially sanctioned behaviors and to alter his or her course of action accordingly. Sullivan went to some lengths to incorporate various forms of learning into his framework and not all of them are connected to anxiety. However, early learning is based on the avoidance of anxiety, and this form of learning is intimately connected with the ability of the self-system to function syntactically.

Sullivan's system is a probabilistic, epigenetic model, although this area is open to theoretical development. Probabilistic epigenesis ultimately rests on bidirectionality in the system, and for Sullivan, this bidirectionality is found in his Meadian approach to interpersonal relationships. The emergent, probabilistic nature of developmental phenomena traces to the bidirectional and complex exchanges taking place between persons. This complexity is enhanced further by the many different interpersonal fields within which development takes place.

**Patterns of Change: The Levels of the System Are Coactional, with Functionally Coordinated Changes Occurring Throughout.** The concept of coaction is implicit in the central concepts of Sullivan's system. He rejected the notion of a free-standing individual, personality, or culture, arguing that the only meaningful sense in which any of these concepts exist is within interpersonal fields, in their coaction. Sullivan's framework is fundamentally concerned with coactions between cultural elements and psychobiological functioning as they take place between individuals. These relationships occur in interpersonal situations, which either integrate or disintegrate. Integrating situations represent the successful coaction of biological needs, the individual's self-system, and cultural elements as they are instantiated in the interpersonal field. More or less acculturated persons interdependently satisfy their needs, encouraging or inhibiting actions in each other with anxiety gradients. Ideally, cultural prescriptions inform the self-system so that how one proceeds to satisfy needs is always consensually validated in the interpersonal field. In these instances, cultural prescriptions and psychobiologically based needs coact: Cultural prescriptions are honored and the individual's needs are satisfied.

On the other hand, psychiatry is concerned with the lack of coaction in the field, the patterned way in which situations disintegrate. Situations disintegrate when individuals fail to validate ongoing experience consensually, to communicate syntactically. This failure reflects a distortion in the self-system of one of the persons in the field; anxiety prompts the self-system to censor experience, and this censoring leads to a failure to define the situation consensually, since one party has but a subset of the relevant field data. To reestablish coactionality, the psychiatrist must enter the field as a participant observer and determine when, during patterned activity, syntactic communication breaks down. This juncture represents the intervention of anxiety, and the task then becomes to understand why anxiety has been triggered, drawing on the individual's tensional history.

**Development: Intellectual and Social Criteria Distinguish the Types of Change That Developmentalists Study.** Sullivan (1945) explicitly identified his internal-intellectual roots in Freud, the psychobiologist and his teacher Adolf Meyer, and his mentor William Alanson White (Blitsten, 1953; Mullahy & Melinek, 1983). External-intellectual influences are also clear: Sapir and Benedict in linguistics and anthropology, Lewin, Cooley, and Mead in social psychology, and Bridgman in the philosophy of science. Many of Sullivan's themes also sit well with American pragmatism, especially the primacy of experience and scientific efforts to understand it.

There were, arguably, social and personal forces at work as well. In examining Sullivan's life history, one finds ample evidence of marginality, including his socioeconomic and religious background, social isolation until he began working at St. Elizabeth's Hospital, sexual confusion, alcoholic tendencies, and possibly schizophrenic episodes (Perry, 1982). In late life Sullivan became familiar with the Chicago school of sociology (especially W. I. Thomas), and he came to view many of his earlier tribulations as reflecting broader social changes taking place in urban areas in the United States. This marginality, and his subsequent realization that it was "legitimate," undoubtedly informed one of the great premises of Sullivan's conceptual framework: that people are more alike than not. Taking this premise seriously, Sullivan developed a legendary reputation as a clinician in his work with schizophrenics.

## Discussion: Looking for Development across Disciplines

In the seminal volume *The Concept of Development*, Harris (1957) notes that the concept of development is fundamentally biological, although applicable to other disciplines. In this chapter we elaborate that assertion: Several basic concepts that have proved useful to the study of development in psychobiology have also been useful in psychology and sociology. These conceptually transposable elements may indicate the influence that biology has had on both developmental psychology (Ford & Lerner, 1992; Gottlieb, in press; Schneirla, 1959, 1965) and sociology (Hodgson, 1991; Smelser, 1988; Wallace, 1988). At the same time, these commonalities may reflect disciplinary convergences on the unity of development in complex systems.

The relevance of biological models is not surprising given that change and development figure prominently in the conceptual history of biology, especially in the realm of embryology. However, the biological sciences have also assumed thought models from the social sciences (e.g., in immunology, see Löwy, 1992). Disciplinary boundaries are constantly being transcended, sometimes resulting in major accomplishments (Crick, 1988), although the institutional structuring of the research enterprise works to fortify disciplinary isolation.

Harris noted that the transposability of biological concepts to developmental science is characterized by a tension between a unity of science position, arguing that general theory can embrace phenomena at all levels of analysis, versus a discontinuity position, arguing that each level is governed by unique laws. Our analysis in this chapter reveals both substantial convergence and unevenness among the disciplines. For example, there is substantial convergence on the use of multiple time frames and their interplay, while the disciplines show marked unevenness in their discussions of bidirectionality.

Some unevenness traces to historical circumstance, while some reflects specificities of the levels of analysis. For example, developmental research studies phenomena that cannot be addressed completely by biology – namely, the symbolic-laden cultural worlds of receptive human beings, seen also as agents of change. Recently, attention has been given to the semiotic level of psychological functioning (Boesch, 1991; Cole, 1990, 1992; Rogoff, 1990; Shweder, 1990; Shweder & Sullivan, 1993). In the sociology of children, an interest in symbols and culture has been a central theme in recent research (Corsaro & Eder, 1994).

Given the biological, psychological, and social dimensions of development, the promotion of a "developmental science" can only refer to multidisciplinary efforts. Clarification of the theoretical profiles of different disciplines plays a critical role in this intellectual enterprise. In the final analysis, a better understanding of the commonalities and unevenness among the disciplines will contribute to the emergence and refinement of a developmental science that both reflects a unity of science framework and capitalizes on disciplinary-specific strengths.

## References

Abbott, A. (1988). Transcending general linear reality. *Sociological Theory, 6*, 169–186.

Andreski, S. (1971). Introductory essay: Sociology, biology and philosophy in Herbert Spencer. In S. Andreski (Ed.), *Herbert Spencer: Structure, function and evolution* (pp. 7–32). London: Michael Joseph.

Anokhin, K. V., Mileusnic, R., Shamakina, I. Y., & Rose, S. (1991). Effects of early experience on c-Fos gene expression in the chick prebrain. *Brain Research, 544*, 101–107.

Bailey, K. D. (1984). Equilibrium, entropy and homeostasis: A multidisciplinary legacy, *Systems Research, 1*, 25–43.

Baldwin, J. M. (1906). *Thought and things: A study of the development and meaning of thought, or genetic logic: Vol. 1. Functional logic or genetic theory of knowledge.* London: Swan Sonnenschein.

Banker, H., & Lickliter, R. (1993). Effects of early and delayed visual experience on intersensory development in bobwhite quail chicks. *Developmental Psychobiology, 26*, 155–170.

Baron, J. N., & Bielby, W. T. (1980). Bringing the firm back in: Stratification, segmentation, and the organization of work. *American Sociological Review, 45*, 737–765.

Benedict, R. (1934). *Patterns of culture.* Boston, MA: Houghton Mifflin.

Berk, R. A. (1988). Causal inference for sociological data. In N. Smelser (Ed.), *Handbook of sociology* (pp. 155–172). Newbury Park, CA: Sage.

Best, J. (1990). *Threatened children: Rhetoric and concern about child victims.* Chicago: University of Chicago Press.

Bidell, T. R., & Fischer, K. W. (1992). Cognitive development in educational contexts. In A. Demetriou, M. Shayer, & A. Efklides (Eds.), *Neo-Piagetian theories of cognitive development* (pp. 11–30). London: Routledge.

Blitsten, D. R. (1953). *The social theories of Harry Stack Sullivan.* New York: William-Frederick.

Boesch, E. E. (1991). *Symbolic action theory and cultural psychology.* Berlin: Springer.

Bronfenbrenner, U. (1979). *The ecology of human development.* Cambridge, MA: Harvard University Press.

Cairns, R. B. (1992). The making of a developmental science: The contributions and intellectual heritage of James Mark Baldwin. *Developmental Psychology, 28*, 17–24.

(1993). Belated but bedazzling: Timing and genetic influence in social development. In G. Turkewitz and D. A. Devenny (Eds.), *Developmental time and timing* (pp. 61–84). Hillsdale, NJ: Erlbaum.

Cairns, R. B., Gariépy, J.-L., & Hood, K. E. (1990). Development, microevolution and social behavior. *Psychological Review*, *97*, 49–65.
Cairns, R. B., MacCombie, D. J., & Hood, K. E. (1983). A developmental-genetic analysis of aggressive behavior in mice: I. behavioral outcomes. *Journal of Comparative Psychology*, *97*, 69–89.
Cairns, R. B., McGuire, A. M., & Gariépy, J.-L. (1993). Developmental behavior genetics: Fusion, correlated constraints, and timing. In D. F. Hay and A. Angold (Eds.), *Precursors and causes in development and psychopathology* (pp. 87–122). New York: Wiley.
Calamandrei, G., & Keverne, E. B. (1994). Differential expression of Fos protein in the brain of female mice [is] dependent on pup sensory cues and maternal experience. *Behavioral Neuroscience*, *108*, 113–120.
Campbell, J. H., & Perkins, P. (1988). Transgenerational effects of drug and hormone treatments in mammals. *Progress in Brain Research*, *75*, 535–553.
Chrousos, G. P., & Gold, P. W. (1992). The concepts of stress and stress systems disorder. *Journal of the American Medical Association*, *267*, 1244–1252.
Cole, M. (1990). Cultural psychology: A once and future discipline? In J. Berman (Ed.), *Nebraska Symposium on Motivation* (pp. 279–336). Lincoln: University of Nebraska Press.
(1992). Context, modularity and the cultural constitution of development. In L. T. Winegar and J. Valsiner (Eds.), *Children's development within social context: Vol. 2. Research and methodology* (pp. 5–31). Hillsdale, NJ: Erlbaum.
Cole, M. (Ed.). (1978). *Mind in society: The development of higher psychological processes, by L. S. Vygotsky*. Cambridge, MA: Harvard University Press.
Coleman, J. S. (1988). Social capital in the creation of human capital. *American Journal of Sociology*, *94*, S95–S120
(1991). *Social capital, human capital, and investment in youth.* Paper presented at the Johann Jacobs Foundation, Marbach, Germany.
Collins, R. (1988). *Theoretical sociology*. San Diego, CA: Harcourt, Brace, Jovanovich.
Corsaro, W. A. (1992). Interpretive reproduction in children's peer cultures. *Social Psychology Quarterly*, *55,* 160–177.
Corsaro, W. A., & Eder, D. (1994). The development and socialization of children and adolescents. In K. S. Cook, G. A. Fine, and J. S. House (Eds.), *Sociological perspectives on social psychology* (pp. 421–451). Boston: Allyn & Bacon.
Crick, F. (1988). *What mad pursuit: A personal view of scientific discovery.* London: Penguin.
Dannefer, D. (1984). Adult development and social theory: A paradigmatic reappraisal. *American Sociological Review*, *49*, 100–116.

Denzin, N. (1977). *Childhood socialization.* San Francisco: Jossey-Bass.
Driesch, H. (1929). *The science and philosophy of the organism.* London: Black.
Durkheim, Emile. (1951). *Suicide.* Glencoe, IL: Free Press.
Edelman, G. M. (1992). *Bright air, brilliant fire.* New York: Basic.
Elder, G. H., Jr. (1986). Military times and turning points in men's lives. *Developmental Psychology, 22,* 233–245.
(1987). War mobilization and the life course: A cohort of World War II veterans. *Sociological Forum, 2,* 449–472.
Elder, G. H., Jr., & Caspi, A. (1990). Studying lives in a changing society: Sociological and personological explorations. In A. I. Rabin, R. A. Zucker, and S. Frank (Eds.), *Studying persons and lives* (pp. 201–247). New York: Springer.
Elder, G. H., Jr., Modell, J., & Parke, R. D. (1993). Studying children in a changing world. In G. H. Elder Jr., J. Modell, & R. D. Parke (Eds.), *Children in time and place* (pp. 1–46). Cambridge University Press.
Fine, R. (1979). *A history of psychoanalysis.* New York: Columbia University Press.
Fischer, K. W. (1980). A theory of cognitive development: The control and construction of hierarchies of skills. *Psychological Review, 87,* 477–531.
Fischer, K. W., & Bullock, D. (1984). Cognitive development in school-age children: Conclusions and new directions. In W. A. Collins (Ed.), *The years from 6 to 12: Cognitive development during middle childhood* (pp. 70–146). Washington, DC: National Academy Press.
Fischer, K. W., Bullock, D. H., Rotenberg, E. J., & Raya, P. (1993). The dynamics of competence: How context contributes directly to skill. In R. H. Wozniak and K. W. Fischer (Eds.), *Development in context* (pp. 93–120). Hillsdale, NJ: Erlbaum.
Fischer, K. W., & Farrar, M. J. (1987). Generalizations about generalization: How a theory of skill development explains both generality and specificity. *International Journal of Psychology, 22,* 643–677.
Fischer, K. W., & Kenny, S. L. (1986). The environmental conditions for discontinuities in the development of abstractions. In R. Mines & K. Kitchener (Eds.), *Adult cognitive development* (pp. 57–75). New York: Praeger.
Fishbein, H. D. (1976). *Evolution, development, and children's learning.* Pacific Palisades, CA: Goodyear.
Flavell, J. H. (1963). *The developmental psychology of Jean Piaget.* New York: Van Nostrand.
Ford, D. H., & Lerner, R. M. (1992). *Developmental systems theory: An integrative approach.* Newbury Park, CA: Sage.
Freud, S. (1933/1937). *New introductory lectures on psychoanalysis.* London: Hogarth and Institute of Psychoanalysis.

Fuller, J. L. (1967). Experiential deprivation and later behavior. *Science, 158*, 1645–1652.

Furth, H. G. (1981). *Piaget and knowledge: Theoretical foundations*. Chicago: University of Chicago Press.

Gariépy, J.-L. (1994). The mediation of aggressive behavior in mice: A discussion of approach–withdrawal processes in social adaptation. In K. E. Hood, G. Greenberg, & E. Tobach (Eds.), *Behavioral development in comparative perspective: The approach–withdrawal theory of T. C. Schneirla* (pp. 231–283). New York: Garland.

Gay, P. (1988). *Freud: A life for our own time*. New York: Norton.

van Geert, P. (1987). The structure of developmental theories: A generative approach. *Human Development, 30*, 160–177.

(1988a). The concept of transition in developmental theories. In W. J. Baker, L. P. Mos, H. V. Rappard, & H. J. Stam (Eds.), *Recent trends in theoretical psychology* (pp. 225–235). New York: Springer.

(1988b). A graph theoretical approach to the structure of developmental models. *Human Development, 31*, 107–135.

Giddens, A. (1976). *New rules of sociological method: A positive critique of interpretative sociologies*. London: Hutchinson.

(1979). *Central problems in social theory: Action, structure and contradiction in social analysis*. London: Macmillan.

(1984). *The constitution of society: Outline of a theory of structuration*. Cambridge: Polity.

(1985). *The nation-state and violence: Vol. 2. A contemporary critique of historical materialism*. Berkeley: University of California Press.

(1991). *Modernity and self-identity: Self and society in the late modern age*. Stanford, CA: Stanford University Press.

(1992). *The transformation of intimacy*. Oxford: Polity.

Gigerenzer, G. (1991). From tools to theories: A heuristic discovery in cognitive psychology. *Psychological Review, 98*, 254–267.

Gigerenzer, G., & Murray, D. J. (1987). *Cognition as intuitive statistics*. Hillsdale, NJ: Erlbaum.

Glick, P. C., & Norton, A. J. (1977). Marrying, divorcing, and living together in the U.S. today. *Population Bulletin, 32*, 15.

Gottlieb, G. (1970). Conceptions of prenatal behavior. In L. R. Aronson, E. Tobach, D. S. Lehrman, and J. S. Rosenblatt (Eds.), *Development and evolution of behavior* (pp. 111–137). San Francisco: Freeman.

(1991a). Experiential canalization of behavioral development: Theory. *Developmental Psychology, 27*, 4–13.

(1991b). Experiential canalization of behavioral development: Results. *Developmental Psychology, 27*, 33–34.

(1992). *Individual development and evolution: The genesis of novel behavior*. New York: Oxford University Press.

(in press). A systems view of psychobiological development. In D. Magnusson (Ed.), *Individual development over the lifespan: Biological and psychosocial perspectives* (pp. 76–104). Cambridge University Press.

Harris, D. B. (1957). *The concept of development: An issue in the study of human behavior*. Minneapolis: University of Minnesota Press.

Hinde, R. A. (1990). The interdependence of the behavioral sciences. *Philosophical Transactions of the Royal Society, London B, 329*, 217–227.

Ho, M.-W. (1984). Environment and heredity in development and evolution. In M.-W. Ho & P. T. Saunders (Eds.), *Beyond neo-Darwinism: An introduction to the new evolutionary paradigm* (pp. 267–289). San Diego, CA: Academic Press.

Hobhouse, L. T. (1927/1969). *Development and purpose*. London: Macmillian.

Hodgson, D. (1991). The ideological origins of the Population Association of America. *Population and Development Review, 17*, 1–34.

Hogan, D. P. (1981). *Transitions and social change: The early lives of American men*. New York: Academic Press.

Hogan, D. P., & Astone, N. M. (1986). The transition to adulthood. *Annual Review of Sociology, 12*, 109–130.

Horowitz, F. D. (1987). *Exploring developmental theories: Toward a structural/behavioral model of development*. Hillsdale, NJ: Erlbaum.

House, J. S., & Mortimer, J. T. (1990). Social structure and the individual: Emerging themes and new directions. *Social Psychology Quarterly, 53*, 71–80.

Janet, P. (1926). *De l'angoisse a l'extase*. Paris: Alcan.

Johnson, E. O., Kamilaris, T. C., Chrousos, G. P., & Gold, P. W. (1992). Mechanisms of stress: A dynamic overview of hormonal and behavioral homeostasis: *Neuroscience and Biobehavioral Reviews, 16*, 115–130.

Kahlbaugh, P. E. (1993). James Mark Baldwin: A bridge between social and cognitive theories of development. *Journal for the Theory of Social Behavior, 23*, 79–103.

Kalberg, S. (1983). Max Weber's universal-historical architectonic of economically-oriented action: A preliminary construction. In S. McNall (Ed.), *Current perspectives in social theory* (pp. 233–258). Greenwich, CN: JAI Press.

Kalicki, B. (1994). Die Normalbiographie als psychologisches Regulativ: Zum subjectiven Bedeutungsgehalt von Lebensereignissen, die vom normalbiographischen Zeitmuster abweichen. Unpublished dissertation, University of Trier, Germany.

Kohn, M. L., & Schooler, C. (1983). *Work and personality: An inquiry into the impact of social stratification*. Norwood, NJ: Ablex.

Kovach, J. K., & Wilson, G. (1988). Genetics of color preferences in quail chicks: Major genes and variable buffering by background genotype. *Behavioral Genetics*, *18*, 645–661.

Kruttschnitt, C., McLeod, J. D., & Dornfeld, M. (1994). The economic environment of child abuse. *Social Problems*, *41*, 299–315.

Kuhn, T. (1970). *The structure of scientific revolutions* (2nd ed.). Chicago: University of Chicago Press.

Lakatos, I. (1978). *The methodology of scientific research programs*. Cambridge University Press.

Langer, J. (1969). Disequilibrium as a source of development. In P. Mussen, J. Langer, & M. Covington (Eds.), *Trends and issues in developmental psychology* (pp. 22–37). New York: Holt, Rinehart, & Winston.

(1970). Werner's comparative organismic theory. In P. H. Mussen (Ed.), *Carmichael's manual of child pscyhology* (pp. 733–771). New York: Wiley.

Lawrence, J. A., & Valsiner, J. (1993). Conceptual roots of internalization: From transmission to transformation. *Human Development*, *36*, 150–167.

Lerner, R. M., & Kaufman, M. B. (1985). The concept of development in contextualism. *Developmental Review*, *5*, 309–333.

Lickliter, R., & Hellewell, T. B. (1992). Contextual determinants of auditory learning in bobwhite quail embryos and hatchlings. *Developmental Psychobiology*, *25*, 17–31.

Löwy, I. (1992). The strength of loose concepts–boundary concepts, federative experimental strategies and disciplinary growth: The case of immunology. *History of Science*, *30*, 376–396.

London, I. D. (1949). The concept of the behavioral spectrum. *Journal of Genetic Psychology*, *74*, 177–184.

Lumsden, C. J., & Wilson, E. O. (1980). Translation of epigenetic rules of individual behavior to ethnographic patterns. *Proceedings of the National Academy of Sciences, USA*, *77*, 4382–4386.

Magnusson, D. (1988). *Individual development from an interactional perspective: A longitudinal perspective*. Hillsdale, NJ: Erlbaum.

Mazlish, B. (1989). *A new science: The breakdown of connections and the birth of sociology*. University Park, PA: Pennsylvania State University Press.

Mazzarello, P., Poloni, M., Spadari, S., & Focher, F. (1992). DNA repair mechanisms in neurological diseases: Facts and hypotheses. *Journal of Neurological Science*, *112*, 4–14.

Mead, M. (1934). *Mind, self, society*. Chicago: University of Chicago Press.

Miller, D. B., Hicinbotham, G., & Blaich, C. F. (1990). Alarm call responsivity in mallard ducklings: Multiple pathways in behavioural development. *Animal Behaviour*, *39*, 1207–1212.

Moen, P., Kain, E. L., & Elder, G. H., Jr. (1983). Economic conditions and family life: Contemporary and historical perpsectives. In R. R. Nelson & F. Skidmore (Eds.), *American families and the economy: The high costs of living* (pp. 213–254). Washington, DC: National Academy Press.

Mullahy, P., & Melinek, M. (1983). *Interpersonal psychiatry.* New York: SP Medical and Scientific Books.

Neugarten, B. L., Moore, J. W., & Lowe, J. C. (1965). Age norms, age constraints, and socialization norms. *American Journal of Sociology, 70,* 710–717.

Parker, S. T., & Gibson, K. R. (1979). A developmental model for the evolution of language and intelligence in early hominids. *Behavioral and Brain Sciences, 2,* 367–408.

Patriarca, S. (1994). Statistical nation building and the consolidation of regions in Italy. *Social Science History, 18,* 357–376.

Pattee, H. H. (1973). Physical problems of the origin of natural controls. In A. Locker (Ed.), *Biogenesis, evolution, homeostasis* (pp. 41–49). New York: Springer.

Perry, H. S. (1982). *Psychiatrist of America: The life of Harry Stack Sullivan.* Cambridge, MA: Harvard University Press.

Piaget, J. (1970). *Structuralism.* New York: Basic.

(1971). *Biology and knowledge.* Chicago: University of Chicago Press.

Porter, T. M. (1986). *The rise of statistical thinking: 1820–1900.* Princeton, NJ: Princeton University Press.

Riley, M. W., Foner, A., & Waring, J. (1988). Sociology of age. In N. Smelser (Ed.), *Handbook of sociology* (pp. 243–291). Newbury Park, CA: Sage.

Rindfuss, R. R., Swicegood, C. G., & Rosenfeld, R. A. (1987). Disorder in the life course: How common and does it matter? *American Sociological Review, 52,* 785–801.

Ritzer, G. (1988). Sociological metatheory: A defense of a subfield by a delineation of its parameters. *Sociological Theory, 6,* 187–200.

Rogoff, B. (1990). *Apprenticeship in thinking: Cognitive development in social context.* New York: Oxford University Press.

Rustak, B., Robertson, H. A., Wisden, W., & Hunt, S. P. (1990). Light pulses that shift rhythms induce gene expression in the suprachiasmatic nucleus. *Science, 248,* 1237–1240.

Sameroff, A. J. (1983). Developmental systems: Contexts and evolution. In P. H. Mussen (Ed.), *Handbook of child psychology: Vol. 1. History, theory and methods* (4th ed., pp. 237–294). New York: Wiley.

Sander, F., & Volkelt, H. (1962). *Ganzheitspsychologie.* Muchic: Beck.

Scarr-Salapatek, S. (1976). Genetic determinants of infant development: An overstated case. In L. Lipsitt (Ed.), *Developmental psychobiology: The significance of the infant* (pp. 59–79). Hillsdale, NJ: Erlbaum.

Schneirla, T. C. (1959). An evolutionary and developmental theory of biphasic processes underlying approach and withdrawal. *Nebraska Symposium on Motivation*, *7*, 1–42.

(1965). Aspects of stimulation and organization in approach/withdrawal processes underlying vertebrate behavioral development. *Advances in the Study of Animal Behavior*, *1*, 1–71.

Shapiro, T. (Ed.). (1991). *The concept of structure in psychoanalysis*. Madison, CT: International Universities Press.

Shweder, R. (1990). Cultural psychology – What is it? In J. W. Stigler, R. A. Shweder, & G. Herdt (Eds.), *Cultural psychology* (pp. 1–43). Cambridge University Press.

Shweder, R., & Sullivan, M. (1993). Cultural psychology – Who needs it? *Annual Review of Psychology*, *44*, 497–523.

Silberman, I. (1981). Balance and anxiety. *Psychoanalytic Study of Children*, *36*, 365–380.

Sjövall, B. (1967). *Psychology of tension: An analysis of Pierre Janet's concept of "tension psychologique" together with an historical aspect*. Nordstedts: Svenska Bokforlaget.

Smelser, N. (1988). Social structure. In N. Smelser (Ed.), *Handbook of sociology* (pp. 103–129). Newbury Park, CA: Sage.

Smith, B. (Ed.). (1988). *Foundations of Gestalt theory*. Munich: Philosophia.

Spitz, R. (1965). *The first year of life*. New York: International Universities Press.

Stern, W. (1938). *General psychology from a personalistic standpoint*. New York: Macmillan.

Sullivan, H. S. (1945). *Conceptions of modern psychiatry*. New York: Norton.

(1953). *The interpersonal theory of psychiatry*. New York: Norton.

Turkewitz, G., & Devenny, D. A. (1993). Timing and the shape of development. In G. Turkewitz & D. A. Devenny (Eds.), *Developmental time and timing* (pp. 1–11). Hillsdale, NJ: Erlbaum.

Valsiner, J. (1987). *Culture and the development of children's action*. Chichester: Wiley.

van der Veer, R., & Valsiner, J. (1991). *Understanding Vygotsky: A quest for synthesis*. Oxford: Blackwell.

Waddington, C. (1971). Concepts of development. In E. Tobach, L. R. Aronson, & E. Shaw (Eds.), *The psychobiology of development* (pp. 17–23). San Diego, CA: Academic Press.

Wahlsten, D., & Gottlieb, G. (in press). The invalid separation of effects of nature and nurture: Lessons from animal experimentation. In R. J. Sternberg & E. L. Grigorenko (Eds.), *Intelligence: Heredity and environment*. Cambridge University Press.

Wallace, W. L. (1988). Toward a disciplinary matrix in sociology. In N. Smelser (Ed.), *Handbook of sociology* (pp. 23–76). Newbury Park, CA: Sage.

Weiss, P. (1959). Cellular dynamics. *Review of Modern Physics*, *31*, 11–20.

Werner, H. (1957). The concept of development from a comparative and organismic point of view. In D. B. Harris (Ed.), *The concept of development* (pp. 125–147). Minneapolis, MN: University of Minneapolis Press.

Wertsch, J. V. (1985). *Vygotsky and the social formation of the mind.* Cambridge, MA: Harvard University Press.

Winegar, L. T., & Valsiner, J. (1992). Re-contextualizing context: Analysis of metadata and some further elaborations. In L. T. Winegar & J. Valsiner (Eds.), *Children's development in social context: Vol. 2. Research and methodology* (pp. 249–266). Hillsdale, NJ: Erlbaum.

Wright, S. (1968). *Evolution and the genetics of population: Vol. 1. Genetic and biometric foundations.* Chicago: University of Chicago Press.

Youniss, J. (1992). Parent and peer relations in the emergence of cultural competence. In H. McGurk (Ed.), *Childhood social development: Contemporary perspectives* (pp. 131–147). Hillsdale, NJ: Erlbaum.

# 3 Ecological Perspectives in Human Development: A Comparison of Gibson and Bronfenbrenner

*Jonathan Tudge, Jacquelyn T. Gray, and Diane M. Hogan*

In this chapter we provide a brief overview of ecological perspectives as they relate to human development, as the background to more extensive discussion of the perspectives taken by two theorists, James Gibson and Urie Bronfenbrenner. Despite their very different foci (Gibson being concerned primarily with perception, Bronfenbrenner with social contexts) and their different levels of analysis, they share basic assumptions and, we shall argue, their perspectives should be viewed as complementary. The assumptions that they share derive from their acceptance of an ecological perspective.

What is an ecological perspective? It is a standpoint for conceptualizing the changing maturing person in relation to a changing environment – social, physical, and psychological. The ecological perspective is shared with other frameworks within which human development is considered, ranging from cultural psychology as represented by Shweder (1990), Rogoff (1990), and Valsiner (1989), through the co-constructionist perspective on development (Tudge, Putnam, & Valsiner, in press; Wozniak, 1993), and encompassing developmental psychobiology (Gottlieb, 1992, in press; Johnston, 1985). Although the ecological perspective, and the term *ecology*, originated (at least in modern day science) in biology, its use spans several disciplines, among which is developmental psychology. There, it is linked most notably to the work of James Gibson and Urie Bronfenbrenner. For both of these theorists an ecological perspective has unique meaning, yet fundamentally they share a belief in the

Preparation of this chapter was facilitated by the award of a National Academy of Education Spencer Fellowship to the first author. We would like to express our appreciation to the members of the Carolina Consortium on Human Development for the intellectual stimulation gained from our weekly discussions, and particularly to Michael Shanahan, Jaan Valsiner, and Timothy Johnston for their insightful comments on an earlier draft.

necessity of viewing the individual and the environment as they relate to and define each other. They have built their theories upon this premise.

Ecology is the study of organism–environment interrelatedness. The coining of the term *ecology* is usually credited to the German zoologist and evolutionist Ernest Haeckel. In 1873 Haeckel proposed a new science (called oekologie, from the Greek word *oik*, for living place or house) to study organisms in their environment, which he believed to be inseparable parts of a whole (Bubolz & Sontag, 1993).

In the late nineteenth century, interest in person–environment interrelatedness grew, accelerating with the emergence of Darwin's theory of evolution and the role of the environment in adaptation and species survival. This was also a time of rapid urbanization, industrialization, and social reform, and there was concern about how individuals and families would fare in the face of such change. The use of the term *ecology* appeared in the study of the family as early as 1892. Ellen Swallow Richards unsuccessfully tried to persuade the cofounders of home economics (the early name of the field devoted to the study of children and families in context) to name the new discipline oekologie, in keeping with their aim of studying individuals as social beings relating to their immediate environments (Bubolz & Sontag, 1993; Clarke, 1973). Other disciplines, such as geography (Barrows, 1923) and sociology (Burgess, 1926; Park, 1936; Thomas & Znaniecki 1918–1920), also incorporated ecological approaches early in the century. The perspective has also appeared in anthropology, economics, and human–environment relations (Bubolz & Sontag, 1993).

## Ecological Ideas in Historical Perspective

The idea that the study of human development must involve consideration of the context or environment in which it takes place is not new. Indeed, it has been around for at least a century (Bronfenbrenner, 1993; Valsiner, 1992; van der Veer & Valsiner, 1988). The study of development in relation to environment can be traced to Germany in the 1870s and the research of Schwabe and Bartholomai on influences of neighborhood environment and the development of concepts in children. These scholars concluded, "It is an undeniable fact that the average individuality of the child in a metropolis . . . is a different one, in consequence of the influence of his surroundings, from that of a child living in a rural district or in a small town" (quoted in Bronfenbrenner & Crouter, 1983, p. 360). Many other scholars have contributed to the emergence of ecological approaches to human development since then, and several of them will be mentioned in the following pages. These scholars have not at any time represented the mainstream of psychology (developmental or otherwise), but their contributions to current trends toward a greater acceptance of contextualism and ecological models should not be underrated.

For example, in U.S. psychology at the turn of the century, James Mark Baldwin (1895) wrote that the question "How does the indivdual organism manage to adjust itself better and better to its environment? . . . [was] the most urgent, difficult and neglected question of the new genetic psychology" (pp. 180–181, quoted in Cairns, 1992, p. 19). In the Soviet Union, similar interest was being shown in the ways in which individual development and the social world were interrelated. Lev Vygotsky's cultural-historical theory clearly linked development with social context. In Vygotsky's theory, learning takes place through interaction with more competent others, and all development is framed within a context that is socially created at both local and broad societal levels and is affected by the developing nature of the individual (Tudge et al., in press; Tudge & Winterhoff, 1993; van der Veer & Valsiner, 1991; Vygotsky, 1978; Wertsch, 1985). Dewey's understanding of development was very close to Vygotsky's in that Dewey (1911) believed that "mind and character require a culture medium in order to develop" (p. 422) and saw development as a process that is related to social practices, beliefs, and ideologies. Both theorists echoed Pierre Janet's idea of sociogenesis – knowledge being first interpersonal and then becoming intrapersonal (van der Veer & Valsiner, 1988; Tudge et al., in press).

Organismic theorists Kurt Goldstein (1939) and Andra Angyal (1941) argued for holism, a related concept. Drawing from Dewey's article "The Reflex Arc Concept in Psychology" (1896), Angyal (1941) held that attempts to separate individual from environment were futile, since, given the complexity of their interpenetration, any resulting separation would create an artificial distinction. Angyal described the total entity, or biosphere (which comprised the biological, social, and psychological individual), "not as interacting parts, not as constituents which have independent existence, but as aspects of a single reality which can be separated only by abstraction" (p. 100).

These perspectives have never been at the forefront of psychology, particularly as practiced in the United States, where it has been and continues to be dominated by an experimental and reductionistic model adopted from the physical sciences, rather than an ecological perspective derived from biology. Although some psychologists have argued for a more holistic approach (considering the interrelatedness of individual, physical, sociohistorical, and cultural aspects of development), the discipline has been dominated by those who have taken a dichotomous stance on the relation between the individual and environment.

The origins of this dichotomous stance can be traced back to the nineteenth century and associationist thought (see, e.g., Boole's *Laws of Thought*, 1854). The dichotomy was instantiated at the time of the official recognition of the discipline as a science, when in 1879 Wilhelm Wundt opened his laboratory in Leipzig, Germany. Wundt distinguished between experiences that are open to individual introspection and those that are social in nature, the latter being, in his view, quite separate (Laboratory of Comparative Human Cognition, 1983). Wundt believed that the study of both was essential and, indeed, complementary (Cole, 1989). However, the rift between empirical and descriptive psychological investigation has endured to the present day. In ensuing years, North American psychologists working in the traditions of functionalism, behaviorism, and experimental and cognitive psychology have striven to "control" context and values in the quest for objectivity (equated with the physical sciences) and the building of a nomothetic science of thought and behavior (Suppe, 1977). Ironically, this positivist perspective was embraced most fully by social scientists during the time when philosophers of science began to seriously doubt its usefulness (Doherty, Boss, LaRossa, Schumm, & Steinmetz, 1993; Suppe, 1977).

To several psychologists, however, it was evident in the early years of the new discipline that a purely experimental and reductionistic methodology could not adequately answer all questions pertaining to psychological phenomena. Criticism of reductionism in the United States can be traced to pragmatists John Dewey (Wertsch, 1991) and William James, and in Germany to Wilhelm Dilthey (Cole, 1979, cited in Bronfenbrenner, 1979). For example, John Dewey (1902) believed development to be the interaction of forces within the maturing child with social values, goals, and meanings of the adult world; "The education process is due to the interaction of these forces" (p. 272, quoted in Cahan, 1992). From an ideology of progress, Dewey emphasized that the social world was dynamic rather than static (Cahan, 1992).

The ideas of Dewey and James laid the foundations for symbolic interactionism, and indeed two of its early leaders, Cooley and Mead, were trained in the tradition of pragmatism. While this group contributed to early excitement with scientific methods in the United States, their principal ideas centered on the social construction of meaning, or socially based development. Symbolic interactionism is premised on the reciprocal nature of person–social environment relationships. Humans are seen as creating together a symbolic world, which in turn shapes their behavior. In Charles Horton Cooley's writing (1902/1956) the process by which the concept of self develops is clearly social and dialectical. The "looking glass self" emerges through interactions with others in the environment; the child acts socially, perceives others' assessments of the behavior, and bases his or her reaction on that perception (1902/1956). Likewise, in George Herbert Mead's view, development of the mind (meaning and consciousness) is a social process. Consensual meaning arises out of interpersonal actions and responses (Mead, 1934/1956). Furthermore, in the immediate settings in which people live there was thought to be continuous mutual influence. Ernest E. Burgess (1926) believed that the behaviors and actions of each family member could, and would, change the interaction patterns of all other members of the family. Thus, symbolic interactionism is about the nature of the interactions between human beings, who act in relation to each other and perceive and interpret each other and themselves (Charon, 1979). It is, in effect, about person–environment interrelatedness.

In midcentury, holistic approaches to the study of development were again put forward, most notably by Kurt Lewin and psychologists working in the Gestalt tradition, the locus of much opposition to reductionism (Gardner, 1985). Wertheimer and Kohler proposed that psychological analysis should start with the perceptual field as a whole. In the Gestalt model, field is differentiated into constituent parts, figure and ground. These parts should be studied not in isolation, however, but in terms of their mutual influence (Hall & Lindzey, 1985). Kurt Lewin shared this Gestalt emphasis on interactions among a totality of factors in a given context (Lewin, 1931). After his death in 1947 two of his colleagues, Roger Barker and Herbert Wright, continued to investigate the role of environmental forces on the "lifespace" of the child (Barker & Wright, 1951; Wright & Barker, 1950).

This, then, was the intellectual climate in which the ecological perspective grew. To illustrate it more fully, we shall discuss two different theories that are both termed *ecological* and that while they have very different emphases, are quite complementary – those of Gibson and Bronfenbrenner. Both theories grew out of dissatisfaction with contemporary approaches to psychology. Gibson (1973), for example, wrote that "experimental psychology today suffers from the defect that what is known is mostly irrelevant and what is relevant is mostly unknown" (quoted in Reed, 1988, p. 6). What was relevant in his view was perception, which he defined as the *relation* between person and environment, a position that derived from the work of the Gestalt theorists. Bronfenbrenner, who himself was strongly influenced by Lev Vygotsky and Kurt Lewin, also rejected the associationist dichotomy and the positivist position that social science needs to be pure (value-neutral and context-free) to be useful and scientific (Bronfenbrenner, 1977, 1979), and stressed the need for social relevance in research. Bronfenbrenner (1977) held that neither scientific rigor nor relevance to the real world need be forgone in the study of human development, stating, "The orientation proposed here rejects both the implied dichotomy between rigor and relevance and the assumed incompatibility between the requirements of research in naturalistic situations and the applicability of structured experiments at an early stage in the scientific process" (p. 194):

> Especially in recent decades, research in human development has pursued a divided course, with each direction tangential to genuine scientific progress. . . . The emphasis on rigor has led to experiments that are elegantly designed but often limited in scope. This limitation derives from the fact that many of these experiments involve situations that are unfamiliar, artificial, and short-lived and that call for unusual behaviors that are difficult to generalize to other settings. (p. 193)

## Gibson's Theoretical Framework

James Gibson was trained as an experimental psychologist at Yale during the 1920s. His intellectual development and experimental work is detailed in the biography *James J. Gibson and the Psychology of Perception*, by Edward Reed (1988), who described Gibson as a "distinguished dissident." Gibson studied human behavior and perception at a time when most psychologists were examining learning in rats. He continued to study perception and during World War II provided a description of the visual information used by pilots to land airplanes. When studying computers became more predominant than studying rats, Gibson remained focused on perception and described his position as an ecological approach to psychology (perception being the primary foundation area to examine). Although surely influenced by the ideas of philosophers and modern scientists (such as Darwin, Russell, Whitehead, Einstein, William James, and Kurt Koffka) as they coincided in the intellectual community in the 1920s (Reed, 1988), Gibson nonetheless departed from many of the ideas of these early influences. Reed (1988) suggests that Gibson's development of his ecological framework was not so much a product of any single incident or idea but rather the progression in his work and thinking about perception up to the publication of his last book, *The Ecological Approach to Visual Perception* (1979). The corpus of Gibson's work represents 50 years of experimental research and conceptual publications. (See Reed, 1988, for the complete list of Gibson's publications.) The following description given by Reed (1988) nicely places James Gibson in historical context:

> As a young man, Gibson was an optimist and a pragmatist, someone who believed that experimentation in the social sciences could help elucidate human behavior and thereby help make the world a better place. Later he came to doubt his early optimism about the value of experimentation in psychology. . . . The story of Gibson's life is the story of this personal transformation and the changes in psychological theory and practice that made him a distingushed dissident. It is the story of someone who learned to see for himself in the heady days of American progressivism and experimentalism and never stopped looking at things in his own way. (p. 25)

James Gibson (1979) concentrated his attention on perception; his theory of perception is prototypically ecological, his position being that perception is understandable only in terms of both the perceived and the perceiver. His belief was that perception is "direct" as opposed to mediated by inference and representation, positions more commonly taken by psychologists. Gibson argued that there is information in the optic array that is directly available to be "picked up" by a perceiver. Perception defines a relationship between an active organism and its environment, development being the change in this relationship over the course of the organism's life. Gibson argued that the information is "inexhaustible" but that more of it becomes known over time through perceptual learning. This type of learning, he believed, is characterized by a process of differentiation, rather than construction (Gibson & Gibson, 1955). Gibson and his wife, E. J. Gibson, argued that meaning does not need to be constructed. To explain why construction was not relevant for perception, the Gibsons used three primary concepts: reciprocity of the organism and its environment, information, and affordances.

Gibson (1979) stated that perception cannot be understood by examining the perceiver alone, but only by examining the relationship between the perceiver and the environment that is the object of perception. One aspect of this reciprocity is the close link in Gibson's theory between perception and action, a link related to the concept of affordances.

An affordance, in Gibson's terms, can be described as the possibility for action on the part of an actor in an environment. The constraints of the actor and the constraints of the environment mutually contribute to such possibilities for action. For example, a rigid surface affords locomotion, a path affords pedestrian locomotion, a stairway affords ascent and/or descent, an object of an appropriate size affords grasping, a rigid object with sharp edge affords cutting, and so on. In each case, however, the affordance relationship between organism and environment is defined simultaneously by properities of the organism and properties of the environment. Thus, a 6-month-old infant would not perceive a large rigid surface as one affording walking, but as one affording crawling. In the case of the object to be grasped, the adjective *appropriate* can be understood only in terms of the organism's characteristics: What is graspable for an adult may not be graspable for an infant. Similarly, exploratory behaviors that allow the organism to "probe the environment . . . reveal information that specifies relevant environmental properties" for the organism (Adolph, Eppler, & E. Gibson, 1993). Accordingly, perception of the environment is necessarily perception of the self. In the course of development, perceivers tune their actions by differentiating the information that is relevant in the environment for the purpose of performing some action or activity. The affordance relationship captures the linkage that James Gibson proposed between perception and action. Action is guided by perception and action over time informs perception.

What, then, is perception? According to Gibson, perception is based on information pickup. An organism, equipped with perceptual systems (visual, auditory, proprioceptive, etc.), picks up information available in the environment (the optic array, the auditory array, etc.). This process is direct and does not require inference or other cognitive processes, a radical departure from more traditional accounts of perception.

Gibson described in great detail the possible information conveyed in the optic array. Observers with perceptual systems (evolved to use just the sort of information specified by the layout, surfaces, and objects in the environment) pick up information that specifies the properties of surfaces and objects (available "in the light"). Gibson (1979) described, from an ecological perspective, an approach to "ecological optics" (as opposed to classical optics) that requires an initial description of the environment "since what there is to be perceived has to be stipulated before one can even talk about perceiving it" (p. 2). Gibson argued that the information in an illuminated medium should not be assumed to "stimulate receptors" as in classical optics, but should be considered information in the light that can activate the perceptual system tuned to pick it up. Thus, perception is not the

> processing of sensory inputs, but the extracting of invariants from the stimulus. . . . The information in ambient light, along with sound, odor, touches, and natural chemicals is inexhaustible. A perceiver can keep on noticing facts about the world she lives in to the end of her life without ever reaching a limit. There is no threshold for information comparable to a stimulus threshold. Information is not lost to the environment when gained by the individual, it is not conserved like energy. (Gibson, 1979, pp. 2, 243)

In sum, Gibson's theoretical framework assumes that the perceiver and the environment are inseparable. As is true of other ecological positions, the strong position is taken that the study of the individual isolated from his or her environment (or, for that matter, of the environment without consideration of the organisms inhabiting that environment) may allow empirical clarity but will not inform understanding of human development.

### *Research within Gibson's Ecological Framework*

Clearly, from Gibson's perspective, perception is an activity that occurs across time. Perception is thus dynamic and is a relationship between an organism and its environment. If there is information to specify the properties of the environment and if the perceiver picks up this information, it then becomes important to identify the information in order to understand how a perceiver uses that information to guide activity. Two questions are relevant: What is information and what is the affordance relationship? Scholars using the Gibsonian framework have conducted research addressing both questions.

What sort of information can be identified? To start, information that is used to perform an action might be empirically described. This information is available in optic flow patterns created by self-motion and perceivers use it to guide activity. Apparently, this type of information is extracted in the course of activity; it does not need to be constructed. Lee (1980) identified the parameter *tau*, which specifies "time to contact." In the case of plummeting gannets, tau specifies when to pull their wings back before "contacting" a body of water. For humans, tau specifies when to apply pressure to one's automobile brakes to avoid collision. Tau (with constant velocity) "is a precise measure of time remaining until the distance between the eye and the surface is reduced to zero" (Neisser, 1988, p. 5). In another line of research, the visual information used by perceivers to perform and judge the aesthetic qualities of human motion has been identified (Gray & Neisser, 1993; Gray, Neisser, Shapiro, & Kouns, 1991; Scully, 1986). Kinematic information (isolated by using point-light displays) in gymnastics (Scully, 1986) and ballet (Gray & Neisser, 1993) specifies the qualitative aspects of some movement. Identifying the information that perceivers use in physical activities or in judging human motion begins to address the first research question.

Other research has identified the information available "in the light" that specifies whether an opening affords passage. Warren and Whang (1987) have shown that perceivers use the ratio of aperture width and eye height to judge whether they can go through a particular doorway. Critical chair heights and riser heights (the vertical distance from one stair to the next) are also specified via visual information relative to the perceiver's eye height (Mark, 1987; Mark & Vogele, 1988). In these cases, the visual information identified specifies a *relationship* between the environment and the perceiver. Furthermore, the activities (avoiding collision, traversing passageways, sitting, or climbing stairs) are guided by the pickup of information that specifies what the environment affords the actor.

A limited amount of developmental research has been conducted to examine the perception of affordances (for a recent review of work supporting an ecological interpretation, see Adolph et al., 1993). In their review Adolph and her colleagues present the guidelines for conducting develomental research within an ecological perspective. First, the affordance itself needs description; second, the information that specifies the affordance should be identified; and third, the perceptual and action capabilities of the perceiver must be assessed.

This third aspect has been little explored in research with either adults or children (but see Adolph, 1993). However, this aspect is essential to Gibson's theory and has been poorly understood. The constraints on both sides of the affordance relation – those of the environment and of the actor – must be described to grasp fully Gibson's contribution to understanding human development. Earlier criticisms of Gibson's theory (Fodor & Pylyshyn, 1981) were based on an assumption that the information that specified an affordance was simply the visual information that specified some property of the environment or of objects. These critics failed to recognize the essentially interactive nature of Gibson's theory – that the actor also must pick up *self*-information to respond to the information provided by the environment. If perception of the environment is coperception of the self, then information that specifies the environment also specifies the self, or the actor's position in the environment. If the environment affords some action for the perceiver, it is in relation to the perceiver's action capabilities or the actor's biomechanical constraints. In brief, the information that specifies the possibility for action resides in the relationship between actor and environment – a quintessentially ecological position.

As we argued in the introduction to this chapter, an ecological perspective in general acknowledges the relationship between organism and environment. Gibson's ecological framework specifies an empirical approach that aids understanding of the relationship between actors and the *physical* environment. Gibson also discussed the relationship between people. For the perceiver, another person provides "the richest and most elaborate affordances" (Gibson, 1979, p. 135). Gibson was keenly aware of the possibilities for action afforded by one person in relation to another, and although the issue of "social affordances" was not so clearly articulated in his theory as that of the affordances of the properties and objects of the physical environment, Reed (1993) has argued that this is because Gibson attempted to "transcend the usual dichotomy between the social and the physical environment" (p. 53). In a later section we shall discuss the ecological perspective of Bronfenbrenner, which concentrates primarily on the relationship between the developing person and the developing *social* environment. The work of E. Gibson (e.g., Adolph et al., 1993; E. Gibson 1969, 1988; E. Gibson & Olum, 1960) and that of Neisser (1988, 1994) is particularly interesting, in that they have taken J. Gibson's work further in two relevant directions, the developmental and the social, and thereby closer to the position taken by Bronfenbrenner. Eleanor Gibson may be said to have "co-constructed" the Gibsonian framework, taking the developmental concepts that were implicit (but not made explicit) in her husband's work and extending them greatly. She also developed a theory of perceptual learning (E. Gibson, 1969). Neisser, on the other hand, has indicated the ways in which an ecological approach to perception can serve as the foundation for a framework that encompasses the social environment. For reasons of brevity, we have decided here to focus solely on Neisser's extensions.

## *The Ecological Self: Extending the Gibsonian Framework*

Neisser (1988, 1993), working from a Gibsonian perspective, has described a framework for understanding the self. Neisser suggests that there are at least five kinds of self-knowledge: the ecological self, the interpersonal self, the extended self, the private self, and the conceptual self. The ecological self is primary, being directly perceived from the start. As one would expect, given its basis in Gibson's theory, the ecological self is coperceived as the environment is perceived. In other words, perception of the environment is perception of the self situated in that environment. According to Neisser (1988), the interpersonal self is also directly perceived. Research on the earliest mother–infant interactions (Stern, 1985; Trevarthen, 1979) is cited as evidence for this claim:

> J. J. Gibson's (1979) principle that all perceiving involves co-perception of environment and self applies also to the social environment and to the interpersonal self, i.e., the self that is established

> in these interactions. Just as the ecological self is specified by the orientation and flow of optical texture, so the interpersonal self is specified by the orientation and flow of the other individual's expressive gestures; just as the ecological self is articulated and confirmed by the effects of our own physical actions, so the interpersonal self is developed and confirmed by the effects of our own expressive gestures on our partner. (Neisser, 1988, p. 10)

Young children are actively engaged with the people, objects, and physical properties of their environments. They are curious and willing to explore their world from a very early age. These explorations and interactions contribute to their acquisition of real-world knowledge and ultimately to an ability to reflect on those interactions. These same explorations and interactions contribute to a child's sense of self (Neisser, 1993). From these earliest experiences, young children begin to develop concepts about physical objects and psychological constructs. These earliest concepts are influenced by the nature of the child's competence in physical actions and by the quality of the earliest social interactions (Neisser, 1993).

Neisser's framework for understanding the development of the self places the ecological self and the interpersonal self as the foundation for the later development of the extended, private, and conceptual selves. This framework represents a promising extension of Gibson's ecological theory of perception into the other areas of human development such as memory, affect, concept formation, and cognition in situated activity.

Neisser has suggested a further theoretical extension to Gibson's direct perception system (Neisser, 1993). In addition to a direct perception system Neisser proposes a second perception system – a recognition system that is distinct from, but complementary to, the direct perception system. This "re-cognition" system allows the perceiver to acquire knowledge about what categories things belong to or to recognize that the present object is an exemplar of other similar objects. While the direct perception system specifies where one is situated in the environment with respect to the physical layout or to social interchanges, the recognition system allows for the acquisition of knowledge about what things are with respect to culturally specified meaning. These two systems are "about different things; use different kinds of information; and provide different kinds of certainty" (Neisser, 1992, p. 23). Further, these two systems surely cooperate in ways perhaps like Rumelhart and McClelland's PDP (parallel distributed processing) networks (1986). Neisser's two-systems view, together with his self-knowledge framework, promises to further distinguish Gibson's important contribution.

How does one move from these theoretical premises to empirical research in human development? Research on affordances is evolving as it addresses such issues as infants' developing locomotion (Adolph, 1993), their manipulation of objects (Eppler, 1990), reaching and grasping (Rochat & Senders, 1990), development of knowledge about intermodal unity (E. Gibson, 1984), the use of tools (Leeuwen, Smitsman, & Leeuwen, in press), and autistic children's understanding of social affordances (Loveland, 1991). For example, infants' developing manipulation skills can be viewed as a continuum progressing from mouthing objects to banging objects to more sophisticated exploration of objects with both hands. Over the course of the first year, as these skills develop, the level of differentiation of the affordances of those objects develops concomitantly (Adolph et al., 1993). Studies within the Gibsons' framework of affordances have direct application to the concerns of those working with young children and their families, although translating the findings from these studies into workable applications remains an important task. For now, we know that adopting the Gibsons' ideas about perception and development requires attention not only to the developing capabilities of the individual, but to the relationship between the developing capabilities of the individual and the properties of the environment and the objects and people in it. As Adolph and her colleagues (1993) suggest, we must describe the affordance relationship inclusive of the constraints of actor and the environment. As the actor, or the developing child, changes in action capabilities, so too will the possibilities for action with respect to the environment – which in effect changes for the individual as more information is differentiated and additional possibilities for activity are revealed. Development, then, is the change in this relationship across the life span. The requisite research methodology will examine the relationship between the actor and his or her environment (physical or social).

Neisser's conceptualization of five kinds of self-knowledge suggests a number of research questions. Perhaps most central is the question of the self and its development. Since Neisser's formulation of self-knowledge differs from Cooley's and Mead's to the extent that not just social but ecological activity is central to a fuller understanding of self, several new lines of research are possible. For example, the competence and sense of agency engendered by activities in and operations on the physical environment become important measures to assess. Measures of positive affect and reciprocity in adult–child or child–child interactions (the interpersonal self, which also is present from the start) could be examined along with measures of the ecological self. The ecological self highlights an additionally important aspect of human development – an aspect not considered by other purely social-based theories of the self. One line of research currently using this framework is attempting to describe the origins of young children's implicit theories of intelligence (Gray, Hogan, Rodarmel, & D'Agostino, in preparation). Framed within Neisser's theory of self-knowledge, these scholars are attempting to identify the origins of at least one aspect of the conceptual self. It is possible that early behavioral patterns that preschool children exhibit (a *mastery* approach or *helpless* approach to solving problems or learning skills) emerge from the ecological and social contexts that young children participate in, and that these patterns are early indicators of young children's implicit theories of intelligence. If children's early ecological and social activities can be linked to the learning goals they assume, it becomes possible to track the development of at least one aspect of their conceptual selves – their emerging, but implicit theories of intelligence.

Within Neisser's framework, it becomes essential to take an ecological perspective in order to understand the origins of beliefs about the world. For example, starting from a position that cultures influence beliefs, one can find differences with respect to a concept like intelligence (Lutz & LeVine, 1983; Stevenson et al., 1989), but little more can be done to identify the origins of these differences apart from invoking preexisting differences in cultural belief systems. However, through an examination of the earliest interactions that individuals have in both their physical and social environments, the contribution of the self as an active agent is highlighted. The individual acts and interacts not only in a social environment, but in a physical environment. The nature and outcome of action and interaction in the physical environment also need to be described in order to understand the development both of the self and of cultural beliefs. Individuals, after all, explore and acquire knowledge about the world in which they live, a world rich in information about possibilities for action within it and about possibilities for interaction with the others who share it. Asking what information is available to the perceiver, how the perceiver uses this information to guide activity, how affordances support action and interaction, how self-knowledge develops and contributes to development, and where beliefs about the self and the world originate are all questions that relate specifically to an ecological framework.

To fully understand human development from an ecological perspective, we might first assume that development occurs within the individual who is not separable from his or her environment. What Neisser has offered is an opportunity to test, empirically, Gibson's claims and to ground other aspects of development in Gibson's ecological theory of perception. As we shall show, what Bronfenbrenner has done is to take a similarly ecological framework, equally interactive, but focused more on the systemic properties of the environment, from the physical and social and extending to the historical and cultural in its local and broadest sociocultural manifestations.

## Bronfenbrenner's Theoretical Framework

The first major difference between Bronfenbrenner's position and that of Gibson has to do with the ways in which they treat the environment. If Gibson's approach to the human–environment relationship is one that has to date focused on perception of the physical environment, Bronfenbrenner's deals primarily with the social environment. A second difference has to do with the notion of direct versus indirect relations. As we have described it, Gibson was primarily concerned with *direct* relations, those aspects of the environment perceived directly and immediately by the individual. Bronfenbrenner believes that although the direct effects of the immediate social and physical environment ("proximal processes" in his terminology) are very important, these cannot be well understood without taking into account more distal processes – historical, cultural, social, and environmental conditions that affect the developing child only indirectly.

A third apparent difference between the ecological positions espoused by these two theorists has to do with the nature of the relations between individual and environment. Gibson's position was quite unequivocal; an understanding of the individual alone or the environment alone is totally impossible. Any understanding of individual function must specify features of the environment, and vice versa. Bronfenbrenner's position is less clear; scholars who draw on his early writings have represented his position as focusing almost exclusively on environmental influences on development (Bubolz & Sontag, 1993). A casual reading of Bronfenbrenner's early writings on the ecology of human development reveals that they are very well developed with regard to the various contexts in which developing humans find themselves, but have little to say about the nature of the developing organisms themselves. As late as 1986, Bronfenbrenner was talking about the "influences" of various contexts on the family, as though developments within the family (or within the developing organism) or influences of the family on the outside world (or influences of child on family) were of less importance.

However, this seemingly unidirectional approach to development (albeit a highly differentiated unidirectional approach) was, we believe, always more apparent than real. As we have argued with regard to Gibson, a theory is never developed outside an intellectual context. Theories are not simply informed by theoretical traditions on which the theorist wishes to build; they are shaped by theorists against which he or she is arguing. At the time when Bronfenbrenner wrote *The Ecology of Human Development* (1979), the vast majority of studies of children's development, particularly in the domain of cognition, treated that development as context-free (see the discussion in Bronfenbrenner, 1989). It was at that time that he made his telling critique of the field: "It can be said that much of developmental psychology is the science of the strange behavior of children in strange situations with strange adults for the briefest possible periods of time"(1977, p. 513). As Bronfenbrenner (1993) later expressed it, "The developmental attributes of the person are defined, both conceptually and operationally, without any explicit reference to the environment in which they occur, and are presumed to have the same psychological meaning irrespective of the culture, class, or setting in which they are observed, or in which the person lives" (p. 9).

Bronfenbrenner's primary goal at that time was thus to provide a much more differentiated and complex sense of the different "systems" that influence the developing person, and the interrelations between them. Using the metaphor of the *matrioshka* (Russian nested doll), Bronfenbrenner (1979) portrayed the developing child as being at the center of an interconnected set of contexts, including those that directly impinged on the child (contexts at the microsystem and mesosystem levels) and those that affected the child indirectly, mediated by those with whom the child came into direct contact (contexts at the exosystem and macrosystem levels).

The various systems were defined as follows. A microsystem is a setting in which the developing person is situated. Microsystem effects relate to the activities in which the person engages and which he or she observes, the roles taken by the participants in those activities, and the interpersonal relations between the person and those around him or her. These interpersonal relations are affected by the personality and temperamental characteristics of the interacting individuals, their belief systems, and so on, all of which are in dynamic flux over the course of development. Family, school, peer group, workplace, church all constitute examples of microsystems, in which the individual develops in conjunction with different sets of social partners.

Individuals inhabit more than one microsystem, however; the child engages in one set of activities at home, another with his or her peers, yet another in church, and yet different activities at school. Interpersonal relations are with one set of people in one such microsystem, with another in another microsystem. In some cases, there are consistencies between activities, interpersonal relations, or both in the various microsystems in which the child exists; in other cases the linkages between them are less consistent. The relations between microsystems constitute the mesosystem.

There are, of course, many contexts with which the developing individual does not have direct contact, but which nevertheless exert an indirect effect. In the case of children, the prototypical such context is the parental workplace; experiences that the parents have at work often have an influence on the activities and interpersonal relationships that the child experiences directly. For example, parents who can exercise a good deal of self-direction at work may be more likely to encourage initiative and independence in their children, whereas those for whom success at work is linked to following directions carefully may be more likely to encourage compliance in their children (for more details, see Tudge & Putnam, Chapter 9, this volume). Linkages of this nature comprise exosystem effects.

The broadest level that Bronfenbrenner discussed is the macrosystem, which also exerts its effects indirectly, mediated by those with whom the developing person comes into contact. Macrosystem effects are those at the cultural level, with culture here considered at both the societal and within-societal levels, including social class, race, and ethnicity (see Tudge & Putnam, Chapter 9, this volume). Belief and value systems, cultural tools and institutions, and material resources and opportunities that are available to the cultural community all affect the developing person, albeit indirectly. For example, industrialized societies have typically removed opportunities for children to learn the skills necessary to become economically self-sufficient through direct participation, and instead required that they learn in specialized institutions (schools) that are far removed from the contexts in which children will eventually be expected to practice those skills. The situation is quite different in technologically simple cultures (hunter-gatherer and simple agrarian groups), in which children are expected to learn through observation of and participation in the tasks they will eventually use quite independently. Such overarching organizations of the cultural group clearly have enormous implications for children's development.

If these various systems constitute the layers of the *matrioshka*, then the chronosystem represents the passage of the doll through time. Chronosystem effects are those that relate to change or stability in the various contexts that have an impact (direct or indirect) on the developing person and changes in the nature and characteristics of that person. Chronosystem effects force attention on the fact that, as the individual changes, he or she does so in an ever-changing set of contexts at every layer of the entire ecological system, from changes within the family to changes at the historical and cultural level (see Shanahan & Elder, Chapter 4, this volume).

In his earlier work, Bronfenbrenner (1979) concentrated almost exclusively on the contexts in which development occurred, paying little attention to aspects of the developing individual and leaving chronosystem effects quite implicit. However, to view Bronfenbrenner's position as espousing a simplistically unidirectional model of development would be totally incorrect. As early as 1983, and in a sightly more differentiated form in 1988, he described a typology of models of development. At about the same time (Bronfenbrenner, 1989), he made quite explicit his concept of development, using this concept as a foundation to discuss these models. Essentially what he did was to expand on Lewin's equation B = f(PE) – that behavior is a function of an interaction between person and environment – by substituting development for behavior. This substitution is, of course, of critical importance. Whereas Lewin's position is concerned with an outcome at a given point in time,

Bronfenbrenner's concern (1989) is with "the set of processes through which properties of the person and the environment interact to produce constancy and change in the characteristics of the person over the life course" (p. 191). The use of "processes" here is also critical; as was true for Lewin, Bronfenbrenner is interested in the processes or mechanisms that "activate or sustain development" (p. 192). His treatment of development is best viewed from the perspective of his critique of models that fail to consider the relations of environment and individual, or the processes linking them, or both.

Bronfenbrenner (1988) identified models ranging from those that dealt with only one portion of the equation to ones that dealt with both person and environment in interaction, and that identified the processes linking them to development (termed the "person–process–context" model). He made quite clear that the latter model was necessary for an adequate study of development. Bronfenbrenner (1988) argued that the most simple models were those that focused exclusively on aspects of the environment ("social address models") or on the person ("personal attributes models"). He argued that these models, though widely used in psychology, are simplistic because they allow no assessment of any interactive relations between individual and environment, while ignoring the processes or mechanisms of development. The assumption implicit in the first model is that development proceeds in the same way for any individual occupying the same social address (racial or ethnic group, socioeconomic status [SES], gender, and so on). The assumption of the second model is that features of the individual such as temperament or IQ are sufficient to "explain" development.

Among models intermediate in complexity Bronfenbrenner identified "sociological niche" models, or those that allow researchers to consider interactions among two or more different social addresses (SES and race, for example). Individuals occupying those niches are still, however, assumed to develop in similar ways. By contrast, "person-context" models include in their design personal attributes as well as different social addresses. Scholars using such a model might consider, for example, different developmental outcomes for boys and girls in different sociological niches.

None of the models so far mentioned include any means of understanding the developmental processes themselves, however – the "f" in Lewin's equation. Bronfenbrenner (1988) discusses three different types of model that allow an assessment of process. The first type he refers to as microsystem (person–process) models, those that posit a causal process that stems from characteristics of the person (studies of genetic transmission or the impact of specific physical or physiological characteristics on later development) or that stem from events in the child's proximal context (studies of the ways in which development occurs in the course of face-to-face interaction or under the influence of particular local or proximal environmental conditions). The second type, called process–context models (and much less used in developmental psychology) allow the assessment of ways in which particular contexts differentially affect developmental processes (such as interpersonal interactions) themselves.

The third and final type of process-related model that Bronfenbrenner (1988) discusses is the person–process–context model, the theoretically and methodologically most complete model to fit the expanded Lewinian formulation that Bronfenbrenner believes to be most useful for developmental research. In brief, this model allows an assessment not only of the interactive nature of individuals and their environments, both proximal and distal, but also of the processes of development that are at work. The person–process–context model requires that researchers consider the interactive ways in which developing individuals are influenced by and simultaneously influence the context that envelops them. Bronfenbrenner (1993) labels these individual characteristics "developmentally instigative" – characteristics that are not expected to remain fixed, but respond to (and effect responses in) the surrounding context. These individual characteristics have to do with such "personal stimulus characteristics" as an infant's fussiness, calmness, liking of being held, and physical attractiveness. These characteristics are, of course, simultaneously personal and social, bringing about responses from those around the infant. Other developmentally instigative characteristics include individual differences in reaction to, interest in, and exploration of the world (social and physical), persistence, and belief systems about the world, particularly beliefs about the extent to which the individual can effect change in that world.

If these are the personal attributes that the model needs to consider, what constitutes the context? As might be expected from our early discussion, context cannot be restricted simply to the microsystem, but must incorporate linkages between the systems, from micro to macro. Bronfenbrenner (1993) describes contexts as also having "developmentally instigative" characteristics that, in interaction with the developing individual's characteristics, serve to facilitate or impede development. Bronfenbrenner has in mind factors such as material, physical, and social resources, the stability of those resources, and the extent to which they are organized or disorganized.

These aspects of the physical, social, and symbolic environment may be viewed at all levels from the most proximal (microsystem) to the most distal (macrosystem). For example, a family can become relatively disorganized with fewer resources in the period surrounding a divorce; similarly, an entire society can experience disorganization and lack of resources, as during a war or in time of economic adversity. Similarly, within any society, prospects for one group may be systematically curtailed. These macrolevel effects clearly have their effects at the exosystem, mesosystem, and microsystem levels, too, as Bronfenbrenner's discussion of the work of Elder and his colleagues (Elder, 1974; Elder & Caspi, 1990) makes clear (see also Shanahan & Elder, Chapter 4, this volume).

Finally, in terms of the person–process–context model, the processes of development must be specified – *how* does a particular type of environment link to a particular outcome with some people but not others? Bronfenbrenner draws on his own earlier studies with Cochran (cited in Bronfenbrenner, 1988) to show how similar environmental conditions affect girls and boys differently. He also discusses the work of Elder and his colleagues indicating that the age at which children experienced the Depression as well as their gender led to very different outcomes. The concern with process, of course, forces attention on aspects of both the developing individual and the developing environment.

As if to compensate for his apparent concentration on the contexts of development (the environmental part of Lewin's equation) in his early writings on this subject (an emphasis occasioned by the contemporary focus solely on aspects of the individual), Bronfenbrenner has subsequently made quite clear the explicitly interactive nature of the system. For example, echoing Marx, Bronfenbrenner (1993) states that "human beings are not only the partial products, but also the partial producers of their environment" (p. 6). To stress its interactive nature, Bronfenbrenner and Ceci (1994) now refer to the model as a "bio-ecological paradigm of human development" (p. 568). This dialectical or transactional approach to human development is echoed throughout the pages of Bronfenbrenner's most recent writings on the subject. Bronfenbrenner and Ceci (1994) argue that "from the moment of conception, the actualization of inherited predispositions for embryological development and physiological activity do not occur in a vacuum, but are differentially responsive . . . to the intrauterine environment" (p. 580). The authors go on to state, moreover, that "the power of innate propensities is in no way reduced after birth, for, as the child begins to interact with persons, objects, and symbols, the external environment becomes genetically loaded as the active organism selects, modifies, and partially constructs its own world" (p. 580). The embedded nature of individual and context is clearly marked; in an earlier discussion of cognitive development, Bronfenbrenner and his colleagues state, "The context in which cognition takes place is not simply an adjunct to the cognition, but a constituent of it" (Ceci, Bronfenbrenner, & Baker, 1988, p. 24). Bronfenbrenner (1993) is thus at pains to point out that the effects of individual and environmental factors are not only not simply additive, but may vary both in strength and direction. The relation between them, he argues, is synergistic.

Unlike Gibson, who collected a great deal of data as he was developing his position, Bronfenbrenner has not been highly active in gathering empirical data. His chosen task, instead, has been to focus on the data gathered by others, illustrating the ways in which their data exemplify one or other of the models discussed earlier. He often goes further, however, pointing out ways in which the scholar could have expanded on the design in such a way as to approximate more closely to the person–process–context ideal. He has focused on research both from a historical perspective (Bronfenbrenner & Crouter, 1983) and in using the most relevant of contemporary research (Bronfenbrenner 1979, 1986, 1989, 1993). His most recent endeavor has been to use research that comes close to using a person–process–context model to indicate the problems underlying the position taken by contemporary behavior geneticists (Bronfenbrenner & Ceci, 1994). In this paper the authors describe microsystem processes as "proximal processes" and draw on research that indicates the presence of synergistic relations between these proximal processes and the broader settings (both cultural and historical) within which these proximal processes are set.

The critical issue in this expanded treatment is that of process – *how* heritability relates to development, and the processes of gene–environment interaction. "At the core of the problem lies . . . the need to identify the *mechanisms* through which genotypes are transformed into phenotypes" (Bronfenbrenner & Ceci, 1994, p. 568). The argument that Bronfenbrenner and Ceci make is predicated on the view that the mechanisms are not simply unidirectional, but interactional or synergistic, and the authors draw on a wide range of studies that support this position (e.g., Gottlieb, 1991; Kandel, Schwartz, & Jessell, 1991). Erlenmeyer-Kimling (1972) argues that "gene–environment interactions are numerous and that treatment effects are frequently reversed in direction for different genotypes" (p. 201), and Wahlsten (1994) makes much the same argument, criticizing heritability analysis as used in behavior genetics, which "requires an assumption that heredity and environment *do not* interact.... [However,] the additive model is not biologically realistic" (pp. 248–249). Instead, aspects of the developing individual and the developing context in which the individual is situated (proximal processes) need to be considered simultaneously in order to understand "dynamic and historically determined processes which give rise to structure and motion by virtue of the dialectical interplay of the internal and the external, the nucleus and the cytoplasm, the individual and society" (p. 254).

As would be expected from our previous discussion of the person–process–context model, the range of heritability is much greater than behavior geneticists have argued, depending on the characteristics of the proximal processes (necessarily an interaction between the developing child and those with whom the child comes into contact) in interaction with developmentally instigative characteristics of the broader context. Specifically, Bronfenbrenner and Ceci (1994) argue that if "proximal processes serve as a mechanism for actualizing genetic potential" (p. 572), contexts in which proximal processes are strong would be those in which most of the expressed variation was related to genetic endowment. Contexts characterized by weak proximal processes, on the other hand, would appear to indicate a much smaller impact of genetic endowment. Bronfenbrenner and his colleagues draw on the research of a number of scholars (Drillien, 1964; Fischbein, 1980; Luster, Rhoades, & Haas, 1989; Moorehouse, 1991; Tulkin 1977; Tulkin & Kagan, 1972 – all cited in Bronfenbrenner & Ceci, 1994) to show how proximal processes as varied as maternal beliefs, the quality of mother–child interaction, the extent of school-related experiences encountered in the home, and the degree of monitoring of adolescents had different impacts on the developmental outcomes for children in poorer environments than for those in more favorable environments. What is particularly striking is that the effectiveness of proximal processes varies according to the outcomes of interest – whether having to do with competence or dysfunction. These effects are difficult if not impossible to interpret within a behavior–genetic framework.

What remains to be clarified in this account, however, is the definition of high versus low levels of proximal processes. During Bronfenbrenner and Ceci's discussion of the work of Drillien (1964), high seems synonymous with "good" or "quality" processes of mother–child interaction, low being equated with "poor process" (1994, pp. 574–575). As a number of scholars (Ogbu, 1981; Tudge et al., in press) have argued, the quality of mother–child interaction (for example) cannot be assessed without consideration of the culturally defined standards of competence – what counts as competent (or quality) interaction in one culture may be defined quite differently in another. The relation between such historically and culturally relevant factors to proximal processes lies at the center of Bronfenbrenner's systemic theory, but makes it difficult to place interactional processes (or any other processes) on a single continuum of development, as Bronfenbrenner and colleagues appear to have done.

## Conclusion

We have examined ecological approaches to development, setting them in their historical and intellectual context, and focusing on two – the theories of James Gibson and Urie Bronfenbrenner. The central concern of all ecological theories is the mutual relationship or mutual reciprocity between developing individuals and their *oik* (environment), and in this respect Gibson and Bronfenbrenner share a common basic assumption. Also, they were both unhappy with the dominant trend in the field of psychology, a trend based on viewing individual and environment as dichotomous entities whose influences on development could be examined separately. The ecological perspective, as such, predated both theorists, as we have shown; whereas Bronfenbrenner (1979) acknowledged that scholars stand "on the shoulders of giants, and mistake the broadened vision for our own" (p. xi), Gibson's application of ecological principles to perception was a radical departure.

If these are the similarities in their positions, what was different about them? At the heart of the Gibsonian position is perception, a basic psychological process – but one that in Gibson's framework intrinsically links the perceiver and the perceived. In Bronfenbrenner's case, the key concept is that of proximal process – that is, relatively enduring "progressively more complex reciprocal interaction between an active, evolving bio-psychological organism and the persons, objects, and symbols in its immediate environment" (Bronfenbrenner & Ceci, 1994, p. 572). It is immediately apparent that while the attention to reciprocity is shared, Bronfenbrenner's focus is at a different level of analysis than that of Gibson. The environment is central to both, but there is a difference at the level of description of the relationship between the individual and the environment. It would be easy to draw a distinction between the two theorists based on a clcavage between the social (Bronfenbrenner) and the physical (Gibson) environments that their research addresses. But both theorists were wiser than that. As we mentioned, Gibson held that perception of any object was simultaneously perception of the self. Moreover, Reed (1988, 1993) has stated that Gibson did not draw a clear distinction between the social and the physical environment, and argues that his theory fits well with aspects of Vygotskian theory. Costall (1989) also argued that "the social context of cognition was indeed a central concern for Gibson, and one which figured in some of his earliest formulations of his theory" (p. 11). However, it is difficult to reconcile Gibson's account of *direct* perception, perception that is unmediated and in no way constructed, with the perception of activities in the social world. Even perception of physical objects may be mediated by the co-construction of beliefs and meanings attributed to such objects within a particular culture. It is interesting to note that Neisser's extension of Gibson, in which the constructed nature of cognitive processes features prominently, may do more than simply extend the theory when proposing that there may be two distinct perceptual systems – a direct system and a recognition system – that can account for culturally constructed knowledge.

In the case of Bronfenbrenner, the social environment does indeed figure prominently (although always, as we have pointed out, in interaction with aspects of the developing individual). However, the physical environment has as great a role to play in his theory. Indeed, the nature of the proximal processes varies in environments characterized as being either rich or poor in material resources. Economic hardship, whether having to do with features of the physical environment (quality of housing, safety of the neighborhood, etc.) or the availability and nutritional quality of food, interacts with proximal processes to have an impact on outcomes for the developing individual. Interestingly, where in some of his early formulations (e.g., Bronfenbrenner, 1979, p. 127) he cites approvingly Thomas's dictum that "if men define situations as real, they are real in their consequences," he has subsequently made clear that material and physical resources have their objective as well as subjective impact (Bronfenbrenner & Ceci, 1994).

We would also like to draw attention to the two theorists' conceptions of development and process. As Siegler and Crowley (1991) argue, any study of developmental processes must include observations that are dense "during the period of change relative to the rate of change of the phenomenon" (p. 607). Development of a skill, such as how to solve a model-copying problem, may take place over a relatively short period of time, whereas development of reading typically takes place over years. Processes of development may thus be observed over microgenetic, ontogenetic, historical, or even phylogenetic time (Tudge et al., in press). Gibson believed that the "process of extracting information" (viewed as increasing differentiation) occurred across the life span, but his concern with perceptual processes was centered at the microgenetic level, developmental processes being captured and described by direct experimentation (Gibson & Gibson, 1955).

By contrast, Bronfenbrenner is interested in the study of processes at each and every level, being concerned with the ways in which processes at macro levels (historical and cultural) through the micro levels (proximal processes) affect development. His perspective necessarily relates development to developing characteristics of the individual, as they interact with developing characteristics of those other individuals and social settings in which the individual plays a part, and to developing aspects of the environment (physical and social) that have an impact, direct and indirect, on the individual and that are, in turn, influenced by the individual. Bronfenbrenner's theory, unlike that of Gibson, clearly fits within the framework presented by Shanahan, Valsiner, and Gottlieb (Chapter 2, this volume); his ecological system has a structure that is both hierarchical and horizontal, relations between levels of the system and between elements at any one level are transactional/dialectical, and time, or processes of development, are viewed in terms of an interplay between historical, ontogenetic, and microgenetic levels.

In conclusion, it seems clear that the theories of both Gibson and Bronfenbrenner are truly ecological, as we have defined that term. The key fact is that, for both, relations between individual and environment are central. These relations are essentially dialectical or synergistic; the criticism leveled at both for having a unidirectional perspective (that Gibson was concerned solely with properties of the physical environment and that Bronfenbrenner was interested only in the effects of the social environment) are simply not tenable. Their theories are necessarily concerned with change over time, and Bronfenbrenner's theory is explicitly developmental, although this has often been ignored by critics. For Gibson, the individual picks up information that simultaneously guides activity and specifies the self. Perception is dynamic and change is inherent in the activity of perception. Again, the relationship between the perceiver and the perceived changes across time. With increasing economy, the perceiver differentiates more or different aspects of the available information. The development of skills and expertise in some domain may be described in this way (Gray & Neisser, 1993). Through activity, then, the individual attains an increasingly differentiated knowledge of the thing being acted on and of the self. Continuing activity is necessarily different since now the object being acted on is better differentiated *and* the individual doing the acting is different – there is a synergistic interplay throughout. For Bronfenbrenner, processes of development are at the core of his theory, with activity between developing individual and social partners the key to understanding both stability and change. These interpersonal interactions, of course, are most fully understood by considering them in broader historical, cultural, and social contexts, and the relations between them are synergistic.

## References

Adolph, K. E. (1993). *Perceptual-motor development in infants' locomotion over slopes*. Unpublished dissertation, Emory University, Atlanta, GA.

Adolph, K. E., Eppler, M. A., & Gibson, E. J. (1993). Development of perception of affordances. In C. Rovee-Collier & A. Lipsett (Eds.), *Advances in infancy research* (Vol. 8, pp. 51–98). Norwood, NJ: Ablex.

Angyal, A. (1941). *Foundations for a science of personality*. New York: Commonwealth Fund.

Baldwin, J. M. (1895). *Mental development in the child and the race: Methods and processes*. New York: Macmillan.

Barker, R. G., & Wright, H. F. (1951). *One boy's day*. New York: Harper.

Barrows, H. H. (1923). Geography as human ecology. *Annals of the Association of American Geographers*, *13*(1), 1–14.

Bronfenbrenner, U. (1977). An experimental ecology of human development. *American Psychologist*, *32*, 513–531.

(1979). *The ecology of human development: Experiments by nature and design*. Cambridge, MA: Harvard University Press.

(1986). Ecology of the family as a context for human development: Research perspectives. *Developmental Psychology*, *22*, 723–742.

(1988). Interacting systems in human development: Research paradigms – Present and future. In N. Bolder, A. Caspi, G. Downey, & M. Moorehouse (Eds.), *Persons in context: Developmental processes* (pp. 25–49). Cambridge University Press.

(1989). Ecological systems theory. In R. Vasta (Ed.), *Annals of child development* (Vol. 6, pp. 187–249). Greenwich, CT: JAI Press.

(1993). The ecology of cognitive development: Research models and fugitive findings. In R. Wozniak & K. Fischer (Eds.), *Development in context: Acting and thinking in specific environments* (pp. 3–44). Hillsdale, NJ: Erlbaum.

Bronfenbrenner, U., & Ceci, S. (1994). Nature–nurture reconceptualized in developmental perspective: A bioecological model. *Psychological Review*, *101*, 568–586.

Bronfenbrenner, U., & Crouter, A. C. (1993). The evolution of environmental models in developmental research. In P. H. Mussen (Ed.), *Handbook of child psychology: Vol. 1. History, theory, methods* (pp. 357–414). New York: Wiley.

Bubolz, M. M., & Sontag, M. S. (1993). Human ecology theory. In P. G. Boss, W. J. Doherty, R. LaRossa, W. R. Schuam, & S. S. Steinmetz (Eds.), *Sourcebook of family theories and methods, a contextual approach* (pp. 419–448). New York: Plenum.

Burgess, E. W. (1926). The family as a unity of interacting personalities. *Family*, *7*, 3–9.

Cahan, E. D. (1992). John Dewey and human development. *Developmental Psychology*, *28*, 205–214.

Cairns, R. (1992). The making of developmental science: The contributions and intellectual heritage of James Mark Baldwin. *Developmental Psychology*, *28*, 17–24.

Ceci, S. J., Bronfenbrenner, U., & Baker, J. (1988). Memory in context: The case of prospective memory. In F. Weinert & M. Perlmutter (Eds.), *Universals and change in memory development* (pp. 243–256). Hillsdale, NJ: Erlbaum.

Charon, J. M. (1979). *Symbolic interactionism: An introduction, an interpretation, an integration*. Englewood Cliffs, NJ: Prentice-Hall.

Clarke, R. (1973). *Ellen Swallows: The woman who founded ecology*. Chicago: Follett.

Cole, M. (1989). Cultural psychology: A once and future discipline? *Nebraska Symposium on Motivation, 37*, 279–335. Lincoln: University of Nebraska Press.

Cooley, C. H. (1956). *Human nature and social order*. Glencoe, IL: Free Press. (Original work published 1902)

Costall, A. (1989). A closer look at "direct perception." In A. Gellatly, D. Rogers, & J. A. Sloboda (Eds.), *Cognition and social worlds* (pp. 10–21). Oxford: Clarendon Press.

Dewey, J. (1896). The reflex arc concept in psychology. *The early works of John Dewey, 1882–1897* (Vol. 5, pp. 96–109). Carbondale: Southern Illinois University Press.

(1902). The child and the curriculum. *The middle works of John Dewey, 1899–1924* (Vol. 2, pp. 271–292). Carbondale: Southern Illinois University Press.

Dewey, J. (1911). Development. *The middle works of John Dewey, 1899–1924* (Vol. 6, pp. 420–422). Carbondale: Southern Illinois University Press.

Doherty, W. J., Boss, P. G., LaRossa, R., Schumm, W. R., & Steinmetz, S. K. (1993). Family theories and methods: A contextual approach. In P. G. Boss, W. J. Doherty, R. LaRossa, W. R. Schumm, & S. K. Steinmetz (Eds.), *Sourcebook of family theories and methods: A contextual approach* (pp. 3–30). New York: Plenum.

Elder, G. H., Jr. (1974). *Children of the Great Depression*. Chicago: University of Chicago Press.

Elder, G. H., Jr., & Caspi, A. (1990). Studying lives in a changing society: Sociological and personological explanations. In A. I. Rabin, R. A. Zucker, & S. Frank (Eds.), *Studying persons and lives* (pp. 201–247). New York: Springer.

Eppler, M. A. (1990). *Perception and action in infancy: Object manipulation skills and detection of auditory–visual correspondences*. Unpublished doctoral dissertation, Emory University, Atlanta.

Erlenmeyer-Kimling, L. (1972). Gene–environment interactions and the variability of behavior. In L. Ehrman, G. S. Omenn, & E. Caspari (Eds.), *Genetics, environment and behavior* (pp. 181–208). New York: Academic Press.

Fodor, J. A., & Pylyshyn, Z. W. (1981). How direct is visual perception: Some reflections on Gibson's ecological approach. *Cognition, 9*, 139–196.

Gardner, H. (1985). *The mind's new science: A history of the cognitive revolution*. New York: Basic.

Gibson, E. J. (1969). *Principles of perceptual learning and development.* New York: Appleton-Century-Crofts.

(1984). Development of knowledge about intermodal unity: Two views. In L. S. Liben (Ed.), *Piaget and the foundations of knowledge* (pp. 19–41). Hillsdale, NJ: Erlbaum.

(1988). Exploratory behavior in the development of perceiving, acting, and acquiring knowledge. *Annual Review of Psychology*, *39*, 1–41.

Gibson, E. J., & Olum, V. (1960). Experimental methods of studying perception in children. In P. H. Mussen (Ed.), *Handbook of research methods in child development* (pp. 311–373). New York: Wiley.

Gibson, J. J. (1979). *The ecological approach to visual perception.* Boston: Houghton Mifflin.

Gibson, J. J., & Gibson, E. J. (1955). Perceptual learning: Differentiation or enrichment? *Psychological Review*, *62*, 32–41.

Goldstein, K. (1939). *The organism.* New York: American Books.

Gottlieb, G. (1991). Experiential canalization of behavioral development: Theory. *Developmental Psychology*, *27*, 4–13.

(1992). *Individual development and evolution: The genesis of novel behavior.* New York: Oxford University Press.

(in press). Contemporary theory in developmental psychobiology. In B. Cairns & G. H. Elder, Jr. (Eds.), *Developmental science.* Cambridge University Press.

Gray, J. T., Hogan, D., Rodarmel, S., & D'Agostino, A. (in preparation). The orgins of young children's implicit theories of intelligence.

Gray, J. T., & Neisser, U. (1993, August). *Aesthetic judgments of biological motion: The role of visual information and expertise.* Paper presented at the Seventh International Conference on Event Perception and Action, University of British Columbia, Vancouver.

Gray, J. T., Neisser, U., Shapiro, B., & Kouns, S. (1991). Observational learning of ballet: The role of kinematic information. *Ecological Psychology*, *3*(2), 121–134.

Hall, C. S., & Lindzey, G. (1985). *Introduction to theories of personality.* New York: Wiley.

Johnston, T. D. (1985). Environmental constraints and the natural context of behavior: Grounds for an ecological approach to the study of infant perception. In G. Gottlieb & N. A. Krasnagor (Eds.), *Measurement of audition and vision in the first year of postnatal life* (pp. 91–108). Norwood, NJ: Ablex.

Kandel, E. R., Schwartz, J. H., & Jessell, T. M. (1991). *Principles of neural science.* New York: Elsevier.

Laboratory of Comparative Human Cognition. (1983). Culture and cognitive development. In P. H. Mussen (Ed.), *Handbook of child psychology: Vol. 1, History, theory, methods* (pp. 295–356). New York: Wiley.

Lee, D. N. (1980). The optic flow field: The foundation of vision. *Philosophical Transactions of the Royal Society of London, B 290*, 169–179.

Leeuwen, L. von, Smitsman, A., & Leeuwen, C. von. (in press). Tool use in early childhood: Perception of higher-order affordance. *Journal of Experimental Psychology: Human Perception and Performance.*

Lewin, K. (1931). Environmental forces in child behavior and development. In C. Murchison (Ed.), *A handbook of child psychology* (pp. 94–127). Worcester: MA: Clark University Press.

Loveland, K. (1991). Social affordances and interaction: Autism and the affordances of the human environment. *Ecological Psychology, 3*(2), 99–119.

Lutz, C., & LeVine, R. (1983). Culture and intelligence in infancy. In M. Lewis (Ed.), *Culture and intelligence in infancy* (pp. 327–345). New York: Plenum.

Mark, L. S. (1987). Eye-height-scaled information about affordances: A study of sitting and stairclimbing. *Journal of Experimental Psychology: Human Perception and Performance, 10*, 683–703.

Mark, L. S., & Vogele, D. (1988). A biodynamic basis for perceiving categories of action: A study of sitting and stairclimbing. *Journal of Motor Behavior, 19*, 367–384.

Mead, G. H. (1956). *On social psychology: Selected papers* (Anselm Strauss, Ed.). Chicago: University of Chicago Press. (Original work published 1934)

Neisser, U. (1988). Five kinds of self-knowledge. *Philosophical Psychology, 1*(1), 35–59.

Neisser, U. (1992, June). *Direct perception and re-cognition. Opposing theories but complementary perceptual systems.* Paper presented at the American Psychological Society, San Diego, CA.

(1993). The self perceived. In U. Neisser (Ed.), *The perceived self: Ecological and interpersonal sources of self-knowledge* (pp. 5–21). Cambridge University Press.

Ogbu, J. (1981). Origins of human competence: A cultural-ecological perspective. *Child Development, 52*, 413–429.

Park, R. E. (1936). Human ecology. *American Journal of Sociology, 42*, 1–15.

Reed, E. S. (1988). *James J. Gibson and the psychology of perception.* New Haven, CT: Yale University Press.

(1993). The intention to use a specific affordance: A conceptual framework for psychology. In R. H. Wozniak & K. W. Fischer (Eds.), *Development in context: Acting and thinking in specific environments* (pp. 45–76). Hillsdale, NJ: Erlbaum.

Rochat, P., & Senders, S. J. (1990, April). Sitting and reaching in infancy. In P. Rochat (Chair), *Posture and action in infancy.* Symposium conducted at the meeting of the International Conference on Infant Studies, Montreal, Canada.

Rogoff, B. (1990). *Apprenticeship in thinking: Cognitive development in social context.* Oxford University Press.

Rumelhart, D. E., & McClelland, J. L. (Eds.). (1986). *Parallel distributed processing: Explorations in the microstructure of cognition: Vol. 1, Foundations.* Cambridge, MA: MIT Press.

Scully, D. M. (1986). Visual perception of technical execution and aesthetic quality in biological motion. *Human Movement Science, 5,* 185–206.

Shweder, R. A. (1990). Cultural psychology – What is it? In J. W. Stigler, R. A. Shweder, & G. Herdt (Eds.), *Cultural psychology: Essays on comparative human development* (pp. 1–43). Cambridge University Press.

Siegler, R. S., & Crowley, K. (1991). The microgenetic method: A direct means for studying cognitive development. *American Psychologist, 46,* 606–620.

Stern, D. N. (1985). *The interpersonal world of the infant.* New York: Basic.

Stevenson, H. W., Lee, S., Chen, C., Stigler, J. W., Hsu, C., & Kitamura, S. (1989). Beliefs and achievement: A study of American, Chinese and Japanese children. Unpublished manuscript.

Suppe, F. (1977). *The structure of scientific theories* (2nd ed.). Urbana: University of Illinois Press.

Thomas, W. I., & Znaniecki, F. (1918–1920). *The Polish peasant in Europe and America* (Vols. 1–5). Boston: Badger.

Trevarthen, C. (1979). Communication and cooperation in early infancy: A description of primary intersubjectivity. In M. Bullowa (Ed.), *Before speech: The beginning of interpersonal communication* (pp. 321–347). Cambridge University Press.

Tudge, J. R. H., Putnam, S. E., & Valsiner, J. (in press). Culture and cognition in developmental perspective: Reading as a co-constructive process. In B. Cairns & G. H. Elder Jr. (Eds.), *Developmental science.* Cambridge University Press.

Tudge, J. R. H., & Winterhoff, P. A. (1993). Vygotsky, Piaget, and Bandura: Perspectives on the relations between the social world and cognitive development. *Human Development, 36,* 61–81.

Valsiner, J. (1989). *Human development and culture: The social nature of personality and its study.* Lexington, MA: Lexington Books.

(1992). *James Mark Baldwin and his impact: Social development of cognitive functions.* Paper presented at the First Conference for Socio-Cultural Research, Madrid.

van der Veer, R., & Valsiner, J. (1988). Lev Vygotsky and Pierre Janet: On the origin of the concept of sociogenesis. *Developmental Review, 8,* 52–65.

(1991). *Understanding Vygotsky: A quest for synthesis*. Oxford: Blackwell.

Vygotsky, L. S. (1978). *Mind in society*. Cambridge, MA: Harvard University Press.

Wahlsten, D. (1994). The intelligence of heritability. *Canadian Psychology*, *35*, 244–260.

Warren, W. H., & Whang, S. (1987). Visual guidance of walking through apertures: Body scaled information for affordances. *Journal of Experimental Psychology: Human Perception and Performance*, *13*, 371–383.

Wertsch, J. V. (1985). *Vygotsky and the social formation of mind*. Cambridge, MA: Harvard University Press.

(1991). *Voices of the mind: A sociocultural approach to mediated action*. Cambridge, MA: Harvard University Press.

Wozniak, R. H. (1993). Co-constructive metatheory for psychology: Implications for an analysis of families as specific social contexts for development. In R. H. Wozniak & K. W. Fischer (Eds.), *Development in context: Acting and thinking in specific environments* (pp. 77–91). Hillsdale, NJ: Erlbaum.

Wright, H. F., & Barker, R. G. (1950). *Methods in psychological ecology*. Lawrence: University of Kansas, Department of Psychology.

PART TWO

# Paradigmatic Statements

# 4 Nested Comparisons in the Study of Historical Change and Individual Adaptation

*Michael J. Shanahan and Glen H. Elder, Jr.*

Sociological studies of human development take a variety of forms, including sequences of comparisons that establish links between the changing social environment and individual adaptation. This chapter focuses on mechanisms linking broader societal patterns to individuals, by beginning with groups defined by social change and proceeding with fully contained subgroups. We specify the conceptual basis for nested comparisons; such an approach is best understood in conjunction with quasi-experimental strategies that capitalize on Bronfenbrenner's (1979) "transforming experiment." We next consider the utility of nested comparisons in formulating research questions within the life course framework. At this point, we extend the strategy of nested comparisons to facilitate the integration of quantitative and qualitative analyses. This integration provides a strategy for linking patterns of adaptation among groups with the diversity of adjustive processes among individuals. Our approach is illustrated with a detailed case study that connects service in World War II with postwar health patterns.

In thematic terms, the connection between social change and the individual represents a foundational issue in the emergence of sociology (Mazlish, 1991) and can be found in many of the early efforts of the Chicago school of sociology (Bulmer, 1984; Faris, 1967). Particularly noteworthy is Thomas and Znaniecki's (1918–1920) exhaustive *The Polish Peasant in Europe and America*, a study of social change in the lives of Polish immigrants to the United States. As Elder (1991) observes, perhaps the most enduring legacy of this effort is its conceptual approach, which emphasizes a processual view of group and individual experience in changing times. In this and other works, Thomas would underscore the importance of context, social change, and life history, as well as the strategic role of comparisons in interrelating these concepts.

In his situational approach, Thomas (1927) argued that the analysis of human behavior begins with an inductive examination of context, in contrast to beginning with biological or psychological presuppositions that can limit discovery. Across his writings, Thomas interrelated social institutions, neighborhoods, groups, the family, and individual experience (Volkhart, 1951). Within this situational approach, the "crisis," a period of rapid and drastic change, represents a strategic research site, since the crisis concatenates through the social system and can initiate enduring, social-structural changes (Thomas, 1909). As Volkhart (1951) notes, "A great depression, a war, may bring new definitions of the situations which persist long after the events that evoked them" (p. 13).

In reference to the crisis, Thomas made two proposals that were noteworthy for the sociology of his time. First, he connected crisis with individual adaptation; the situational approach links concrete settings with "adaptive strivings and the processes of adjustment" (Thomas, 1931, p. 177). Second, he cautiously argued for approximations of experimental designs to study behavior. Thomas rejected unqualified analogies between the natural and social sciences, simplistic notions of causality, and the possibility of measuring the full complexity of the situation or of implementing complete controls in natural settings (1927, 1939; Thomas & Thomas, 1932). However, he viewed control groups as a necessary element of social science methodology. In the final analysis, he seemed committed to some elements of the experimental design in concrete settings, with results providing a tentative basis for explanation.

His methodological strategy included the constant interplay between these results and life histories. This interplay was necessary because the experimental method could not examine the personal history and subjective experience of the individual, integral features of the situation. As he observed in his Presidential Address to the American Sociological Society, "Behavior patterns . . . are overwhelmingly conditioned by the types of situations and trains of experience encountered by the individual in the course of his life" (1927, p. 1).

In his discussions of context, social change, and the use of comparisons, Thomas stands as a prescient figure in efforts to interrelate history and the individual. Yet research since his time affords a more refined view, which includes insights from the life course paradigm, the ecology of human development, and quasi-experimental methodology.

## The Conceptual Basis for Historical Change–Individual Linkages

Given a paradigmatic interest in social structural change, sociologists often study historical events because of their pervasive effects on the organizational and relational patterns in a social system. The task is to identify precisely what organizational and relational changes follow from historical change, beginning with features of the society at large, and tracing through institutions, organizations, and small groups.

Comparisons enable us to link such change with individual adaptation, although these linkages are complicated in two respects. First, researchers lack control over historical events, which rules out formally designed and executed experiments. Instead, analysts use a combination of strategies to simulate an experimental design. Second, the linking of historical and personal change extends across different levels of analysis, ranging from social forces at the societal level to socially based processes that constitute the everyday life of an individual. An economy in decline is eventually felt by the family and child as it slows local industries, increases the unemployment rate, and gives rise to barter. Linkages between macro- and microevents can be accomplished with nested comparisons.

### *Historical Change as a System-wide Experiment*

The use of comparisons to generate knowledge became prominent with the emergence of the modern experimental method of comparing experimental and control groups (Boring, 1954). Especially since the publication of Fisher's (1925) *Statistical Methods for Research Workers*, a widely accepted feature of the experimental method has been the preexperimental equalization of the control and experimental groups through random assignment. The experimental group is then exposed to a manipulation, and subsequent tests of difference between the two groups permit the imputation of causality with statistical efficiency. Several experimental designs, as well as their corresponding strengths and weaknesses, have been identified (Campbell & Stanley, 1963).

Perhaps the most basic experimental design involves the pretest–posttest control group:

$$\begin{array}{l} R\ O_1\text{—}X\text{—}O_2, \\ R\ O_3\text{————}O_4, \end{array}$$

where R stands for randomization, X for a manipulation, and O for an observation, or measurement. Individuals are randomly assigned to one of two groups and measured on some attribute. The experimental manipulation is then introduced and each group is reassessed. A difference between $O_2$ and $O_4$ is considered attributable to X, since the two groups differ only by X.[1] For example, a random (R) group of civilians are drafted into a war: How does war service (X) affect marital relationships (O)?

How this idealized process actually occurs in studies of historical change and individual adaptation is complicated by a lack of control over group membership and the experimental manipulation. Control over group membership is necessary for the random assignment of individuals to the "treatment group," those experiencing historical change. When randomization is possible, the distribution of X is probably independent of the distributions of other Xs that might affect O, thereby eliminating alternative explanations for $O_1$–$O_2$ changes. In fact, the specific ways in which history manifests itself in the lives of individuals is often selective. Civilians are not randomly drafted into wars.

Control over the experimental manipulation is necessary to ensure that the change being studied is well understood (Lipsey, 1993). Yet historical events cannot be controlled; indeed, historical change should be viewed as a manipulation only in the sense that both represent changing circumstance. War is a myriad of both objective and subjective experiences. Lack of control over group assignment and change therefore represents a fundamental challenge to the validity of studies linking history and individuals.

This lack of control necessitates the use of quasi-experimental designs, strategies that attempt to generate scientific information from situations in which the researcher lacks control over "the scheduling of experimental stimuli (the when and to whom of exposure and the ability to randomize exposures)" (Campbell & Stanley, 1963, p. 34). The use of such designs is advocated when true experiments are not feasible and is therefore appropriate in the study of historical change and adaptation.

The value of quasi-experimental knowledge is promoted from a Popperian philosophy of science that emphasizes the *probative* value of experiments to theory. From this perspective, the design that is most capable of eliminating alternative explanations (and is possible, given the available data) is utilized. Subsequent studies – with other data, measures, and methods (Cook, 1993; Shadish, Cook, & Houts 1986) – can then be used to evaluate the existing body of empirical findings. As Campbell and Stanley (1963) note, scientific knowledge is the "cumulation of selectively retained tentatives" (p. 4). Causal inferences stemming from quasi-experimental designs are strengthened by confirmation (Marini & Singer, 1988).

In the study of historical change, true experiments are rarely feasible, although conditions approaching an experimental design are sometimes found in the course of events. Bronfenbrenner's (1979) "transforming experiment" occurs with a "restructuring of existing ecological systems in ways that challenge the forms of social organization, belief systems, and lifestyles prevailing in a particular culture or subculture" (p. 41). History is often equated with big events such as economic crises or wars, which restructure ecological systems and begin as relatively discrete occurrences in individual lives. These types of changes are well suited to a quasi-experimental framework, which emphasizes the causative role of abrupt change or discontinuous process (Caporaso, 1973). However, less discrete forms of historical change are also possible. A society's compositional and spatial organization may change, as well as patterns of transportation, communication, and education; indeed, complex arguments have been advanced, linking modernization with patterns of everyday life (Giddens, 1991). These types of historical changes are not as well suited to quasi-experimental strategies. They may involve a discontinuous process, but their gradual, diffuse nature with respect to the individual makes operational tests linking society and personal development exceedingly difficult.

Even within a quasi-experimental approach to abrupt change, however, a number of problems threaten the validity of comparisons. Many turns in history are unanticipated, thereby negating the possibility of a pretest observation. The following design, the posttest-only control group, was frequently used in early-twentieth-century agricultural research (Fisher, 1925):

$$R\ X\text{———}O_1,$$
$$R\text{————}O_2.$$

The use of this design rests on the power of randomization: If the groups are truly random in their membership, they probably differ only with respect to the effects of X. Unfortunately, historical change is often pervasive, and this means that the "treatment" is not randomly distributed across members of a society. At first glance, this leaves us with a preexperimental design, what Campbell and Stanley (1963) call a "one-shot case study":

$$X\text{———}O.$$

For example, the Great Depression (X) affects the entire U.S. society, and then measurements (O) of individuals within that society are taken. On its face, the design lacks an experimental and control group, as well as randomization between them, and so is "of almost no scientific value" (p. 6).

Fortunately, this preexperimental design can be strengthened considerably, using a range of strategies. Campbell and Stanley recognize efforts to approximate "the intrinsic symmetry of the 'true' experimental designs" as "patch-up designs." Patch-up designs approximate experiments through the coordination of data reconstruction and statistical methods to eliminate rival explanations. A common set of strategies can be found in the Life Studies Project, which draws on a number of archives, including the Berkeley Guidance Study and Oakland Growth Study data sets. Research questions are modified in terms of the available data and the data are recast in terms of the research question.

Patch-up designs often require the supplementation and conceptually driven recoding of existing data sets (Elder, Pavalko, & Clipp, 1993). For example, studies based on the Stanford–Terman Sample of Gifted Children have utilized the archive's newspaper clippings, letters from the participants, death certificates, and field notes, in addition to the collected questionnaire data.

Patch-up designs are exemplified in the Great Depression studies, which capitalize on a transforming experiment, the rapid economic decrement that households experienced during the 1930s. In the case of the Berkeley sample, data were collected as the Great Depression took place, allowing for pretest measurements. Still, a control group seems improbable for a generalized historical event like the Great Depression: All Americans living in the 1930s experienced the event in some respect. However, some groups experienced specific aspects of the Depression, while others did not. Thus, conceptually defined control groups are possible.

If one's interest lies in the effects of economic decrements in the household economy, then groups can be defined by whether families experienced such a decline. In the Depression studies, families with a 35% or more reduction in assets were classified as having experienced decline. Such a cutoff is somewhat arbitrary, but the sensitivity of the conclusions to the 35% level can be tested. Ideally, considerations of this kind come together to approximate a quasi-experimental strategy, the nonequivalent control group design:

$$O_1\text{—}X\text{—}O_2,$$
$$O_3\text{———}O_4.$$

Control and experimental groups are defined conceptually, and given data collection before the Depression, pre- and post-"test" observations can be compared. This design differs from the highly favored pretest–posttest design previously mentioned only in its lack of randomization.

Threats to validity involving interactions among selection, maturation, and the manipulation are especially noteworthy for this type of comparison. For example, differences between $O_2$ and $O_4$ can be due to a change process unique to the experimental group, not due to the hypothesized effect of X. If lower-status men were more likely to be drafted into a war, then a study of the effects of mobilization (X) on postwar income patterns ($O_2$–$O_4$) would confound a prewar difference that predicted both mobilization and lifetime income trajectory. Also, interactions between selection and the effect of X can occur, whereby X has an effect, but only because of unique attributes of the experimental group. In both cases, a premanipulation difference in the group explains a postmanipulation group difference.

These threats stem from selective forces that sort specific types of people into the control and experimental groups. In practice, researchers strive to minimize biases resulting from selection, although with varying degrees of success (Reichardt & Gollob, 1986). Some critics argue that selection is so intrinsic to the processes that social scientists study that the elimination of alternative hypotheses by way of statistical controls is rarely feasible and can easily generate misleading results (e.g., Lieberson, 1985). From this perspective, there are many areas of inquiry that simply represent "undoable science."

The ability to statistically control selection and other alternative explanations that would otherwise be ruled out by randomization has been the source of persistent and serious controversy over the merits of quasi-experimental strategies in general and the nonequivalent control group design in particular (e.g., see Bryk & Weisberg, 1977; Weisberg, 1979; for an application, see Bryk, 1981; Murnane, 1981). Most commentary is skeptical, if not pessimistic, about the use of statistical controls to adjust for initial group differences.

However, while Campbell and Stanley argue against the proliferation of "pseudo research," they also assert that quasi-experimental research designs are "sufficiently probing ... *where more efficient probes are unavailable*" (p. 35). They note that every quasi-experimental design has specific threats to its validity and the researcher must address these when possible (see also Cook & Campbell, 1979). Indeed, the issue of selection has received considerable attention, resulting in statistical procedures to correct this class of bias (Winship & Mare, 1992); however, whether such procedures actually eliminate biases due to selection is subject to doubt (e.g., Stolzenberg & Relles, 1990). Moreover, a preoccupation with the "pure effects" of events net of selection processes can be misguided when linking history with individuals. Selection processes are often substantively important to explanations of historical change and individuals.

Experimental and statistical controls are important because, across studies, they can eliminate rival hypotheses. But other criteria – empirical cues – also inform inferences about causal relationships. As Marini and Singer (1988) explain, "Empirical cues suggest that a causal inference may be justified, although none constitutes indisputable evidence for or against the causal hypothesis, and none is *sine qua non.* A subjective element in judging the causal evidence from empirical cues is an unavoidable aspect of causality assessments" (p. 366). These cues typically include considerations surrounding temporal ordering, covariation, proportionality of cause and effect, contiguity, and congruity (Einhorn & Hogarth, 1986; Marini & Singer, 1988). This approach to causation shifts attention from concern for detecting causation as an ontological characteristic to the multiple bases for causal beliefs that persuade scientists.

Contiguity and congruity prove particularly important in studies linking historical change and individual adaptation. Contiguity requires that purported causes and their effects occur closely in time and space. This is frequently not the case in life course studies and is well illustrated in Clausen's (1991) research on the long-term implications of adolescent planfulness. He reports relationships spanning over three decades between adolescent planfulness and adult career disruption, marital problems, and feelings of alienation and depression.

Congruity requires similarities between the cause and effect in strength, duration, and structural resemblance. In fact, the life course paradigm alerts our attention to the long-term effects of social change, which frequently are not congruous in strength or duration (Elder, George, & Shanahan, in press). The theme of interlocking lives also alerts the analyst to the possibility that change reverberates through a social system by way of social relationships. In this way, the effects of social change can be quite different in their structural manifestations. Economic crisis can shape socioeconomic and political values, as well as alter family relationships, pose strains and stresses for individuals, and affect a range of childhood outcomes (Elder, 1974; Moen, Kain, & Elder, 1983).

Establishing links between history and individual adaptation is especially challenging given a lack of congruity and contiguity between social changes and personal functioning. These issues are addressed by nested comparisons, which seek to link broader change with individuals by specifying processes and mechanisms at different levels of analysis.

### *Nested Comparisons across Levels of Analysis*

Quasi-experimental methods can be used within a nested comparisons framework to link more macro levels of social change to individual patterns of adaptation. While quasi-experimental strategies are methodological in their concern for attributes of the available data and the use of appropriate designs, the nested comparisons strategy is conceptual, providing a way to think through levels of aggregation and address the problems of congruity and contiguity.

As noted, nested comparisons focus on mechanisms linking broader societal patterns to individuals, by beginning with groups defined by social change and proceeding with fully contained subgroups. Significantly, nested comparisons and quasi-experimental methods come together in linking historical change and individual lives: Nested comparisons trace broader change to lower levels of aggregation, always comparing a conceptually defined control group with a group experiencing change associated with the historical event.

A simple example involves how World War II affected postwar marital satisfaction among Americans. A fundamental distinction involving war is whether an individual is mobilized for military service and, if so, at what stage in the life course. Differentiating among veterans by age of entry into the service, one can further study war-related experiences, whether the recruit was sent overseas, and, among those who were, whether combat was experienced. Among combat veterans, one may further nest by symptoms of Post Traumatic Stress Disorder. By making "thought experiments" at various levels, we begin to appreciate the specific aspects of war that are related to individual outcomes. Indeed, Pavalko and Elder (1990) report that both entry into the service after age 30 and combat experiences increase the likelihood of divorce after the war.

Thus, nested comparisons identify subgroups of individuals defined with respect to structural location as that has been changed by a particular historical transformation. This strategy can be used for the identification and refinement of strategic research questions through a hypothetical expansion or contraction of groups.

For example, studies of the Great Depression found that fathers' precrisis emotional instability increased their inconsistent behavior toward their children (Elder & Caspi, 1988). The nesting (among fathers, those who experienced economic decline, and among deprived fathers, those with and without pre-Depression emotional instability) can be expanded or narrowed in theoretically meaningful ways. One conceptual expansion of the nest asks whether this finding applies to all economic disruptions of family life, ranging from the recessionary malaise of the 1970s to the contemporary farm crisis of the rural United States. Here the original Depression group of families with emotionally unstable fathers is expanded to include other economic downturns. A possible contraction of the nest occurs when we ask whether this finding applies equally to all families irrespective of kinship or neighborhood ties, which might act in compensation. Thus, among families who experienced decline and had a father with pre-Depression emotional instability, we can further classify families according to their social support networks.

## Nested Comparisons in Life Course Analysis

Nested comparisons involve the use of subgroups that are defined in terms of historical change. But how are such subgroups systematically

Table 4.1. *Forms of Life Course Nested Comparisons*

| Life Course Causal Mechanism | Nested Comparison | Focus of Comparison |
|---|---|---|
| Situational imperatives | Structural | Social location |
| Life stage principle | Temporal | Timing of event |
| Accentuation principle | Personal | Psychological |
| Interdependent lives | Relational | Primary group |
| Control cycles | Reactive | Adaptation |

identified? The life course paradigm recognizes five causal mechanisms, which can be used to define five unique types of nested comparisons, as shown in Table 4.1. The general strategy is to specify causal mechanisms that link changes in social structure to adaptive patterns; nested groups are defined by these mechanisms.

*Situational imperatives* refer to the demand characteristics of an environment; as such, situational imperatives are not a causal mechanism per se, but rather a family of processes that link social structure to personal functioning. From the dated socialization literature, situational imperatives were viewed as complex schedules that promoted specific forms of learning; sociologists have emphasized the schedules of learning (i.e., contextual attributes) as opposed to the actual learning mechanisms implicit in their paradigm. A more contemporary approach emphasizes both context and a diverse set of mediating mechanisms that link environments with personal functioning (House & Mortimer, 1990).

From a comparative perspective, interest in situational imperatives reflects a concern for how environments are transformed with historical change. Frequently, structural comparisons are made by examining individuals who, by virtue of their social location, experience events from markedly different vantage points; these social locations are theoretically relevant because they define different sets of opportunities, risks, obligations, and expectations. In this sense, structural comparisons represent a starting point for sociological analysis, detailing how a historical event has altered context, including both broader social connections and patterns of everyday life. In our experimental notation, structural comparisons direct our attention to X, the manipulation, and the processes that it might implicate.

The primary difficulty with the structural comparison is that individuals who are affected differently in times of drastic change are often dissimilar in many ways. This raises the possibility of preexperimental differences confounding the effects of change. Thus, structural comparisons require close attention to the issue of prechange differences.

For example, studies of the Great Depression began by defining groups of families according to the extent of their economic loss – families experiencing a 35% reduction in assets were classified as having experienced economic decline. However, were certain types of families more likely to experience decline? In actuality, very few differences were observed between these types of families. Had differences been observed that were related to outcomes of interest, these systematic differences between families experiencing and not experiencing decline would need to be identified. However, as noted, selection is not merely a source of statistical bias. Rather, it can be an integral, substantive part of explanations linking history and persons.

In terms of structural comparisons, the Depression studies largely focused on family processes in an ecology defined by economic circumstance: A direct nesting linked the economic macroevent to family process, with a distinction between families from different classes. Other intervening structural nests are also possible. For example, the father's employment can be defined by economic sector (e.g., manufacturing or personal services). While families in both sectors experienced decline, their adaptive strategies may have varied considerably. Fathers in the personal service sector (e.g., a dentist) often bartered their services for goods and other services, so that even a 35% reduction in assets may not have amounted to a severe disruption within the family. On the other hand, fathers in the industrial sector may have lost their jobs completely, leading to serious tension within the family.

The *life stage principle* holds that the influence of historical change on the life course of an individual depends on the stage at which the individual experiences the event. The stage may be defined by the family cycle or by measures of lifetime achievement (e.g., career stage). The life stage principle locates the family and the child within the life course and its age-graded tasks and experiences. Thus, temporal comparisons are involved, often by situating individuals with reference to an event by way of their age.

Studies of families and children in the Great Depression were based on a natural experiment involving the life stage principle, the nesting of those experiencing the event by age. A series of analyses compared the life course of Californians who were born at opposite ends of the 1920s, members of the Oakland cohort (birthdates 1921-1922) and members of the Berkeley cohort (birthdates 1928–1929). As children during the prosperous 1920s, the Oakland Study members were old enough to help their families and did not leave home until the crisis had passed. By contrast, members of the Berkeley cohort experienced the Depression at a younger, more vulnerable age and experienced adolescence during the unsettled times of World War II. Even within families, the life stage principle could be seen: Siblings only 5 years apart in 1940 were as different in history as the difference between combat experiences on the island of Bougainville in the South Pacific and a class party at Berkeley High School (Elder, 1991).

One difficulty with this type of comparison is its assumption of homogeneity of experience within age strata: Individuals sharing a reasonably common age are assumed to be more alike than those with different ages. However, this assumption is rarely tested (see Riley, Foner, & Waring, 1988). A second problem reflects maturation: "Effects" linked to social change may in fact be typical changes occurring across the age period studied. Perhaps a group of older children became more efficacious during the Great Depression, when compared with a younger group; these changes could reflect the ontogeny of mastery, not the Depression. Thus, temporal comparisons require within-age-strata control groups.

The *accentuation principle* holds that historical change will increase the salience of individual and relational attributes that were prominent before the transition. This mechanism is reflected in the comparison of groups defined by psychological or relational attributes of its members. What is striking about personal comparisons is their strategic violation of the experimental design: Whereas experiments are based on preexperimental equalization of the groups, personal comparisons are based on a systematic inequality between groups before the event of interest. This principle is well illustrated by studies showing how men with explosive tendencies fared poorly during the Great Depression (e.g., Liker & Elder, 1983). During times of stress, explosive men experienced decrements in the quality of the marital relationship and increased the arbitrary and punitive character of parental discipline. Other tensions accentuated by pre-Depression explosiveness included marital discord (Elder, 1979) and parent–child conflict (Elder, Caspi, & Van Nguyen, 1986).

Personal comparisons run a serious risk of selection bias given their deliberate use of unequal groups before the historical event. Because the groups differ on one theoretically important parameter and given the high correlations often observed in developmental systems (Cairns, McGuire, & Gariepy, 1993), the groups may well differ in many ways, some of which are related to the outcome of interest. For example, were explosive men more likely to experience more serious levels of economic deprivation? Given patterns of affinity in marriage, did explosive men have explosive wives? Or were fathers more explosive because their children had hostile temperaments? Personal comparisons also raise the issue of maturation: Did the crisis really accentuate the effects of explosivity or did more pronounced effects reflect the ontogeny of explosiveness? Comparisons involving personal attributes need to pay particular attention to alternative explanations arising from selective and maturation processes.

*Interdependent lives* refer to the social intermeshing of lives and involve relational comparisons that focus on the role of network attributes in dealing with change. Sociological research has traditionally placed a special emphasis on the family, since it responds as a unit to social change and constitutes the proximal environment within which developmental processes take place (Furstenberg, 1985); intergenerational kinship networks, neighborhoods and communities, work groups, voluntary associations, and friendships may also be relevant. Relational comparisons are similar to Coleman's (1988) notion of social capital – social ties that facilitate action. From this perspective, groups are compared based on differences in the availability of relationships that help and hinder the implementation of strategies of adapation. Again, biases due to selection and maturation are distinct possibilities. For example, perhaps prosocial individuals are more likely to have well-developed networks. This raises the possibility that $O_2$–$O_4$ differences may not be due to X, but rather to the unique ontogeny of O among prosocial individuals.

Finally, the notion of *control cycles* is based on W. I. Thomas's early writings on social change. The control cycle centers on the connection between the individual's loss of and efforts to regain control in times of change. Control cycles are a useful way to think about social change, since change frequently brings with it the disparity between claims and resources to which control cycles respond (see Elder & Caspi, 1988). However, historical change can prompt a number of reactive strategies and these constitute the focus of reactive comparisons. What strategies are used in response to economic decline? Strategies define roles and their enactment may have lifelong implications. Reactive comparisons begin with a typology of adaptive strategies and then consider how these strategies differentially affect roles in the family. For example, studies have examined the developmental implications of children's contributions to the household economy in times of need (Elder, 1974; Elder, Foster, & Ardelt, 1994).

These life course mechanisms prove useful in empirical efforts to link social change with patterns of individual adaptation among groups. Given a historical event, the analyst asks whether the social structure has been modified in ways that require adaptive measures on the part of individuals or groups. Are there personality traits that would help or hinder such adaptive efforts? How would such adaptive patterns affect individual members based on their position in the life course? What attributes of an individual's social network facilitate or hinder adaptive change? And what are the short- and long-term consequences of various adaptive strategies?

At the same time, these types of questions have limited the inquiry to the effects of changing social structures on groups of individuals, to the neglect of individuals' active responses to and influences on social organization. Most comparisons have been structural, temporal, or personal, and these tend to depict similarly located individuals as responding similarly to change, whereas people are capable of more active, creative responses, reflecting human agency. These adaptations can also be studied by extending nested comparisons into qualitative data, through the use of strategically defined case studies.

## Nested Case Studies of Socially Based, Individual Adaptation

A fundamental tension in the use of comparisons involves the distinction between analytic and holistic orientations (Ragin, 1987). Analytic procedures establish the common elements that a series of cases share, while holistic strategies emphasize the unique relationships among many factors in every case. As Griffin (1992) notes, most comparative research drawing on historical settings negotiates a paradox: "finding diversity in the midst of uniformity and producing regularities from differences" (p. 264).

Sociologists and political scientists studying comparative history (e.g., the emergence of revolutions) have engaged in lively debate about the merits of these approaches (Kiser & Hechter, 1991; McMichael, 1992), and the debate is informative to developmental science since the two fields of inquiry share a common problematic: the qualitative transformation of complex entities over time (see, e.g., Amenta, 1991, on comparative approaches to the developmental history of welfare states). Much of the discussion centers on "synthetic strategies" that use quantitative and qualitative comparisons simultaneously to generate knowledge that is both particular and generalizable (Ragin, 1991, especially the chapter by Janoski on internal and external analysis).

The analytic orientation is evidenced by stochastic models such as those frequently used by sociologists in the study of social change. Such models reflect a paradigmatic orientation: Sociologists are frequently interested in patterns that characterize groups. On the other hand, the socialization paradigm implicit in this approach has been undergoing substantial revisions, which emphasize human agency and the heterogeneity of responses to the environment (Elder & O'Rand, 1994). Social change and adaptation can be depicted in both modal and unique terms through the integration of quantitative and qualitative comparisons.

Thus far we have noted the use of nested comparisons, defined by life course mechanisms, which describe adaptive patterns typical of groups. Yet the nested comparison strategy offers a systematic method for linking quantitative findings with qualitative case studies: Once an empirical generalization has been established about groups, diversity can be explored through further nestings. For example, among families that experienced decline, children fared poorly if fathers had unstable emotional profiles before the crisis. This finding, based on quantitative analyses, involves two groupings, economic decline and father's emotional stability, plus the child's outcome. If we assume that each grouping can be operationalized dichotomously (e.g., explosive fathers versus stable fathers), then the number of possible groups is $2^3$, or 8, distinct nested groups. We can then identify cases that appear to be "anomalous" based on our quantitative results: for example, families that experienced a decrement, had explosive fathers, but whose children had positive developmental outcomes.

In itself, this strategy represents the qualitative study of *outliers*. However, the life course framework offers a refinement of this process. The researcher has some leverage on the direction the case study should take: Case studies should begin with comparisons not made in the quantitative analyses. Thus, findings with respect to explosive fathers were based on a personal comparison (emotional instability) nested within a structural comparison (35% decline in assets).

The case studies should begin with temporal, relational, and reactive comparisons. For example, the children with positive outcomes but explosive fathers may have had close relationships with grandparents (a relational comparison); they may have been slightly older (temporal) and thus less susceptible to parental influences; or these children may have played an active role in helping their families through hard times (reactive), which offset the negative effects of their fathers' emotional instability. In this way, nested comparisons within a life course framework can generate hypotheses to be explored by way of case studies.

As noted, all of the Depression studies relied on structural comparisons to identify families by decline, and most of these studies explored nestings involving temporal or personal comparisons. One promising extension of these studies that would capture the heterogeneity of individual responses and agency of the actors would be to use reactive and relational comparisons to explore the dynamic of control cycles and interdependent lives. Control cycles often reference individuals and their sense of efficacy (e.g., Bandura, 1982), although, when conceptually joined with interdependent lives, control cycles refer to adjustive patterns within stable relationships, most often the family. Control cycles and interdependent lives can be considered concurrently by studying how individuals, as part of a collectivity such as the family, seek to reestablish a sense of equilibrium in a system disrupted by social change.

From this perspective, social change disrupts the primary group, which then responds by collectively seeking a new definition of the situation, in both material and normative terms. Case studies document both the nature of the disruption caused by historical change and the individual as part of a primary group, negotiating circumstances to reestablish a stable and consensually based pattern of everyday living. These case studies focus life histories on how the individual and his or her primary group respond to challenges posed by social change to reestablish a sense of control. The purpose of these case studies is to detail the variable ways in which individuals adapt to challenging circumstances; they are a source of empirical and theoretical elaboration and not, as sometimes asserted, a way of validating quantitative findings.

## Linking War and American Men's Lives

The use of quasi-experimental methods and nested comparisons can be illustrated by a study that explores the effects of war on men's health, as mediated by life course disorganization. Typical of many studies linking history and personal change, this research question suggests relationships that are neither congruous nor contiguous – war experiences and lifetime patterns of health.

World War II was a naturally occurring experiment that allowed for a consideration of this issue, since it pulled men and women from families, careers, and community. One would expect less positive health outcomes for men who entered the service, an expectation based on evidence linking stressors associated with life course disorganization with less favorable health. Based on previous research, we expect that this relationship holds primarily among those who entered the service later in life, in their 30s. As opposed to younger men, these older entrants had established well-defined career trajectories and were less able to begin a new line of work after the war (Elder, 1986, 1987).

### *Analytic Comparisons of Groups*

Elder and his colleagues (Elder, Shanahan, & Clipp, 1994) examine how military service affected lifetime physical health trajectories with men from the Stanford–Terman Sample of Gifted Children, a longitudinal sample initiated in 1922 with 12 follow-ups through 1976. Table 4.2 shows two logistic regression models testing these ideas; the equations predict a negative physical health trajectory (1 = yes, 0 = no; Clipp, Pavalko, & Elder, 1992) from the end of the war in 1945 to death or 1976, whichever came first. Our fundamental interest lies in the effects of early (ages 18–32) and late (33–41) entry into the military on health patterns. Since our reference category is

Table 4.2. *Effects of Time of Entry into World War II on Postwar Physical Health Trajectory*

| Variable | Model 1 | Model 2 |
|---|---|---|
| Intercept | 1.64*** | 1.73*** |
| | (.47) | (.48) |
| Early entry | –.43 | –.40 |
| | (.31) | (.31) |
| Late entry | 1.00*** | .58 |
| | (.28) | (.36) |
| Younger cohort[a] | .19 | .25 |
| | (.20) | (.21) |
| Years lived postwar | –.05*** | –.05*** |
| | (.01) | (.01) |
| Education 1940 | –.22*** | –.23*** |
| | (.06) | (.06) |
| Postwar career | –.04 | –.20 |
| | (.20) | (.22) |
| Late career (interaction term) | | .99[†] |
| | | (.54) |
| $\chi^2$, df | $53.9_6$*** | $57.37_7$*** |

*Note:* Logistic coefficient/standard error reported. Based on a logistic regression predicting poor health trajectory. $N = 552$. Reference is nonveterans.
[†] $p < .10$; * $p < .05$; ** $p < .01$; *** $p < .001$.
[a] 1 = born 1910–1924. Reference is men born 1900–1909.

nonveterans, the comparisons directly simulated by these equations are between nonveterans (who experienced no life course disorganization) and groups defined by age of entry (with later entrants experiencing more disruption). We control membership in the younger cohort, years lived after the war, and education, all factors thought to influence health patterns.

As Model 1 shows, the late entrants are significantly more likely to show a negative pattern of health (odds ratio = 2.72, $p < .001$). Model 2 introduces a late career interaction term between late entry and a variable measuring work life progression (1 = stable or downward pattern, 0 = upward progression) after the war. Its effect is positive and marginally significant, indicating that late entry into the service coupled with a poor postwar work life leads to poor health. Significantly, in analyses not reported here, the models control for physical health in 1940 and the results are substantially the same. The inclusion of this variable eliminates the alternative explanation that postwar health trajectories are due to prewar differences in health.

These results illustrate how patch-up designs begin to simulate experiments – in this case, a patch up comparable in many respects to a nonequivalent control group design:

$$\begin{array}{l}(R)O_{1a}\text{—}X\text{—}O_{2b}\\(R)O_{3a}\text{———}O_{4b}.\end{array}$$

In many instances, even after archival data have been recast, exact measures do not exist for both pre- and postevent time periods, resulting in a less favorable variation of the nonequivalent control group design. Thus, $O_a$ (physical health in 1940) is used to establish pretest equivalence of physical health, although $O_b$ (physical health trajectory) is used to measure test effects. Our reference category is composed of nonveterans, men who did not experience the "experimental manipulation" (service in the war) and so constitute our conceptually defined control group. Randomization is partially simulated by the inclusion of control variables that represent alternative explanations to postwar patterns in health. Particularly threatening to the study's validity is that older entrants would be expected to show poorer health than early entrants; we cover this possibility with the inclusion of birth cohort as a predictor. A statistical adjustment was also introduced to control selective biases due to attrition: perhaps $O_2$–$O_4$ differences reflect a select group of individuals dropping out of the sample. However, the substantive conclusions remain unchanged.

The example also reflects the use of nested comparisons. Model 1 shows that late entrants were more likely to experience a negative health trajectory than nonveterans. Model 2 shows that it is actually late entry coupled with poor postwar career progression that explains health patterns; those men who entered late and experienced poor work life progression were about 2.7 times more likely to exhibit a poor health trajectory. The structural comparison involved veterans and nonveterans. The causal mechanism of interest is life course disruption: Nonveterans would have negligible disruption since they were not mobilized, while that intensity of disruption would vary among veterans by time of entry, a temporal comparison.

Further nests would be necessary to link life course disorganization with physical health. For example, previous research suggests connections between stressors and immune functioning, and among social dislocations, material deprivations, status inconsistencies, loss of self-identity, and a range of indicators of well-being (Elder et al., in press). At this juncture, our evidence suggests a plausible connection between life course disorganization and physical well-being, although further research is clearly needed.

### *Holistic Comparisons through Life History Records*

To capture the heterogeneity of postwar experiences, we extend these analyses to case studies. Our primary quantitative finding shows that late-entering veterans with unfavorable postwar careers experienced negative physical health trajectories – a finding derived from three nestings (veteran status, age of entry, and career pattern). These three nestings define eight (i.e., $2^3$) specific subgroups of interest. A specific example will illustrate how life course causal mechanisms can focus the life histories: late entrants with bad careers and good health. We suggested that the use of relational and reactive comparisons in tandem would be a valuable starting point. Thus, the initial focus of the life histories is how late entrants with bad careers and good health retained a sense of control over their lives through group-based adaptive strategies.

Drawing on life histories of the Terman men constructed as part of the Life Studies Project, we note one such case, a veteran who entered the service late. This individual reported in 1972 that "I have always had excellent physical health." At the same time, he had no career to speak of before the war; after the war, he remained in the same position for many years, then was forced into early retirement. He showed greater than average turnover toward the end of his career.

However, consistent with our general expectations, there is evidence that noncareer factors gave meaning to his life, especially religion and family. He reports involvement in church-related activities before the war, and religion was continually mentioned throughout his record. He had five daughters after the war and reports in 1960 that his leisure time is spent with them. Most telling is his short bout with depression, reflected upon in 1972: "The concern of my wife and family – plus what I believe was real help from 'upstairs' – I came out of it improved." His 1977 life review notes that "watching the personal development of our children (and giving them support) has provided new personal insight" and that "I feel that [my wife] and I are constantly growing in our mutual love and respect and in our ability to develop increasingly pleasant patterns of living. We have a most rewarding life and a bright future!" In a comparative framework, it would be particularly appropriate to contrast this case with the case of a late entrant with a disrupted career, poor family life, and good health to identify noncareer factors.

Other life history patterns could also be studied – for example, nonveterans or early entrants with bad health and good careers. Given our framework, these life histories would focus on the presence of noncareer factors contributing to life course disorganization. A cursory examination of such cases suggests that postwar alcoholism and divorce were two such factors. These examples begin to illustrate how life histories can be nested within generalizations derived from quantitative analyses and then studied within the life course paradigm.

## Exploring the Legacy of W. I. Thomas

History undoubtedly affects patterns of human life, and this is vividly illustrated in times of dramatic and sudden change. Yet specifying exactly how such change affects the individual's adaptive strategies is a complicated enterprise, requiring the interplay of quasi-experimental strategies and nested comparisons. The research enterprise is best served by acknowledging the limitations of one's comparisons and compensating for these when possible.

The most pervasive threat to these studies is initial differences in the "control" and "experimental" groups, differences that raise the possibility of alternative explanations, including selection and maturation biases. From a methodological standpoint, these biases probably become more serious as the number of nestings increases. However, substantively, such processes explain why certain groups experience events in specific ways and are thus a critical component to explanations linking individuals and history. Analytic comparative approaches will attempt to remove the effects of all plausible, alternative explanations to estimate the pure effects between variables. A more holistic approach will include selection and maturation as an integral part of the substantive explanation.

Implicit in our approach is the assumption that basic social psychological processes that describe reactions to historical change generalize through time (Elder, 1993). Research stemming from this assumption is not unqualifiably deterministic (cf. Zuckerman, 1993), nor does it purport to offer transhistorical laws in an expansive sense (cf. Gergen, 1973). Rather, this research looks for similarities that characterize reactions to reasonably comparable historical changes, allowing for peculiarities across research settings. This position reflects a tension in ecological approaches to human development: Time and place condition the course of human development, yet cross-situational generalizations are possible.

For example, Elder's (see Elder & Caspi, 1988) program of research studying the effects of economic hardship on the family initially relied on quasi-experimental studies of the Berkeley and Oakland data sets; from these studies a theoretical model was formulated linking deprivation with intrafamilial processes, a model that specified how economic problems lead to psychological disturbances among the parents and, in turn, affect the marital and parent–child relationships (Moen et al., 1983).

Many of the insights from this model have been tested and supported in other settings: in a sample of Iowans during the farm crisis of the 1970s (Conger et al., 1992, 1993; Conger & Elder, 1994), as well as in a national probability sample (McLeod & Shanahan, 1993). While these studies also relied on quasi-experimental designs, the increased rigor of sampling, measurement, and methods renders them more stringent tests of a model initially formulated on the best available data at the time. The basic mechanisms linking economic hardship with family process and adjustment operate in these other settings. Despite methodological and conceptual difficulties, programmatic studies of historical change and individual development can lead to a better understanding of context, social change, and individual adaptation.

Over 60 years have elapsed since the penetrating work of W. I. Thomas on social change and the individual. Drawing on the life course paradigm, quasi-experimental methods, and the ecological approach to human development, we can refine his early insights. Yet with further advances in conceptual models and methods, we will return to historical data and rediscover the past once more.

## Note

1. This is slightly oversimplified. For example, as Leamer (1983, p. 32) points out, "Randomization does not assure that each and every

experiment is 'adequately mixed' but randomization does make 'adequate mixing' probable."

## References

Amenta, E. (1991). Making the most of a case study: Theories of the welfare state and the American experience. In C. Ragin (Ed.), *Issues and alternatives in comparative social research* (pp. 172–194). Leiden: Brill.

Bandura, A. (1982). The psychology of chance encounters and life paths. *American Psychologist, 37*, 747–755.

Boring, E. (1954). The nature and history of the control group. *American Journal of Psychology*, *67*, 573–589.

Bronfenbrenner, U. (1979). *The ecology of human development: Experiments by nature and design.* Cambridge, MA: Harvard University Press.

Bryk, A. S. (1981). Disciplined inquiry or policy argument? *Harvard Educational Review*, *51*, 497–509.

Bryk, A. S., & Weisberg, H. I. (1977). Use of nonequivalent control group design when subjects are growing. *Psychological Bulletin*, *84*, 950–962.

Bulmer, M. (1984). *The Chicago school of sociology: Institutionalization, diversity and the rise of sociological research.* Chicago: University of Chicago Press.

Cairns, R. B., McGuire, A. M., & Gariépy, J.-L. (1993). Developmental behavior genetics: Fusion, correlated constraints, and timing. In D. F. Hay & A. Angold (Eds.), *Precursors and causes in development and psychopathology* (pp. 87–122). New York: Wiley.

Campbell, D. T., & Stanley, J. G. (1963). *Experimental and quasi-experimental designs for research.* Boston: Houghton Mifflin.

Caporaso, J. A. (1973). Quasi-experimental approaches to social science. In J. A. Caporaso & L. L. Roos (Eds.), *Quasi-experimental approaches* (pp. 3–38). Evanston, IL: Northwestern University Press.

Clausen, J. (1991). Adolescent competence and the shaping of the life course. *American Journal of Sociology*, *96*, 805–842.

Clipp, E. C., Pavalko, E. K., & Elder, G. H., Jr. (1992). Trajectories of health: In concept and empirical pattern. *Behavior, Health and Aging*, *2*, 159–179.

Coleman, J. S. (1988). Social capital in the creation of human capital. *American Journal of Sociology, 94*, S95–S120.

Conger, R. D., Conger, K. J., Elder, G. H., Jr., Lorenz, F. O., Simons, R. L., & Whitbeck, L. B. (1992). A family process model of economic hardship and adjustment of early adolescent boys. *Child Development*, *63*, 526–541.

(1993). Family economic stress and the adjustment of early adolescent girls. *Developmental Psychology*, *29*, 206–219.

Conger, R. D., & Elder, G. H., Jr. (Eds.). (1994). *Families in troubled times: Adapting to change in rural America.* New York: Aldine.

Cook, T. D. (1993). A quasi-sampling theory of the generalization of causal relationships. In L. B. Sechrest & A. G. Scott (Eds.), *Understanding causes and generalizing about them* (pp. 39–82). San Francisco: Jossey-Bass.

Cook, T. D., & Campbell, D. (1979). Quasi-experimental methods. New York: Prentice-Hall.

Einhorn, H. J., & Hogarth, R. M. (1986). Judging probable cause. *Psychological Bulletin, 99,* 3–19.

Elder, G. H., Jr. (1974). *Children of the Great Depression: Social change in life experiences.* Chicago: University of Chicago Press.

(1979). Historical changes in life patterns and personality. In P. B. Baltes & O. G. Brim (Eds.), *Life-span development and behavior* (pp. 118–159). New York: Academic Press.

(1986). Military times and turning points in men's lives. *Developmental Psychology, 22,* 233–245.

(1987). War mobilization and the life course: A cohort of World War II veterans. *Sociological Forum, 2,* 449–472.

(1991). The life course, social change and the Chicago tradition. Mimeo. Life Studies Project, Carolina Population Center.

(1993). Time, human agency, and social change: Perspectives on the life course. *Social Psychology Quarterly, 57,* 4–15.

Elder, G. H., Jr, & Caspi, A. (1988). Human development and social change: An emerging perspective on the life course. In N. Bolger, A. Caspi, G. Downey, & M. Moorehouse (Eds.), *Persons in context: Developmental processes* (pp. 77–113). Cambridge University Press.

Elder, G. H., Jr., Caspi, A., & Van Nguyen, T. (1986). Resourceful and vulnerable children: Family influences in hard times. In R. K. Silbereisen, K. Eysferth, & G. Rodinger (Eds.), *Development as action in context: Problem behavior and normal youth development* (pp. 167–186). New York: Springer.

Elder, G. H., Jr., Foster, E. M., & Ardelt, M. (1994). Children of the household economy. In R. D. Conger & G. H. Elder Jr. (Eds.), *Families in troubled times* (pp. 127–146). New York: Aldine.

Elder, G. H., Jr., George, L. K., & Shanahan, M. J. (in press). Psychosocial stress over the life course. In H. Kaplan (Ed.), *Perspectives on psychosocial stress.*

Elder, G. H., Jr., Pavalko, E. K., & Clipp, E. C. (1993). *Working with archival data: Studying lives.* Newbury Park, CA: Sage.

Elder, G. H., Jr., & O'Rand, A. M. (1994). Adult lives in a changing society. In K. Cook, J. House, & G. Fine (Eds.), *Handbook of social psychology: Sociological perspectives* (pp. 452–475). New York: Basic Books.

Elder, G. H., Jr., Shanahan, M. J., & Clipp, E. C. (1994). When war comes to men's lives: Patterns in the life course. *Psychology of Aging*, *9*, 5–16.

Faris, R. L. (1967). *Chicago sociology: 1920–1932*. San Francisco: Chandler.

Fisher, R. A. (1925). *Statistical methods for research workers* (1st ed.). London: Oliver & Boyd.

Furstenberg, F. F., Jr. (1985). Sociological ventures in child development. *Child Development*, *56*, 281–288.

Gergen, K. J. (1973). Social psychology as history. *Journal of Personality and Social Psychology*, *26*, 309–320.

Giddens, A. (1991). *Modernity and self-identity: Self and society in the late modern age*. Stanford, CA: Stanford University Press.

Griffin, L. J. (1992). Comparative-historical analysis. In E. Borgatta & M. Borgatta (Eds.), *Encyclopedia of sociology* (pp. 263–271). New York: Macmillan.

House, J. S., & Mortimer, J. T. (1990) Social structure and the individual: Emerging themes and new directions. *Social Psychology Quarterly*, *53*, 71–80.

Kiser, E., & Hechter, M. (1991). The role of general theory in comparative-historical sociology. *American Journal of Sociology*, *97*, 1–30.

Leamer, E. E. (1983). Let's take the con out of econometrics. *American Economic Review*, *73*, 31–43.

Lieberson, S. (1985). *Making it count*. Berkeley: University of California Press.

Liker, J. K., & Elder, G. H., Jr. (1983). Economic hardship and marital relations in the 1930's. *American Sociological Review*, *48*, 343–359.

Lipsey, M. (1993). Theory as method: Small theories of treatments. In L. B. Sechrest & A. G. Scott (Eds.), *Understanding causes and generalizing about them* (pp. 5–38). San Francisco: Jossey-Bass.

Loehlin, J. C. (1987). *Latent variable models: An introduction to factor, path, and structural analysis*. Hillsdale, NJ: Erlbaum.

Marini, M. M., & Singer, B. (1988). Causality in the social sciences. *Sociological Methodology*, *16*, 347–411.

Mazlish, B. (1991). *A new science: The breakdown of connections and the birth of sociology*. University Park: Pennsylvania State University Press.

McLeod, J. D., & Shanahan, M. J. (1993). Poverty and children's distress. *America Sociological Review*, *58*, 351–366.

McMichael, P. (1992). Rethinking comparative analysis in a post-developmentalist context. *International Journal of Social Science*, *133*, 351–365.

Moen, P., Kain, E. L., & Elder, G. H., Jr. (1983). Economic conditions and family life: Contemporary and historical perspectives. In R. R. Nelson & F. Skidmore (Eds.), *American families and the economy: The high costs of living* (pp. 213–259). Washington, DC: Academy Press.

Murnane, R. J. (1981). Evidence, analysis, and unanswered questions. *Harvard Educational Review, 51*, 483–489.

Pavalko, E. K., & Elder, G. H., Jr. (1990). World War II and divorce: A life course perspective. *American Journal of Sociology, 95*, 1213–1234.

Ragin, C. (1987). *The comparative method: Moving beyond qualitative and quantitative strategies.* Berkeley: University of California Press.

Ragin, C. (Ed.). (1991). *Issues and alternatives in comparative social research.* Leiden: Brill.

Reichardt, C. S., & Gollob, H. F. (1986). Satisfying the constraints of causal modelling. In W. M. K. Trochim (Ed.), *Advances in quasi-experimental design and analysis* (pp. 91–107). San Francisco: Jossey-Bass.

Riley, M. W., Foner, A., & Waring, J. (1988). Sociology of age. In N. Smelser (Ed.), *Handbook of sociology* (pp. 243–290). Newbury Park, CA: Sage.

Shadish, W. R., Jr., Cook, T. D., & Houts, A. C. (1986). Quasi-experimentation in a critical multiplist mode. In W. M. K. Trochim (Ed.), *Advances in quasi-experimental design and analysis* (pp. 29–46). San Francisco: Jossey-Bass.

Stolzenberg, R. M., & Relles, D. A. (1990). Theory testing in a world of constrained research design: The significance of Heckman's censored sampling bias correction for nonexperimental research. *Sociological Methods and Research, 18*, 395–415.

Thomas, W. I. (1909). *Source book for social origins.* Boston: Badger.

(1927). The behavior pattern and the situation. *Publications of the American Sociological Society, 22*, 1–13.

(1931). The relation of research to the social process. In W. F. G. Swann et al. (Eds.), *Essays on research in the social sciences* (pp. 175–194). Washington: Brookings Institution.

(1939). Comment by W. I. Thomas. In H. Blumer, *Critiques of research in the social sciences: Vol. 1. An appraisal of Thomas and Znaniecki's "The Polish peasant in Europe and America"* (pp. 1–81). New York: Social Science Research Council.

Thomas, W. I., & Thomas, D. S. (1932). *The child in America.* New York: Knopf.

Thomas, W. I., & Znaniecki, F. (1918–1920). *The Polish peasant in Europe and America* (Vols. 1 and 2). Chicago: University of Chicago Press.

Volkhart, E. H. (1951). Introduction: Social behavior and the defined situation. In E. H. Volkhart (Ed.), *Social behavior and personality: Contributions of W. I. Thomas to theory and social research* (pp. 1–32). New York: Social Science Research Council.

Weisberg, H. I. (1979). Statistical adjustments and uncontrolled studies. *Psychological Bulletin, 86*, 1149–1164.

Winship, C., & Mare, R. D. (1992). Models for sample selection bias. *Annual Review of Sociology, 18*, 327–350.

Zuckerman, M. (1993). History and developmental psychology, a dangerous liaison: A historian's perspective. In G. H. Elder Jr., J. Modell, & R. D. Parke (Eds.), *Children in time and place: Developmental and historical insights* (pp. 226–240). Cambridge University Press.

# 5 The Value of Comparisons in Developmental Psychology

*Debra Mekos and Patricia A. Clubb*

Group comparisons are a ubiquitous phenomenon in developmental psychology. Empirical efforts abound with analyses of age, gender, and ethnic differences, as well as comparisons between securely and insecurely attached infants, peer-rejected and popular children, and authoritarian and authoritative parents. A survey of studies published in *Child Development* over the past 50 years bears this out; 68% to 88% employed cross-sectional and group comparison designs (Redmond, 1994). Given the discipline's penchant for this typological mode of inquiry, questions arise as to what we can expect to learn about development from an examination of differences between groups. Do group comparisons mask processes of change? Or can they be used to highlight developmental mechanisms that would otherwise be obscured in analyses of individual differences or single-subject case studies of growth?

The purpose of this chapter is to discuss the potential value of group comparisons for studying development. Although some have criticized the study of group differences as nondevelopmental (e.g., Valsiner, 1984), we argue that there is nothing inherent in this approach to warrant such a conclusion. Instead, we hope to show that group comparisons can serve an important function in the programmatic study of developmental phenomena. We focus on three types of comparisons: gender, atypical children, and age group differences. Although by no means a comprehensive set, we believe the issues they raise extend to other, more topic-specific comparisons (e.g.,

The writing of this chapter was supported by a Carolina Consortium postdoctoral fellowship to the first author and a predoctoral fellowship to the second author. We would like to thank members of the Carolina Consortium on Human Development for their insights and suggestions, especially Carol Eckerman, Glen Elder, Gilbert Gottlieb, Peter Ornstein, Michael Shanahan, Raymond Sturner, Jonathan Tudge, and Jaan Valsiner.

abused versus nonabused children) as well. In illustration we present three exemplary studies, each involving a specific type of comparison, that gain strength and clarity because of their attention to group differences in the phenomenon of interest. Noting the strengths and limitations of group comparison approaches, we conclude with a discussion of the utility of combining within-person and group comparison designs.

## Criticism of Group Comparative Methods

In a sense, the research enterprise always involves some form of comparison, be it a cross-sectional study of group differences or a longitudinal study of a single person's performance over time. The critical question, of course, is whether the comparisons enrich our understanding of development. Taking Kurt Lewin's (1933) lead, several authors have raised objections to the practice of examining group differences to study development, arguing that analysis at the level of the individual is the only avenue suitable to the task (Lightfoot & Folds-Bennett, 1992; Valsiner, 1984).

Typically, group comparisons involve the classification of individuals on a single attribute (e.g., gender, ethnicity, family structure), under the assumption that individuals can be placed into bounded, discrete categories that are stable across context and time. A mean group score representing the prototypic quality on the domain of interest is derived by averaging across the behavior of individuals within a group. Group means are then compared and any statistically significant differences between means are taken as evidence for the influence of the classificatory attribute on the domain of interest, assuming other factors are held constant.

The central criticism of this approach is that by averaging across behavior within a group, the variability across individuals and contexts is lost (Valsiner, 1984). Deviations from the prototypic mean are viewed as noise or error variance, and individuals with highly discrepant scores are treated as outliers rather than central to our understanding of the phenomenon. According to this view, group comparisons are ill-suited for examining individual development because they yield information about a mathematical average that may not correspond to the dynamics of behavior for any individual within that group (Lightfoot & Folds-Bennett, 1992). In short, inferences about the behavior and development of specific individuals interacting in specific contexts cannot be drawn from the study of group differences.

However, this criticism ignores the possibility that developmental processes may be linked to the attribute on which groups are defined. For argument's sake, suppose that aspects of the person's gender or ethnicity play a pivotal role in development of a particular domain of behavior. One could study the domain in terms of the pattern of development for a single person, the general pattern for a large sample of persons, or individual differences in the pattern of development among persons. However, because neither gender nor ethnicity varies within an individual, a focus on intraindividual change would in essence ignore the relevance of these attributes for the developmental process. Studies of individuals and individual differences would yield descriptive information about the timing, rate, and sequencing of development, but could not adequately identify how change emerges if gender and ethnicity were not taken into consideration. Only through a comparison of gender or ethnic differences in the patterns of change would one begin to understand the mechanisms that underlie the observed changes in behavior. For some developmental phenomena, this scenario may be reality. In such instances, group comparisons may be essential for flagging developmental mechanisms that would otherwise be obscured in single-person case studies or studies of individual differences.

## Group Comparisons within a Systems View of Development

The value of group comparisons for understanding processes of change becomes more crucial if one takes a systems view of development. This theoretical framework has appeared under a variety of guises, including developmental contextualism (Lerner, 1984), life span development (Baltes, 1987), interactionism (Magnusson, 1988), person–process–context model (Bronfenbrenner, 1988), transactionalism (Sameroff, 1983), dynamic systems (Thelen & Ulrich, 1991), and probabilistic epigenesis (Gottlieb, 1992). Although differing in detail, these perspectives share the same core organizing assumption that development represents the continuous reorganization and integration of multiple levels of experience that induce, constrain, facilitate, and maintain behavior over the course of a person's life (for more detail, see Winegar, Chapter 1, Shanahan,

Valsiner, & Gottlieb, Chapter 2, and Tudge, Gray, Hogan, Chapter 3, this volume).

Two corollaries of this view are central to our argument concerning the value of group comparisons. First, development is an emergent process that depends on the confluence of many asynchronously changing elements, rather than a prescriptive process in which a single element within or outside the organism produces change. Thus, no single component of the system is solely sufficient or responsible for development in any domain. Instead, development arises from the way in which the multiple components organize themselves to produce novel forms of behavior or maintain current forms of functioning.

Second, the course of development is probabilistic rather than deterministic. In other words, there is a considerable amount of plasticity in development, resulting in multiple pathways to the same outcome and multiple outcomes resulting from similar processes. For any single individual, the actual developmental pathway is always a product of transactions between their developmental history and current functioning and experience. Thus, not all persons would be expected to follow the same developmental trajectory, despite surface similarities in functioning at a given point in time. This is not to say that the range of possible developmental trajectories is limitless, however. Components of the developing system are mutually interdependent, with alterations in one component influencing alterations in others, and it is this interdependence that sets limits on the rate and direction of growth.

A systems view entails an approach to the study of development that emphasizes the diversity in patterns of change over the life span, both within and across persons. Rather than focusing on the prediction of outcomes or end states from one time to the next, this perspective calls for detailed description of the interweaving of experience at all levels – physiological, psychological, social, cultural – as an individual moves through time. And yet because of its multifaceted and dynamic quality, our efforts to immobilize development long enough to describe and understand it in detail will always be limited. Herein lies the dilemma. Given the ephemeral nature of development, accurate understanding of the phenomenon does not easily lend itself to the practice of extracting discrete categories at discrete points in time from the ongoing stream of change (Cairns, 1986; Nesselroade &

Ford, 1987). Yet in order to gain insight into what is occurring, we must strive to do just that. As Robert Hinde (1988) has noted, we can only observe change and variability from the backdrop of continuity and stability.

At first glance, one might conclude that group comparisons, with their emphasis on developmental homogeneity among individuals within groups, would be antithetical to a systems view of development, with the latter's emphasis on plasticity in individual patterns of change. However, group comparisons may be a valuable means of representing the multifaceted nature of developmental systems. In criticism of the traditional variable-centered approach to developmental research, Magnusson and Bergman (1988) argue that examination of developmental processes requires the analysis of persons as integrated totalities comprising a configuration of biological, social, and contextual factors. Similarly, Thelen and Ulrich (1991) emphasize the importance of identifying what they term the "collective variable," representing a compression of the many possible ways in which the components of development could be organized. Finally, Cairns and colleagues (Cairns & Cairns, 1991; Cairns, McGuire, & Gariépy, 1993) argue that the experiences that shape behavior do not operate in isolation, but instead represent an interdependent system of correlated constraints that collaborate to guide development in some directions and not others. Particular configurations set limits on what the organism can do and influence the timetable for what behaviors will emerge at what points in the life course.

In our view, many of the typologies used in developmental psychology to examine group differences implicitly acknowledge the existence of correlated constraints contained within the categories of age, gender, and the like. From a developmental systems perspective, adequate understanding cannot be gleaned from an examination of a person's status on a single attribute, but rather must be assessed from the vantage point of a particular configuration of components. It would be difficult, if not impossible, to assess all these components directly. However, they may be conveniently contained within the classificatory attributes on which groups are defined. In some respects, the identification of group membership and examination of group differences may be the only tools at our disposal for freezing in time and space the myriad interdependent influences that direct the course of development. We argue that group comparison serves an important heuristic function for summarizing particular configurations of components – biological, psychological, social, cultural, historical – that accompany group membership. Moreover, implicit in the use of group comparisons is the notion that this configuration in some way matters, that the multiplicity of pathways that development can take is constrained in similar ways by what differentiates one group from another.

For example, much effort has been devoted to the identification of processes underlying gender differences in math and science achievement (see Jacklin, 1989, for a review). It is reasonable to assume that gender differences exist at all levels of the developmental system – in brain structure, hormonal activity, spatial perception and cognition, social expectations of parents, teachers, and peers, as well as societal, cultural, and historical differences in the value placed on math and science achievement for boys and girls. Furthermore, it is reasonable to expect differences at each level to influence and be influenced by gender differences at other levels. We would argue that the failure to consider the confluence of gender differences at all these levels and the ways in which they are organized has hindered our understanding of the complex processes involved.

To be sure, noting an achievement difference between boys and girls and stopping at that point tells us nothing about the processes that give rise to this difference. Indeed, there is a real danger in attributing causal status to the attribute on which groups are defined, as Bronfenbrenner (1988) points out in his criticism of social address models. However, while gender differences have no explanatory power of their own, they are informative to the extent that they provide clues about the relevant processes involved. We are not advocating the wholesale use of group comparisons, yet for some domains there may be good reason to suspect that constraints on development are as much a reflection of group membership as of individual attributes. The systematic use of group comparisons can facilitate the detection of these constraints and their contribution to developmental change. Moreover, when combined with within-person comparisons, they can serve an explanatory function as well, by pointing to potential processes through which development arises. To better illustrate the value of group comparisons for understanding development, we now turn to a more specific discussion of their use in studies of gender, atypical children, and age group differences.

## Group Comparisons in Developmental Psychology

### *Gender Comparisons*

References to typological differences between males and females date back to the time of Aristotle, when women were characterized as compassionate and envious and men as courageous and valiant (Ruble, 1984). These stereotypic beliefs in maleness versus femaleness have permeated Western thought throughout the centuries, but it has only been since the 1960s that developmental psychologists have seriously considered gender differences an important domain of inquiry (Jacklin, 1989). The past three decades have witnessed a virtual explosion of research on the issue, to the point that many studies now include an analysis of gender differences as a matter of course (Ruble, 1984). Unfortunately, increments in our perfunctory use of gender comparisons in research have outpaced our theoretical conceptualizations of how and why gender differences develop.

There are a variety of reasons for expecting developmental differences between males and females, given the biological and sociocultural differences that exist (Maccoby, 1988; Ruble, 1984; Whiting & Edwards, 1973). However, our commonsense belief that boys and girls are more different than alike has, for the most part, not been supported by research on the issue (Feingold, 1988; Hyde & Linn, 1988; Maccoby & Jacklin, 1974). This discrepancy between belief and evidence may stem in part from the way in which studies of gender differences are typically done (Jacklin, 1981; Ruble, 1984).

For example, many studies show a lack of sensitivity to the role of social context and cultural belief systems in eliciting or prohibiting the expression of gender-relevant behavior. Yet context plays a critical role, as illustrated by cross-cultural research on the social behavior of male and female children (Edwards & Whiting, 1988) and research on cross-situational variability in a person's gender-linked behavior within a given culture (Deaux & Major, 1987). Another limitation is the strong focus on quantitative differences in levels of behavior between males and females and the neglect of qualitative differences in the structure or function of behavior between gender groups. A third limitation concerns the issue of timing in the expression of gender-relevant behavior in development. Cross-sectional designs are by far the most common method for assessing gender differences. The problem with this practice is that it ignores the possibility that gender differences, though not apparent when behavior is examined at a single point in time, may emerge when longitudinal patterns are examined.

One notable example of how gender comparisons can inform the study of development is an investigation by Cairns and colleagues (Cairns, Cairns, Neckerman, Ferguson, & Gariépy, 1989), which examined patterns of continuity and change in aggression from childhood to adolescence. This study assessed a sample of boys and girls over a 6-year period, using peer and teacher reports, as well as self-ratings, of aggressive behavior. Of particular interest for our purposes are the factor analysis results for aggression in 4th and 7th grades.

What emerged was an interesting pattern of gender differences in the developmental course of aggression over this period. Specifically, boys showed an increasing consolidation of what defines aggression, with separate factors for self-ratings and peer/teacher ratings of physical confrontation in 4th grade merging into a single self/other factor of physical confrontation by 7th grade. In contrast, the developmental pattern for girls indicated a diversification in what constitutes aggressive behavior. The pattern for girls was characterized by a qualitative shift from separate factors of self-ratings and peer/teacher ratings of physical confrontation in 4th grade to two functionally distinct factors by 7th grade – physical confrontation and a more subtle form of social aggression involving gossip, ostracism, and alienation.

What these results suggest is a divergence in the development of aggressive behavior for boys and girls from preadolescence to early adolescence. Many have noted the gender difference in levels of aggression and the declines in girls' aggressive behavior with age. However, these results suggest the opposite conclusion, that girls' aggression does not decline over time as much as it becomes more diversified in form and function. With its attention to both quantitative and qualitative change, this study helped to clarify the meaning of gender differences in aggression and provided some clues to the processes involved.

For example, one of the most interesting results concerns the emergence of girls' social aggression in 7th grade, a period that coincides with pubertal changes in the neuroendocrine system (Buchanan, Eccles, & Becker, 1992), cognitive changes in reasoning and critical thinking (Keating, 1990), elaboration of one's self-concept (Harter, 1990), and school-related changes in the structuring of peer groups and activities (Brown, 1990). Changes at all these levels could be implicated in the observed emergence of social aggression in girls. What the explicit examination of gender differences in this study provided was some direction as to where and when to search for critical processes. Any adequate explanation for the development of aggression from childhood to adolescence will need to take these differing pathways into account.

### *Comparison of Normal and Atypical Development*

The comparison of normal and atypical development has a long history in psychology, tracing back to psychoanalytic theory and the work of Sigmund Freud (1954). Its most recent incarnation, the field of developmental psychopathology (Cicchetti, 1984; Rutter & Garmezy, 1983), takes as a fundamental tenet the notion that both atypical and normal development will be best understood when studied in concert, with research on one informing and enriching research on the other.

In many ways the definition of what is considered atypical depends directly on a comparison between the normal course of growth and deviations from that course. Thus, the study of atypical development focuses explicitly on the identification and explanation of developmental plasticity, and how experience serves to deflect development from a more adaptive course to a less adaptive one (Radke-Yarrow & Zahn-Waxler, 1990; Sroufe, 1990). However, definitions of adaptive and maladaptive are not viewed as absolutes. Instead, there is a strong emphasis on the social, cultural, and historical contexts in which behavior is observed and how these contexts, in relation to the developing person, co-define a continuum from normal to atypical functioning. Rutter (1987, 1989), in particular, has argued that vulnerability and resilience constitute processes of reciprocal transaction between persons and their environments, rather than fixed attributes contained within persons or environments. What determines the relative level of adaptation or maladaptation at a given point in time depends in large part on these transactive processes.

What gains in our understanding of development can be made from a comparison of normal and atypical patterns of growth? First, the study of atypical growth can shed light on processes of normal development. In many respects, atypical patterns can be viewed as naturally occurring experiments, in that processes which result in adaptive development are either absent or deficient in some individuals and some contexts. Through close examination of the pathways and intermediate outcomes of atypical individuals, we can begin to understand the role that such processes may play in producing adaptive growth. An excellent example of this can be found in the work by Cicchetti and colleagues (Cicchetti & Beeghly, 1990; Cicchetti & Sroufe, 1978) on reflexive responses in infants born with or without Down syndrome. Through a comparison of infants with and without this cognitive impairment, Cicchetti and colleagues were able to identify the occurrence and timing of two distinct processes involved in the development of defensive reactions, one reflexive and emerging early in infancy, and the other a result of cognitive and maturational factors.

Research on normal–atypical differences has also redirected our questions to issues of timing in development. For example, the discovery that some individuals are strengthened by exposure to stress while others are not has shifted our attention to how a person's developmental level can alter the impact of stressful experiences. A notable example is Elder's work (Elder, 1974; Elder & Caspi, 1988; see also Shanahan & Elder, Chapter 4, this volume) concerning the long-term consequences of the Great Depression on children's development. Contrary to the view that economic hardship is consistently detrimental, this research shows that the age at which children experienced economic uncertainties and family strains played an important role in determining whether they would be strengthened or weakened by the experience. Specifically, adolescent boys were more likely to become an integral part of the family's efforts to generate income for the household, giving them an increased sense of personal worth and responsibility for others that was then carried through their adult years. Preadolescent boys, on the other hand, were more vulnerable to the inconsistency or absence of parental support and guidance, factors related to lower levels of achievement and more limited aspirations throughout life.

Comparisons between normal and atypical groups have also led to the study of normative development arising from nonnormative histories – the examination of so-called resilient individuals who demonstrate adaptive forms of functioning despite a history of biological and/or environmental insult (Masten, Best, & Garmezy, 1990). Research on resilience and how it arises in development has called into question the deterministic view that experiences early in life invariably lead to particular outcomes. Instead, it has redirected our attention to how various levels of the organismic system combine to alter the probability of a particular outcome.

An excellent example of this approach is an ongoing program of research by Eckerman and colleagues (Eckerman, Sturm, & Gross, 1985; Gross, Oehler, & Eckerman, 1983). Using comparisons between full-term and preterm very-low-birthweight (VLBW) infants, these investigators have begun to map the diverse developmental pathways associated with preterm birth. The research focuses on a group of full-term infants and four groups of VLBW infants defined in terms of prenatal and neonatal head growth: (1) microencephaly at birth/less postnatal head growth, (2) microencephaly at birth/more postnatal head growth, (3) normocephaly at birth/less postnatal head growth, and (4) normocephaly at birth/more postnatal head growth. Assessments of medical complications, neurological and physical growth deficits, and behavioral and cognitive functioning have been obtained at 6, 15, and 24 months of age.

The results indicate drastically different patterns of growth for the five groups of infants. Interestingly enough, the VLBW infants with normal pre- and postnatal head growth tended to be indistinguishable from their full-term counterparts in terms of developmental pathways and outcomes. On the other hand, the microencephalic/less postnatal head growth infants evidenced severe delays in psychomotor and cognitive development at 24 months, as well as a pattern of continued delay from 6 to 24 months. The other two groups of VLBW infants tended to fall within the middle range of developmental outcomes. However, it is interesting to note that the normocephalic/less postnatal head growth infants showed the greatest variability in developmental pathways, with some infants showing continued delays from 6 to 24 months, others showing a pattern of developmental catch-up by 24 months, and still others showing no developmental delay until 24 months.

What is noteworthy about this research is its explicit attention to the issue of plasticity in development, even within an "at-risk" group. Indeed, a key assumption informing this work is that differences in early biological status do not determine the course of later development. By comparing variations in the developmental pathways *among* VLBW infants, as well as between this group and full-term infants, the research provided vital descriptive information on the developmental sequelae of premature birth. It also raises new questions about the processes that define these distinctive pathways, demonstrating that simple comparisons between preterm and full-term infants will mask rather than illuminate the processes involved.

### *Age Group Comparisons*

Age comparisons constitute the cornerstone of developmental psychology. As early as the 1880s, Wilhelm Preyer was carrying out detailed comparisons of his different aged offspring to explore the development of senses, will, and intellect (Cairns, 1983). Age group comparisons continue to represent the bulk of empirical work in developmental psychology (Redmond, 1994), despite the strong consensus that comparisons of children of different developmental ages are a poor substitute for longitudinal studies that follow a group of children as they develop over time (Applebaum & McCall, 1983; Kessen, 1960; Wohlwill, 1970; see Shanahan, Valsiner, & Gottlieb, Chapter 2, this volume). However, in some instances age group comparisons may provide more information on developmental processes than can be gleaned solely from studies of within-person change over time. We begin with a discussion of the problems associated with age group comparisons, and then present an example of how these methods were used to clarify developmental processes.

The exemplary group comparison studies we have presented up to this point share a common strength – group differences studied within a longitudinal framework. This strength represents the major limitation in age group comparisons, which by definition are cross-sectional. Simply put, cross-sectional methodologies do not allow one to assume that differences observed between two age groups at one point in time reflect processes of change for a single individual across those two ages. Yet more often than not, researchers use evidence of mean differences between age groups to make statements that go beyond the assertion that a sample of *X*-year-olds differs from a sample of *Y*-year-olds on the domain of study.

The assumption implicit in this practice is that chronological age alone underlies the observed difference in behavior, that the various age groups are equivalent in all other respects. However, Schaie (1965) and Baltes (1968) have demonstrated the fallacy of this assumption, pointing out that age effects are always confounded with cohort and history effects at any single time of measurement. Moreover, for certain developmental phenomena chronological age may not be the best marker of developmental (Wohlwill, 1970). An excellent example of this is Magnusson's (1988) research on the importance of pubertal timing, a measure of biological age, in understanding patterns of psychosocial development in girls from adolescence to young adulthood.

Perhaps the most critical limitation of age group comparisons is the fact that age has no explanatory value of its own. Demonstrating that 6-year-olds perform better than 4-year-olds on a particular task tells us nothing about why older children do better than younger children or how this improvement emerges over time. Attributing causal status to the classificatory attribute is a potential criticism of all group comparison methods, but it may be especially problematic for age group comparisons. In a particularly strong indictment of age group comparison as a means of studying development, Wohlwill (1970, 1973) argued that age-related change is a given in any developmental inquiry and should be considered a dimension along which development is studied, rather than a proxy for mechanisms that influence its rate and form.

How can researchers avoid these limitations while still conducting age group comparisons? One profitable strategy, illustrated in the work of Michelene Chi and colleagues, is to test hypotheses regarding possible mechanisms by manipulating theoretically relevant variables, employing multiple measures within studies, and supplementing findings of age differences with case studies of individual children. In other words, in a programmatic study of a phenomenon, "what" questions answered by age group comparisons (i.e., What age differences exist?) can be followed by "why" questions (i.e., Why do they occur within particular individuals?).

One of the most pervasive findings in cognitive developmental research is that older children and adults remember more than younger children. However, there is less consensus as to why age-related differences in memory abilities exist. Possible explanations include greater sophistication in the use of memory strategies such as rehearsal (Harnishfeger & Bjorklund, 1990), changes in short-term memory storage (Case, 1984), and changes in a person's knowledge base of information about the world and how such information is structured (Chi & Ceci, 1987). Evidence for age-related changes in individual components of memory has been documented; however, interpreting the meaning of such findings is complicated by the fact that many changes in the memory system are related to age. How can an understanding of each component be achieved if memory is to be viewed as a developing system? No single research design, statistical tool, or task can provide an answer.

The general question guiding the research of Chi and colleagues concerns the role of the knowledge base in memory development. Chi (1978) disagreed with the conclusions of other researchers that the expansion of working memory capacity underlies age changes in memory performance, arguing instead that prior work in this area confounded the person's age with his or her knowledge of the task stimuli used. She also argued that changes in strategy use could not completely account for the age changes observed, because the training studies typically used to enhance younger children's performance were never able to eliminate age differences completely. To tease apart the roles of strategy use, working memory capacity, and the knowledge base in memory development, Chi (1977, 1978) utilized age group comparisons in two inventive research designs.

In the first study, Chi (1977) employed a "reversal of training" procedure to investigate whether differences in memory performance could be due to changes in working memory capacity. The logic underlying typical training studies is that children can be experimentally provided with instructions or experiences thought to underlie developmental changes in the behavior of interest. To the degree that children show more advanced forms of behavior after the experimental manipulation, inferences can be drawn concerning the hypothesized developmental mechanism (Harnishfeger & Bjorklund, 1990).

The "reversal of training" procedure, in contrast, modifies the experimental task in order to elicit childlike performance from adults. Chi (1977) argued that if it were possible to equate the performance of children and adults by experimentally controlling for level of strategy use, knowledge, and encoding, such findings would call into question the existence of age-related changes in working memory capacity. Faces were chosen as stimuli in order to control for familiarity and to prevent subjects from grouping the material into a larger single unit to be remembered. Strategy use and encoding were constrained in adults by decreasing the amount of time available to view the stimuli, and by asking adults to refrain from using other task-specific strategies. Given the possibility that adults might have multiple ways to encode information about order, ordered recall of the stimuli was not required. When these alterations in the memory task were made, the recall of children and adults did not differ.

Chi turned again to age group comparisons to determine whether children might actually perform better than adults under some conditions. In this study, Chi (1978) reported striking and counterintuitive age differences between adults' and children's ability to remember chess positions. The children, who were chess experts, outperformed the adults, who were novices to the game, on measures related to initial memory for chess positions after a brief 10-second exposure to the stimuli. In a repeated memory task, young chess experts required fewer trials to achieve perfect performance than did adults. On the other hand, adults outperformed children when more traditional stimuli, such as strings of random digits, were used. Examination of age differences on the two types of tasks, which presumably rely on different memory processes, was instrumental in clarifying the question of age differences in memory and what those differences represent. The study's contribution would have been more limited if either the chess position task, which taps the level of the knowledge base, or the random digit task, which taps the capacity of working memory, had been excluded.

To further explore the role of the knowledge base in memory development, Chi and Koeske (1983) employed a case study approach to examine in greater detail the nature of the knowledge base for an individual child. The study focused on the knowledge base of a 4-year-old dinosaur expert. Despite the child's acknowledged expert status, the investigators found much diversity in the child's knowledge base, with some domains of dinosaur knowledge more extensively developed than other domains. Using this approach, Chi and Koeske (1983) were able to more precisely determine how the structure of the knowledge base, defined in terms of nodes and linkages, differed across various subdomains of knowledge, and how such distinctions relate to memory.

## Within-Person Comparisons

Our focus until this point has been on cross-sectional between-person comparisons. Although by far the primary modes of comparative analysis in developmental psychology (Redmond, 1994), they are by no means best suited to assessing developmental change. Examination of change in a single person's behavior across time involves a type of comparison that may be especially fruitful for understanding development.

Two types of within-person comparisons are considered: single-subject longitudinal methods and single-subject microgenetic methods. Both types involve the sequential analysis of an individual's behavior over a specified period of time, allowing for a more direct assessment of the rate, direction, and form of growth. However, they differ in the length of the observation period and the spacing between observation intervals. Single-subject longitudinal methods typically involve multiple assessments at regular intervals over a period of days, weeks, or months (Nesselroade & Ford, 1985). The assessments represent discontinuous, discrete units rather than a continuous sampling of the ongoing stream of behavioral change taking place. In contrast, microgenetic methods involve the continuous assessment of behavior occurring in real time in the context of a specific task or activity (Siegler & Crowley, 1991). Limited by the pragmatics of continuous observation, microgenetic methods typically focus on change during the course of hourly periods, often spread over multiple sessions (Siegler & Jenkins, 1989). What distinguishes single-subject longitudinal and microgenetic studies from other longitudinal methods is the higher concentration of observations obtained during the period of change (Siegler & Crowley, 1991). Both types of within-person comparison can be potentially powerful tools for the explication of mechanisms, but their differing observational time frames make them uniquely suited to different kinds of developmental phenomena.

The single-subject longitudinal method, or P-technique as it is formally known (Cattell, 1952), has a long tradition in developmental psychology. Over the past 40 years, a number of investigators have taken advantage of its potential for examining intraindividual change (Nesselroade, 1991a). The method involves repeated measurements of a single person using a battery of measurement devices (e.g., questionnaires, Q-sorts, structured interviews), with each device representing one or more variables on the domain of interest. The density of observations, normally hourly or daily assessments, is usually far greater than the density of variables. Variables are covaried across occasions of measurement, and factor analysis is used to construct dimensions of change for that individual. What the method yields are indicators of intraindividual variability across a selected period of time (e.g., 3 months), reflecting coherent, systematic patterns of fluctuation in a person's behavior. P-technique has enabled researchers to identify coherence in intraindividual variability for several psychological attributes, including locus of control, self-concept, depression, temperament, and cognitive abilities (Jones & Nesselroade, 1990; Nesselroade & Ford, 1985).

The method has several advantages over traditional longitudinal approaches to assessing within-person change. First, it utilizes multiple measures of the phenomenon of interest to assess qualitative change in the patterning and organization of behavior, in addition to the more traditional assessment of quantitative changes in behavior over time. Second, the method involves assessments over a large number of occasions closely spaced in time. This practice has distinct advantages over the monthly or yearly assessment schedule common to most longitudinal research because it provides far more information on the temporal aspects of development, including intraindividual variability and intraindividual change. Third, the method makes possible the disentanglement of intraindividual variability from intraindividual change. While many investigators dismiss intraindividual variability as noise or random error, Nesselroade (1991b) has cogently argued that this cyclical fluctuation contains important information about a person's base condition from which other aspects of developmental change and stability can be compared. The central idea is that persons as developing systems experience two forms of change simultaneously, one reflecting relatively rapid and reversible oscillations in behavior and the other reflecting nonreversible, relatively enduring change. To understand the developmental process, attention must be given to how these two components are integrated within the person to produce behavior. These two components are always confounded at any single occasion of measurement. Multiple assessments across short intervals of time can help to separate more enduring developmental change from the momentary variability reflecting the "steady state hum" of the organism.

Another type of within-person comparison is the microgenetic method, which can be traced back to the 1920s, when Heinz Werner (1948) first began to conduct what he referred to as "genetic experiments." Recognition of its value for studying development has waxed and waned since that time (Catan, 1986). However, this method has experienced a recent resurgence by investigators intent on explicating the mechanisms underlying cognitive development (Rogoff & Lave, 1984; Siegler & Crowley, 1991).

The method can be defined in terms of three key properties. First, observations span the entire period of behavior from when change begins to when it reaches relative stability. Second, the method involves a trial-by-trial analysis to detect when change initially occurs, what steps lead to the initial appearance of change, what steps are involved in its stabilization, and which aspects are quantitative and which are qualitative. Third, the density of observations must be high relative to the rate of change of the phenomenon of interest. Because of the high density of observations, this method is best suited to developmental changes that occur over relatively short periods of time. To induce changes in functioning that might not ordinarily occur during brief periods, researchers often present a novel task or provide experiences that are hypothesized to lead to change. For example, in a microgenetic study of children's acquisition of memory strategies, children were provided with training in the use of novel rehearsal and organization strategies to hasten the developmental process (Paris, Newman, & McVey, 1982).

Although some have criticized the method for its focus on short-term change, Siegler and Crowley (1991) argue that the patterns revealed represent more than task-specific learning. They assert that the processes observed, such as inconsistencies in the use of newly acquired modes of behavior, may contain clues about mechanisms critical to the kind of long-term generalized change traditionally viewed as development. The strength of this method lies in its ability to make minute-by-minute comparisons of a person's behavior as it unfolds in real time. As a means of observing events involved in transitions from one state to the next, the microgenetic method has no equal.

## Combining Within-Person and Group Comparison Approaches

Many have noted that the gains made in our description of states (e.g., *what* people of a particular age can and cannot do) are more than offset by our meager understanding of mechanisms, of *how* people systematically move from one state to the next (Bronfenbrenner, Kessel, Kessen, & White, 1986; Hinde & Bateson, 1984; Wohlwill, 1973). In our view, explication of the mechanisms involved in transitions and reorganizations across the life course remains the primary goal in developmental psychology. Some have argued that an understanding of mechanisms requires the use of single-subject longitudinal and microgenetic designs (Lightfoot & Folds-Bennett, 1992). However, the specter of nongeneralizability that haunts these methods constitutes a major limitation. While within-person comparisons allow for more detailed study of the change process, it is essential to demonstrate that the processes observed are systematic for particular people interacting in particular contexts, rather than idiosyncratic to a particular person at a particular point in time and space. Such a view calls for an approach to research that continually moves from within-person to between-person comparisons, recognizing and building on the strengths that each method can provide.

The purpose of this chapter has been to illustrate how group comparisons can serve to move developmentalists closer to an explication of mechanisms. Attention to group differences in the phenomenon of interest allows investigators to examine how the configuration of components that differentiates one group from another could influence the range of pathways observed. This descriptive function represents an important first step in the programmatic study of developmental phenomena. For example, attention to gender differences in the function of aggression as it changes from preadolescence to early adolescence in the Cairns study highlights a critical transition point that would have gone undetected if changes in aggression across a sample of children had been assessed. Because of its focus on gender differences in patterns of change, this study was able to uncover two distinct developmental pathways in aggression, one an increased consolidation of overt physical strategies over time and the other a diversification of aggressive behavior involving overt confrontation on the one hand and covert, social ostracism on the other. To be sure, documentation of this interesting gender difference tells us nothing about how these two pathways arise. However, combining within-person and group comparison methods may be a fruitful second step.

For example, gender comparisons could be used in tandem with microgenetic methods as a means of trying to induce social aggression prior to its normal emergence, either with early adolescent boys or preadolescent girls. It is as yet unclear what those mechanisms might be, but our knowledge of gender differences in peer interaction and socialization should provide some clues (Eder & Parker, 1987; Maccoby, 1988). If the manipulation of potential mechanisms succeeds in changing a child's behavior, we can begin to speculate about processes that give rise to the emergence of social ostracism as it occurs naturally in girls' development. This approach to identifying developmental mechanisms has proved quite successful in other domains (see, e.g., Siegler & Jenkins, 1989; Thelen & Ulrich, 1991). But again we emphasize that the focus on gender differences is crucial for elucidating what those potential mechanisms might be.

Similar efforts to combine within-person and group comparison designs might be useful in identifying the processes that underlie the developmental plasticity of preterm infants found in Eckerman's research, or children's acquisition of expert knowledge found in Chi's work. For example, examination of intraindividual variability in postnatal head growth over short periods of time for different groups of preterm infants might help to clarify what patterns of neurological change, within a particular infant, are related to developmental delays in psychomotor and cognitive skills. Applications of microgenetic methods in conjunction with comparisons of children and adults might also be instructive in identifying the steps that young children take in the process of acquiring expertise in a particular domain of knowledge, and the extent to which these steps differ for adults as they acquire expertise in the same domain.

In our view, group comparison approaches are necessary for clarifying the findings of within-person studies and narrowing the search for developmental processes that move individuals from one state to the next. Of course, the value of group comparison will always be dependent on the willingness of researchers to move beyond descriptions of differences between groups. But at the same time, group comparison may be our only means of representing the myriad interdependent influences that direct the course of development. These interdependent influences are implicitly acknowledged in any group comparative design. The task now before us is to make the implicit explicit.

## References

Appelbaum, M. I., & McCall, R. B. (1983). Design and analysis in developmental psychology. In P. H. Mussen (Series Ed.) & W. Kessen (Vol. Ed.), *Handbook of child psychology: Vol. 1, History, theory, and methods* (pp. 415–476). New York: Wiley.

Baltes, P. B. (1968). Longitudinal and cross sectional sequences in the study of age and generation effects. *Human Development*, *11*, 145–171.

(1987). Theoretical propositions of life-span developmental psychology: On the dynamics between growth and decline. *Developmental Psychology, 23*, 611–626.

Bronfenbrenner, U. (1988). Interacting systems in human development: Research paradigms – Present and future. In N. Bolger, A. Caspi, G. Downey, & M. Moorehouse (Eds.), *Persons in context: Developmental processes* (pp. 25–49). Cambridge University Press.

Bronfenbrenner, U., Kessel, F., Kessen, W., & White, S. (1986). Toward a critical social history of developmental psychology: A propaedeutic discussion. *American Psychologist, 41*, 1218–1230.

Brown, B. B. (1990). Peer groups and peer cultures. In S. Feldman & G. Elliott (Eds.), *At the threshold: The developing adolescent* (pp. 171–196). Cambridge, MA: Harvard University Press.

Buchanan, C. M., Eccles, J. S., & Becker, J. B. (1992). Are adolescents the victims of raging hormones: Evidence for activational effects of hormones on moods and behavior at adolescence. *Psychological Bulletin, 111*, 62–107.

Cairns, R. B. (1983). The emergence of developmental psychology. In P. H. Mussen (Series Ed.) & W. Kessen (Vol. Ed.), *Handbook of child psychology: Vol. 1. History, theory, and methods* (pp. 41–102). New York: Wiley.

(1986). Phenomena lost: Issues in the study of development. In J. Valsiner (Ed.), *The individual subject and scientific psychology* (pp. 97–111). New York: Plenum.

Cairns, R. B., & Cairns, B. D. (1991). Social cognition and social networks: A developmental perspective. In D. Pepler & K. Rubin (Eds.), *The development and treatment of childhood aggression* (pp. 249–278). Hillsdale, NJ: Erlbaum.

Cairns, R. B., Cairns, B. D., Neckerman, H. J., Ferguson, L. L., & Gariépy, J. L. (1989). Growth and aggression: 1. Childhood to early adolescence. *Developmental Psychology, 25*, 320–330.

Cairns, R. B., McGuire, A., & Gariépy, J. L. (1993). Developmental behavior genetics: Fusion, correlated constraints, and timing. In D. F. Hay & A. Angold (Eds.), *Precursors and causes in development and psychopathology* (pp. 87–122). New York: Wiley.

Case, R. (1984). The process of stage transition: A neo-Piagetian view. In R. J. Sternberg (Ed.), *Mechanisms of cognitive development* (pp. 19–44). New York: Freeman.

Catan, L. (1986). The dynamic display of process: Historical development and contemporary uses of the microgenetic method. *Human Development, 29*, 252–263.

Cattell, R. B. (1952). The three basic factor-analytic research designs: Their interrelationships and derivatives. *Psychological Bulletin, 49*, 499–520.

Chi, M. T. H. (1977). Age differences in memory span. *Journal of Experimental Child Psychology*, *23*, 266–281.

(1978). Knowledge structures and memory development. In R. S. Siegler (Ed.), *Children's thinking: What develops?* (pp. 73–96). Hillsdale, NJ: Erlbaum.

Chi, M. T. H., & Ceci, S. J. (1987). Content knowledge: Its role, representation, and restructuring in memory development. In H. W. Reese (Ed.), *Advances in child development and behavior* (Vol. 20, pp. 91–142). Orlando, FL: Academic Press.

Chi, M. T. H., & Koeske, R. (1983). Network representation of a child's dinosaur knowledge. *Developmental Psychology*, *19*, 29–39.

Cicchetti, D. (1984). The emergence of developmental psychopathology. *Child Development*, *55*, 1–7.

Cicchetti, D., & Beeghly, M. (1990). *Children with Down syndrome: A developmental perspective.* Cambridge University Press.

Cicchetti, D., & Sroufe, L. A. (1978). An organizational view of affect: Illustration from the study of Down syndrome infants. In M. Lewis & L. Rosenblum (Eds.), *The development of affect* (pp. 309–350). New York: Plenum.

Deaux, K., & Major, B. (1987). Putting gender into context: An interactive model of gender-related behavior. *Psychological Review*, *94*, 369–389.

Eckerman, C. O., Sturm, L. A., & Gross, S. J. (1985). Different developmental courses for very-low-birthweight infants differing in early head growth. *Developmental Psychology*, *21*, 813–827.

Eder, D. J., & Parker, S. A. (1987). The cultural production and reproduction of gender: The effect of extracurricular activities on peer group culture. *Sociology of Education*, *60*, 200–213.

Edwards, C. P., & Whiting B. B. (1988). *Children of different worlds.* Cambridge, MA: Harvard University Press.

Elder, G. H., Jr. (1974). *Children of the Great Depression: Social change in life experience.* Chicago: University of Chicago Press.

Elder, G. H., Jr., & Caspi, A. (1988). Economic stress in lives: Developmental perspectives. *Journal of Social Issues*, *44*, 25–45.

Feingold, A. (1988). Cognitive gender differences are disappearing. *American Psychologist*, *43*, 95–103.

Freud, S. (1954). *Collected works, standard edition.* London: Hogarth.

Gottlieb, G. (1992). *Individual development and evolution: The genesis of novel behavior.* New York: Oxford University Press.

Gross, S. J., Oehler, J. M., & Eckerman, C. O. (1983). Head growth and developmental outcome in very-low-birthweight infants. *Pediatrics*, *71*, 70–75.

Harnishfeger, K. K., & Bjorklund, D. F. (1990). Children's strategies: A brief history. In D. F. Bjorklund (Ed.), *Children's strategies: Contemporary views of cognitive development* (pp. 1–22). Hillsdale, NJ: Erlbaum.

Harter, S. (1990). Self and identity development. In S. Feldman & G. Elliott (Eds.), *At the threshold: The developing adolescent* (pp. 352–387). Cambridge, MA: Harvard University Press.

Hinde, R. A. (1988). Continuities and discontinuities: Conceptual issues and methodological considerations. In M. Rutter (Ed.), *Studies of psychosocial risk: The power of longitudinal data* (pp. 367–385). Cambridge University Press.

Hinde, R. A., & Bateson, P. (1984). Discontinuities versus continuities in behavioral development and the neglect of process. *International Journal of Behavioral Development, 7*, 129–143.

Hyde, J., & Linn, M. (1988). Gender differences in verbal ability: A meta-analysis. *Psychological Bulletin, 104*, 53–69.

Jacklin, C. (1981). Methodological issues in the study of sex related differences. *Developmental Review, 1*, 266–273.

(1989). Female and male: Issues of gender. *American Psychologist, 44*, 127–133.

Jones, C. J., & Nesselroade, J. R. (1990). Multivariate, replicated, single-subject, repeated measures designs and P-technique factor analysis: A review of intraindividual change studies. *Experimental Aging Research, 16*, 171–183.

Keating, D. (1990). Adolescent thinking. In S. Feldman & G. Elliott (Eds.), *At the threshold: The developing adolescent* (pp. 352–387). Cambridge, MA: Harvard University Press.

Kessen, W. (1960). Research design in the study of developmental problems. In P. H. Mussen (Ed.), *Handbook of research methods in child development*. New York: Wiley.

Lerner, R. M. (1984). *On the nature of human plasticity*. Cambridge University Press.

Lewin, K. (1933). Environmental forces. In C. Murchison (Ed.), *Handbook of child psychology* (pp. 590–625). Worcester, MA: Clark University Press.

Lightfoot, C., & Folds-Bennett, T. (1992). Description and explanation in developmental research: Separate agendas. In J. B. Asendorpf & J. Valsiner (Eds.), *Stability and change in development: A study of methodological reasoning* (pp. 207–228). Newbury Park, CA: Sage.

Maccoby, E. (1988). Gender as a social category. *Developmental Psychology, 24*, 754–765.

Maccoby, E., & Jacklin, C. N. (1974). *The psychology of sex differences*. Stanford, CA: Stanford University Press.

Magnusson, D. (1988). *Individual development from an interactional perspective: A longitudinal study*. Hillsdale, NJ: Erlbaum.

Magnusson, D., & Bergman, L. R. (1988). Individual and variable-based approaches to longitudinal research on early risk factors. In M. Rutter (Ed.), *Studies of psychosocial risk: The power of longitudinal data* (pp. 45–62). Cambridge University Press.

Masten, A. S., Best, K. M., & Garmezy, N. (1990). Resilience and development: Contributions from the study of children who overcome adversity. *Development and Psychopathology*, *2*, 425–444.

Nesselroade, J. R. (1991a). Interindividual differences in intraindividual change. In L. M. Collins & J. L. Horn (Eds.), *Best methods for the analysis of change: Recent advances, unanswered questions, future directions* (pp. 92–105). Washington, DC: American Psychological Association.

(1991b). The warp and the woof of the developmental fabric. In R. M. Downs, L. S. Liben, & D. S. Palermo (Eds.), *Visions of aesthetics, the environment, and development: The legacy of Joachim F. Wohlwill* (pp. 213–240). Hillsdale, NJ: Erlbaum.

Nesselroade, J. R., & Ford, D. H. (1985). P-technique comes of age: Multivariate, replicated, single-subject designs for research on older adults. *Research on Aging*, *7*, 46–80.

(1987). Methodological considerations in modeling living systems. In M. E. Ford & D. H. Ford (Eds.), *Humans as self-constructing living systems: Putting the framework to work* (pp. 47–79). Hillsdale, NJ: Erlbaum.

Paris, S. G., Newman, R. S., & McVey, K. A. (1982). Learning the functional significance of mnemonic actions: A microgenetic study of strategy acquisition. *Journal of Experimental Child Psychology*, *32*, 490–509.

Radke-Yarrow, M., & Zahn-Waxler, C. (1990). Research on children of affectively ill parents: Some considerations for theory and research on normal development. *Development and Psychopathology*, *2*, 349–366.

Redmond, S. M. (1994, Spring). A scientometric analysis of the journal *Child Development. Newsletter of the Society for Research in Child Development.*

Rogoff, B., & Lave. J. (1984). *Everyday cognition: Its development in social context.* Cambridge, MA: Harvard University Press.

Ruble, D. N. (1984). Sex-role development. In M. H. Bornstein & M. Lamb (Eds.), *Developmental psychology* (pp. 325–372). Hillsdale. NJ: Erlbaum.

Rutter, M. (1987). Psychosocial resilience and protective mechanisms. *American Journal of Orthopsychiatry*, *57*, 316–330.

(1989). Pathways from childhood to adult life. *Journal of Child Psychology and Psychiatry*, *30*, 23–51.

Rutter, M., & Garmezy, N. (1983). Developmental psychopathology. In P. H. Mussen (Series Ed.) & E. M. Hetherington (Vol. Ed.), *Handbook of child psychology: Vol. 4. Socialization, personality, and social development* (pp. 775–911). New York: Wiley.

Sameroff, A. (1983). Developmental systems: Contexts and evolution. In P. H. Mussen (Series Ed.) & W. Kessen (Vol. Ed.), *Handbook of child psychology: Vol. 1. History, theory, and methods* (pp. 237–294). New York: Wiley.

Schaie, K. W. (1965). A general model for the study of developmental problems. *Psychological Bulletin*, *64*, 92–107.

Siegler, R. S., & Crowley, K. (1991). The microgenetic method: A direct means for studying cognitive development. *American Psychologist*, *46*, 606–620.

Siegler, R. S., & Jenkins, E. (1989). *How children discover new strategies.* Hillsdale, NJ: Erlbaum.

Sroufe, L. A. (1990). Considering normal and abnormal together: The essence of developmental psychopathology. *Development and Psychopathology*, *2*, 335–347.

Thelen, E., & Ulrich, B. D. (1991). Hidden skills: A dynamic systems analysis of treadmill stepping during the first year. *Monographs of the Society for Research in Child Development*, *56* (Series No. 223).

Valsiner, J. (1984). Two alternative epistemological frameworks in psychology: The typological and variational modes of thinking. *Journal of Mind and Behavior*, *5*, 449–470.

Werner, H. (1948). *Comparative psychology of mental development.* New York: International Universities Press.

Whiting, B. B., & Edwards, C. (1973). A cross-cultural analysis of sex differences in the behavior of children aged 3 to 11. *Journal of Social Psychology*, *91*, 171–188.

Wohlwill, J. F. (1970). The age variable in psychological research. *Psychological Review*, *77*, 49–64.

(1973). *The study of behavioral development.* New York: Academic Press.

# 6 Implications from Developmental Cross-cultural Research for the Study of Acculturation in Western Civilizations

*Beth Kurtz-Costes, Rona McCall, and Wolfgang Schneider*

Cross-cultural research in developmental psychology has traditionally focused on two areas: cultural comparisons, in which two or more cultural groups are studied and contrasted on variables of interest, and studies of acculturation, in which the focus is the culture change of individuals and groups as two diverse cultures meet. Although at first glance these two areas of study may seem to have little in common, both are concerned with culture, and both are comparative in nature. In this chapter, we first discuss some of the theoretical and methodological issues associated with developmental, cultural comparative research. Second, we explore research in acculturation. Based on research in acculturation with adults, we develop a preliminary model explaining acculturation in children. Finally, we describe a research project currently in progress that is charting the acculturation of Eastern European immigrant children who have recently arrived in a West German community.

## Cultural Comparisons in Developmental Psychology

Cultural comparative investigations in developmental psychology have typically been driven by two seemingly opposing purposes: On the one hand, some of these studies have sought to identify universals in human behavior, thus attempting to establish that research results found with one cultural group hold true for other groups. Conversely, other cultural comparative research programs have deliberately sought to identify and explain phenomena that vary across cultures (Berry, Poortinga, Segall, & Dasen, 1992; Triandis, Malpass, & Davidson, 1972). In the section that follows, we outline some of the potential pitfalls associated with cultural comparative investigations.

In particular, we discuss five issues: (1) the use of culture as an independent variable, (2) problems of ethnocentrism in cultural comparisons, (3) (in)equivalence of research materials across cultural groups, (4) issues related to sample selection, and (5) an integration of differences and similarities in theories about cultural variation. Before we begin, we would like to note that one of the great disputes in cross-cultural work, and one that crosses disciplinary lines (e.g., psychology, anthropology, sociology), concerns the definition of *culture* (Brislin, 1990; Shweder, 1990). It is well beyond the scope of this chapter to enter that debate. Instead, we use the term *culture* as it is generally used in cross-cultural psychology – to represent the values, traditions, behaviors, and beliefs characteristic of a group of people.

## *Theoretical and Methodological Issues in Cultural Comparative Research*

The first challenge to cross-cultural research that we discuss concerns the use of *culture as an independent variable.* Traditionally, cultural comparative studies have defined their samples by national borders. In some studies, groups are subdivided within countries by geographic, racial, or ethnic characteristics (e.g., rural vs. urban; African-American vs. Caucasian American). Whether comparisons are conducted within or across national boundaries, using culture as an independent variable for these subject populations is often a misnomer. The major danger is that subject samples may differ from one another in more ways than the researcher intends. For instance, a researcher who is studying memory development in Indian and German children may have interviewed two groups of children who differ not only in country of origin, but also in educational background, religious beliefs, parental marital status, prior exposure to other ethnic groups, prior travel experiences, and a host of other factors. In this case, the use of culture as an independent variable is misleading at best and clouds interpretation of differences between the two groups.

Two problems emerge from this use of culture as an independent variable. First, many cultural comparative investigations fail to identify what it is about the cultural groups under investigation that would lead one to assume behavioral differences between them. For instance, researchers may measure personality characteristics in peoples of two or more cultures with little a priori explanation of why cultural differences are anticipated. A second, related problem emerges when behavioral differences are anticipated between two cultural groups because of a particular cultural characteristic, but researchers fail to establish that other factors that may or may not vary across the two cultural groups are not responsible for the effect. In this type of investigation, culture is used as a proxy variable, while the actual focus of the study is a much more specific independent variable that is assumed to vary across the two groups. This design is problematic when researchers fail to establish equivalence of the groups on other key characteristics.

These points may be illustrated by drawing from the classic study of the Müller–Lyer illusion. Using subjects from the United States and 14 non-European countries, Segall, Campbell, and Herskovits (1966) studied perceptual illusions of length using the Müller–Lyer illusion (i.e., two horizontal lines equal in length, one with arrow tips at both ends and one with inverted arrow tips at both ends) and the horizontal–vertical illusion (i.e., a vertical and horizontal line intersecting perpendicularly). Segall et al. found support for their hypothesis that environmental demands reinforce the use of cues to interpret an illusion. Specifically, U.S. subjects showed better performance on the vertical–horizontal illusion, whereas non-European subjects performed better on the Müller–Lyer illusion. Segall et al. explained these results by pointing to cultural differences in architecture: Western society is designed around geometric relationships and distance perceptions, whereas non-Western societies are limited by both linear figures and distance cues. However, in contrast to their explanation (Segall et al. 1966) of perceptual differences with reference to characteristics of architectural structures, subsequent research has shown that other variables, such as eye pigmentation, geographic location, and Western influence within a country may account for the results orginally reported (Jahoda, 1966, 1971; Pollack, 1970). Thus, while Segall et al. identified one set of culturally linked variables as responsible for differences in illusion susceptibility, in fact, other characteristics of the cultural groups were more likely the causal agents underlying the cultural differences in perception.

Cultural comparisons can be both meaningful and useful when researchers focus on a specific variable that is known to differ across the cultural groups. In these investigations, cultural differences provide a sort of natural experiment enabling the researchers to draw conclusions about the influence of the variable on performance or development. Therefore, the unit of analysis is the specific variable of interest rather than the global construct *culture*. For instance, in the middle part of this century, most Western countries had mandatory formal education for young children, while many non-Western countries did not. Thus, investigations of the influence of formal education on cognitive development turned appropriately to societies where schooling was not mandatory (Rogoff, 1981). Another example comes from a recent examination of cultural variations in infants' sleeping arrangements, in which middle-class U.S. and Highland Mayan parents' attitudes and values regarding their infants' sleeping arrangements and emotional development were examined (Morelli, Rogoff, Oppenheim, & Goldsmith, 1992). In this study, sleeping habits (i.e., whether an infant slept alone or with a parent) and beliefs about healthy social-emotional development were the foci of the study, rather than a charting of differences across the two cultures. Thus, the two samples were selected to participate because of their attitudes toward infants' sleeping habits, rather than because of cultural background per se.

An area in which these types of comparisons (i.e., examination of a variable that differs across cultures) have been especially fruitful is that of language characteristics. Miura, Okamoto, Kim, Steere, and Fayol (1993) investigated the influences of language characteristics on cognitive development. In this study, French, Japanese, Korean, Swedish, and U.S. first graders' ability to represent numbers and understand place value were evaluated. The results showed that cognitive representations and place value understanding varied across samples. Miura et al. (1993) suggested that their findings could be explained by the different numerical languages these children speak. In particular, Japanese and Korean children are taught a canonical base 10 number representation (i.e., they see the written number as tens and ones), whereas Swedish, French, and U.S. children see a written number as a collection of individual units. The Korean and Japanese languages enhance these children's understanding of place value. Even though the Korean children had not yet learned place value, they showed better performance on the tasks than U.S., French, and Swedish first graders, many of whom had already received instruction in school about place value.

As these examples illustrate, cultural comparisons can be useful when investigators have targeted particular groups because they are known to differ on a specific variable. Nonetheless, as outlined, cultural comparisons too often carry a great danger of *nuisance* variables confounding the results. In any investigation, researchers must assume either that the target groups do not differ other than on the independent variable or that differences on other variables are not responsible for the observed behavioral differences. These two assumptions, each of which is formidable in itself, are unfortunately too often taken for granted in cultural comparative investigations. This danger is exacerbated by the fact that cultural comparative research can be most interesting when the cultures under investigation vary dramatically from each other. However, the greater the disparities between the cultural groups, the greater the risk of misattribution of reasons underlying cultural differences in performance outcomes.

A second potential pitfall in cultural comparative research is the danger of *ethnocentrism*. Whether researchers begin with the goal of finding universals or of pinpointing differences in behavior, their work usually originates in one cultural setting. That is, researchers generally begin a project with knowledge of what constitutes "normal" behavior in one culture and take their expectations and presumptions with them to the second cultural setting. Given this starting point, too many researchers have approached their results with the attitude that *their* standards were *the* standards for normal behavior (cf. Berry et al., 1992), with little sensitivity to the mores and beliefs of other groups. As Triandis (1990) notes, all peoples have tendencies to think of what goes on in their own culture as "natural" and "correct," and to think of what happens in other cultures as "unnatural" and "incorrect" (cf. Brewer & Campbell, 1976). Given this slant, it is not surprising that the first several decades of cultural comparative studies frequently portrayed members of the researchers' society in a position of superiority, and members of other societies as inferior (see, e.g., Hendrikz, 1975; Lasry, 1975).

Fortunately, the wind has changed, leading to a number of investigations that have done precisely the opposite. For example, in an investigation of visual-spatial memory in desert Aboriginal and white Australian adolescents, Kearins (1981) showed that when asked to remember the location of an array of objects, the Aboriginese consistently outperformed the other group, even when given an array of objects that were considered to be less familiar to the Aboriginese adolescents. The Aboriginese adolescents also showed better verbal recall for wild animals. Kearins concluded from these results that both interest and prior experience were responsible for the superior performance of the Aboriginal subjects.

However, the point here is not to find who is superior; rather, the point is to shed one's own cultural clothing enough to understand another culture. Ethnocentrism has the potential to plague all facets of cultural comparative studies, including research methods, instruments, interpretation of research results, and, in fact, the research questions that are asked to begin with.

A third potential problem for cultural comparisons concerns the *equivalence of research materials* across groups. If research participants speak different languages, verbal research materials must be translated. However, most bilingual individuals will agree that "translation" of texts is not a simple matter of noting one-to-one correspondences across the two languages. Often an exact equivalent of a verbal expression does not exist in the second language; if it does exist, it might carry different nuances than in the first language, be of a different word length, or have a different frequency of occurrence in daily conversation. Thus, rather than simply translating research instruments, researchers must aim for a good fit between instrument and subject-in-context (Tronick, 1992).

Establishing this fit is by no means straightforward. A simple example might be drawn from a research project conducted in India that did not involve cultural comparisons, but did require the adaptation of U.S. measures to a non-Western society (Kurtz, Borkowski, & Deshmukh, 1988). In this investigation of the influences of home characteristics on children's cognitive development, Kurtz et al. used an adapted form of Caldwell and Bradley's (1984) HOME scale. One item in the scale evaluates the size of the child's home relative to the number of individuals in the family. The Indians collaborating in this project suggested modifying this item, arguing that only the very wealthiest of Indian families resided in houses with as many square feet per person as the average U.S. household. On another item, the home environment was to receive a positive ranking if the mother openly praised her child in the course of the one-to-two-hour interview (cf. Caldwell & Bradley, 1984). However, this item also raised a red flag for our Indian (Marathi) colleagues, who reasoned that only an ill-bred Indian mother would compliment her child in front of a strange adult; therefore, this item was dropped from the scale.

As these two examples illustrate, cultural comparisons are by no means straightforward, and development of equivalent materials can be a formidable undertaking. Because cultural differences, especially those between widely varying cultural groups, can be so varied and subtle, it is advisable that cultural comparative studies be conducted by individuals who intimately know both cultures under investigation.

A fourth issue related to cultural comparative investigations is that of *sample selection.* Selection or identification of the groups and of the particular individuals who will participate in the study determine both the conclusions that can be drawn from the results and the potential generalization of those results to other groups. With regard to the individuals from a cultural group who are selected, researchers should clearly define their cultural groups, and then determine what individuals are representative of those groups. For instance, when comparing Japanese school children with U.S. school children, what Americans should be selected? Should Japanese-American children be eliminated? Are the researchers' needs best suited by obtaining a sample of strictly Caucasian Americans, or would a mixed racial group that is more representative of the U.S. population be better? Are other subject characteristics besides race important to selection (e.g., religion, urban vs. rural, social status)? Obviously, such questions must be answered anew in each investigation, since factors that would confound the results of one study will not be problematic in another. The point here is twofold: First, subjects should be representative of their cultural group, and second, as discussed earlier, researchers should be wary of confounding variables.

A second important point related to subject selection concerns the search for universals in behavior. As we outlined in our introductory paragraphs, some cross-cultural investigations are designed not to note differences between cultural groups, but rather to identify similarities (i.e., culture-general phenomena), thus establishing that theories developed in one cultural setting also hold elsewhere. Sample selection is obviously important when trying to establish the culture-generality of developmental phenomena, since similarities are far more likely to be found in highly similar cultures than in those that differ. For instance, cross-national research by Boehnke, Silbereisen, Eisenberg, Reykowski, and Palmonari (1989) has identified similar patterns in social-emotional development for children from four nations. Boehnke et al. (1989) investigated the development of prosocial motivation in 7- to 18-year-olds from West Germany, Poland, Italy, and the United States. Participants responded to the Prosocial Motivation Questionnaire, in which situations are presented and children identify potential motives for a prosocial action (e.g., helping a friend clean his or her room). The results of Boehnke et al. indicate that intrinsic motives (e.g., task and other orientation) were valued over extrinsic motives (e.g., hedonism and self-interest) by children in all four countries. Further, developmental patterns in prosocial behavior were similar across nations. For instance, hedonistic responses decreased with age, while task orientation increased. Although these results support universal similarities in prosocial development, it should be noted that West Germany, Poland, Italy, and the United States are all industrialized Western countries, and thus conclusions about universality would best be left to tests with cultural groups that differ more dramatically from one another.

Certainly in any research endeavor, the characteristics of the sample determine the range and limits of generalizability of the results. Nowhere is this more evident than in cultural comparative research. With regard to research illustrating cultural differences, it is appropriate to question the generality of a phenomenon within each culture, since differences can often be found within cultural/national boundaries that are just as great as those found across cultural/national boundaries. Cautious investigators do not speak in terms of research on "universals," but rather in terms of "similarities" or "culture-general phenomena" (cf. Brislin, 1990), since a research design that is inclusive enough to actually establish a universal is unlikely to be carried out. Here again, the selection procedures – regarding what groups to include, as well as what individuals represent each group – are critical in determining the conclusions and their generality.

The final issue in cultural comparisons we will discuss concerns the *integration of cultural differences and universals in theory*. Although some behaviors and some aspects of development might be expected to vary across cultures, other developmental phenomena are highly similar across cultures. Therefore, comprehensive theories should deal with both similarities and differences. Similarly, well-guided research programs define both the similarities and the differences in the cultural groups under study.

In a four-nation study of maternal speech to infants, Bornstein et al. (1992) identified both culture-specific and culture-general characteristics of mothers' speech. These researchers studied mothers' language use with 5- and 13-month-old infants, distinguishing between language intended to express affection versus language with a didactic purpose. Although mothers from all four countries (Argentina, France, Japan, and the United States) used all types of speech categories and spoke more to older than to younger infants, numerous cultural differences were also noted in the results. For instance, French mothers in the study, unlike mothers from the other three countries, used less affect-salient speech to older infants than to younger infants. Japanese mothers increased overall production of speech to older children as did mothers from the other countries, but unlike other mothers, their speech continued to be more affective than didactic in content (Bornstein et al., 1992). These results highlight the fact that the universal/cultural-difference distinction in many ways is an artificial one, and that we should attempt to build theories that explain both similarities and differences in development across cultural groups.

This discussion has elaborated five challenges to comparative cultural research: the use of culture as an independent variable, ethnocentrism, equivalence of research materials, sample selection, and implications for theory. In the next section, we discuss the second primary focus of cross-cultural psychology: research in acculturation.

## Research in Acculturation

*Acculturation* may be defined as culture change that results from continuous, firsthand contact between two distinct cultural groups (Redfield, Linton, & Herskovits, 1936). Although this definition implies that change is bidirectional, it is nonetheless acknowledged that the greatest changes usually occur in the nondominant rather than the dominant cultural group. Acculturation is both an individual and a group phenomenon; thus, continuous contact between two cultural groups will result in changes in the shared cultural values and traditions of the two groups involved, and also in the culturally linked values and traditions of individuals in those groups (Berry, 1989, 1991). As Berry (1989) has outlined, immigrant groups may become acculturated to their host society with or without maintaining their own cultural identities.

Acculturation as a process of group and individual change is a developmental phenomenon, and we would argue that it cannot be effectively studied without focusing on the process of change itself. Given that acculturation is a process of *changing*, that is, of becoming rather than of being, it is ironic that the vast majority of studies of acculturation utilize cross-sectional, single-measurement interviews. In most of these studies, the investigators measure an immigrant group on one or more dimensions of interest and compare their performances/responses to those of a native, dominant culture group. These studies have compared immigrant and receiving groups in domains such as school achievement (e.g., Brandon, 1991; Gibson, 1987), psychosocial adjustment (e.g., Kinzie, Tran, Breckenridge, & Bloom, 1980; Nicassio, 1985), family interaction styles (e.g., Schönpflug, Silbereisen, & Schulz, 1990), and acculturation (e.g., Smither & Rodriguez-Giegling, 1982; Wong-Rieger & Quintana, 1987).

In a second type of acculturation study, the investigators compare two or more groups of immigrants, usually of the same cultural background, but who differ in the amount of time they have spent in the new cultural setting (e.g., Lindgren & Yu, 1975; Padilla, Wagatsuma, & Lindholm, 1985; Rosenthal & Feldman, 1990; Sharma, 1984). For example, in an investigation of first-, second-, and third-generation Japanese-American students, Padilla et al. (1985) found that first-generation students were lower in self-esteem and experienced more stress than third-/later-generation students. Differences in stress and self-esteem were related to acculturation. Similarly, Rosenthal and Feldman (1990) studied first- and second-generation Chinese immigrants in the United States and Australia, adolescents from the two host cultures, and adolescents from Hong Kong. Rosenthal and Feldman focused on family environment – in particular, the extent to which the adolescent perceived the family environment as structured and controlling. Results of the study indicated a continuum, with Chinese in Hong Kong reporting the greatest family regulation of adolescent behavior, the two nonimmigrant host groups (i.e., Australian and U.S.) reporting the least control, and the immigrant groups reporting intermediate levels.

Although these investigations are more revealing of the actual processes at work in acculturation than are studies that simply contrast immigrant and receiving society groups, we would still argue that such designs are not nearly as effective in capturing the processes underlying acculturation as are longitudinal studies. That is, cross-sectional studies are actually measuring *differences* among groups – in this case, among groups who have spent more or less time in the receiving culture – rather than measuring *changes* that occur in individuals as they become more acculturated to a society. As Schneider

(1989) has outlined, the problems associated with longitudinal research are many, including *practical problems* such as cost and long-term recruitment of staff, *conceptual problems* regarding the definition of change, and *methodological problems* concerning the assessment of change and stability over time. However, given the limitations of cross-sectional designs, the process of acculturation will not be well understood without longitudinal research. We will return to this point later in the chapter.

## A Model of Acculturation in Children

Borrowing from research conducted primarily with adults, we now outline a model of acculturation that may be applied to children. This model is intended to represent various characteristics of the child, the receiving culture, and the sending culture that influence an immigrant child's acculturation and adaptation to the receiving culture. Our list is by no means intended to be exhaustive, but rather is a first attempt at building a theory that may then be tested and further developed through research. Characteristics of the child that we believe are likely to influence a young immigrant child's acculturation include: age at migration, language facility, gender, personality characteristics, and contact with the receiving culture. Societal factors that influence acculturation include the child's premigration experiences, reasons for migration, disparity between the sending and receiving cultures, and characteristics of the receiving society (Figure 6.1). We do not suggest that these factors operate independently of one another; for instance, a child's age at migration is likely to influence language facility, and language facility will obviously be related to contact with the host culture. However, we posit each as a unique factor contributing to the child's acculturation. Each factor will be described in turn.

### *Age at Migration*

Of the few studies of acculturation that have focused on children, most have had age as a primary focus. Most of these studies have indicated that children who arrive in the receiving society at a younger age adapt more easily and more completely than individuals who arrive at a later age (Goldlust & Richmond, 1974; Szapocznik, Scopetta, Kurtines, & Aranalde, 1978).

We suggest that age influences the acculturation process in a num-

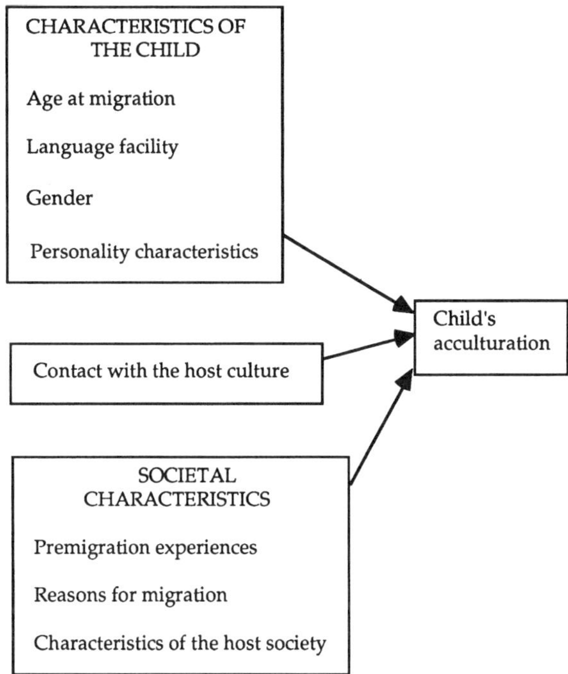


**Figure 6.1.** A model of acculturation in children.

ber of ways. One primary way is through its relationship to second-language acquisition. Lenneberg (1967) proposed that because the nervous system loses its flexibility with maturation, language development occurs primarily in childhood. When acquisition of a second language is the focus of study, adults seems to acquire both phonology and syntax more quickly than children in the short term. However, when adults and children are compared on long-term attainment, those individuals who acquired language early in childhood show clear advantages over adult learners, both in phonology and in syntax (e.g., Oyama, 1976, 1978; Patkowski, 1980). In a recent examination of second-language learning as a function of age, Johnson and Newport (1989) tested native Chinese and Koreans who had emigrated to the United States. These individuals ranged in age from 3 to 39 years and had lived in the United States between 3 and 26 years when they were tested. Johnson and Newport reported a strong advantage in English proficiency for immigrants who had arrived in early childhood. Further, the authors provided evidence that the age effect was not due to differences in amount of exposure to English, motivation, self-consciousness, or identification with American culture.

In addition to its relationship to eventual language attainment, age at migration is likely to also influence the acculturation process in that younger children presumably have weaker or less-defined cultural identities than do older children and adults. Since a younger child has had less experience with his or her native culture than an adult, culturally related values, beliefs, and customs are not as firmly embedded in the child at the point of migration; thus, adaptation to the receiving society likely occurs more readily. Relatedly, an individual who has migrated as a child is less likely than an adult migrant to have strong ties to his or her native culture. Older individuals, because of ties "back home," are more likely to maintain contact with relatives and friends in their native culture, thereby maintaining their own cultural identity.

A third example of how age at migration may influence the individual's acculturation is through its relationship to amount of contact that he or she has with the receiving society. Children who attend school will of necessity encounter members of the host culture with greater frequency than children or adults who stay at home. Contact with the receiving society will be discussed in greater detail later.

### *Language Facility*

A second factor related to the acculturation process is language skill. In the psychiatric literature, low host-language proficiency has frequently been linked to greater incidence of depression and other psychiatric disorders, and overall lower levels of adaptation (e.g., Nicassio, 1985). Kim (1977, 1978) has outlined a model illustrating the centrality of effective communication in acculturation. In this model, interpersonal communication and use of mass media are viewed as central to the immigrant's acculturation, and both are posited to be dependent on the immigrant's language competency. Kim has tested her model with Korean immigrants and has found that English competence and mass media availability were linked to reported interpersonal communication and mass media consumption, which were, in turn, linked to perceptual complexity (i.e., the degree of complexity with which members of the host society were viewed, which was assumed to be a measure of acculturation).

Language facility most likely influences acculturation both because of the communication (thus, exchange of ideas) that it permits and because of its motivating characteristics. In other words, greater language fluency enhances the motivation both to communicate with receiving society members and to watch television and read newspapers. In a recent study of two generations of Asian and European immigrants in the United States, language skills were highly related to acculturation for the Asian-Americans, and acculturation, in turn, predicted academic achievement (Kurtz-Costes, Goldman, & Ngo, 1993).

### *Gender*

With a few exceptions, most contemporary large-scale migrations are occurring from developing countries to developed, industrialized countries. Children's acculturation may be expected to vary along gender lines primarily because of the contrasts between predominant gender roles in developing countries and those in industrialized countries. Although attitudes are gradually changing everywhere, women in Third World countries are more likely than their First World counterparts to assume major domestic responsibilities at an early age and are less likely to select marriage partners independently, to be politically active, to pursue higher education, or to own property (Bennett, 1983; Davis, 1983; Keats, 1989; Smith-Hefner, 1993).

Given these differences in traditional gender roles, immigrant females are more likely than males to be restricted in their contacts with members of the receiving society and are more likely to marry within their ethnic group. For example, in an investigation of Indian immigrants in British society, Sharma (1984) found significant gender differences in autonomy: While first- and second-generation Indian boys did not differ from English boys, Indian girls showed less autonomy in their everyday lives and perceived greater expectations from their parents to play a responsible role in household activities than did English girls. Similarly, Smith-Hefner (1993) has documented the differential treatment of daughters versus sons by Khmer immigrant parents and the resulting impact on the daughters' education. In her ethnographic study Smith-Hefner found that because of concerns regarding the daughters' sexual purity, Khmer adolescent girls frequently marry while they are still in high school and are then forced to drop out of school because of pregnancy.

However, our generalizations should not be too broad when considering gender differences in acculturation, since parents' attitudes toward gender differences in the acculturation of their children vary across cultural groups. Although some ethnic groups may be far more resistant to the assimilation of their female children, other groups may show the reverse pattern. For instance, because Japanese and Indian women leave their birth homes at the point of marriage and are expected to care for their husbands' parents for the rest of their lives, Japanese and Indian parents might be more concerned about their sons' retention of cultural values than of their daughters'.

### *Attitudes and Personality Characteristics*

A review by Hannigan (1990) summarizes literature examining personality and attitudinal predictors of acculturation (or "intercultural effectiveness," in Hannigan's terms). Although Hannigan focused specifically on the cross-cultural effectiveness of Peace Corps volunteers and international students, who are usually temporary sojourners rather than permanent immigrants in a receiving country, much of his model can be applied to immigrants. Hannigan classified adaptation factors into three categories: skills, attitudes, and personality traits. According to this rubric, skills and attitudes are subject to change, or training, while personality traits are assumed to be established in the individual, and are thus less likely to change. Skills that facilitate acculturation include communication skills, flexibility (i.e., the ability to deal with different communication styles), and the ability to establish and maintain relationships. Attitudes that enhance acculturation or international effectiveness include orientation to knowledge (i.e., realizing that others may possess valuable knowledge rather than viewing oneself as an expert); a positive attitude toward the new culture and a willingness to distance oneself from one's own culture; a nonjudgmental attitude (i.e., highly respectful of the host culture); and cultural empathy (i.e., the ability to put oneself in another's shoes, the ability to understand and to use nonverbal communication in the host culture).

Hannigan's list of personality traits that enhance acculturation include patience, tolerance, ability to deal with stress, persistence with flexibility (e.g., recognition of when to follow through on a task and when to be sensitive to host culture priorities), self-confidence, and healthy self-esteem. Several personality traits that Hannigan argues are negatively associated with cross-cultural effectiveness include perfectionism, rigidity, dogmatism, ethnocentrism, and dependent anxiety.

Hannigan's (1990) summary of research dealing primarily with sojourners (i.e., those who are residing in a culture different from their own, but who do not intend to stay) is consistent with research examining the influence of personality factors on immigrants' and refugees' acculturation. For instance, Smither and Rodriguez-Giegling (1982) reported that acculturation of Vietnamese refugees in the United States was better predicted by personality factors (conscientiousness and likability) than by time in the country, education, or age. Other research has linked negative self-perceptions and a greater perceived distance between self and the receiving culture to greater adjustment difficulties on the part of refugees (Nicassio, 1985). However, it should be noted that causality between these two factors might operate in both directions: If negative self-perceptions hinder acculturation, a lack of acculturation might also lead to negative self-perceptions. In fact, in the study mentioned earlier by Padilla and his colleagues (1985), first-generation Japanese-Americans were found to have lower levels of self-esteem than third-/later-generation Japanese-Americans, a finding that the authors attributed to lower levels of acculturation in the first-generation group. Lower levels of acculturation, on the other hand, might influence attitudes toward the new culture. Thus, for many children, positive experiences with a culture enhance self-esteem, which in turn better enable the child to step forth assertively in new situations, leading to greater acculturation, and so the cycle continues.

## *Contact with the Receiving Culture*

If interpersonal communication is central to the acculturation process, then the immigant's contact with the receiving culture will be an important conduit for such interpersonal communication to take place. Immigrant families who reside in ethnically homogeneous neighborhoods have less opportunity for contact with members of the receiving society than families who settle in an area with few others from their ethnic background. Thus, an immigrant who is isolated from his or her native culture will of necessity acquire the host language more quickly, befriend members of the receiving culture, and live in proximity to host culture members. These factors will, in turn, facilitate the acculturation and assimilation of the individual (Wong-Rieger & Quintana, 1987).

For children, amount of contact with the receiving society is especially related to living arrangements, schooling, and attitudes and behaviors of parents. In the case of living arrangements, as described earlier, some immigrant groups may remain in an ethnically homogeneous area for generations, such as the Chinese living in San Francisco's Chinatown. In contrast, others are virtually isolated from their native culture. Relatedly, in areas where a large number of immigrants from a particular country have settled, children's adjustment in the school setting is buffered by the presence of siblings and friends who not only share the mother tongue of the child, but who also understand the child's cultural behaviors and assumptions. In some cases, as has occurred in the United States with Hispanic groups, a sufficient number of immigrants in an area have altered the school system itself, increasing the likelihood that an immigrant child's teacher and principal have the same ethnic/cultural heritage as the child. Although schools often serve as the main institution for acculturation of immigrant children, Bhatnagar (1985) concluded in his review of bilingual education programs that cognitive outcomes are better for immigrant children who receive instruction in their mother tongue while gradually acquiring the host language. However, it remains unclear what the social and emotional outcomes are for children who continue to be immersed in their native culture and language versus those who are plunged totally into the receiving society earlier on. On the one hand, maintenance of mother language and culture might protect the child's self-esteem and promote a healthy pride in ethnic identity. On the other hand, such contacts might serve to distance the child from the receiving culture and impede the process of acculturation.

Attitudes and lifestyle of the immigrant child's parents also influence the child's acculturation, since parents occupy a central role and position of power for their children. Especially in communities where a number of immigrant families from one ethnic background reside, parents may vary widely in the extent to which they encourage their children to have contact with members of the host culture. For instance, Gibson (1987) showed in her study of Punjabi Sikh families that parents of boys pushed their sons toward higher education, while parents of daughters actively discouraged the girls from taking college preparatory classes, because they believed that too much education would ruin their daughters' prospects for marriage. Although Gibson focused on academic achievement, it may be concluded from her ethnographic study that parental attitudes – in this case, attitudes related to gender – differentially influenced the amount of contact their children had with members of the host society. In the following sections, we will discuss societal characteristics that influence children's acculturation.

### *Premigration Experiences and Reasons for Migration*

A fundamental distinction must be made in studies of acculturation between involuntary and voluntary migrants. Voluntary migrants who have willingly left their homelands, usually with expectations of furthering their education and/or improving their standard of life, would presumably have very different characteristics than refugees, who have left their homelands because of fear, war, starvation, or persecution (Nicassio, 1985). Many involuntary migrants have endured severe trauma prior to their departure from their homelands, and many have similarly lived months or even years in difficult circumstances before arriving at their final destination. For instance, many Southeast Asians fleeing their homelands in the 1970s spent months or years in refugee camps in Thailand or the Philippines.

Individuals who are fleeing war or persecution have often become separated from family members, and thus are deprived of support and nurture from loved ones at a moment in their lives when such support is desperately needed. Even if an entire family has successfully arrived in the receiving society intact, if they are involuntary immigrants it is likely that they may have lost contact with extended family at home and also see little possibility of returning to visit family members in the future. This estrangement is likely not only to cause psychosocial stress, thus interfering with healthy adjustment, but also to disrupt the refugee's view of his or her native culture. This disruption accentuates the erosion of cherished cultural traditions that may have begun prior to departure, when many refugees have witnessed marked transformations of their native lands. In Berry's (1991) model of refugee adaptation, predeparture stressors include war, famine, torture, imprisonment, loss of civil rights, camp life, loss of property, loss of family, and uncertainty about the future. These are formidable obstacles to healthy adjustment in a society that may be insensitive to the refugee's needs, at best, and xenophobic, at the worst.

For children, reactions to traumatic stressors are related to the degree of violence experienced, presence or absence of personal injury, age of the child, and access to family support (Athey & Ahearn, 1991). As was noted earlier, loss is a defining characteristic of refugee status. Refugees lose their homes, their possessions, and frequently their loved ones. For children, loss of parents can be overwhelming; stress related to the loss is exacerbated if the child witnessed the parent's torture or death (Pynoos & Eth, 1985).

Two points should be clarified regarding the relationship between premigration experiences and acculturation. First, although we have made the distinction between voluntary and involuntary migrants, wide variability is found in the premigration experiences of involuntary groups. Although some refugees have experienced war, extreme deprivation, and torture, others have endured relatively benign religious or political persecution. Second, reactions to premigration experiences are undoubtedly mediated by postmigration conditions. For instance, in a study of 46 severely traumatized Cambodian children in California, Kinzie and Sack (1991) found no direct relationship between specific reported experiences (e.g., witnessing the death of a family member, seeing people beaten, suffering severe starvation) and adjustment, but did find a strong relationship between current living situation and psychiatric diagnosis. Children who were living with one or more family members were much less likely to be diagnosed as severely disturbed than children who were living with Cambodian or U.S. foster families. Kinzie and Sack (1991) concluded that contact with family members mitigated the symptoms of severe trauma.

### *Characteristics of the Receiving Society*

One way in which characteristics of the receiving society influence the child's acculturation is the similarity or disparity between the sending and receiving societies. If religion, customs, and lifestyle are more rather than less similar across the two societies, acculturation should occur more easily. Thus, migrants who are moving from Iraq to Germany (or vice versa) would be expected to have very different acculturation experiences than individuals moving from France to the United States.

A second receiving society characteristic influencing acculturation involves the attitudes of host society members toward the immigrant group. In this vein, the degree to which a group is welcomed by a receiving society depends in part on the economic and political role of the immigrant group in their new homeland. Immigrants are more likely to be well received if they collectively provide a needed source of labor or occupy an important political or moral role in the receiving society (e.g., Eastern Europeans migrating to the United States during the Cold War). The economic or political role of the immigrant group and disparity between sending and receiving cultures influence the reception that immigrants receive. This reception – which can range from a warm welcome at one end of the spectrum to xenophobia, legal discrimination, and interpersonal violence at the other end – will of course shape the immigrant child's orientation toward and acculturation to the receiving society (cf. Jiobu, 1988).

A third characteristic of the receiving society that influences the child's acculturation is the degree of cultural pluralism in the receiving society. Adjustment of a new immigrant will be particularly enhanced by the presence of social agencies that facilitate cultural pluralism, such as governments that consider the special needs of linguistic and religious minority groups to be a priority, and business services, recreational facilities, radio and television, and schools that provide special services to ethnic minority groups (cf. Goldlust & Richmond, 1974).

## *Discussion*

We have outlined a model that details factors influencing the acculturation of immigrant children. Two points should be made about applications of the model. The first has to do with the distinction between the individual and the group. Our model of acculturation was designed to describe the individual's adjustment and assimilation into the receiving society. As psychologists, we are interested primarily in individuals; however, we would argue that many of the principles we have discussed may also be applied to the acculturation of groups into a host society. For instance, the language characteristics of the group as a whole will determine to what extent individual members can continue to survive without learning the host language; experiences prior to migration are commonly shared by a group of migrants; attitudes toward gender will influence the probability of intermarriage, which strongly affects a cultural group's assimilation into the host culture. Thus, although space limitations prevent a detailed discussion of the matter, we suggest that much of what we have written about individuals might also be applied to the acculturation of groups.

A second point regarding the model has to do with the bidirectionality of acculturation. We began the section on acculturation by stating that it is a process involving cultural change in two groups resulting from prolonged contact with each other; however, we have discussed acculturation in a unidirectional fashion. We would like to note here that any cultural change, whether between groups or individuals, almost always leaves both sides in a changed state. However, the degree of change will vary, with something approaching a synthesis of the two cultures occurring at one extreme, to very little change occurring in the dominant culture at the opposite extreme. An illustration in terms of individual acculturation might be a marriage between individuals of two different societies, each of whom spends several years in the native culture of the spouse and becomes "fluent" not only in the other's native language, but also in the other's culture. At the opposite end of the spectrum is the individual who migrates to a new setting and becomes very much a part of that society without changing the cultural traditions and values of members of that society. Parallels can easily be imagined in the acculturation of groups. The point is that although acculturation is a bidirectional process, the degree to which change will occur in the dominant culture varies tremendously.

Next we describe a study currently in progress that is guided by our model of acculturation in children. Given the paucity of longitudinal studies of acculturation, we have undertaken a long-term study of immigrant children, hoping to follow them for a number of years. We will describe our methodology here as an example of how longitudinal studies may help us better understand the acculturation process.

## A Longitudinal Study of Acculturation

Since the Berlin Wall came down in 1989, thousands have migrated from the former Soviet Union and Eastern Bloc countries into Western Europe. Some of these people were fleeing persecution; others were simply seeking a better life and/or reunion with relatives. We designed this study to follow the adaptation of a group of Eastern European immigrant children in a West German community. We were especially interested in the following factors: (1) the role of language in the children's adaptation, (2) the influence of social context variables (e.g., current living situation, contact with individuals in birth country) on the child's adaptation, (3) the interplay between academic achievement and social-emotional adjustment, and (4) the developmental progression of acculturation and assimilation in our two immigrant groups.

## *Method*

A total of 157 9- to 10-year-old children participated at the first measurement point. We recruited the following four groups of children: (1) East European children currently living near the West German city Würzburg whose mother tongue is German (these children are mostly from the former East Germany), (2) East European children currently living near Würzburg whose mother tongue was a language other than German, (3) West German children whose families have resided near Würzburg for at least two generations, and (4) children born and currently residing in the East German city Erfurt (these children have not migrated).

Participating children complete questionnaires assessing the following: fluency in German; attitude toward school; attributional beliefs about academic outcomes; school-related anxiety; and academic self-concept. The children's parents complete questionnaires regarding migration information; parents' employment status; parents' education; family living situation; parents' educational aspirations for the child; parents' perceptions of the child's abilities; family lifestyle characteristics relevant to the child's academic performance (e.g., Do you have particular rules for your child regarding homework completion?); amount/type of contact the family maintains with individuals in their homeland; and language use in the home. In the first year of data collection, children completed the measures at three points separated by about 4-month intervals.

This research project was designed in part as an initial attempt to test our proposed model of acculturation. Obviously the study is a partial test of the model. However, by beginning to synthesize within one study some of the child and societal characteristics that have been addressed individually in past studies, we hope to gain a more comprehensive understanding of the acculturation process for children. In particular, we are measuring how language skills, personality characteristics (e.g., attributional beliefs, self-concept, school anxiety), and contact with the host culture influence and are influenced by the child's acculturation. Further, our parental assessments enable us to tap experiences that occurred prior to immigration, amount and quality of contact with the host society, and reasons for migration.

Our inclusion of four distinct groups in the study permits us to make a number of comparisons. First, we are able to evaluate the acculturation processes of two Eastern European groups who have different linguistic and historical links to West Germany. Second, our inclusion of a comparison group in Erfurt will allow us to note differences between children who have migrated and those who have not. Although it is often acknowledged that voluntary migrants are a self-selected group who might differ in important ways from members of a society who do not migrate, studies of acculturation rarely attempt to include a nonmigratory comparison group. Finally, the inclusion of a West German group will give us a same-age database to which we can compare the other groups.

The longitudinal aspect of this project will allow us to observe directly the ways in which the immigrant children change as they adjust to life in West Germany. Further, the longitudinal design allows for testing the bidirectionality operating among factors. For instance, we will be able to note the degree to which a positive self-concept is predictive of acculturation and, in turn, to what extent greater acculturation enhances self-concept. Most important, we hope to document both the predictors and the rate of acculturation and adaptation of these two groups of immigrant children.

## Summary

We have outlined five methodological and conceptual issues that are central to cultural comparisons in developmental psychology. In particular, we discussed the use of culture as an independent variable, ethnocentrism, difficulties in developing research materials that are equivalent across cultural groups, problems associated with sample selection, and the theoretical integration of culture-specific and culture-general phenomena.

Research in acculturation investigates the changes that occur over time when two or more cultures interact. Unfortunately, most prior research in acculturation has neglected to use longitudinal designs, which are best suited for examining change over time. Furthermore, few investigators have addressed acculturation in children. Therefore, we outlined a model that might guide investigations of acculturation in children. Characteristics of the child that were posited to influence acculturation included age at migration, language facility, gender, and personality characteristics. Societal factors that influence the child's adjustment include premigration experiences, reasons for migration, and characteristics of the receiving society. Amount of contact the child has with the host culture also influences the child's acculturation.

Finally, we described a research project currently in progress that investigates the acculturation and assimilation of Eastern European children who have recently migrated to a West German community. This study is one of the first longitudinal attempts to trace the acculturation process in children and also provides a preliminary test of our model of acculturation in children.

## References

Athey, J. L., & Ahearn, F. L. (1991). The mental health of refugee children: An overiview. In F. L. Ahearn and J. L. Athey (Eds.), *Refugee children: Theory, research, and services* (pp. 3–19). Baltimore: Johns Hopkins University Press.

Bennett, L. (1983). *Dangerous wives and sacred sisters.* New York: Columbia University Press.

Berry, J. W. (1989). Acculturation and psychological adaptation. In J. P. Forgas & J. M. Innes (Eds.), *Recent advances in social psychology: An international perspective* (pp. 511–520). North Holland: Elsevier Science.

(1991). Refugee adaptation in settlement countries: An overview with an emphasis on primary prevention. In F. L. Ahearn and J. L. Athey (Eds.), *Refugee children: Theory, research, and services* (pp. 20–38). Baltimore: Johns Hopkins University Press.

Berry, J. W., Poortinga, Y. H., Segall, M. H., & Dasen, P. R. (1992). *Cross-cultural psychology: Research and applications.* Cambridge University Press.

Bhatnagar, J. (1985). Language maintenance programmes for immigrant children. *International Review of Applied Psychology, 34*, 503–526.

Boehnke, K., Silbereisen, R. K., Eisenberg, N., Reykowski, J., & Palmonari, A. (1989). Developmental patterns of prosocial motivation: A cross-national study. *Journal of Cross-Cultural Psychology, 20*, 219–243.

Bornstein, M. H., Tal, J., Rahn, C., Galperín, C. Z., Pêcheux, M.-G., Lamour, M., Toda, S., Azuma, H., Ogino, M., & Tamis-LeMonda, C. S. (1992). Functional analysis of the contents of maternal speech to infants of 5 and 13 months in four cultures: Argentina, France, Japan, and the United States. *Developmental Psychology*, *28*, 593–603.

Brandon, P. R. (1991). Gender differences in young Asian-American's educational attainments. *Sex Roles*, *25*, 45–61.

Brewer, M. B., & Campbell, D. T. (1976). *Ethnocentrism and intergroup attitudes.* New York: Wiley.

Brislin, R. W. (1990). Applied cross-cultural psychology: An introduction. In R. W. Brislin (Ed.), *Applied cross-cultural psychology* (pp. 9–33). Newbury Park, CA: Sage.

Caldwell, B. M., & Bradley, R. H. (1984). *Administration manual: Home observation for measurement of the environment.* Little Rock: University of Arkansas Press.

Davis, S. S. (1983). *Patience and power.* Cambridge, MA: Schenkman.

Gibson, M. A. (1987). The school performance of immigrant minorities: A comparative view. *Anthropology and Education Quarterly*, *18*, 262–275.

Goldlust, J., & Richmond, A. (1974). A multivariate model of immigrant adaptation. *International Migration Review, 8*, 193–216.

Hannigan, T. P. (1990). Traits, attitudes, and skills that are related to intercultural effectiveness and their implications for cross-cultural training: A review of the literature. *International Journal of Intercultural Relations*, *14*, 89–111.

Hendrikz, E. (1975). Spatial reasoning and mathematical and scientific competence. In J. W. Berry & W. J. Lonner (Eds.), *Applied cross-cultural psychology* (pp. 219–223). Amsterdam: Swets & Zeitlinger.

Jahoda, G. (1966). Geometric illusion and environment: A study in Ghana. *British Journal of Psychology*, *57*, 193–199.

(1971). Retinal pigmentation, illusion susceptibility and space perception. *International Journal of Psychology*, *6*, 99–208.

Jiobu, R. M. (1988). *Ethnicity and assimilation.* Albany: State University of New York Press.

Johnson, J. S., & Newport, E. L. (1989). Critical period effects in second language learning: The influence of maturational effects on the acquisition of English as a second language. *Cognitive Psychology*, *21*, 60–99.

Kearins, J. M. (1981). Visual spatial memory in Australian Aboriginal children of desert regions. *Cognitive Psychology*, *13*, 434–460.

Keats, D. M. (1989). Adolescents: An Australian-Asian cross-cultural view. In J. P. Forgas & J. M. Innes (Eds.), *Recent advances in social psychology: An international perspective* (pp. 529–534). New York: Elsevier.

Kim, Y. Y. (1977). Communication patterns of foreign immigrants in the process of acculturation. *Human Communication Research*, *4*, 66–77.

(1978). A communication approach to the acculturation process: A study of Korean immigrants in Chicago. *International Journal of Intercultural Relations*, *2*, 197–224.

Kinzie, J. D., & Sack, W. (1991). Severely traumatized Cambodian children: Research findings and clinical implications. In F. L. Ahearn and J. L. Athey (Eds.), *Refugee children: Theory, research, and services* (pp. 20–38). Baltimore: Johns Hopkins University Press.

Kinzie, J. D., Tran, K., Breckenridge, A., & Bloom, J. (1980). An Indochinese refugee psychiatric clinic: Culturally accepted treatment approaches. *American Journal of Psychiatry*, *137*, 1429–1432.

Kurtz, B. E., Borkowski, J. G., & Deshmukh, K. (1988). Metamemory development in Maharashtrian children: Influences from home and school. *Journal of Genetic Psychology*, *149*, 363–376.

Kurtz-Costes, B., Goldman, J., & Ngo, P. (1993). *Achievement striving and achievement behaviors of Americans of Asian and European heritage.* Paper presented at the annual meetings of the American Educational Research Association, Atlanta.

Lasry, J. C. (1975). Cross-cultural comparisons of a mental health scale. In J. W. Berry & W. J. Lonner (Eds.), *Applied cross-cultural psychology* (pp. 123–129). Amsterdam: Swets & Zeitlinger.

Lenneberg, E. (1967). *Biological foundations of language.* New York: Wiley.

Lindgren, H. C., & Yu, R. (1975). Cross-cultural insight and empathy among Chinese immigrants to the United States. *Journal of Social Psychology*, *96*, 305–306.

Miura, I. T., Okamoto, Y., Kim, C. K., Steere, M., & Fayol, M. (1993). First graders' cognitive representation of number and understanding of place value: Cross-national comparisons – France, Japan, Korea, Sweden, and the United States. *Journal of Educational Psychology*, *85*, 24–30.

Morelli, G. A., Rogoff, B., Oppenheim, D., & Goldsmith, D. (1992). Cultural variation in infants' sleeping arrangements: Questions of independence. *Developmental Psychology*, *28*, 604–613.

Nicassio, P. M. (1985). The psychosocial adjustment of the Southeast Asian refugee. *Journal of Cross-Cultural Psychology*, *16*, 153–173.

Oyama, S. (1976). A sensitive period for the acquisition of a non-native phonological system. *Journal of Psycholinguistic Research*, *5*, 261–285.

(1978). The sensitive period and comprehension of speech. *Working Papers on Bilingualism*, *16*, 1–17.

Padilla, A. M., Wagatsuma, Y., & Lindholm, K. J. (1985). Acculturation and personality as predictors of stress in Japanese and Japanese-Americans. *Journal of Social Psychology*, *125*, 295–305.

Patkowski, M. (1980). The sensitive period for the acquisition of syntax in a second language. *Language Learning*, *30*, 449–472.

Pollack, R. H. (1970). Müller–Lyer illusion: Effect of age, lightness, contrast and hue. *Science*, *170*, 93–94.

Pynoos, R. S., & Eth, S. (1985). Children traumatized by witnessing acts of personal violence: Homicide, rape, or suicide behavior. In S. Eth and R. S. Pynoos (Eds.), *Post-traumatic stress disorder in children* (pp. 17–43). Washington, DC: American Psychiatric Press.

Redfield, R., Linton, R., & Herskovits, M. J. (1936). Memorandum on the study of acculturation. *American Anthropologist*, *38*, 149–152.

Rogoff, B. (1981). Schooling's influence on memory test performance. *Child Development*, *52*, 260–267.

Rosenthal, D. A., & Feldman, S. S. (1990). The acculturation of Chinese immigrants: Perceived effects on family functioning of length of residence in two cultural contexts. *Journal of Genetic Psychology*, *15*, 495–514.

Schneider, W. (1989). Problems of longitudinal studies with children: Practical, conceptual, and methodological issues. In M. Brambring, F. Lösel, & H. Skowronek (Eds.), *Children at risk: Assessment, longitudinal research, and intervention* (pp. 313–335). New York: de Gruyter.

Schönpflug, U., Silbereisen, R. K., & Schulz, J. (1990). Perceived decision-making influence in Turkish migrant workers' and German workers' families. *Journal of Cross-Cultural Psychology*, *21*, 261–282.

Segall, M. H., Campbell, D. T., & Herskovits, M. J. (1966). *The influence of culture on visual perception*. Chicago: Bobbs-Merrill.

Sharma, S. M. (1984). Assimilation of Indian immigrant adolescents in British society. *Journal of Psychology*, *118*, 79–84.

Shweder, R. A. (1990). Cultural psychology: What is it? In J. W. Stigler, R. A. Shweder, & G. Herdt (Eds.), *Cultural psychology* (pp. 1–43). Cambridge University Press.

Smith-Hefner, N. J. (1993). Education, gender, and generational conflict among Khmer refugees. *Anthropology and Education Quarterly*, *24*, 135–158.

Smither, R., & Rodriguez-Giegling, M. (1982). Personality, demographics, and acculturation of Vietnamese and Nicaraguan refugees to the United States. *International Journal of Psychology*, *17*, 19–25.

Szapocznik, J., Scopetta, M. A., Kurtines, W., & Aranalde, J. A. (1978). Theory and measurement of acculturation. *Interamerican Journal of Psychology*, *12*, 113–130.

Triandis, H. C. (1990). Theoretical concepts that are applicable to the analysis of ethnocentrism. In R. W. Brislin (Ed.), *Applied cross-cultural psychology* (pp. 34–55). Newbury Park, CA: Sage.

Triandis, H. C., Malpass, R., & Davidson, A. R. (1972). Cross-cultural psychology. *Biennial Review of Anthropology*, *1*, 1–84.

Tronick, E. Z. (1992). Introduction: Cross-cultural studies of development. *Developmental Psychology*, *28*, 566–567.

Wong-Rieger, D., & Quintana, D. (1987). Comparative acculturation of Southeast Asian and Hispanic immigrants and sojourners. *Journal of Cross-Cultural Psychology*, *18*, 345–362.

PART THREE

# Comparisons at the Level of Data

# 7 The Co-development of Identity, Agency, and Lived Worlds

*Dorothy C. Holland and Debra G. Skinner*

Within the discipline of anthropology, the concept of culture has undergone a major revision. The notion of culture as a homogeneous, bounded entity has been replaced by a notion of cultures as heterogeneous and unbounded, contested and emergent. The former perspective, sometimes labeled "objectivist," has given way to a "practice" view of culture. In the paradigms that predate practice theory, especially structuralism and structural functionalism, the important analyses were those that happened after the culture had been analytically segregated, so to speak, from the flow of daily life. The point was to understand culture as a system, separable and significant unto itself. A whole generation of criticism has led practice theorists to take a different direction. These theorists no longer seek an abstract and generative model of culture, postulated to "underlie" social action. The point instead is to understand collective meaning systems as *situated* in social action, education and individual development as they occur in *practice*, and linguistic forms as they are used in *performance*.[1] In the older paradigms, one started with moments of cultural

This chapter draws on a number of studies, particularly one funded by the National Science Foundation (BNS-9110010). Although we have not always had the space to accommodate their suggestions, we have learned from and appreciated the comments of a number of thoughtful readers, including Steve Parish, Margaret Eisenhart, William Lachicotte, Julia Thompson, and the editors of this volume. We thank the staff of the Publications Office at the Frank Porter Graham Child Development Center at the University of North Carolina of Chapel Hill for their help in designing the figures used here. We also thank our research associates and assistants in Nepal, especially G. B. Adhikari, Renu Lama, and Sapana Sharma, as well as Govinda Sharma, who shared his collection of Tij songs with us. We are very appreciative of the many people in Naudada who were patient with us and helped us in many ways. Although we tried, in turn, to contribute to their lives in several ways, their gifts to us are by far the greater.

production, episodes of the joint production of conversation, incidents of practice, and episodes of performance only because they were the convenient, observable points of entry to the important objects of study; practice theorists start from and stay with these moments because they are where human life happens. They are the sites where social formations, cultures, mental states, and languages exist. To step back from them, as Bourdieu (1977, 1990) says repeatedly, is to lose the actor's understanding of his or her world.

Today, sociocultural anthropologists focus on the cultural practices and discourses that people engage in and embody, and the production of these practices within sociocultural constraints, which are themselves subject to reproduction and change through such human activities. Time depth and historical scope are now more likely to be included in anthropological descriptions and analyses than in the past (e.g., Fox, 1991), and accounts of the concrete activities, interpretations, and struggles of specific individuals and groups are favored over generalizations that seem vacuous because they remove cultural practices from the richness and reality of social life and the interrelationship of individual variation, novelty, and cultural creation (e.g., Abu-Lughod, 1991, 1993).[2]

Harkness (1992) notes that recent work in anthropology and human development, located in the subdisciplines of psychological anthropology or cultural psychology (see Schwartz, White, & Lutz, 1992; Stigler, Shweder, & Herdt, 1990), has also moved away from broad generalizations and cross-cultural comparisons of the effects of child-rearing practices on personality and behavior. Contemporary studies emphasize instead the processes of children's language socialization and the importance of linguistic forms in children's acquisition of cultural dispositions (e.g., Ochs & Schieffelin, 1984) and in the socialization of affect and social identity (e.g., Lutz, 1988; Miller & Moore, 1989; Miller, Potts, Fung, Hoogstra, & Mintz, 1990; Miller & Sperry, 1987; Skinner, 1989). Much of this research illustrates the ways in which cultural forms or models act as vehicles that shape and inform the developing individual's cultural knowledge and notions of self. It takes a practice-oriented approach to human development.

Through this emphasis on process, we get a clearer view of how individuals draw upon, personalize, and develop through the cultural meanings that are embedded in everyday discourses and practices. However, little attention has been directed to the processes whereby individual and group reconstructions work back to transform these collective discourses and the cultural models that inform them. Sociogenetic researchers in contemporary psychology and anthropology argue that human development is social in origin, constituted in interactions that are located in particular historical, cultural, and social sites or activities, but few studies address how these levels and sites come together in an actual case to produce transformations. Still fewer psychological theories propose a bidirectional process of development, that is, one which explains the ways individuals and groups introduce novelty and transformations on the collective level (but see Valsiner, 1993; see also Tudge & Putnam, Chapter 9, and Shanahan, Valsiner, & Gottlieb, Chapter 2, this volume).

In this chapter, we introduce a model that elaborates how changes at the individual and collective level take place through bidirectional and interlinked processes. Specifically we direct attention to the *co*-development of identity, agency, and lived worlds. We trace out a case of co-development using an ethnographic, longitudinal case study of women's production of songs for a Nepalese festival. These songs, as cultural products, and the production of them are at the same time part and parcel of both individual and collective development. Such cultural products, we argue, are a central medium through which co-development occurs. Since our focus is on *process*, the model we propose compares individuals and groups with themselves across time; likewise, it compares cultural forms with themselves across time, and the same for lived worlds. This emphasis on processes of development that take place at individual and collective levels and how these are intermeshed with, or mediated by, cultural artifacts over time reintroduces broader historical and sociocultural conditions to anthropological studies of development.

In our efforts to elaborate this model, we have drawn inspiration from the cultural-historical school of psychology. Specifically, Vygotsky's conception of the intermeshing of simultaneously developing levels – for him, the ontogenetic, microgenetic, phylogenetic, and sociohistoric – initially spurred us to think about the relation between sociohistoric development, or cumulative change, and that of individuals. His emphasis on mediating devices, especially those that are collectively produced (cultural), further suggested a key means by which these two levels are articulated.

Vygotsky's genetic perspective centered on *process*. In particular, he wrote about the development of higher psychological functions such as sign-mediated memory, cognition, motivation, and goal-directed thought. For Vygotsky, these sign-mediated functions permitted consciousness and introduced the possibility of self-regulation and self-control (1978; also in Wertsch, 1985, chap. 2). Through the use of signs as mental tools, humans are able to affect their own mental states and gain some degree of self-direction. Without this ability we would be subject to whatever stimuli appeared in the environment; we would lack *agency*.[3]

We emphasize, as did Vygotsky (1978, 1987), the importance of symbolic mediation in the creation of higher-order knowing, particularly cultural knowing. In this view, signs or symbols are cultural-historical products that the developing individual encounters in social interactions. When the individual begins to take these signs as meaningful for him- or herself, they potentially become "mediating devices," or mental tools, for organizing knowledge about the individual and various aspects of the world (Vygotsky, 1978; Holland & Valsiner, 1988). These cultural forms play an important role in the development of identity and agency (for one example, see Cain, 1991) and, we would add, are a medium whereby the lived worlds in which these identities and agencies have meaning are created and changed.

## Identity, Agency, and Lived Worlds

By *lived worlds*, we allude to the importance of meaning in human life, as emphasized by cultural and social anthropologists. Humans live in worlds that are culturally and socially constructed. These worlds are brought to life daily by individuals and groups who have (and/or remember): (1) a history of social interactions and, so, are socially related; (2) a history of coproduced (past) practices; and (3) a history of coproduced discourses for talking about (interpreting) themselves, their relationships, and their practices.[4] These discourses are informed by cultural models (conventional standards of reference or meaning; see Quinn & Holland, 1987). Moreover, these worlds are constructed by individuals who have identities in these worlds, or notions of self to which they are emotionally attached (see later).

Lived worlds are produced under changing social and material constraints. Thus, they are also historical constructions, existing in time.[5] Examples of lived worlds that have been or could be studied include the world of romance on two campuses in the southern United States in the late 1970s to early 1980s (Holland & Eisenhart,

1990), the world of political action in Nepal in the early 1990s after the pro-democracy movement (Holland & Skinner, 1995), the world of Alcoholics Anonymous in the late 1980s (Cain, 1991), and the world of *ludruk* (a type of drama) in mid-1960s Java (Peacock, 1968). In this chapter, we examine the Tij festival and its relation to the lived worlds of domestic relations and of political action in the early 1990s in Naudada – an area of central Nepal.

Lived worlds are populated or figured by culturally constructed types of roles, or what postmodernist writers might call *subject positions*. A subject position is a view of the person that discourses and practices create, determine, and offer for the individual. Subject positions are given by the social structure and are exhibited or inhabited by individuals (Smith, 1988). The world of romance alluded earlier included couples, dates, boyfriends, for example, as well as an extensive vocabulary for describing characters in the world of romance including *hunk*, *jerk*, *prick*, and *gay* for males (Holland & Skinner, 1987). The world of political action in Nepal included the discredited *panchas*, the ascendant Nepali Congress officials, supporters of the various Communist parties, as well as words for other types of political actors, such as *mandalay* (rowdy tough guys who, for a price, stir up trouble at election time). In the world of domestic relations we find a variety of people including wives, husbands, co-wives, mothers-in-law, and husbands' older brothers.

These social and cultural constructions constitute one of the bases for the identities of individuals who participate in these lived worlds. But the concept of subject position cannot be equated to what we call identities. In the conceptualization of subject position, the individual's creation and understanding of his or her own position, identity, and subjectivity and how these develop in history are *not* the focus. Rather, a subject position is understood as one's *subjection* and placement within particular forms of control and discourse. Understood from a neo-Vygotskian and Bakhtinian perspective, identities (or selves) are psychocultural and psychosocial formations that develop as individuals and groups engage in activity in a lived world. They are perspectives on the world that are formed in experience and are named or symbolized for the self through verbal and visual depictions and other cultural devices. In one study in the United States, for example, a woman worried over whether or not she really was a "loose woman," trying on the designation, but eventually rejecting it (Holland, 1985). In another study in Nepal, women presented themselves as "good daughters-in-law" (Skinner, 1990). These types of identities are certainly not completely stable or fixed, but they are part of the person's (consciously and unconsciously) remembered history that is brought to the present and so affects the interpretation of the present. We disagree, in other words, with discourse theory in anthropology and psychology that too readily equates identity with subject positions in discourse and practice (see, e.g., Davis & Harré, 1990; Harré & Van Langenhove, 1991; Kondo, 1990).[6] Being subjected to such positions, being treated as though one fit such positions, *are* crucial events in the individual's development of identity, but as any developmental approach would argue, the individual must be recognized as having a *history-in-person.* That is, identities are developed over time in experience. They are not totally redefined at the instant one is exposed to another discourse and a different subject position. Discourse theory disregards development.

An identity, which could be called a *lived identity* to signify its association with the kind of world described earlier, entails having an ongoing point of view, an ongoing place that provides a view from somewhere (as opposed to the view from nowhere celebrated in most Western notions of cognition as separate from emotion). Having a lived identity means having a sense of one's interests and feelings related to those interests, and it means having an ongoing sense of what sort of actor one is – who one is or where one stands in the world. An identity may be composed simply of the kind of sense that Bourdieu (1977, 1990) discusses – an unarticulated "gut" sense of one's capital or standing in social interactions – or it may be more developed, more available to consciousness as in the case of the woman who heard voices accusing her of being a "loose woman" and against which she defended herself.[7] In other words, an identity could hypothetically be encompassed in Bourdieu's "habitus" (i.e., out-of-awareness; embodied, rather than linguistically mediated; dispositions sedimented from experience), but they are probably always objectified to some extent.

Aspects of lived identities (i.e., one's perspective, interests, and place in a lived world) can become more or less objectified through representation in a variety of symbolic forms, from a song to a remembered stroll through the woods to a diagnosis from the DSM-IV (*Diagnostic and Statistical Manual of Mental Disorders*, 4th ed.) To the extent that the formations are objectified and available for reflection and for use in self-regulation, the identity is a conscious one. It is difficult to imagine conscious identities or even out-of-awareness lived identities that are unassociated with emotion. Thus, we define (conscious) identities to be understandings of the self to which one is (negatively or positively) emotionally attached (see Holland et al., in preparation).

To the extent that identities are conscious, agency, in the minimum sense of being able to regulate one's own behavior in the lived world, becomes a possibility. Conceivably one could participate in a lived world without any conscious awareness of one's position, without any means of symbolizing to oneself who one is in that world. Drawing on Vygotsky's notions of higher-order psychological functions, however, we would guess that such a person would be unable to direct his or her own activity in that world and so simply be buffeted about, depending on what others are doing (for such a case, see the description of a neophyte to the world of romance in Holland, 1992). Although such a lived identity is enough to propel behavior in a lived world, it is not enough for agency. Participation in a lived world results in a perspective, a sort of rudimentary identity. Consciousness (and, hence, agency) and some modicum of self-control develop gradually through the lever of semiotic mediation.

## The Co-development of Identity, Agency, and Lived Worlds

To illuminate how identity, agency, and lived worlds are interrelated and co-developing, we will begin with a model (Figure 7.1) that we have adapted from Johnson (1987). Johnson originally developed this model to portray the circulation of and processes associated with cultural forms. He wanted to depict the ways in which *collectives* create and appropriate cultural forms. However, we find that with certain modifications this figure is useful for the depiction of processes that go on at the individual as well as the collective level.

At first we will limit our discussion to the development of identity and agency at the individual level. At Point 1 in Figure 7.1, under a particular set of social and historical conditions, an individual produces a text. *Text* is used in a broad sense here to mean a representation or description. The produced text could be in the form of a book, or it could be a sermon, a lecture, a song. It could also be a simple statement, a drawing, chart, figure, pantomime, dance, or whatever, as long as it represents some aspect of the world.[8]

In producing a text, private thoughts and feelings are externalized,

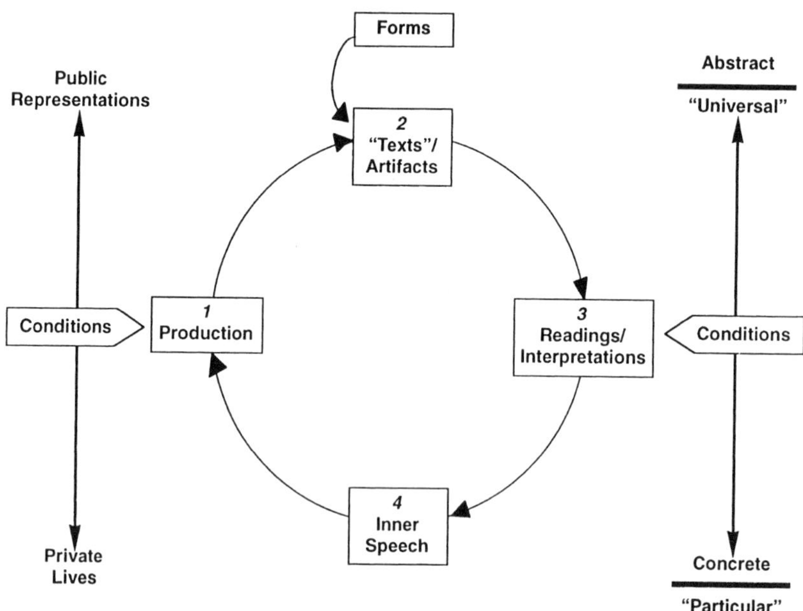


**Figure 7.1.** Development of lived identities through cultural forms. (Adapted from Johnson, 1987.)

subject to personal histories as well as the social and material conditions at hand (see Vološinov's 1986 example of representing hunger), and the text becomes public. Usually the process of turning private, internal thoughts and feelings into text is one of realizing them in conventional forms that make them more accessible to other people. Building upon notions of inner speech (Vygotsky, 1987) we might imagine that one's thoughts and feelings are represented for one's self in cryptic, condensed forms, or perhaps only in inchoate sensations. Externalizing them, then, is putting them into the form of cultural conventions or genres that are recognized and understood by others in one's social world. Academics struggle to externalize their thoughts through conventionalized forms of presented papers, refereed journal articles, and seminars. Bedouin women put sentiments that are not allowed expression in everyday discourse into a genre of poetry called *ghinnawa* (Abu-Lughod, 1986). Nepalese women use Tij songs and other song genres to tell others about their hardships and to criticize those who mistreat them. These songs are representations of the position of women in Nepalese society (see Holland & Skinner, 1995; Skinner, 1990; Skinner, Holland & Adhikari, 1994).

The externalized text – the academic paper or talk, or the Tij song – tends to be structured and presented in particular ways in accordance with specific cultural forms, but its outcome is not totally predictable. Novelty can emerge through the dialectical interplay of personal experience and cultural forms and through practices (re)produced under changing social and historical conditions (for examples, see Barth, 1987; Bourdieu, 1977, 1990; Egnor 1986; Holland & Skinner, 1995; Obeyesekere, 1981; Skinner, Valsiner, & Basnet, 1991).

Once placed in public space, the texts are "read" by others as these others are affected and informed by sociohistorical conditions. *Reading* here means interpreting, understanding, or taking in what is presented. The producer reads what he or she has generated. So do others. They interpret the text in certain ways, and these interpretations are incorporated, along with other readings of other texts, back into the individual producer's inner life or inner speech.[9] Perhaps these interpretations or readings of others become resources for thinking about something in the world, or ways to evoke particular feelings (Holland & Valsiner, 1988). These readings as particularized and privatized in the individual become part of the new cycle of production and externalization. Obviously, as one participates in these worlds via these genres, one's thoughts and feelings are likely to develop in relation to these genres in a way such that, over time, inner speech is affected.

Here we must make another modification of Johnson's figure. He was concerned to present the chief moments in the circuits of cultural forms, not to make the additional point that these forms continue and change or develop through time and acquire a history. Theories of cultural production assume that the circuit of cultural products produces qualitative change in subjectivities. To better understand the dynamics of this process, it is useful to imagine Johnson's circle as a spiral moving in time. In Figure 7.2, the bottom spiral represents the development of individual identity as mediated by cultural forms. These forms, as resources for thinking and feeling about events in the world and selves in the world, contribute to the development of an individual's subjectivity, identity, and understanding of self as a particular type of self and agent. We will illustrate this process with an example from our fieldwork in Nepal.

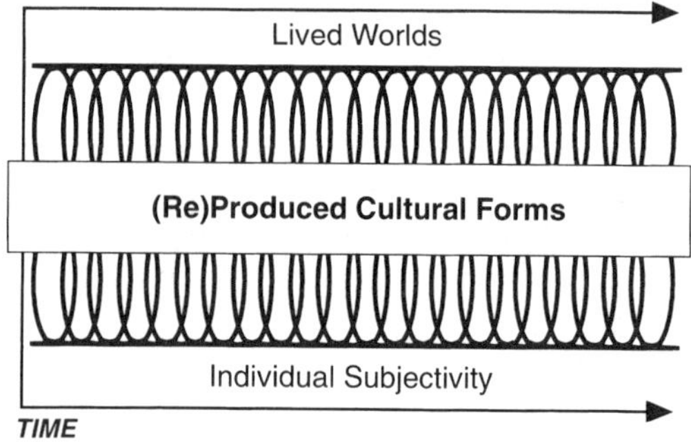


**Figure 7.2.** Co-development of individual agency and lived worlds.

## The Development of Identity and Agency in Tij

In Naudada, a Hindu mixed-caste, rural community where we have done intensive research, and in many other parts of Nepal, girls and women produced and performed songs for the annual Tij festival.[10] These songs were part of a much larger ritual complex that is described at length elsewhere (Bennett, 1983; Holland & Skinner, 1995; Skinner, Holland, & Adhikari, 1994). During this festival, women, primarily from the two highest castes (Bahun and Chetri), carried out a series of rituals and activities over a 4-day period.[11] On the day of Tij itself, they dressed in their finest apparel and jewelry and danced and sang in front of a large audience of men, other women, and children. All the while they underwent a stringent fast to ensure the health and long life of their (future) husbands. Two days later, on Rishi Panchami, the ritual complex ended with an intricate bathing rite done by the women, to absolve themselves of any sins they may have committed because of menstruation, and with a final worship ceremony performed by a Hindu priest.[12]

What is of interest to us here are the songs that the women produced and practiced for several weeks before the festival and then sang on the day of Tij. We will use Figure 7.1 to discuss the development of identity of a Naudadan woman through this cultural form of Tij songs.

Renu, a Chetri[13] woman who was in her mid-twenties in 1991, lived in her *māita* (natal home) in one of the hamlets that made up the community of Naudada. Renu never attended school, but her parents arranged for her to marry an educated man. According to Renu, her husband soon came to have contempt for her because she was uneducated. This, coupled with his being a drunkard, forced her to leave her husband's home (*ghar*) and return to her natal home to live and find support. After her return, she composed several songs for Tij, which she and her friends and female relatives performed for the festival. Her songs included autobiographical references and seemed to be a medium she deftly used to externalize her inner thoughts and emotions. The following song is one that Renu composed for the 1991 Tij festival:[14]

*Song No. 1*

I worked all day on the flat lands of Salyantar.
On that long road, no one was there.
Though I say no one, my husband was walking with me.
He didn't say a single word on this long road.
I walked ahead and my husband walked behind.
My husband did not scold me [i.e., although angry, as indicated by his silence, he did not scold her].
If he didn't like me, why did he marry me?
If I walk ahead and behind, why did he turn his eyes away from me [i.e., why was he angry]?
When I went inside and out, my mother-in-law didn't want to see me.
Though it was a time of drought, my tears created a lake.
You knead flour in a plate and [separate] oil from water.[15]
If my husband doesn't like me, he will return the *sindūr* (vermilion powder).
By fate, you are [as] the brother and I am [as] the sister.
Then I'll say I'm unmarried and go to the river.

In these verses, Renu expressed her distress at her husband's and mother-in-law's contempt for her. Her husband was so angry that he could not even speak to her; her mother-in-law could not bear to look at her. She worried that her husband would take away the vermilion powder (*sindūr*) that women wear in their hair as a symbol of being married. If he did this, she threatened to "go to the river," a very literal reference to suicide (village women sometimes committed suicide by throwing themselves in rivers swollen by monsoon rains).

In a song that Renu composed the year before, in 1990, she sang of a husband who was a drunkard and who squandered the family's wealth and property on alcohol. She criticized the inheritance system that keeps property in the patriline and relegates women to being "outsiders" in both their husband's house and their natal home:

*Song No. 2*

In Pokhara, [there is] an electricity line;
Listen to the description of the drunken husband.
Rising in the morning, he goes down to the hotel;
Who will do the household chores?
The hotel girl has probably [already] made the tea [for the day].
The *raksī* [distilled alcohol] has finished all the money.
The household wealth has all gone to the *hironī* [a cinema role – refers to a hotel girl here].
The most fertile land is all finished because of his drinking *raksī*.
Whatever money you have, it is not enough;
Two or even four bottles of *raksī* are not enough for you.
If I say, "Don't drink," he replies, "I'm not drinking your father's [property]."
The most fertile land is gone and still he does not know [how much he has spent].
The best land is gone because of the drunkard husband;
How will we spend our lives?
The whole day the husband king drinks a jar [of *raksī*];
[The wife says,] You don't need to return home after drinking there in the evening.
In Pokhara bazaar, [there is] an electricity line;
The household property is not mine.
The housewife is an outsider;
All the household property is needed [for *raksī*].
If this wife is not enough, you can get another;
The head of the cock will be caught [i.e., with two wives he'll have problems].
Why do you hold your head [looking worried]? Go sell the buffalo and pigs;
If you don't have enough money [for *raksī*], you will even sell your wife.
After selling his wife, he'll become a *jogī* [here, a beggar without a wife].
I, the daughter, will go stay at my *māita* [natal home].
If I want a man, I can find one just like you;
For my parents' reputation, I have to stay with you.

Renu became an expert at producing Tij songs of a certain type, the *dukhako gīt* (song of hardship), and indeed, her two songs chronicled and criticized the suffering and difficulties she had experienced. This type of song is a cultural form that Renu had learned from joining other women in the activities of the Tij festival, where these songs were sung and produced. It is a conventionalized form that is immediately recognizable through its lyrics, meter, and rhyme as both a song of hardship and a Tij song. It is a cultural form, but Renu's externalizations into this genre included her own creative productions about her experiences and understandings of her life.

Renu and other women described to us the process of creating the songs. Renu told us that the songs came forth from her *man* (heart, mind, seat of emotions located in the center of the chest).[16] She "placed" and "stored up" thoughts and feelings in her *man*, where they "churned about" and "poured forth" in the verses of Tij songs. She also told us that once she composed these songs, she kept them in her *man* and often sang them to herself, even after the time of Tij had passed.

She drew on her experiences, recalled in inner speech, to produce verses in the form of a song that was made public and read by her audience. In fact, her songs did evoke comments by the larger group. Several women were moved by the second song, especially. Some women wept when they heard it. One woman spoke of it making her own *man* churn. For this woman, it evoked memories and emotions associated with her own husband's drinking and gambling. Women in the audience interpreted Renu's song as representative of the hard times that women face in moving to their husband's home upon marriage, where they become servants to the household, where their fates are uncertain, and where husbands and in-laws, especially mothers-in-law, may mistreat them. Renu certainly heard these audience responses. They perhaps entered into her ongoing interpretations of her life to be externalized again in the form of new songs.

Renu, like other women in Naudada (Skinner 1989, 1990), had appropriated Tij songs as a way of thinking and feeling about her life as a woman in this society. The songs contributed to the development of her identity, her understanding of herself as female. These songs, these cultural forms, and the way they were produced and used in women's interaction with other women in the Tij song groups, affected women's understanding of themselves as females in the lived world of family and domestic relations.

These songs were also important forms whereby women developed agency. Through these songs plus exposure to other cultural forms, women developed a particular consciousness of themselves in the world of domestic relations as they were construed in Nepal. They became, through the medium of Tij songs, critical commentators on their lives in families and their various roles as daughters, sisters, daughters-in-law, and wives. For many of those who became engaged with the women's Tij groups and with composing and singing the songs, the role of commentator was salient. Over the course of our research (Skinner first watched Tij sessions in Naudada in 1986), we watched young girls in households that participated in Tij hover on the periphery of the practice sessions and gradually start to take on a larger role. Over the years they became proficient in producing critical commentaries, and they, inferring from their descriptions of their concerns and choices in life, developed identities or self-understandings informed by this critical stance on women's positions within the family (see Holland & Skinner, 1995; Skinner & Holland, in preparation). As the cycle of song production continued, these girls developed not only expertise and cultural knowledge about the domestic worlds in which they participated as daughters, sisters, and, eventually, young wives, but also a sense of themselves as participants symbolized through Tij songs.

The idea that identity and agency, along with expertise and saliency, co-develop in lived worlds has several implications.[17] First, it is likely that comparisons of a number of different women over time would show that some girls never became intensely engaged with the Tij groups and with the songs. While some women developed into proficient songwriters called *sipālu* (experts), others were content to sing along with the group, but not develop proficiency in creating new songs. Those who were less caught up with the songs did not view their lives in the same way as those who were more engaged. Since Tij was (until the recent advent of political discourse on women's position) one of the few sources of critical reflection on women's roles, the cultural knowing of critical perspectives among these relatively uninvolved girls and young women, one would suppose, was simply less developed. Another implication is that their understanding of themselves in the world of family relations was different from that of the girls and women who were involved with the Tij groups' song production and performance. One overall conclusion we draw from our work, in other words, it that there is likely to be significant variation within a cultural group depending upon the ways in which individuals are brought into socially interacted, lived worlds via cultural forms.

## The Development of Lived Worlds

Analogous developmental processes also occur at the collective level: Cultural forms mediate the development of lived worlds. In the case of Tij, the lived world mediated by the Tij *dukha* songs related to the world of family relations. In Naudada and elsewhere in Hindu Nepal, family relations were shaped by a number of practices and expectations. Girls were expected to be good, hard-working, and obedient daughters who would eventually marry. Upon marriage women left their natal homes (*māita*) for the home of their husbands (*ghar*). At the *ghar*, daughters-in-law were expected to be obedient, respectful, and diligent in their household and agricultural duties, laboring from dawn to dark for the in-laws. As wives, women were expected to devote themselves to their husbands, seeing to their needs and obeying their demands. A woman was valued more highly when she gave birth to sons who would carry on the patriline. Only as a mother of sons was she likely to attain more status in the household. With the marriage of her own sons, she gained even more status and power as she directed the activities of the daughters-in-law (Skinner, 1990).

As women moved through this life trajectory from daughter to wife to mother-in-law, they experienced the hardships that came from being under the control of fathers, husbands, and in-laws and from a system that privileged males. Girls, for example, were less likely to have access to schools than were their brothers. They saw their brothers receiving preferential treatment and better clothes and food, they worked longer hours at home and in the field while their brothers played or went to school, and they were aware that the system of inheritance provided their brothers with property, while they received none (Skinner, 1990).

*Dukha* (hardship, suffering) songs provided a critical discourse on these family relations. They were a commentary on the problems women faced in this type of social world and a protest against the system that relegated them to the least powerful levels. Specific *dukha* songs criticized parents for sending sons instead of daughters to school, for giving sons more clothes, and for marrying them off to husbands who came from impoverished households or who gambled, drank, and beat their wives. They criticized their malefactors – the mother-in-law or husband or father who treated them with contempt, no matter how much work they did. In verse, women castigated the system of marriage that made daughters only guests in their natal homes until they were sent away to a husband. They called into question the system of inheritance that gave women only very limited rights to parental and spousal property and increased their constant vulnerability to having to share their husband's affection and resources with a co-wife (see Skinner et al., 1994).[18]

The development of these lived worlds, though intermeshed with individual development of identity and agency, occurs on a collective level. Turning to Figure 7.3, which modifies Figure 7.1 to fit the collective process, we can think of individuals working together in various ways to produce cultural texts. Although novel Tij songs were developed out of private lives and personal senses, they were most often turned into culturally accessible forms through collaborative or cooperative efforts (see Holland & Skinner, 1995; Holland & Skinner, in press; Skinner et al., 1994). The texts were made public and read (Point 3), and then were incorporated into the lived culture (Point 4). This lived culture, or the ways that people actually bring texts into everyday life, into concrete social situations with all the complexities, ambiguities, tensions, emotions, negotiations, and struggles this entails, in turn shapes the discourses and practices of people, some of which may emerge in the next round of cultural production, in new combinations, extensions, or elaborations. Culture as lived goes on to produce cultural forms that are responses to the social and material conditions at hand. These productions, in turn, are appropriated into and mediate change in the collective world. Lived worlds can be developed in new directions by a novel cultural form (Holland & Valsiner, 1988).

For the Tij case, we have songs produced in Naudada and elsewhere in Nepal from four different years (the festival is held annually toward the end of August or beginning of September): 1986, 1990, 1991, and 1992.[19] Comparing those songs and knowing what events were occurring in the community and the larger region and nation, we argue that the cultural forms of Tij songs were important in developing the collective sense of women's rights and so affected the development of the lived worlds of politics and family life such that constructions of women's roles in those worlds were changing.

Nepal, in 1990, was very much affected by an important political

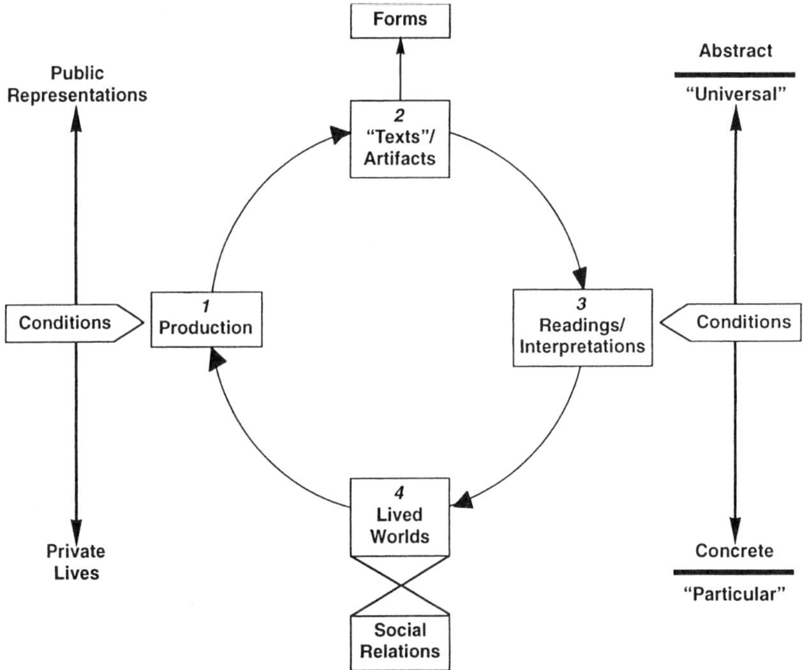


**Figure 7.3.** Development of collective identities through cultural forms. (Adapted from Johnson, 1987.)

event. A people's movement for democracy succeeded in abolishing the panchayat, or one-party, system of government that had been installed by the king some 30 years earlier. Further, the king of Nepal relinquished some of his powers under the new constitution. Nepal's government was transformed from an absolute monarchy to a constitutional monarchy, and political parties became legal and gained strength. This new era ushered in a feeling of freedom and a call for human rights. Beginning in 1990 after the revolution and especially in 1991 after the establishment of the multiparty system and general elections, political Tij songs became much more widely sung in Naudada and throughout Nepal.

These political, or *rājnīti*, songs were significant in producing, on the individual level, a different kind of identity and agency than that associated with *dukha* songs, and, on the collective level, an orientation to the world of politics. *Dukha* songs provided commentary on domestic relations; *rājnīti* songs provided commentary on the government's treatment of women. The people's movement removed people's fear of expressing political opinions. Women were less afraid to sing *rājnīti* songs in public. What we saw in the Tij festival of 1991, the year after the uprising, was a burgeoning of songs that criticized the former panchayat government as well as the Nepali Congress Party (the party that was victorious in winning a majority of positions in the new government) for their treatment of women.[20]

Although the Tij groups were the same, we found a different set of participants stepping forward to write the *rājnīti* songs. Kamala, a 13-year-old Chetri girl, provided an example. Kamala lived in the same area as Renu, but unlike Renu, she had been to school. In 1991, at the time of our in-depth study of Tij, she was attending the eighth grade. She revealed a strong sense of herself as a student and was clearly developing, as were many of her sister schoolgirls, a view of herself as a politically active person. Like Renu, she was recognized as an expert at song composition, but her songs were oriented to a different arena or field of action than were Renu's songs. Kamala composed *rājnīti* Tij songs that were critical of regional and national politics and that called for equal rights before the law and in government policy for women and the poor.[21] In the following song, produced and performed by Kamala and her Tij song group, we find verses that condemn the old political system for exploiting women and call for a new political party that will give women equal rights under the law:

*Song No. 3*

Oh, dominated sisters of Nepal,
We have so much tyranny.
The *panchas* [officials of the former one-party panchayat system]
ate the flesh and also the blood [of the people];
At last we have the multiparty system.
The thirty-year panchayat reign gave so much trouble to women;
They [the *panchas*] drank liquor by selling unmarried girls.
They sold our innocent sisters
And filled their bellies with liquor and chicken.
For even a small thing, they call a meeting [to get money];
*Panchas* took bribes – their reign is like this.
The administration [*panchas*] was like this,
The *panchas* dominated women.
Now this type of rule cannot be tolerated.
Women will no longer tolerate what they did in the past.

Understanding these things, we moved forward;
We fought in the people's movement.
Rise up, women, now we don't have to fear,
Clapping cannot be done by a single hand.
On the day of Baishak, 29, 2048,
There will be a general election.
There are so many parties in the multiparty system,
At last we need the party that benefits us.
A party called the Democratic Party was established;
It deleted the name panchayat and deceived the people.
If this party wins, it will be the same as before;
Women will not have rights and they will have to weep all of
their life.
There is a party called Congress;
If this party wins, women will have to suffer more.
There is another party called Communist;
If this party wins, women will get rights.
The symbol of Communists is the sickle and hammer;
Women, let's publicize the Communist symbol.
Though I want to stop my pen, it doesn't stop;
Goodbye to my respected listeners.

In song, officials of the former panchayat system were accused of selling women as prostitutes to India, taking bribes, and exploiting the people. The singers assailed two political parties as abusers of women's rights, and promoted the Communist Party as the only one that would bring justice to women. In the next song, sung in 1992 by Kamala and her group, women demanded equal access to education and jobs and a recognition that women are as capable as men in developing the country:

*Song No. 4 – Tyranny over Women*

Listen sisters, listen society;
Today I am going to speak about tyranny over women.
The male and female born from the same womb
Do not have equal rights.
The son gets the ancestral property at the age of fourteen,
Whereas the daughter has to get married when she is only twelve.
Parents engage in great trickery,
Sending their daughter weeping to her husband's house.
Parents send the son to school,
Whereas they are afraid to provide education to the daughter.
Father bought books and pens for my younger brother,

> Whereas he wove a basket [for carrying loads] for me, the daughter.
> My name is Kamala, who has studied only to the eighth grade,
> But who has a great desire for further education.
> Parents, don't take me out of school,
> See if I can study well or not.
> Parents, if you provide me an education, I won't fail,
> And after study, I can live by myself.
> Parents, provide me an education at any cost,
> And later when I hold a job, I will repay you.
> We women are also energetic and want justice;
> We also have the right to hold a job.
> A red ribbon tied around black hair,
> We women are always deprived in Nepal.
> Women have even climbed Mt. Everest and reached the moon;
> Women have done so many things in this world.
> Women of other countries are pilots;
> We Nepalese women will be happy if we get the chance to be great women.
> Therefore, women of Nepal, this is not the time to be silent;
> Let's fight to obtain our rights.

Political songs such as these were involved in a different construction of being female – a different way of understanding one's self and other women as figures in a world affected by the government and party politics. As they produced and incorporated political song texts, Kamala and the other women in her Tij song group were developing ways of conceptualizing themselves as politically aware actors and activists in a political world.[22]

These *rājnīti* songs, we argue, were important in the formation of individual identity and agency, as postulated for *dukha* songs, but they, as had the *dukha* songs, also affected the Tij groups as whole. The songs described women as actors in the world of politics who were creating a new role for women in that world. In place of the criticism of mothers-in-law and husbands found in *dukha* songs, these songs had to do with the political world of voting, elections, and processions. In 1991 in Naudada, a women's procession formed and marched through several hamlets. The women shouted demands: "Men, stop drinking alcohol! Stop gambling! Don't marry your daughters so young! Give women equal rights!" About this time, there was also an incident in Naudada in which a posse of 15 women armed with sticks surrounded a man who had beaten his wife. These women threatened that if he ever beat his wife again, they would beat him. Some of the demands and concerns expressed in the procession and by the posse were clearly related to the themes of past *dukha* songs, but the demands for change and action were even more evident in the *rājnīti* songs. The following song, which was sung in 1991, combines both the *dukha* song's concern with a drunkard husband with the *rājnīti* song's concern for action to procure a betterment of women's position:

*Song No. 5*

Our brothers of Ward Two,
It is our request that you don't drink *raksī.*
In Ward Two of our village, don't drink *raksī* in this area.
Brothers, you keep this in your mind;
You remove *raksī* and gambling from here.
The drunkards are treated as animals;
People will give them grass to eat.
The dignity of our village is gone;
You are not allowed to sell *raksī* in the shops.
Otherwise you are not allowed to keep a shop;
After drinking *raksī* you people walk, saying nonsense.
The oxen [drunkards] are used for plowing fields;
From now you quit playing cards [gambling] and drinking *raksī.*
You move forward to bring the revolution;
You wasted rice making *raksī.*
You killed the poor people;
*Raksī* was free in the panchayat period.
Star beer [a specific brand] was started in the Congress period;
Communism is needed to stop *raksī.*
We can get rights only when Communism comes.

From these verses, we see that Tij songs not only served as a means for self-understanding and the development of identity on the individual level; they also served as a means of expressing and developing a collective sense of action.

## Conclusion

We have argued that years and years of Tij songs have been important at both the individual and collective level. During some period in the past, perhaps from their inception, Tij songs became a medium for describing women's worlds and the position of women in those worlds. Women's groups, in preparing songs for the Tij festival, at some point began to articulate a critical commentary on the world of domestic relations and, much more infrequently until the people's movement, on the world of political action. These songs provided a means though which individual women's identities developed. Individual women could and did use the songs to form an articulate sense of their position, interests, and criticisms of the world of domestic relations in Naudada. Recently, some of the groups, or at least some members of the groups, began the same process with respect to the world of political action.

Lived worlds themselves can become more or less vibrant, more or less encompassing of the lives of their members. The Tij festival was (and at the time of this writing, still is) the site of cultural production of an important genre of songs; it was also the site, during the period of song practice, of a world in itself. For a brief period at the time of the festival, the women got together in practice sessions and welcomed home their out-married sisters who were permitted to return for the festival. Some of the practice sessions occurred at night at one or another member's house. The sessions had an air of joviality, festivity, and sentimentality that was out of the ordinary; married women did not often get to come back home, nor did the women of Naudada have much opportunity to go about at night. As we argue elsewhere (Holland & Skinner, 1995; Skinner et al., 1994), a special atmosphere was created at the time of Tij – a sort of a time-bound world of the festival.

Over the period of our research, this time-bound world began to expand. Women in the Tij groups became less circumscribed in time by others as to when they could make up Tij songs, the songs produced by the groups became more widely circulated in both handwritten versions and published songbooks, and the relations between the women in many of the groups became more multistranded. That is, some of the women in the Tij groups began to relate to one another not just as sisters and friends, but also as political actors and, in one case, as a literacy teacher promoting equal rights.

Women in these groups also became more expansive as agents in the worlds of domestic relations and political action. The women from the Tij groups who instigated and/or participated in the march and/or the posse became more demanding in both the world of political action and the world of domestic relations. The influence of these Tij groups extended outside of Tij Day by forms (songbooks) that carried their songs to other arenas and across broader expanses of time.

If we had limited our study to either the sociohistorical or ontogenetic level, we would have missed the ways that each level dynamically informed and motivated the other. We would have missed the ways that cultural forms drive qualitative change in lived worlds and, at the same time, inform individual identity and agency. The identities of Renu and Kamala and their possibilities for agency were crucially formed through similar processes revolving around the same cultural genre of Tij songs, but this genre itself was a medium for change in the lived worlds important to them. When Renu began to participate in Tij, the possibilities for political action were tightly controlled for most of the men of Naudada, not to mention the women. Kamala was growing up in a period of less government repression and at a time when the subjectivities developed, in part, through Tij songs were important in the reconstruction of the political world. As a consequence, Renu and Kamala developed very different gender identities, very different senses of themselves as women in the lived worlds they inhabited. Despite the fact that they sang similar songs in the same public area on the day of the Tij festival, they participated from the basis of very different histories-in-person. Just as we have argued against approaches such as discourse theory that depend on a nondevelopmental view of individuals, we argue against developmental approaches that depend on a nondevelopmental view of the lived worlds of individuals and that rely on a nondynamic view of culture.

## Notes

1. Linguistics has undergone a similar development. Sociolinguists view language from the vantage point of language in practice. For an overview on anthropology's shift to practice theory, see Ortner (1984).
2. An example of this reformulation can be seen in the changing treatment of comparative questions, such as the cross-cultural variation of personhood. In an 1984 article, Shweder and Bourne set forth to answer the question, Does the concept of the person vary cross-culturally? They summed up decades of research on the issue, answered affirmatively that concepts do vary, and characterized one of the major dimensions along which selves vary across culture. Since then a number of articles (Ewing, 1990; Holland,

1992; Holland & Kipnis, 1994; Murray, 1993; Spiro, 1993) have challenged these generalizations primarily because they sacrifice any understanding of dynamics and process, and so obscure much more than they reveal.

3. Note that the view of agency envisioned through Vygotsky's concepts is one that is both constrained and enabled by cultural forms and social interaction. This view is far afield from the usual Western notion of free will.
4. *Discourse* is broadly defined to include forms other than talk – e.g., songs.
5. Bourdieu's (1990) "fields" are one way of analyzing or characterizing these lived worlds, a way that emphasizes power relations. As with Bourdieu's notion of fields, we conceptualize lived worlds as interrelated with one another.
6. Actually, Kondo's (1990) ethnographic account shows a more subtle analysis than presented in her discussion of her theoretical stance.
7. Bakhtin's notion of voices is important for our concept of identity. Identity is not necessarily a settled or uncontested topic, but may be more of a matter of self-discussion (see also Holland et al., in preparation).
8. Although none has yet occurred to us, we clearly need a term better suited to our purposes than *text*. As Steve Parish pointed out to us, the term *text* has associations with printed matter, with a fixed form, with a fait accompli. We agree; these associations are counter to the way in which many cultural forms that we subsume under *text* are encountered. The cultural forms that we emphasize in this chapter, for example, are songs. They are produced and performed in a context that is part of their effect, and they lack the fixity that we associate with printed matter.
9. The dimensions of inner speech and the nature of the intersection of multiple voices can probably best be characterized using Bakhtinian notions such as heteroglossia, voices, dialogicality, and authorship (Bakhtin, 1981, 1984). These ideas and their applications to the "space of authoring" (i.e., the space within which voices are intersecting and being manipulated by the authoring process) are elaborated at length in Holland, Lachicotte, Skinner, Cain, and Prillaman (in preparation). See also Skinner and Valsiner (in preparation) for a discussion of the extent to which Bakhtinian ideas are useful for understanding the development of this authoring or orchestrating process.
10. Although we are certain that many of the practices and activities noted here are still descriptive of the current situation in Naudada,

because of the concern in anthropology about writing in the "ethnographic present" and hence freezing people in time, we employ the past tense.

11. Tij is associated in the literature and in people's thinking with Bahun and Chetri women. Women from these two castes have been the central participants in the rituals and song performance of Tij. Yet our observations in Naudada and elsewhere in Nepal, as well as those of Ahearn (1991) in the Tansen region, indicate that some women from other castes and ethnic groups sang, composed, and performed Tij songs. For the area we observed, we have described the differential participation in Tij by women of different ages, caste/ethnic groups, interests and skills in Holland and Skinner (1995) and Skinner et al. (1994).
12. The Tij–Rishi Panchami festival is complex in both its associations with Hindu texts and Brahmanical ideology and its actual enactments in practice. More details can be found in Bennett (1983), Bista (1969), Bouillier (1982), and Skinner et al. (1994).
13. From the viewpoint of Hindu caste ideology, Chetri is one of the two highest castes in Nepal. Bahun, or Brahman, claims the highest ranking.
14. We collected verses from and/or information about more than 1,000 songs. A sample of songs, including this one, are both translated and transliterated in romanized Nepali in Skinner et al. (1994).
15. A confusing line, but Naudadans thought it meant that the daughter-in-law and mother-in-law do not get along.
16. See Parish (1991) and McHugh (1989) for accounts of somewhat similar concepts used by the Newar and Gurung, respectively, in Nepal.
17. See Holland (1992) for an exposition and another case of the co-development of identification, expertise, and saliency.
18. This critical discourse mediated by *dukha* songs was not the only type of discourse that existed concerning the world of family relations. Brahmanical texts and rituals mediated a discourse and ideology more in line with the traditional life path, one that exhorted the good woman and urged her to carry out her duties cheerfully and religiously.
19. We also interviewed women about songs they remembered from long ago and we saw similar collections that others had made (see Skinner et al., 1994).
20. There were also pro-Congress Tij songs and ones that criticized the various communist parties in Nepal and practices of communist

governments abroad, although these were fewer in number. See Holland and Skinner (1995) and Skinner et al. (1994) for more details on the types of political songs and the composition of the groups that performed them.

21. *Rājnīti* songs were in the repertoire of Tij song groups before the pro-democracy movement. After the movement, it was less dangerous to sing them. They proliferated in great number (see Holland & Skinner, 1995).
22. For the importance attached to "awareness" or "consciousness" in relation to Nepal's political and social history, see Holland and Skinner (1995) and Skinner and Holland (1996).

## References


Abu-Lughod, L. (1986). *Veiled sentiments: Honor and poetry in a Bedouin society*. Berkeley: University of California Press.

(1991). Writing against culture. In R. Fox (Ed.), *Recapturing anthropology: Working in the present* (pp. 137–162). Santa Fe, NM: School of American Research Press.

(1993).*Writing women's worlds: Bedouin stories.* Berkeley: University of California Press.

Ahearn, L. (1991, November). *The emergence of cultural meaning in a Nepali women's songfest.* Paper presented at the 20th Annual South Asia Meetings, Madison, Wisconsin.

Bakhtin, M. (1981). *The dialogic imagination.* Austin: University of Texas Press.

(1984). *Problems of Dostoevsky's poetics.* Minneapolis: University of Minnesota Press.

Barth, F. (1987). *Cosmologies in the making: A generative approach to cultural variation in inner New Guinea.* Cambridge University Press.

Bennett, L. (1983). *Dangerous wives and sacred sisters: Social and symbolic roles of high-caste women in Nepal.* New York: Columbia University Press.

Bista, K. (1969). Tîj ou la fête des femmes. *Objets et Mondes*, *9*, 7–18.

Bouillier, V. (1982). Si les femmes faisaient la fête: A propos des fêtes feminines dans les hautes castes Indo-Nepalaises. *L'Homme*, *22*, 91–118.

Bourdieu, P. (1977). *Outline of a theory of practice.* Cambridge University Press.

(1990). *The logic of practice.* Stanford, CA: Stanford University Press.

Cain, C. (1991). Personal stories: Identity acquisition and self-understanding in Alcoholics Anonymous. *Ethos*, *19*, 210–253.

Davis, B., & Harré, R. (1990). Positioning: The discursive production of selves. *Journal for the Theory of Social Behavior*, *20*, 43–64.

Egnor, M. (1986). Internal iconicity in Paraiyar “crying songs.” In S. Blackburn & A. Ramanujan (Eds.), *Another harmony: New essays on the folklore of India* (pp. 294–344). Berkeley: University of California Press.

Ewing, K. (1990). The illusion of wholeness: Culture, self, and the experience of inconsistency. *Ethos*, *18*, 251–278.

Fox, R. (Ed.). (1991). *Recapturing anthropology: Working in the present.* Santa Fe, NM: School of American Research Press.

Harkness, S. (1992). Human development in psychological anthropology. In T. Schwartz, G. White, & C. Lutz (Eds.), *New directions in psychological anthropology* (pp. 102–122). Cambridge University Press.

Harré, R., & Van Langenhove, L. (1991). Varieties of positioning. *Journal for the Theory of Social Behavior*, *21*, 391–407.

Holland, D. (1985). From situation to impression: How Americans use cultural knowledge to get to know themselves and one another. In J. Dougherty (Ed.), *Directions in cognitive anthropology* (pp. 389–411). Urbana: University of Illinois Press.

(1992). How cultural systems become desire: A case study of American romance. In R. D’Andrade & C. Strauss (Eds.), *Human motives and cultural models* (pp. 61–89). Cambridge University Press.

Holland D., Lachicotte, W., Skinner, D., Cain, C., & Prillaman, R. (in preparation). Emerging selves: Identities forming in and against cultural worlds. Cambridge, MA: Harvard University Press.

Holland, D., & Eisenhart, M. (1990). *Educated in romance.* Chicago: University of Chicago Press.

Holland, D., & Kipnis, A. (1994). Metaphors for embarrassment and stories of exposure: The not-so-egocentric self in American culture. *Ethos*, *22*, 316–342.

Holland, D., & Skinner, D. (1987). Prestige and intimacy: The cultural models behind Americans’ talk about gender types. In D. Holland & N. Quinn (Eds.), *Cultural models in language and thought* (pp. 78–111). Cambridge University Press.

(1995). Contested ritual, contested femininities: (Re)forming self and society in a Nepali women’s festival. *American Ethnologist*, *22*, 279–305.

(in press). Not written by the fate-writer: Activity theory and women’s critical commentary in Nepal. *Folk: The Journal of the Danish Ethnographic Society*, *37*.

Holland, D., & Valsiner, J. (1988). Cognition, symbols and Vygotsky’s developmental psychology. *Ethos*, *16*, 247–272.

Johnson, R. (1987). What is cultural studies anyway. *Social Text: Theory/Culture/Ideology*, *16*, 38–80.

Kondo, D. (1990). *Crafting selves: Power, gender, and discourses of identity in a Japanese workplace.* Chicago: University of Chicago Press.

Lutz, C. (1988). *Unnatural emotions.* Chicago: University of Chicago Press.

McHugh, E. (1989). Concepts of the person among the Gurungs of Nepal. *American Ethnologist, 16,* 75–86.

Miller, P., & Moore, B. (1989). Narrative conjunctions of caregiver and child: A comparative perspective on socialization through stories. *Ethos, 17,* 43–64.

Miller, P., Potts, R., Fung, H., Hoogstra, L., & Mintz, J. (1990). Narrative practices and the social construction of self in childhood. *American Ethnologist, 17,* 292–311.

Miller, P., & Sperry, L. (1987). The socialization of anger and aggression. *Merrill-Palmer Quarterly, 33,* 1–31.

Murray, D. (1993). What is the Western concept of the self? On forgetting David Hume. *Ethos, 21,* 3–23.

Obeyesekere, G. (1981). *Medusa's hair: An essay on personal symbols and religious experience.* Chicago: University of Chicago Press.

Ochs, E., & Schieffelin, B. (1984). Language acquisition and socialization: Three developmental stories. In R. Shweder & R. LeVine (Eds.), *Culture theory: Essays on mind, self, and emotion* (pp. 276–320). Cambridge University Press.

Ortner, S. (1984). Theory in anthropology since the sixties. *Comparative Studies in Society and History, 26,* 126–166.

Parish, S. (1991). The sacred mind: Newar cultural representations of mental life and the production of moral consciousness. *Ethos, 19,* 313–351.

Peacock, J. (1968). *Rites of modernization.* Chicago: University of Chicago Press.

Quinn, N., & Holland, D. (1987). Culture and cognition. In D. Holland & N. Quinn (Eds.), *Cultural models in language and thought* (pp. 3–40). Cambridge University Press.

Schwartz, T., White, G., & Lutz, C. (Eds.). (1992). *New directions in psychological anthropology.* Cambridge University Press.

Shweder, R., & Bourne, E. (1984). Does the concept of the person vary cross-culturally? In R. Shweder & R. LeVine (Eds.), *Culture theory: Essays on mind, self, and emotion* (pp. 158–199). Cambridge University Press.

Skinner, D. (1989). The socialization of gender identity: Observations from Nepal. In J. Valsiner (Ed.), *Child development in cultural context* (pp. 181–192). Toronto: Hogrefe & Huber.

(1990). *Nepalese children's understanding of themselves and their social world.* Ph.D. dissertation. Department of Anthropology, University of North Carolina at Chapel Hill.

Skinner, D., & Holland, D. (1996). Schools and the cultural production of the educated person in a Nepalese hill community. In B. Levinson, D. Foley, & D. Holland (Eds.), *The cultural production of the educated person: Critical ethnographies of schooling and local practice* (pp. 273–299). Albany: State University of New York Press.

Skinner, D., & Holland, D. (in preparation). Contested selves, contested femininities: Selves and society in process. In D. Skinner, A. Pach, & D. Holland (Eds.), *Selves in time and place: Identities, experience, and history in Nepal.*

Skinner, D., Holland, D., & Adhikari, G. B. (1994). The songs of Tij: A genre of critical commentary for women in Nepal. *Asian Folklore Studies, 53*, 257–303.

Skinner, D., & Valsiner, J. (in preparation). *Voices and the orchestration of self.*

Skinner, D., Valsiner, J., & Basnet, B. (1991). Singing one's life: An orchestration of personal experiences and cultural forms. *Journal of South Asian Literature, 26*, 15–43.

Smith, P. (1988). *Discerning the subject.* Minneapolis: University of Minnesota Press.

Spiro, M. (1993). Is the Western conception of the self "peculiar" within the context of world cultures? *Ethos, 21*, 107–153.

Stigler, J., Shweder, R., & Herdt, G. (Eds.). (1990). *Cultural psychology: Essays on comparative human development.* Cambridge University Press.

Valsiner, J. (1993). Bi-directional cultural transmission and constructive sociogenesis. In W. de Graff & R. Mair (Eds.), *Sociogenesis re-examined* (pp. 47–70). New York: Springer.

Vološinov, V. (1986). *Marxism and the philosophy of language.* Cambridge, MA: Harvard University Press.

Vygotsky, L. (1978). *Mind in society: The development of higher psychological processes.* Cambridge, MA: Harvard University Press.

Vygotsky, L. (1987). *Thinking and speech* (N. Minick, trans.) New York: Plenum.

Wertsch, J. (1985). *Vygotsky and the social formation of mind.* Cambridge, MA: Harvard University Press.

# 8 Sociocultural Promotions Constraining Children's Social Activity: Comparisons and Variability in the Development of Friendships

*Paul A. Winterhoff*

## Introduction

> . . . children's friendships exist within a broad ecological, societal, cultural, and historical context which cannot be ignored if we are to attain a satisfactory general understanding of [the development] of friendship in childhood. (Allen, 1981)

The social activities and social relationships of children are selectively promoted by the adult caregivers in the children's social group (Winegar, 1989). These promotions are based on socioculturally and historically constructed preferences and beliefs about the developmental needs of children and the appropriate life goals of members of the particular culture.

One way that sociocultural promotions are made concrete is by the organization and structuring of social settings for children. In this chapter I contend that such promotions of different cultural groups may be contrasted, but that their contrasting natures do not guarantee heterogeneity of children's action or development across cultures. Also, I will demonstrate that within very similar activity settings in one culture, high variability of social relationship development is prevalent. In most psychological and developmental research studies, comparisons are made to point out similarities. However, here I wish to examine developmental systems in which comparisons, both across and within sociocultural groups, tend to affirm individual differences in relationship development. The affirmation of such differences calls

The writing of this chapter was partially supported by an NICHD predoctoral traineeship awarded to the author through the auspices of the Carolina Consortium on Human Development. Thanks are due to Jonathan Tudge for support and advice, to Martie Skinner for help with data management, and to Michael Shanahan, Debra Skinner, and Jaan Valsiner for helpful comments on earlier drafts.

into question unidirectional cultural transmission models of social development.[1]

First, I will try to make plain my own metatheoretical orientation, define some key terms, and compare two metatheoretical approaches that guide research into friendship development. Subsequently, I will outline developmental theory that attempts to account for children's *active reconstructions* of sociocultural promotions. Finally, I will make comparisons of constraints on friendship development at the broad sociocultural level and the individual level within one sociocultural group. These latter comparisons are based on observational data recently collected in two U.S. kindergarten classrooms.

## *The Social Nature of Development*

The chief metatheoretical assumption of this chapter is that social activity leads development. In the case of the current subject matter this implies that individual psychological meanings and understandings concerning the functions and importance of social relationships arise from social activity taking place within socioculturally and historically organized systems (Holland & Skinner, Chapter 7, this volume; Rizzo & Corsaro, 1988; Vygotsky, 1978).[2] In fact within-group psychological constructions of, for example, the *good child* or the *friendly child* are the result of adult intersubjective understandings constructed through persons' lifelong social activity. Through their participation in socially promoted and organized settings, children actively reconstruct these adult cultural meanings and understandings about such things as friendship. In light of these active reconstructions we may view the adult–child developmental system as an open one, constantly being transformed by the interplay between sociocultural guidance and individual and collective action.

## *Open Systems of Development and Constraining Subsystems*

Since human development in all cultures is a dynamic process involving multiple levels of interaction between persons and environments, models of development are best described as open systems (von Bertalanffy, 1950). "Open systems are dependent on exchange relationships with their environments, and their structural organization is maintained or enhanced by these relationships" (Valsiner, 1987, p. 20) Within the open developmental system, socioculturally based understandings promote particular activity settings and available social others for children. Since promoted activity settings and customary child management practices constitute *partial* aspects of the general open system of development, they are best described as *subsystems*. They "share the common function of mediating the individual's developmental experience" (Super & Harkness, 1986, p. 552) and can be characterized as being enhancing, maintaining, or limiting subsystems in which development occurs (Whiting & Edwards, 1988). One might assume that the term *constraining* carries with it only the function of limiting, but the fact is that a culture's constraining organizations can also be seen as enhancing (or "enabling"; see Winegar, 1989) the person's possibilities to embark on a variety of developmental paths.

With regard to children's formation of lasting social relationships, including friendships, there are three constraining structural subsystems (Super & Harkness, 1986) that may differentially influence the enhancement, maintenance, or limitation of social-developmental processes in sociocultural systems. These subsystems are part of a network that dynamically interrelates in the larger sociocultural system of development. The constraining subsystems are (1) the pool of possible companions, (2) children's social activity settings, and (3) the control network made up of the people who actually exert influence over children's immediate activity. This particular collection of constraining subsystems may be included within the broader category of "developmental niche" proposed by Super and Harkness (1986). One might best think of this niche as a moving structure, not as a static one, fitting around the child and organized by the culture. Within this niche, development may be enhanced, maintained, and limited in accord with sociocultural norms. The developmental niche framework was introduced as a method for "examining the cultural structuring of child development" and to help developmentalists avoid conceiving of children as "decontextualized, universal" beings (p. 545). The niche provides anthropologists and psychologists with a common structure for understanding developmental process across cultures. In this chapter I will contrast the concrete physical and social organization subsystems of two sociocultural systems. These subsystems make up an important part of the niche structure.

## Metatheoretical Approaches to Friendship Formation

Before describing sociocultural constraining, I want to identify and compare two metatheoretical approaches to friendship development, and to social relationship development generally (see Winegar, Chapter 1, this volume). Simply stated these may be styled the outcome approach and the process approach. The first of these presents relationships as if they were static entities and may well seek to find some universal definition of friendship, while the second seeks to explain the development of relationships as if they were historical-temporal phenomena. I want to introduce the reader to this additional *comparison* because I believe it may be useful in guiding scrutiny of developmental researchers' implicit or explicit "as ifs" (Vaihinger, 1925).

### *The Outcome Approach*

A common and time-honored metatheoretical strategem of psychologists is to abstract observed phenomena from a fluid developmental process and treat these abstractions as if they were *verifiable things* – outcomes. This practice has been described by Bloom (1981) in terms of linguistic analysis, yet it also applies to the operationalizing of developmental psychologists (Valsiner, 1992). Bloom described the process by which English speakers "entify" verbal or adjectival forms into noun forms. For example, some particular temporally situated "important" event comes to be described as having "importance" at other times, perhaps when it no longer is important. Bloom (1981) describes the shift from the descriptions of actions such as "befriending" to their description as the entity of "friendship" in the following terms:

> The shift . . . signals movement from description of the world as it is primarily understood in terms of actions, properties, and things, to description of the world in terms of *theoretical entities* that have been conceptually extracted from the speaker's baseline model of reality and granted, psychologically speaking, a measure of reality of their own. (p. 37, emphasis added)

This shift results in the creation of a useful fictional construct. This fiction is quite often "justifiable" given the communicative or "operational" purposes at hand, but because of the fluid nature of human development, "verification" of such fictions is impossible. (See Vaihinger, 1925, for a detailed account of the genesis of fictions.)

Once psychological researchers have accomplished this shift with regard to transforming specific prosocial actions into friendship as an entity, they may deal with friendship as if it were a unitary and definable concept – an outcome. Subsequently, empirical researchers can state unequivocally whether or not children "have it." I raise questions about the operationalizing of friendship not to say that this effort should not be undertaken, but rather to say that the metatheoretical outcome approach accepts or assumes a particular form of cultural construction of friendship. In many studies such assumptions are made without the explicit acknowledgment of the culture-bound nature of the researcher's shift from description of action-in-the-world to a "conceptually extracted" theoretical entity (see Winegar, Chapter 1, this volume). The outcome approach fits nicely with a unidirectional transmission model of friendship development. Since adults and caregivers know the parameters of the *friendship entity*, they may transmit it to the children in their care.

The outcome approach to friendship development often posits that having friendship is good for children, and that its absence or presence in early to middle childhood has a profound effect on healthy development. Researchers taking this view recognize some collection of behaviors between members of any given group, and often some collection of statements from group members, as affirming or denying the existence of friendship with other group members. For example, toddlers who spend a great deal of time together in common activity, who occasionally share play material, and who laugh and smile together are recognized as friends (Howes, 1988). In this way a rigid or entified definition of friendship *as an outcome* is adopted a priori in many psychological studies. This definition may be valid at any one point in time for any particular collection of friends, but it may not be valid for use within other sociocultural settings. Additionally, as we shall see, such a definition may ignore the wide variability in the ways that developing children reinterpret and actively reconstruct adult definitions of friendship. Therefore, at different times within the same sociocultural setting, psychologically entified (operational) definitions of friendship may become invalid.

### *The Process Metatheoretical Approach*

This approach to friendship formation involves recognizing its developmental fluidity *along with* its genesis as a socioculturally promoted construction and explaining its temporal flow within the main current (system) of socioculturally promoted activities and skills (Harkness & Super, 1983; Ogbu, 1981; Weisner, 1984). Within this metatheoretical view, individuals, in the process of internalizing socioculturally promoted skills and knowledge, "constructively transform" (Lawrence & Valsiner, 1993) the intersubjective understandings of their culture and remake them as their own subjective understanding.[3] It is because of this transformation that friendship is so difficult to define as an entified construct (Lewis & Feiring, 1988; Mannarino, 1980). It is also a plausible theoretical explanation of the wide variability in the understanding and expressions of friendship within samples of school children in the technocratic culture of the United States (Hartup, 1988).

In this chapter I take a metatheoretical process approach to understanding the formation of friendships (or more inclusively stated, peer social relationships) because it frees one from the rigid operationalizing of the friendship/peer relationship as a static entity. This approach melds congenially with the theoretical assertion that, over time, friendship is co-constructed by children in both physical and verbal activity.

I will compare the social activity and caregiver control subsystems organized for children across two broadly characterized sociocultural groups. I will also compare highly variable processes of friendship formation in a particular setting within one of these groups (kindergarten classrooms in the United States technocracy). By the comparisons and the descriptions included here I hope to contribute to "enlarging our understanding of the processes linking the macro-levels of society and culture with the micro-levels of individual development" (Jahoda & Lewis, 1988, p. 15).

## Adults' Constructions and Children's Reconstructions of Promoted Subsystems

In rejecting models of development involving simple cultural homogeneity and unidirectional transmission of culture, I build on the work of Corsaro (Corsaro, 1992; Corsaro & Rizzo, 1988) and

Valsiner's (1987) developmental theory. These writers emphasize the importance of individual and collective reconstructions of cultural promotions. The sociocultural messages (promotions) received by children are not taken in and reproduced copy-like; rather, they are constructively translated by children in their social activity and reexpressed in the family and peer cultures. In Corsaro's (1992) language these are "*interpretive* reproductions."

In discussing peer interaction in an Italian *scuola materna* (including children ages 3 to 6) Corsaro and Rizzo (1988) cite three "layers" of analysis that help explain the child's active role in the appropriation of cultural meanings and the interpretive reproduction of a peer culture. Their focus is on how these reproductions influence young Italian children's understandings about friendships. However, their analysis of layers taken in a general sense provides a theoretical framework for understanding the development of social relationships within particular sociocultural systems. Their third layer affirms the importance of what I refer to as cultural promotions and, in so doing, may be seen as the layer of analysis where the child's developmental niche, and its constraining subsystems, are subject to careful scrutiny.

The examination of the first layer concerns the sociolinguistic interpersonal exchanges (*discussioni*) of children who are friends and how those exchanges reveal children's understandings about friendship and social norms. The second layer places the discussion routines in the peer culture, describing how these routines contribute to children's joint reconstructions and creations of meaning within this peer culture. The third layer reveals how children "'appropriate' certain elements of adult culture to deal with practical problems" (Corsaro & Rizzo, 1988, p. 881).

As I have stated, it is at this last layer (or level) of analysis that the focus of the present comparative account of sociocultural organization lies. Corsaro and Rizzo quote Merton (1968) in explaining the theoretical import of children's appropriation of adult culture. Specifically, Mertons' assertion that children *informally* and *unwittingly* appropriate adult cultural meanings is emphasized. This point is illustrated by Corsaro's transcripts of children's conversations that refer to their incorporation of adult understandings about the importance of age grading (especially with regard to the transition from the *scuola materna* to the older grouping of the *scuola elementare*). This age grading is one aspect of the socioculturally promoted organization and setting subsystem of modern Italian school culture.

Through an analysis of friends' discussions, Corsaro and Rizzo show how children transform their understandings of the age-grading organization to fit with their own interpretation of peer cultures. In a very simplified retelling – two friends tell a third that the skill with which he uses a construction toy will be useless once they hit the "big time" – the next and more rigorous level of school. Children's understandings of the importance of age grading and what to expect at the next level of school were promoted through a series of teacher and parent organized activities. The boys are using appropriated adult-promoted understandings about their future school lives for their own aims, to help them decide what activities to partake in as friends – to accept some activities as appropriate and to reject others as "too baby."

Two points are important to emphasize at this juncture. First, one obvious way that caregivers supply children with the implicit "cultural uniformities" that Merton describes (Corsaro & Rizzo, 1988) is in the structuring of settings and organizations that directly affect children's social relationships (such as socioculturally promoted and expected transition points from one cultural setting and organization to another). These may be seen from a nondevelopmental (cultural transmission) perspective simply as cultural information to be appropriated by the child. From a developmental perspective, verbally and physically active children, members of a social group, translate or interpret these uniformities, and then reinterpet them within the peer culture. A second point extending Corsaro's notion of interpretive reproduction of adult-promoted sociocultural information can be made. It is precisely at this level of analysis, of children's creative reconstruction of cultural roles and norms, that the fiction of unidirectional transmission of intact and homogeneous cultural meanings from caregiver to child begins to break down (Jahoda & Lewis, 1988). Interpretive reproduction raises the possibility of all sorts of within-group variation of understanding and action among children about such questions as "How do friends act?" or, from a boy, "Is it still all right to play with my sister?" or "How will the presence of a different caregiver change my way of playing?"

Corsaro and Rizzo's analysis is undertaken through careful examination of sociolinguistic exchanges and understandings. However, further understanding of social relationship development can be achieved by also examining the differences that promoted settings and organizations make for children's social development within sociocultural systems. That is, we may look at how children's activity in particular promoted settings or with particular caregivers influence their own interpretations and co-constructions of the meanings and purposes of these constrainers of activity as they are developing social relationships. An in-depth analysis of sociolinguistics and meaning-making among children is crucial for understanding the socialization process, but it does seem that one runs the risk of "missing the forest for the trees" if one does not first fully understand how the settings and organizations that adults introduce to children constrain and guide development toward particular meanings or understandings. Corsaro and Rizzo introduce an example of this type of constraining organization by showing how the age-grading organization of the schools is creatively reconstructed by children.

Stepping back from Corsaro's close analysis of interpersonal exchanges, here I ask, "What differences can sociocultural promotions of activity settings, control structures, and possible playmates make in the development of friendship or other close social relationships?" To facilitate answering this question I will employ the developmental niche structure, incorporating my collection of three socioculturally promoted subsystems as specific examples of constrainers of development within the social worlds of children.

## Comparing Agrarian and Technocratic Systems of Constraint

Two broadly defined sociocultural-historical systems influencing child development will be discussed here. The constraining organizations and settings of these systems will then be shown to have potential for both the limitation and the enhancement of developing social relationships among children. What I am here calling *sociocultural systems* are made up of many different social and cultural groups. These groups are united by similar orientations toward the roles of parents, other kin, and institutions in the development of children and in the organization of activities that contribute to family subsistence.

The concommitant subsystems that are the focus of this comparative analysis involve sociocultural settings and organizations constraining children's activity at the level of *observable* interactions with peers and caregivers. These constraining subsystems are historically formed, and because of this fact we can view them from a "diachronic perspective" (Begnini & Valsiner, 1993). In essence this means we do not have to "get inside" particular cultures to understand adequately the genesis of subsystems; rather, as Begnini and Valsiner assert, we may understand sociocultural systems as "organized systems that have arrived in their present state by way of transformation of their organization over time" (p. 37). Therefore, we may assume that the differences between the systems compared here are the result of the different historical processes that produced them.

We can look at children's activity in particular societies within each of these two sociocultural systems and identify general cross-cultural contrasts in the settings for social activity – limits on the pool of possible social partners – and in those persons designated as appropriate overseers of children's activity.

### *Agrarian Sociocultural Systems*

For the definition of this group of cultures I follow LeVine and White (1986).[4] "Agrarian populations raise their own food through the cultivation of crops, the rearing of domesticated animals, or a combination of the two, while residing in small rural communities" (p. 27). Additionally, Levine and White state that agrarian societies are "dependent on the economic contributions of child labor," and because of this dependence "women and their mates do not deliberately curtail their period of child bearing" (pp. 27, 29). This second factor, known as "natural fertility," is adaptive for agrarian populations in that it provides children as laborers as well as a set of older siblings capable of caring for younger family members in both ordinary and extraordinary circumstances. An example of the latter might be the early death of a parent. The adaptive function of natural fertility in relation to child care becomes important to this chapter as we consider the caretaker-control organizations of agrarian societies.

Examples of agrarian cultures include the Kipsigis of rural Kenya (Super & Harkness, 1986), the Tahitians of the Society Islands (Levy, 1973), Western Samoans (Ochs, 1982, 1988), and the Mixtecan Indians of rural Mexico (Romney & Romney, 1963). Despite the sophistication of the technocratic sociocultural systems "agrarian life – with domestically organized food production as its basis – remains the majority condition of humanity" (LeVine & White, 1986, p. 24).

## *Technocratic Sociocultural Systems*

In this grouping the subsistence activities of the vast majority of people are far removed from the direct production of food or other necessities of life. The economic activity that sustains the family takes place largely away from the home and commonly involves the mass production, promotion, and distribution of services or goods. Children are expected to learn many of the relevant rules of social behavior and the skills needed for their own future support through the institution of the school. Increasingly, children younger than the traditional school age (6 or 7) are also cared for in schoollike settings. In contrast to the agrarian sociocultural system, family size is limited, not expanded, due to economic demands.

The word *technocratic* is borrowed from Illich (1973). It serves several relevant purposes as a name for this group of cultures. It overcomes the lack of meaning of *Western* or even *Westernized* in that peoples from all over the globe from Minneapolis to Kiev to Tokyo are part of this grouping. It also conveys more of the historical recency of this evolving group. I rejected the words *technological*, which may apply to cultures that use tools of widely varying complexity, from stick plows to fiber optic cable, and *industrial*, which historically refers to economies dominated by the production of goods without implying inclusion of the more recent advent of the promotion of services. Finally, technocratic conveys the sense of the predominance of "experts," whether political, educational, technological, or scientific, in all organizational aspects of the nominally democratic, and certainly bureaucratic, societies in question.

## *Transitional Societies*

In the historical development of sociocultural systems there are temporally and circumstantially related changes just as there are in individual development, and there are cultural groups that may be considered transitional. Singhal (1980) described friendship development in two samples of Indian children. They are members of cultural groups that are infused with many traditional agrarian understandings of the social needs of children, but that nonetheless have embraced technocratic schooling methods. Additionally, there are urban cultural settings that retain the flavor of village life – in which agrarian sociocultural practices still predominate and schooling is not well established. Farver and Howes (1988) describe their subjects from Jakarta, Indonesia, in such a way. Within highly diverse cultural collectives, such as the United States, one is sure to identify social groups undergoing profound transitions. The agrarian Amish people of central Ohio, for example, cling to their tried-and-true simple lifestyles, yet a speeding car tragically killing several of their children (June 1993) cannot help but force them to make further necessary allowances for the encroachment of the mainstream technocracy.

## Contrasting Sociocultural Promotions of Constraining Subsystems

The process of friendship formation is essentially one subclass of a larger group of explicitly promoted activities within many of the technocracies. The promotion of friendship takes a more implicit form (see my earlier discussion of Merton) in agrarian sociocultural systems because friendlike relationships develop in the normal course of subsistence activities. The need to belong (Carini, 1982; Ladd, 1990) that is so strongly promoted and felt in the technocracy (e.g., United States) is less of an issue in the agrarian system because the child knows that he or she "belongs" to a kin group, and his or her productive participation in that kin group is promoted from an early age.

Other promoted activities that seem to require more explicit constraining in the technocracies include sleep habits, eating habits, and "appropriate" expressions of emotion. In agrarian systems the baby sleeps beside the mother and nurses on demand, and once the next child is born the toddler's sleeping place is moved to an area with other older siblings (LeVine & White, 1986). In the technocracy sleep is considered an activity to promote so that generally speaking the baby is sleeping alone and for as long as possible as early in life as possible (Morelli, Rogoff, Oppenheim, & Goldsmith, 1992). Meals occur because of neccessity and with little choice of foods in most agrarian societies (Valsiner, 1987). However, in the wealthier technocracies proper nutrition is more of an articulated concern and particular healthy or natural diets are promoted. Also, all sorts of ingenious devices have been designed to help promote the acquisition of eating skills (Valsiner, 1987).

Emotional expression is responded to as representative of immediate need in early life and virtually ignored by adults as the infant moves to childhood in some agrarian societies (Harkness & Super, 1983). In technocracies emotional expression is often promoted as healthy. The emotional expressions of young children are often listened to and responded to carefully by adults (Kostelnik, 1988), although, paradoxically, attempts are often made earlier in infancy to train away such expression – "Let him cry so he won't always expect you to respond."

## Comparisons of Constraining across Cultural Systems: Examples of Variability

In open developmental systems there are numerous possibilities for constraining subsystems to be either enhancing or limiting at different times, or simultaneously so for different individuals. In this section comparisons of the constraining subsystems of the two broader sociocultural systems will make this clear. Specific examples from U.S. kindergarten classrooms (featuring 5- to 6-year-olds) will demonstrate that variability is quite possible within highly similar constraining circumstances. Prior to making the cross-system comparisons and citing examples of within-system variability, I will describe the subjects and outline the data collection methods that were used.

## Methods Used in a Study of Friendship Development in Kindergarten

### *Subjects*

The participants were 40 children who attended two kindergarten classes in a public school in the Piedmont section of North Carolina. This sample included 17 girls (mean age 65.0 months, ranging from 60 to 69 months) and 23 boys (mean age 67.6 months, ranging from 62 to 77 months). Of these, 28 children were Caucasian, 7 were African-American, and 5 were of East Asian, Middle Eastern, or South Asian origin.

The study was longitudinal – data were gathered across the course of an entire school year. Observational data were collected simultaneously and on identical schedules in the two kindergarten classes. Data collection during children's free-play time outside and during their lunch periods began during the first week of school in both classes and continued for two weeks. After the initial period of children's adjustment to the new routines of their classes, observers began to collect data during other times inside and outside both classes. At the end of the initial 3 weeks of school, children were asked to name two classmates whom they played with frequently at school. Teacher nominations of the two most frequent playmates for each child were also collected. Nominations of this sort continued to be recorded at regular intervals until the beginning of the winter school holiday. Regular observations and nominations in both classes continued after this holiday and extended through early February. Duing this January–February coding period, one nomination of favored playmates was recorded from teachers and students. A final observational and nomination period extended from the last week of April to the end of the school year to assess long-term stability of playmate relationships and friendships.

To summarize, three methods were employed for the assessment of interaction patterns commonly understood as friendship: contextualized spot observations, child nominations of commonly favored playmates, and teacher nominations of favored playmates.

### *Observational Assessment*

Trained coders observed each class for 4 hours per week during the study period. Coders observed all study participants in random order (changing each day) using a combination of modified spot observational and time-sampling methods (Bakeman & Gottman, 1986; Ellis, Rogoff, & Cromer, 1981; Whiting & Edwards, 1988). Each class was observed 2 days per week throughout the study period. All observations took place during midweek (Tuesday, Wednesday, or Thursday). Observations of individual children were gathered every minute, with the 20 seconds before the observation being used to make sense of (contextualize) the activity underway. The remaining 40 seconds were used to code, take brief notes, then locate the next child and observe the context of his or her interaction. Coding continued in this fashion through the entire list of class participants, repeating four observations per child through a particular day's coding period. Each child was observed approximately 208 times.

Observers coded the target child's physical setting (outside or inside, structured or free choice of activity), the social setting (solitary, small group, or large group), whether or not a teacher was involved in the interaction, the identification numbers of the two children most closely involved with the target child in "interactive episodes" (Corsaro, 1985; Hinde, Titmus, Easton, & Tamplin, 1985; Rizzo, 1989), and one of eight classes of peer interactions.

The target child's activity was considered the starting point for coding the following interactions: (a) *Negative reciprocal* interactions were recorded if the target child and his or her partner(s) mutually hit, kicked, called each other names, and so on. (b) Two classes of *negative nonreciprocal* interactions were recorded depending on whether the target child or the partner acted or spoke negatively toward companion(s) but the behavior was ignored or the companion(s) exercised restraint. (c) *Propinquity* was recorded if the target child was within the interactive space of any other children but not actively involved with them. (d) Two classes of *positive nonreciprocal* interactions were recorded (as with negative nonreciprocal) if the target or partner attempted to engage a companion positively but the other was unresponsive. (e) *Joint activity* was recorded if the child and partner(s) engaged in activity marked either verbally or motorically by mutual interest. These were situations in which children were jointly focused on the same game, toy, or common work activity, or were engaged in extended conversation. (f) *Positive reciprocal* interactions were recorded when children engaged in joint activity marked by signs of positive affective involvement. (g) *Solitary* activity was also noted and coded.

### *Reliability Data*

Reliability data on 25% of all spot observations were gathered at regular intervals during the entire study period. Tests of agreement using Cohen's Kappa were calculated on all coding categories and were as follows: .725 for teacher presence, .903 for physical setting, .779 for social setting, .922 for the target child's first interaction partners, and .751 for the interaction codes of those partners.

### *Peer and Teacher Nominations*

At regular intervals during the observational period of the study, children were asked to respond (in private) to the following questions: "When you can choose who you want to play with, like at center time or at recess time, whom do you play with most at school?"

and then "Whom else do you play with?" After the child had responded, the experimenter asked, "Are ___ and ___ the children you play with the most?" allowing the child to think about and affirm or change his or her choices. Codes of the nominated friends were recorded in the order of preference that the child gave.

On the same days as the children's nominations, lead classroom teachers were asked to report in writing: "Which child in your class does (target child) play with most at school? Please name one other classmate whom (target child) plays with frequently." Teachers also reported in December (midstudy) on their relative awareness of each child's classroom activity. That is, they were asked to choose one of five categories from *I am very aware of this child's activity in the classroom* to *I am seldom aware of this child's activity*. It is expected that higher positive correlations between teacher and child nominations will be found for children who were better known by their teachers.

An additional question was added to the final nomination session. After they were asked the standard question about common playmates, both teachers and children were asked to respond to an appropriate form of the following: "Among all the children you play with at home and at school, who is your best *friend*? Are any of the other children whom you know good *friends*?" This additional question allowed for an assessment of the extent to which the children and teachers treated the term *friend* and the phrase *the child played with most at school* as synonymous. It also provided direct evidence of the identification of particular classmates as strong friends.

## Cross-cultural Comparison of Constraining Subsystems

I will now return to the comparative analysis of cultural constraint systems. After each general comparison, examples of within-culture variability will be cited from the aforementioned study of friendship development in kindergarten classrooms.

### *Pool of Possibles*

The subsystem governing access to the pool of possibles in agrarian cultures seems to be a limiting constraint. The kin or village group (often one in the same) is exclusive. As LeVine and White (1986) and Weisner (1984) point out, the social relationships of agrarian peoples are "permanent," in that large family and kin groups maintain ties and working relationships throughout life. Parents would not consider the possibility of allowing children to interact with someone from an out-group (Weisner, 1984). The age range of peer groups is generally wide and the home-centered social networks of children (including adults) are comparatively large when contrasted with the technocratic system.

As noted earlier, it might be said that the *pool of possibles* – possible social partners – may constitute an enhancing developmental subsystem in the Untied States. Most likely, however, this subsystem would be highly variable across all the technocratic cultures. Since peer interaction contexts exist largely within school settings, the bureaucratic and legal governance of school attendance would have a lot to do with the homogeneity of school populations. In all technocracies the centrality of the school as a highly probable location of social contact, along with the relative mobility of families, provides the child with a wide variety of nonkin (although most often same-age) playmates as potential friends. In contrast, at home and in the neighborhood, social networks generally (and thus contacts with peers or possible playmates) are comparatively limited when contrasted with those of agrarian cultures (Farran, Mistry, Ai-Chang, & Herman, 1992).

## *Pool of Possibles: Variability within Kindergartens*

In my longitudinal study of friendship development in two kindergarten classrooms it became apparent that children differentially responded to the constraint on their pool of possible friends set up in the kindergarten classroom. Two examples from this study give a partial indication of this variability (names are fictitious).

Jane and Joan were two girls with no friendship history prior to kindergarten. They were assigned to the same worktable at the beginning of the school year and quickly identified each other as mutual playmates. Teachers encouraged their developing relationship by allowing them to select activities together during free choice times (periods when assigned work was finished). They used this time together to extend and develop their friendship and, at the end of the school year, unhesitatingly identified each other as favored playmates.

Myrtle and Frieda were placed in similar circumstances and, again, at first and through most of the year, identified each other as mutual playmates when asked. They too were not restricted from mutual activity during free choice times and, again, spent much of this time playing together. However, at the end of the study period when asked to identify their best friends each of these girls named other people. One named her big sister – "because she does cartwheels with me" – and the other named a child from another class. The constraining subsystem of the pool of possibles seemed to contribute to the formation of friendship in one case, while in the other, despite external appearances, it did not.

### *Activity Settings*

A chief function of cultures is as the "provider of [activity] settings" (Whiting, 1980). These settings are constituted by the actual physical spaces in which children interact. They are constraining to the development of social interaction in obvious and concrete ways, and they change with time and culture.

The physical activity settings promoted in agrarian sociocultural systems are not highly prescribed or structured. In these societies and within the geographic bounds of the village/community, children between the ages of 2 and 6 have opportunities to work and play in more open and varied settings not likely to be constrained directly by adults (LeVine & White, 1986). Children generally interact with a wide age range of companions and with caregivers engaged in a variety of productive activities (Valsiner, 1989).

In agrarian cultures, after the age of 6 and through middle childhood the adult constraining of activity is still not direct, although increasingly children are involved in gender-specific cooperative economic activity most commonly guided by older siblings or designated kin (Fortes, 1970; Weisner, 1984). With regard to the development of reciprocal social relationships, this socioculturally promoted subsystem of settings may be considered as generally enhancing in the agrarian sociocultural system.

In technocratic cultures, settings are often designed specifically for the purpose of managing children's activities and supplied with materials specifically engineered and produced to be used by children. These designed spaces and engineered materials may well be limiting children's social interaction possibilities in that they overstructure children's activity and focus it on the "things" one needs to learn or to play with, rather than on the other people with whom one can create. Also, the activities of contact between peers in these settings are often immediately constrained and controlled by adults in technocratic cultures. In the United States, for example, the primary settings for activity are school or some other institutionalized setting: child day care facility, community after-school programs, karate class, dance class, or soccer practice sessions. In most such settings activity is directly prescribed by adult professionals.

### *Activity Settings: Variability within Kindergartens*

Two of the classrooms observed in my longitudinal study of friendship development were somewhat different physically. Both were mobile classrooms (manufactured specifically for schools). One was a single large room with worktables interspersed and "centers" (curricular or play-oriented activity stations) located on the periphery. The other was divided into two rooms with a connecting hallway so that half the children were always visually separate from the other half. More "academic"-oriented activities were located in one room of this second class, while more "play"-oriented activities were located in the other.

Morning time schedules were quite similar in each class. Both had early morning catch-up work or free choice times, a 40-minute session with an outside-of-class activity (music, library time, art, or physical education), and a period of approximately 1 hour and 15 minutes for teacher-led academic-oriented work in beginning language skills, math, and "social studies." In both classes this period was reterred to as "center time." When children in the single-room class were finished with a morning's assigned work, they were allowed to choose from center or play materials around the periphery of the room. In the two-room class, children were assigned to either the "play" room or the "work" room of the class at the beginning of the day, alternating by days.

Bob and Jon were two friends in the single-room class. They were assigned to the same "work time" table and so were placed together by the organized structure of the class whenever work time took place. They often finished work at about the same time and so began their period of free choice at almost the same time every day. After a short period in school it began to seem as if they *tried* to finish together, and then would go right to the construction toys together.

There they would construct "ships" from plastic construction toys and "fly" them together, often crashing them and also carrying them around the room while making accompanying engine noises. This activity became somewhat disruptive, and so teachers changed the boys' worktables in the hope that they would not finish their work at the same time. This change in activity setting did encourage the boys to play with others, and they were observed after that as less frequent playmates. However, they continued to see each other all through the morning, to play together outside, and to eat lunch next to each other. They also continued to nominate each other as frequent playmates and finally as friends. In this case the single room allowed the boys to maintain visual contact and sustained interest in each other's activity. The structure of the activity setting helped them to maintain their friendship.

Bill and Tom were also initially placed at the same worktable. They were in the two-room class. They, like Bob and Jon, often finished work together and played together in an occasionally disruptive manner. However, in this case teachers decided to separate them more definitely by placing them in different rooms for morning center time. This change practically eliminated their indoor interaction time together, and they seemed to take up with other friends, even to the extent of not playing together much during outside time. As the year went on they stopped naming each other as favored playmates. Variability in friendship development in these two cases seemed to be influenced by the different physical structures of the children's classrooms. This was true even though both pairs continued to have adequate opportunities to spend time together (at outside time, "resource time," and lunch).

## *Control Networks*

"It is the caregivers who gradually guide the older and younger siblings into the development of interpersonal relationships" (Valsiner, 1989, p. 230). Vygotsky (1987) has made famous a parallel assertion with regard to the importance of the guidance of more competent social others for children's development of higher mental functions. Valsiner's statement about familial caregiver guidance toward relationship development applies as well to the caregivers in extrafamilial activity settings and typifies the importance of the constraining subsystem that I have designated as the control network. Again, differences are apparent when we consider the broadly categorized agrarian and technocratic sociocultural systems.

In agrarian sociocultural systems adults do not often directly oversee the activities of children, although as noted earlier there are structural controls on the pool of possibles based on the community-kin structure. Young children are most often looked after by older siblings or kin who are in the process of completing some necessary task (LeVine & White, 1986; Whiting & Edwards, 1988). For this reason the control structure may be seen as an enhancing subsystem for the development of reciprocal social relationships. What the children see, and soon begin to appropriate through involvement as they are carried or follow along with a particular working group, is a process of cooperative and goal-directed activity. Further, in agrarian cultures the interactions of children after the age of 6 may be largely centered around cooperative work tasks as opposed to organized play or schooling. It follows that play activities tend to be more spontaneously organized during the course of daily tasks (Schwartzman, 1978). This may also enhance the development of social relationship skills because children negotiate with each other to determine the parameters of play.

Also following from the influence of work roles on the pool of possibles is the fact that gender segregation is more commonly maintained in agrarian cultures as children grow to middle childhood (Whiting & Edwards, 1988). Children in the United States may have more oppurtunity to play with members of the opposite sex, because they are not constrained in most common institutionalized settings by explicit role assignment. However, there seems to be a more subtle and implicit constraining of cross-gender interaction leading to friendship (Daniels-Beirness, 1989).

In technocratic cultures the social control network for children consists of one or another authoritative adult – the parent, the teacher, the instructor – or groups of adults. These adults exert a direct influence on the social interaction potentials of children, so that it is conceivable that the structures and organization of the setting dictated by adults would limit the child's selection of companions from the pool of possibles (Innocenti et al., 1986; Super & Harkness, 1986). For example, seating arrangements and demands for task completion might determine children's physical and temporal presence in certain classroom areas in schools, and parental work schedules often dictate children's ability to play with friends at home.

Within the scheme of enhancing and limiting subsystems of constraining, this control network in technocracies would seem to be a limiting subsystem. However, it is also an example of the possibilities for both limitation and enhancement within one subsystem since children may be exposed to a variety of subtly different behavioral rules from different overseeing adults. This exposure could provide some children with an opportunity to expand their repertoire of activity and to learn to respond distinctively to different adults in particular situations. This is exactly what occurs for many children from minority subcultural groups when they are placed into educational settings governed by dominant culture assumptions (Harrison, Wilson, Pine, Chan, & Buriel, 1990). It is also relevant to note that, as children grow older, challenging the control network is often a "strong feature" of the local peer culture (Corsaro, personal communication, November 1993).

Contributing perhaps to the limiting nature of the technocratic control system, participants in control functions must often earn some type of credential, and even those who are "naturally" members of the control group (parents) are often considered to be in need of extra training in order to exercise rational control. The acquisition of a set of control skills often serves to emphasize group control at the expense of individual freedom. This tension is apparent in the oft-heard school query/credo, "But what if I let everybody do it?" The role of the teacher – even the kindergarten teacher – is to impart academic skills. The strong belief is that this can be accomplished only if the teacher controls behavior, that is, limits it to a prescribed set of appropriate-for-school manifestations. Therefore, a limiting subsystem is set up with regard to the free interaction of children and the possible formation of friend groups and pairs during a large majority of their time at school. Across all 4,401 observations of the structuring of children's school activity in the current study, 68% were coded as being explicitly controlled by teacher direction. This was true even though coders scheduled their classroom presence to be during periods of the school day with the maximum possible amount of potentially "free" choice time. Of course, children in school do manage to form friendships – but often in spite of institutional, organizational-structural constraining rather than because of it (see also Rizzo, 1989).

## *Control Networks: Variability within Kindergartens*

The teachers in the kindergarten classrooms that I studied had quite similar attitudes about friendship formation as reported in audiotaped, structured interviews. For example, all felt strongly that kindergarten children did develop significant and lasting reciprocal relationships that went beyond simple enjoyment of similar activity or simple propinquity. All took a case-by-case approach to allowing friend pairs or groups to work together – that is, they used behavioral standards to guide them in separating friends during activity times. Friends who could enjoy each other's company without getting "silly" were allowed to work together; those who could not were separated. Teachers also felt that it was appropriate for them to attempt to promote friendships, especially for children who seemed "left out" or solitary.

To cite examples from two classrooms, the first teacher, Carol, controlled children in her classroom primarily by a "divide and conquer" strategy. If behaviors started to be unruly she would quickly identify the offending child or group of children and separate them from the scene of action. In this way she maintained control more by moving children around than by expecting children to work through difficulties or by "getting to the bottom" of a conflict or unruly behavior herself. She also expressed a strong belief that many children did not form close friendships with one or two others, but rather that there were many children in her class who she said were "friends with everyone." Jim, whose inquisitive behavior and verbal ability contributed to his frequent question asking and movement, was often assigned by Carol to another space or room to do his work. Jim nominated many different children as his favored playmates through the course of the year. At the end of the observational period of the study in his class, we rarely observed Jim playing frequently with any one or two children. In this case it is likely that teacher constraining of his activity contributed to his lack of companionship formation.

The second teacher, Nan, was also prone to use isolation and "time-out" as ways to control what she considered unruly behavior; however, her use of this strategy seemed to decrease as the year went on. It seemed that she consciously used stricter discipline at the beginning of the year than at the middle or end of the year. Ronnie was a child who was isolated in time-out practically every day early in the study period. Study research assistants actually had some concern that he was being coded often in solitary activity due to teacher constraining, rather than to his actual social skills. However, even in the face of this highly limiting teacher control behavior, Ronnie consistently nominated and, in turn, was nominated by two mutual playmates. As the study period progressed it became obvious that one of these two was definitely a close friend to Ronnie, and at the end of the study they called each other close friends. In this case the limiting of child activity did not seem to prevent the formation of close friendship, while in the case of the child in Carol's class, the limiting of activity seemed to encourage him to establish a pattern of many different short-term play interactions.

The foregoing comparisons have made the general case for differential socialization resulting from the broad sociocultural systems' promotion of "subsystems" that constrain activity. However, although comparative generalizations as a basis for analysis of cultural differences may be appealing, what we found when we looked closely at within-culture activity was obvious variation in the way that children acted within the constraining subsystems of the particular culture (for another example, see Holland & Skinner, Chapter 7, this volume). It is not that these constraints do not make for definite differences across sociocultural systems, but that they cannot be treated as guarantors of unidirectional transmission of cultural norms (Lawrence & Valsiner, 1993).

Individual variability with regard to the development of social relationships may be the rule rather than the exception. This "rule of variability" has often been ignored by developmental psychology (Lightfoot & Folds-Bennett, 1992; Mekos & Clubb, Chapter 5, this volume), and this is just as true with regard to friendship development as with regard to other phenomena. We must look within cultures to determine if subsystems constraining children's activity make for some restricted homogeneity of developmental patterns (Weisner, 1988).

## Conclusion

Throughout this chapter I have tried to maintain a wide view of social relationship development, purposefully attempting to demonstrate the myriad and often uncontrollable influences on this process as it flows along in different sociocultural systems.

I have described the profoundly different constraining subsystems that guide – but do not determine – the development of social relationships in two broadly conceived sociocultural systems. These differences, profound as they are, should not tempt us to assume homogeneity of action within cultural groups, nor absolute heterogeneity across sociocultural systems. I have tried to demonstrate this by describing the outlines of different developmental paths that children seemed to follow within one consistently organized cultural setting.

Anecdotal reports of children's activity in relation to the three constraining subsystems were considered. They demonstrated that teacher attitudes and practices about social relationships generally, and friendship specifically, as well as teacher structuring of the activity settings influenced friendship development patterns. Following the ideas of both Corsaro and Rizzo (1988) and Lawrence and Valsiner (1993), the variability in developmental patterns described here and elsewhere (Hartup, 1988; Lewis & Feiring, 1988) are offered as additional evidence against a cultural transmission model of relationship development.

In developed or technocratic societies the social relationship of friendship is socially promoted. In everyday activity children in technocracies translate and redefine friendship for themselves, retaining some of the adult cultural meaning that this relationship carries, but bringing along some of their own individually and collectively constructed understanding as well (Corsaro & Rizzo, 1988). The constraining role of the control structure, in this case made up of teachers and their activity-limiting rules, seems to be an important influence on the development of friendships within the particular classroom cultures. Combining the variability of teacher constraining with individual children's own constructive transformations of cultural understandings about friendship makes for a rich and varied picture of friendship formation during the kindergarten year.

The constraining subsystems of a child's developmental niche certainly *influence* development. However, neither a general nor a highly particular sociocultural address will bestow homogeneous developmental patterns on individuals with regard to friendship development:

> The particular ways of acting by children and adults are not determined in any strict way *within* the constraints that are set up to canalize their development. Within the constrained structure of child–environment relationships indeterminacy of particular actions is rampant, but the construction of the constraints that set the

> boundary conditions for children's action development is a deterministic and goals-oriented process. In sum psychological development, both in ontogeny and in history, can be considered deterministically indeterministic. (Valsiner, 1987, p. 238)

The present analysis shows that this deterministic indeterminism can be demonstrated not only by close analysis of variations in symbolic mediation a la Corsaro and Rizzo (1988), but also by longitudinal observations of individual variation in social interaction activity within relatively homogeneous cultural settings. The evidence I am gathering points to the weakness of traditional assumptions about within-culture homogeneity of action derived from unidirectional transmission models of development, and to the fictional character of treating any culturally promoted phenomenon as a static entity.

## Notes

1. The recognition of these contrasting promotions between cultures can contribute to greater understanding about the wide diversity of human thought and action. Additionally, recognition of the lack of within-culture homogeneity in developmental patterns militates against the destructiveness of cultural chauvinism and exclusivity.
2. Here *historical* is meant to be taken inclusively, considering not only the long-term cultural history of a social group, but also the individual's history of personal relationships (Corsaro & Rizzo, 1988). Vygotsky emphasized the methodological importance of considering the child's personal developmental history in cultural context. He quotes P. P. Blonsky to emphasize this point: "Behavior can only be understood as the history of behavior" (Vygotsky, 1978, p. 65).
3. This analysis of development as including "constructive transformations" by the agent runs parallel to Corsaro's analysis of "interpretive reproductions" (Corsaro & Rizzo, 1988).
4. Under LeVine and White's broad definition of *agrarian*, there are three subclasses of societal organization – horticulturalist, pastoralist, and agrarian.

## References

Allen, V. L. (1981). Self, social group, and social structure: Surmises about the study of children's friendships. In S. R. Asher & J. M. Gottman

(Eds.), *The development of children's friendshps* (pp. 182–203). Cambridge University Press.

Bakeman, R., & Gottman, J. M. (1986). *Observing interaction: An introduction to sequential analysis*. Cambridge University Press.

Begnini, L., & Valsiner, J. (in press). "Amoral familism" and child development: Edward Banfield and the understanding of child socialization in Southern Italy. In J. Valsiner (Ed.), *Comparative-cultural and constructivist perspectives: Vol. 3. Child development within culturally structured environments* (pp. 34–46). Norwood, NJ: Ablex.

Bloom, A. H. (1981). *The linguistic shaping of thought: A study in the impact of language on thinking in China and the West*. Hillsdale, NJ: Erlbaum.

Carini, P. (1982). *The school lives of seven children: A five-year study*. Grand Forks: University of North Dakota Press.

Corsaro, W. A. (1985). *Friendship and peer culture in the early years*. Norwood, NJ: Ablex.

(1992). Interpretive reproduction in children's peer cultures. *Social Psychology Quarterly*, *55*, 160–177.

Corsaro, W. A., & Rizzo, T. A. (1988). *Discussione* and friendship: Socialization processes in the peer culture of Italian nursery school children. *American Sociological Review*, *53*, 879–894.

Daniels-Beirness, T. (1989). Measuring peer status in boys and girls: A problem of apples and oranges. In B. H. Schneider, G. Attili, J. Nadel, & R. P. Weissberg (Eds.), *Social competence in developmental perspective* (pp. 107–120). Boston: Kluwer Academic.

Ellis, S., Rogoff, B., & Cromer, C. C. (1981). Age segregation in children's social interactions. *Developmental Psychology*, *17*, 399–407.

Farran, D. C., Mistry, J., Ai-Chang, M., & Herman, H. (1992). Kin and calabash: The social networks of preschool part-Hawaiian children. In R. Roberts (Ed.), *Coming home to preschool: The sociocultural context of early education* (pp. 42–58). Norwood, NJ: Ablex.

Farver, J. A., & Howes, C. (1988). Cross cultural differences in social interaction: A comparison of American and Indonesian children. *Journal of Cross Cultural Psychology*, *19*, 203–215.

Fortes, M. (1970). Social and psychological aspects of education in Taleland. In J. Middleton (Ed.), *From adult to child: Studies in the anthropology of education* (pp. 14–74). New York: Natural History Press.

Harkness, S., & Super, C. M. (1983). The cultural construction of child development: A framework for the socialization of affect. *Ethos*, *11*, 221–231.

Harrison, A. O., Wilson, M. N., Pine, C. J., Chan, S. Q., & Buriel, R. (1990). Family ecologies of ethnic minority children. *Child Development*, *61*, 347–362.

Hartup, W. W. (1988). Behavioral manifestations of children's friendships.

In T. J. Berndt & G. W. Ladd (Eds.), *Peer relationships in child development* (pp. 46–70). New York: Wiley.

Hinde, R. A., Titmus, G., Easton, D., & Tamplin, A. (1985). Incidence of "friendship" and behavior toward strong associates versus nonassociates in preschoolers. *Child Development*, *56*, 234–245.

Howes, C. (1988). *Peer interaction of young children*. Chicago: Society for Research in Child Development.

Illich, I. (1973). *Tools for conviviality*. New York: Harper & Row.

Innocenti, M. S., Stowitschek, J. J., Rule, S., Killoran, J., Striefel, S., & Boswell, C. (1986). A naturalistic study of the relation between preschool setting events and peer interaction in four activity contexts. *Early Childhood Research Quarterly*, *1*, 141–153.

Jahoda, G., & Lewis, I. M. (1988). Introduction: Child development in psychology and anthropology. In G. Jahoda & I. M. Lewis (Eds.), *Acquiring culture: Cross cultural studies in child development* (pp. 1–34). London: Routledge.

Kostelnik, M. J. (1988). *Guiding children's social development*. Cincinnati, OH: South-Western.

Ladd, G. W. (1990). Having friends, keeping friends, making friends, and being liked by peers in the classroom: Predictors of children's early school adjustment? *Child Development*, *61*, 1081–1100.

Lawrence, J. A., & Valsiner, J. (1993) Conceptual roots of internalization: From transmission to transformation. *Human Development*, *36*, 150–167.

LeVine, R. A., & White, M. I. (1986). *Human conditions: The cultural basis of educational development*. New York: Routledge & Kegan Paul.

Levy, R. I. (1973). *Tahitians: Mind and experience in the Society Islands*. Chicago: University of Chicago Press.

Lewis, M., & Feiring, C. (1988). Early predictors of childhood friendship. In T. J. Berndt & G. W. Ladd (Eds.), *Peer relations in child development* (pp. 246–273). New York: Wiley.

Lightfoot, C., & Folds-Bennett, T. (1992). Description and explanation in developmental research: Separate agendas. In J. B. Asendorpf & J. Valsiner (Eds.), *Stability and change in development: A study of methodological reasoning* (pp. 207–228). Newbury Park, CA: Sage.

Mannarino, A. P. (1980). The development of children's friendships. In H. C. Foot, A. J. Chapman, & J. R. Smith (Eds.), *Friendships and social relations in children* (pp. 45–64). Chichester: Wiley.

Merton, R. K. (1968). *Social theory and social structure*. New York: Free Press.

Morelli, G., Rogoff, B., Oppenheim, D., & Goldsmith, D. (1992). Cultural variation in infants' sleeping arrangements: Questions of independence. *Developmental Psychology*, *28*, 604–613.

Ochs, E. (1982). Talking to children in Western Samoa. *Language in Society, 11*, 77–104.

(1988). *Culture and language development: Language acquisition and language socialization in a Samoan village*. Cambridge University Press.

Ogbu, J. U. (1981). Origins of human competence: A cultural-ecological perspective. *Child Development, 52*, 413–429.

Rizzo, T. (1989). *Friendship development among children in school.* Norwood, NJ: Ablex.

Rizzo, T., & Corsaro, W. (1988). Toward a better understanding of Vygotsky's process of internalization: Its role in the development of the concept of friendship. *Developmental Review, 8*, 219–237.

Romney, K., & Romney, R. (1963). *The Mixtecans of Juxtlahuaca, Mexico.* In B. B. Whiting (Ed.), *Six cultures: Studies of child rearing.* New York: Wiley. (Reprinted as a separate volume, 1966)

Schwartzman, H. (1978). *Transformations: The anthropology of children's play*. New York: Plenum.

Singhal, S. (1980). Home and school context of friendship expectation development in school children in India. *Psychologia, 23*, 105–115.

Super, C. M., & Harkness, S. (1986). The developmental niche: A conceptualization at the interface of child and culture. *International Journal of Behavioral Development, 9*, 545–569.

Vaihinger, H. (1925). *The philosophy of "as if."* London: Kegan Paul, Trench, Trubner.

Valsiner, J. (1987). *Culture and the development of children's action.* Chichester: Wiley.

(1989). *Human development and culture.* Lexington, MA: Heath.

(1992). Interest: A metatheoretical perspective. In A. K. Renninger, S. Hidi, & A. Krapp (Eds.), *The role of interest in learning and development* (pp. 27–41). Hillsdale, NJ: Erlbaum.

von Bertalanffy, L. (1950). The theory of open systems in physics and biology. *Science, 111*, 23–29.

Vygotsky, L. S. (1978). *Mind in society: The development of higher psychological processes.* Cambridge, MA: Harvard University Press.

(1987). *The collected works of L. S. Vygotsky: Vol. 1. Problems of general psychology*. New York: Plenum.

Weisner, T. S. (1984). Ecocultural niches of middle childhood: A cross-cultural perspective. In W. A. Collins (Ed.), *Development during middle childhood* (pp. 335–369). Washington, DC: National Academy Press.

(1988). Comparing sibling relationships across cultures. In P. G. Zukow (Ed.), *Sibling interaction across cultures: Theoretical and methodological issues* (pp. 11–25). New York: Springer Verlag.

Whiting, B. B. (1980). Culture and social behavior: A model for the development of social behavior. *Ethos, 8*, 95–116.

Whiting, B. B., & Edwards, C. P. (1988). *Children of different worlds: The formation of social behavior*. Cambridge, MA: Harvard University Press.

Winegar, L. T. (1989). Organization and process in the development of children's understanding of social events. In L. T. Winegar (Ed.), *Social interaction and the development of children's understanding* (pp. 45–65). Norwood, NJ: Ablex.

# 9 The Everyday Experiences of North American Preschoolers in Two Cultural Communities: A Cross-disciplinary and Cross-level Analysis

*Jonathan Tudge and Sarah E. Putnam*

An understanding of everyday lived experience, as well as of the culture that underlies it, shapes it, and is simultaneously shaped by it, is important for the study of human development. Traditional psychological methods, such as observation or experimentation in controlled laboratory and laboratory-like settings, or the use of questionnaires and surveys, have yielded data regarding how people perform in certain circumstances, what they say they do, and how they respond to questions. But a growing number of contemporary psychologists, responding to challenges to the relevance and ecological validity of these methods and seeking a fresh approach to the understanding of human development, have begun to expand their theoretical and methodological repertoire. Scholars are more commonly focusing on studying children and adults in the settings in which they are typically situated – at home, in the classroom, or in the workplace – treating the context in which development is occurring as necessarily integrated with that development (see, e.g., Corsaro, 1985; Dunn, 1988; Heath, 1983; Lave, 1988; Rogoff, 1990; Valsiner, 1987).

Portions of this chapter were first presented at the biennial meetings of the International Society for the Study of Behavioral Development, Recife, Brazil (July 1993). Preparation of this chapter was facilitated by the award of a National Academy of Education Spencer Fellowship to the first author and a Carolina Consortium on Human Development predoctoral fellowship to the second author. We are indebted to Judy Sidden, who collaborated with us in the design of the coding scheme and who collected some of the data, and to the families and children who gave so generously of their time. We would also like to express our appreciation to the members of the Carolina Consortium on Human Development for their intellectual stimulation and to Michael Shanahan and Melvin Kohn for their feedback on an earlier draft of this chapter.

In doing so, these scholars are drawing on models and methods that have been used in other disciplines, notably cultural anthropology and some of the more qualitative approaches in sociology. The ideas incorporated in these methods are not new to psychology, however, but are to be found in the work of several early-twentieth-century theorists, including Janet, Baldwin, Vygotsky, Werner, Dewey, and Mead (Cairns, 1992; Glick, 1992; Tudge, Putnam, & Valsiner, in press; van der Veer & Valsiner, 1988). These ideas are also to be found in the work of some who have taken an ecological position on human development (see Tudge, Gray, & Hogan, Chapter 3, this volume). Although the specific positions of each theorist and each strand of thought are by no means identical, all view social life and individual activity and development as tightly interconnected, encompassing different levels of analysis (e.g., the individual, the immediately surrounding social and physical environment, and the broader level of culture). They also emphasize, albeit in different ways, that to investigate individual development requires understanding of the relations between individuals and the sociocultural world they inhabit.

This ecological and sociocultural perspective is the one that we have adopted in our research, having drawn from related frameworks from several disciplines. From psychology we have been influenced by the cultural-historical school of Vygotsky and his followers and by the ecological position taken by Bronfenbrenner, from sociology by the work of Kohn, and from cultural anthropology by the work of Whiting, Edwards, and their colleagues. In the first part of this chapter we describe the theoretical frameworks relevant to our research, and then indicate the ways in which they have informed this research. In the second part, we discuss the research itself.

## Theoretical Frameworks

### *Vygotsky's Cultural-Historical Theory*

Vygotsky was explicitly concerned with the social, co-constructive nature of cognitive development. Certain core concepts of his cultural-historical theory of human mental development are central to the present argument: that cultural and social structures, institutions, symbol and meaning systems, tools, and activities are closely interwoven with an individual's mental development; that higher mental functions, such as thinking and memory, are formed in the course of engaging in activities in the physical and social world; that the original form of higher mental activity is external and social, which is then appropriated by the individual in the course of activity (particularly activity in collaboration with others who have greater competence); and that sign and symbol systems, such as language, are essential tools of culture for the extension and development of human consciousness (Tudge et al., in press; Tulviste, 1991; van der Veer & Valsiner, 1991, 1994; Vygotsky, 1978, 1987; Wertsch, 1985, 1991). These postulates led Vygotsky to seek a unit and a method of analysis that would retain the integrity of the system he envisioned.

Vygotsky called social activity "the principal source of development" (quoted in Davydov & Zinchenko, 1989, p. 29), but it is clear that by social activity he considered the interrelatedness of an individual's independent level of functioning, interaction between the individual and others in the course of activity, and the sociocultural historically shaped context that gives meaning to the activity (Cole, 1985; Tudge & Winterhoff, 1993; van der Veer & Valsiner, 1991, 1994; Wertsch, 1985). For example, when conceptualizing social interaction, Vygotsky was interested in the relationship between the individual's level of functioning independently and level of functioning when working in collaboration with someone else, particularly someone more competent at the skill or tool use being learned. He called the "zone of proximal development" the difference between what an individual can achieve independently and what he or she can achieve in the course of collaboration, and argued that it is *created* in the course of activity, primarily with a more competent partner, but also in the course of individual play (Nicolopolou, 1993; Vygotsky, 1978). As Cole (1985) put it, it is within the zone of proximal development that the individual becomes social, and the social becomes individual.

This theoretical position necessarily involves an interweaving of levels of analysis – the individual, the interpersonal, and the cultural. The position taken by Vygotsky and his followers (primarily Luria and Leont'ev) is that an understanding of development will be incomplete if scholars concentrate solely on what the individual brings to bear on any problem (the individual level – what the person can achieve independently) and on the interpersonal level (joint activity that creates a zone of proximal development). The very nature of interactions between people, the interactional forms considered appropriate, the types of activities in which they jointly participate, and the tools they use in the course of activity can be fully understood only by reference to the cultural level. Vygotsky proposed that psychological processes first occur on the social plane and then are appropriated (made one's own while being transformed in the process) to the psychological plane. Since social interactions are culturally organized and internally transformed, the internalized psychological processes are simultaneously culturally, interpersonally, and internally co-constructed and organized. Development is thus viewed as the co-creation of world and mind on the basis of a history of actions that individuals perform in the world, actions that are shaped and given meaning simultaneously by people around them and by culture and history. At the same time, as some scholars have pointed out (Corsaro, 1985, 1992; Holland & Skinner, Chapter 7, this volume), cultures themselves undergo transformation in the course of their own reproduction.

Saying that "any fundamentally new approach to a scientific problem inevitably leads to new methods of investigation and analysis" (1978, p. 58), Vygotsky sought a new method with which to test his theories. He thought that the new method should retain the quality of that being studied and sought a structural method for the analysis of human mental development (Davydov & Zinchenko, 1989). Just as you cannot better understand water by breaking a molecule into its constituent parts for observation, Vygotsky felt that the unit for studying mental processes must retain the relationship between these processes and their cultural, historical, and institutional settings.

### *Bronfenbrenner's Ecological Systems Theory*

Bronfenbrenner, in many recent publications (e.g., Bronfenbrenner, 1988, 1989, 1993; Bronfenbrenner & Ceci, 1994), has argued that an ecological perspective forces scholars to consider the interrelationships between the developing individual and the physical and social setting in which the individual is developing, with social setting considered at both the proximal and the distal levels (see Tudge, Gray, & Hogan, Chapter 3, this volume). From this perspective, scholars would need to identify some proximal processes through which developmental change is brought about (such as interpersonal interaction in the course of joint activity), the personal characteristics of the persons involved in the processes (e.g., gender or some other biological or psychological characteristic), and when and how those processes vary as a function of a broader context in which the processes take place (with context considered as incorporating such things as culture, social class, physical features of the environment, historical cohort, racial or ethnic group).

Bronfenbrenner argued that it is essential to consider the processes linking contextual factors (of either a proximal or distal nature) and characteristics of the individual. Simply differentiating two or more groups of children on the basis of some "variable" such as social class, race, or gender in terms of some developmental outcome or test score is of limited utility. Bronfenbrenner argued that studies that did no more than this were based on "social address" models (see Mekos & Clubb, Chapter 5, this volume). He thought that such comparisons drew unwarranted inferences on the basis of little more than environmental labels. Social class is among the most common social addresses in the research literature (Bronfenbrenner & Crouter, 1983), usually with no attention given to the physical and social environment, what activities are taking place, what the processes involved might be, or how these things could affect the development of the individual (Bronfenbrenner, 1988). Not surprisingly, given Bronfenbrenner's indebtedness to Vygotsky and his followers (Bronfenbrenner, 1993), his theory also involves methodology that draws from the individual, interpersonal, and cultural levels of analysis.

### *Cultural Anthropology and Cultural Psychology*

Among cultural anthropologists, particularly those interested in children's social development, and developmental psychologists interested in culture, it is in the course of everyday routine activities that children gain cultural knowledge – ways of behaving and thinking considered important in their cultural community (Edwards & Whiting, 1980; Harkness & Super, 1985, 1986; LeVine & White, 1986; Mead, 1961; Morelli & Tudge, 1989; Ochs & Schieffelin, 1984; Rogoff, 1981; Tudge, Putnam, & Sidden, 1993, 1994; Valsiner, 1989; Whiting & Edwards, 1988). Competent members of the community engage in activities viewed as important, and make those activities more or less available for children to participate in. In technologically simple cultures, the type of adult activities in which children will be expected to become competent occur around the children. For example, in hunter-gatherer and agrarian groups, a girl is more likely to be involved in helping her mother in such activities as tending to the crops, cooking, and learning to weave, and from an early age will be involved in caring for younger siblings. By contrast, a boy is much more likely to be encouraged to learn how to hunt (in the course of observation and participation to the extent of his capability) and from 6 or 7 will be expected to look after the animals. (Ember's, 1973, discussion of a counterexample occurred only where the group had a large preponderance of boys.)

By contrast, in industrialized societies much of the work that is critically important for economic self-sufficiency occurs away from the home, and children therefore have to learn the skills they need to become self-sufficient in specialized institutions (various types of child care centers and schools). Nevertheless, work also occurs in and around the home, and children are in some instances encouraged to participate (helping to set the table, for example) and in others are not (lighting the fire). Children, simultaneously, strive to get involved in the activities that are going on around them. They seek opportunities to participate in ongoing activities, to start new activities, and recruit others to participate with them. The availability (and lack of availability) of activities and the extent to which children are involved are thus mutually determined by culturally and historically related factors, the values and beliefs of more competent members of the culture (who arrange different types of activities for their young, and encourage them in different ways and to different extents to participate in them), and by the children's own active attempts to participate in and start activities (Fischer & Fischer, 1966; Goodnow, 1984; Goodnow & Collins, 1990).

There are clearly points of connection between these cultural-anthropological and cultural-psychological perspectives and the theoretical positions presented earlier (Vygotsky's cultural-historical theory and Bronfenbrenner's ecological systems theory). However, the relationship between culture and the outcomes of interest are not always established by those interested in cultural issues. Just as Bronfenbrenner was critical of the use of social address models, Whiting (1976) has criticized reliance on "packaged variables." Many cross-cultural researchers, particularly but by no means exclusively in psychology, treat culture as a packaged variable – a variable that is used simply to differentiate one group from another, one culture from another – with no attempt to elucidate the features, mechanisms, and processes that serve to translate culture into the different practices or beliefs that are the focus of attention (Shweder, 1990). Whiting (1976) explicitly called for cultural anthropologists and psychologists interested in cross-cultural issues to "unpackage" culture so as to shed light on the processes important for understanding development in different cultural settings.

### *Sociology*

From sociology we have found particularly useful the work of Kohn and his associates, who have explored the relationship between social class, parental workplace experiences, and child-rearing beliefs and practices (Kohn, 1977, 1979; Kohn & Schooler, 1983; Kohn & Slomszynski, 1990; Luster, Rhoades, & Haas, 1989). In its packaged form social class frequently appears in multiple regression models as an independent variable and, in fact, has considerable predictive value. Nonetheless, the meaning of the variable *social class* is little understood, its processes cloaked behind a descriptive label. Kohn's research began the task of discovering the meaning of belonging to a particular social class by examining values and beliefs of middle-class and working-class parents.

Kohn (1977) found that class, statistically controlling a set of other major social variables, was more powerfully related to parental values than was the *totality* of such other major social variables as race, religion, region, and national background, controlling for class. Kohn found that the higher the parents' (particularly the fathers') social class position, the higher the value the parents placed on their children's self-direction, the use of initiative, and independent thought and judgment. Why should social class (or, to be more explicit, position in the social stratification system – Kohn & Slomszynski, 1990) be related to these values? Kohn argued that occupations higher in the social structure are more likely to be substantively complex, to be relatively free of supervision by others, to allow self-direction and initiative, and to be involved with people rather than things. Kohn argued that there were two relevant consequences. The first was that as parents are likely to try to instill in their children the qualities that have enabled them to be competent in their work, there will be a tendency for behavior exemplifying those qualities to be encouraged in their children. The second is that parents who view self-direction and initiative as possible and efficacious are likely to believe that the same will be true for their children, and therefore encourage it. By contrast, parents who are more closely supervised at work are more likely, Kohn found, to value conformity and obedience in their children. An additional point is that the more that men are controlled in their everyday lives, the more they are likely to try to exercise control in the one place where they have power – within the family (Tudge, 1982).

Social class is more than workplace practices, of course. Kohn (1977) argued that it constitutes a complex of conditions, including occupational circumstances, education, levels and stability of income that "structure men's view not only of the occupational world, but of social reality in general" (p. 164). In a footnote, he claims that "it is not just that class is related to men's capacities to perceive and to judge, but that class shapes the reality that is there to be seen and to be judged" (p. 187). Social class thus shapes the goals parents have for their children, their methods of discipline, parent–child relationships, and, by extension, their views of what is appropriate for girls versus boys. One consequence is that children tend to learn the very values that fit them into the types of occupations that their parents have (Tudge, 1982; Willis, 1977).

What Kohn has thus accomplished is to move discussion of social class from a social address position to one that posits the processes or mechanisms that serve to translate membership in social class to child-rearing practices, and thus to reproduce class-related practices from one generation to the next. We would argue that different social classes within any society have different values, beliefs, and meaning systems that are instantiated in parental practices and reproduced in the next generation. Social class, like culture considered in broader terms as nations or societies, embodies systematically differentiated conditions of life that profoundly affect people's views of reality and provides guidelines by which values and orientation of the social structure are translated into individual action. On the basis that meaning systems and conditions of life are not only different in different social classes, but are reproduced from generation to generation, we would argue that there is a clear connection between membership in a social class and membership in any cultural group. As Bronfenbrenner (1989) expressed it, cultures (whether considered across or within societies) may be distinguished by the fact that "the patterns of belief and behavior characterizing the macrosystem are passed on from one generation to the next through processes of socialization carried out by various institutions of the culture" (p. 229). To this statement we would have to add that those being socialized are simultaneously highly active in the process of socialization themselves, co-constructing or collectively reproducing their culture.

## Methodology

We argued at the outset that our research has been informed by theory drawn from a number of different disciplines although, as is clear, the particular exemplars we have found useful have much in common. In what ways have we incorporated them into our research? At the theoretical level, the greatest influence has been from Vygotsky and Bronfenbrenner. Elsewhere (Tudge et al., 1993, 1994) we have discussed this research from the perspective of Vygotskian theory. In this chapter, therefore, we shall concentrate on drawing the connections to Bronfenbrenner. Kohn's research has been influential in focusing our attention on social class and the mediating connection with workplace experiences (the exosystem level in Bronfenbrenner's terminology). The work of cultural anthropologists and cultural psychologists (particularly Whiting and her colleagues, and Rogoff and her colleagues) is seen most clearly in the methods we used to collect our data.

To exemplify the type of ecological person–process–context model discussed by Bronfenbrenner (for more details see Tudge, Gray, & Hogan, Chapter 3, this volume), these data should allow simultaneous understanding of "developmentally instigative" characteristics of the person, "developmentally instigative" characteristics of the environment, and analysis of the processes of development. As was made clear in Chapter 3, Bronfenbrenner's model is based on Lewin's famous equation [$B = f(PE)$], but was expanded to state that development (rather than simply behavior) is a function of the interaction of the person and the environment. Bronfenbrenner's model is thus built on the premise that understanding of human development cannot be based solely on characteristics of the individual or of the environment, but rather on their synergistic interaction.

In the data we shall discuss in this chapter we satisfy the minimum requirements of the person side of the equation in two ways, by examining who it is that initiates activities and involvement in activities, and we look separately at males and females. Gender constitutes a developmentally instigative characteristic – indeed, from the moment of birth parents' reactions and activities seem to differ, depending on the sex of the infant (McFarland, cited in Cole & Cole, 1992). Moreover, as Bronfenbrenner (1988, 1993) makes clear, the very processes of development differ by gender. For example, Bronfenbrenner (1988) cites studies by Bronfenbrenner and Cochran (1979) and Cochran and Woolever (1982) which found that the relationship between joint mother–child activity and subsequent school outcomes was significantly stronger for boys than for girls and, interestingly, that the mother's joint activity facilitated the child's performance in elementary school only if the mother herself had some education beyond high school. The more education beyond high school she had, the stronger the effect of her joint activity on the child's achievement in school. The joint impact of education and activity was significantly greater for boys than for girls.

The processes of development in which we are interested are the everyday activities in which our participants engage, in conjunction with their partners in those activities. Our particular interests are in the differing extents to which activities are made available to children and the manner in which the children become involved in those activities (under their own instigation or that of another person).

Then there is the environment side of the equation. In Bronfenbrenner's ecological systems theory (1989), environment must be considered at a number of intersecting levels, from the microsystem to the macrosystem. At the first, or microsystem, level we are talking about the activities in which children engage and the face-to-face interactions that they have with their partners. Specifically, in this chapter we concentrate on their lessons, attempts to impart information (albeit implicit) or to receive information (in the case of a child asking a question). The children inhabit different microsystems, however – home and child care setting constitute the two that we examine, focusing on the different extents to which children are involved in lessons in each type of setting, and the different types of lesson in which they are involved. At this second level of analysis we are dealing with what Bronfenbrenner has called mesosystem relations.

The third level consists of the exosystem – those contexts in which the child does not directly participate but which nevertheless exert an indirect influence. This research was built in part on Kohn's research that membership in a social class plays an important role in child-rearing practices at least in part because of the different beliefs and values held by parents with different workplace experiences. As discussed earlier, Kohn's data suggest that parents who believe that self-direction and initiative is important for economic self-sufficiency are likely to encourage their children to exhibit more self-direction at home. By contrast, parents whose jobs are more closely supervised are more likely to value conformity and obedience in their children. Our expectation was that children whose parents differ in their workplace experiences are likely to initiate lessons differentially and to initiate their own involvement in those lessons differentially.

Finally, at the macrosystem level, we must consider broad cultural values, beliefs, institutions, and resources, both physical and social, that are held in common by a group. "From this perspective, social classes, ethnic or religious groups, or persons living in particular regions, communities, neighborhoods, or other types of broader social structures constitute a subculture whenever the above conditions [shared belief systems, conditions of life, etc., that are reproduced from generation to generation] are met" (Bronfenbrenner, 1989, p. 229). At the level both of community and of socioeconomic status our research relates to the macrosystem. Data collected in Korea (Lee & Tudge, 1995; Tudge, Lee, & Putnam, in press), Russia (Hogan, Tudge, Snezhkova, & Kulakova, 1996; Tudge, Kulakova, & Snezhkova, 1996), and Estonia (Tammeveski, Meltsas, & Tudge, in press) (divided similarly between children whose fathers are either professionals or blue-collar workers) will allow a broader examination of macrosystem factors, at both the cross-societal and within-societal levels.

We adopted our methods of gathering data from those more commonly used by cultural anthropologists such as Whiting and Edwards (1988) and their colleagues and cultural psychologists such as Rogoff (1990) and her colleagues. The spot observational methodology is one that requires observers to pick a point in time and note, for the person who is the focus of attention, what that person is doing, who any partners are in that activity, the physical setting, who else is in that setting, and so on. Typically many such observations are taken of each "focal," or target, individual at different times of the day, so as to get a good sense of the varied settings inhabited by the targets, their activities, and their partners. (For more detail, see Ellis, Rogoff, & Cromer, 1981; Munroe & Munroe, 1971; Rogoff, 1978; Whiting & Edwards, 1988.)

The methodological techniques most commonly employed by developmental psychologists to assess the nature and processes of adult– (typically mother–)child interaction and activities differ in crucial ways from those used by cultural anthropologists. For the most part, Western researchers interested in young children's activities and in adult–child interactions have collected a vast amount of data in laboratory settings or in the course of structured or semistructured home observations. Observation of adult–child activity (whether in the home or laboratory) is often deliberately structured so as to ensure a minimum of interruption; it occurs at a time when the adult (typically the mother) does not intend to cook dinner, go shopping, entertain friends, clean the house, watch television, or do any of the myriad activities that typically occur. Thus, the implicit or explicit message communicated to mothers by researchers is to interact or play with their children, as time is set aside for mothers to engage their children and be child-oriented, at least to the extent to which this is a part of their normal behavioral repertoire. Yet the adult-oriented activities that are a regular part of the fabric not only of her life but of her child's are precisely those areas in which children are most likely to be exposed to and participate in adult life in that community. By restricting the "disruptions," developmental psychologists may thus have presented a misleading picture of the extent to which adults engage their children in the ongoing adult-oriented activities available in their communities. Richards (1977) has argued that, as a result, we know more about the naturally occurring activities of non-Western children than about those in this country – at least in part because methodological techniques designed to document and understand the activities of non-Western children have rarely been employed in research on North American children.

Most of the studies that focus on everyday activities of children in the United States, for example, draw explicitly on cultural anthropology. The best examples are Fischer and Fischer's (1966) observations in Orchard Town as part of the Six Cultures Study, the Claremont spot observational study reported by Whiting and Edwards (1988), and the use of spot observations to describe patterns of age and gender segregation in Salt Lake City (Ellis et al., 1981). Other studies use a similar methodology, such as the longitudinal studies of social interaction conducted by Clarke-Stewart (1973) and Carew (1980), but these are rare. A somewhat different methodology, focusing on one child and attempting to report all that that child did during one day, was used by Barker and his colleagues (Barker & Wright, 1951).

Ethnographic accounts of children's activities and behavior in school are easier to find (e.g., Corsaro, 1985; Dumont & Wax, 1976; Erickson & Mohatt, 1982; Hood, McDermott, & Cole, 1980; Lubeck, 1985; McDermott, Gospodinoff, & Aron, 1978), and children's naturally occurring play in different cultural communities has received some attention (Bloch & Pellegrini, 1989; Dunn & Wooding, 1977; Schwartzman, 1978, 1986; Smilansky, 1968), but studies like these do not attempt to cover the full range of children's everyday activities.

It should be clear, then, that the spot observational methods we employed to observe children's activities differed from those used by Kohn and his associates, who used survey and interview techniques. Kohn was interested in data on parental values and beliefs about child rearing, rather than in an examination of what the parents (or their children) actually did, which was our focus. The data presented in this chapter complement Kohn's rather well, and data recently collected (Hogan et al., 1996; Tudge et al., in press) make the connection yet stronger.

In summary, one goal of our research (the Cultural Ecology of Young Children Project) is to retain the dynamic relationship between the children's activities and the cultural, historical, and institutional settings within which and with respect to which they are organized. The unit of analysis, like the metatheoretical and theoretical assumptions undergirding the research, must be one that crosses levels. Our unit is thus conceptualized as "child in activity within a culturally constructed setting," a unit that retains the interrelated nature of human beings and their environments.

## Participants and Methods

In this chapter we focus on the activities, partners, and settings of 20 Caucasian preschoolers who ranged in age from 28 to 45 months. The children were drawn from two cultural communities (one named "Holden" in which parents tend to work in professional occupations and one named "Summit" in which parents tend to work in the nonprofessional sphere) in a southeastern city in the United States. The Holden group of children consisted of 6 girls and 5 boys, and the Summit group consisted of 5 girls and 4 boys.

Participants were located in the following manner. *Community* was defined as an area of town bounded on all sides by relatively clear boundaries (major roads, railway line, etc.), with no major roads cutting through the area, relatively small in size (1½–2 square miles), and judged to be fairly homogeneous in terms of types of housing and racial makeup. A list was then generated from the birth records of all children born in that area between 2 and 4 years earlier. Letters were sent to all families who appeared still to be living in the area (information derived from the telephone book and/or city records) and were followed by a screening call. In order to participate, the family still had to be living in the area, and had to fit education and occupation criteria. For the Holden community, at least one parent had to have a minimum of a college degree and have an occupation judged to be professional according to Hollingshead criteria; for the Summit community neither custodial parent could have a degree (one nonresidential, divorced father had a degree).

Of the 28 families contacted in Holden, 10 declined to participate, 7 were willing to participate but did not meet our requirements, and 11 participated. The minimum median family income (families responded to an income range rather than a precise amount) for this group was $70,000 (ranging from $40,000 to more than $85,000), and the median Hollingshead ranking for all working parents (excluding the 6 mothers who worked at home) was 8 (administrators, lesser professionals), range 7–9. The mothers' median educational attainment was a bachelor's degree (ranging from some college to graduate degrees), and their average years of full-time education after age 14 was 8.1 (SD = 1.23). The fathers' median (and minimum) educational attainment was also a bachelor's degree, but two had doctoral degrees, and their average years of full-time education after age 14 was 8.9 (SD = 1.7).

Of the 18 families contacted in Summit, 4 declined to participate, 5 were willing to participate but did not meet our requirements, and 9 participated. The minimum median family income for this group was $25,000 (ranging from $10,000 to $40,000), and the median Hollingshead ranking was 4 (skilled manual workers), range 2–5 (all mothers but one worked outside the home). The mothers' median and maximum educational attainment was "some college" and all had finished high school. On average, these mothers completed 4.9 years of full-time education after age 14 (SD = 1.54). The fathers' median educational attainment was completion of high school and ranged from "less than high school" to "some college," and their average years of education after age 14 was 4.6 (SD = 1.62).

The percentage of families who wished to participate was high, given the intrusiveness (20 hours of observation of each child) of the study (64% of the Holden families and 78% of Summit families), perhaps a reflection of the fact that each family that participated received a $250 savings bond in the child's name. Seven of the 10 Holden families that declined to participate gave busy schedules as the reason. When pressed, 1 family also cited the intrusiveness of the research, the primary reason given by the other 3 Holden families. Of the 4 Summit families that were unwilling to participate, 2 had in-home babysitters who refused to be observed, 1 had a newborn and was planning to move out of the neighborhood, and in 1 the father cited his occupation in law enforcement. The reasons given for not participating appear to indicate that those individuals who were feeling more stress or were less comfortable with the idea of having a stranger in their homes were unlikely to participate. The families that participated were also quite busy, as evidenced by the wide variety of activities and settings in which observations were made, but they may have been better able to cope with their busy schedules and more relaxed with the presence of an outsider.

Families were asked to keep their daily routines unchanged as much as possible during the observation period. Each child was observed, wherever he or she was, for 20 hours over the course of a week to capture the equivalent of an entire waking day. Observations were continuous in 2- and 4-hour blocks, but activities, partners, respective roles, and so on were only coded during 30-second "windows" every 5½ minutes, using the modified spot observations discussed earlier. Activities were coded as being "available to" the child if they occurred within his or her ear- or eyeshot. Children were coded as being "involved in" the activities if they were physically participating or were observing.

The activities in which we were interested were lessons (4 categories), work (5 categories), play (10 categories), conversation (3 categories), and "other" (6 categories, including sleeping and eating). (For full details of the coding scheme, please refer to Tudge, Sidden, & Putnam, 1990.) In brief, *lessons* were defined as involving the deliberate attempt to impart or receive information in four areas: academic (spelling, counting, learning shapes and colors, etc.); interpersonal (teaching etiquette or "proper" behavior); skill/nature (how things work, why things happen); and religious. *Work* was defined as "activities that either have economic importance or contribute to the maintenance of life" (Tudge et al., 1990) and was broken down into work involving no technology, technology modified for a child's use, or "adult" technology. *Play* (including exploration and entertainment) was defined as activities that were being engaged in for fun or for their own sake, with no apparent curriculum (which would constitute a lesson) or sense that the activity had economic importance (work). Thus, a child looking at a book or being read to would be coded as engaging in play with an academic object, whereas the child asking what a particular word was or being asked to name the colors would be coded as being involved in an academic lesson. *Conversation* was defined as talk that was not related to the ongoing activity and had a sustained or focused topic. Talking that accompanied play, work, or a lesson was not coded as conversation. During any 30-second window, more than one activity could occur and could be coded.

## Results

### *Activities Coded*

A total of 3,584 observations were taken of these 20 preschoolers, 1,967 of the Holden group (11 children) and 1,617 of the Summit group (9 children). Because we coded all activities that occurred in the child's immediate vicinity (irrespective of the child's involvement) and because during the 30-second period a child could change activities, a total of 5,799 activities were coded: 2,676 for the Summit group and 3,123 for the Holden group. However, some of the observations took place while the children were sleeping (98 for the Summit group, 212 for the Holden group), and the activities taking place at those times (a total of 304, not including sleep as an activity) were clearly not available to the children. This left 5,185 activities that were potentially available to the children, 2,453 for the Summit group (47% of the total) and 2,732 (53%) for the Holden group. Because both groups featured one more girl than boy, the proportion of observations on girls was somewhat higher in both communities (55:45).

### *Activities: Availability and Involvement*

Many activities occurred within easy ear- and eyeshot of the children, and were therefore potentially available to them, even if the children did not get involved in them. In both the Holden group (where the parents worked in the professional sphere) and Summit group, play (including exploration and entertainment) was the most common activity occurring around these children (about 40% and 45% of the activities observed in the two groups, respectively). Conversation was more likely to occur around the Holden children than their Summit counterparts (17% vs. 8%, respectively), whereas work was somewhat less likely to occur (15% vs. 22%, respectively). Lessons occurred least often (about 7% and 4%, respectively).

Turning to activities in which the children were actively involved (either as participant or observer), play occurred with even greater frequency, particularly so in the Summit group (62% vs. 48% for the Holden children). The children from the two groups were involved to the same extent in work (approximately 8% of all activities in which they were involved), but the Holden children were more involved than their Summit counterparts in both conversation (14% vs. 7%, respectively) and lessons (8% vs. 5%, respectively). The remaining activities in which the children were involved fell into the category of *other*.

### *Lessons*

Our focus for the remainder of this chapter will be on the lessons in which children were involved. Lessons were available 279 times and children were involved in 232 of them, either as active participants or as careful observers. As seen in Figure 9.1, the Holden children engaged overall in more lessons than their Summit counterparts, particularly with regard to academic lessons (lessons about reading, numbers, colors, etc.) and skill/nature lessons (such as tying shoes or learning about the workings of nature). Interpersonal lessons (dealing with manners, getting along with others, etc.) were more evenly distributed, but it is clear that these lessons constituted the majority of lessons in which the Summit children were involved (58% of their total lessons), whereas the Holden children's lessons were more evenly distributed across the three types of lessons. (It is also interesting that the Holden children were far more likely than those from Summit to play with academic objects – looking at books or playing games with explicitly academic purposes – 108 vs. 60 instances.)

The following examples are illustrative of academic lessons in the two communities:

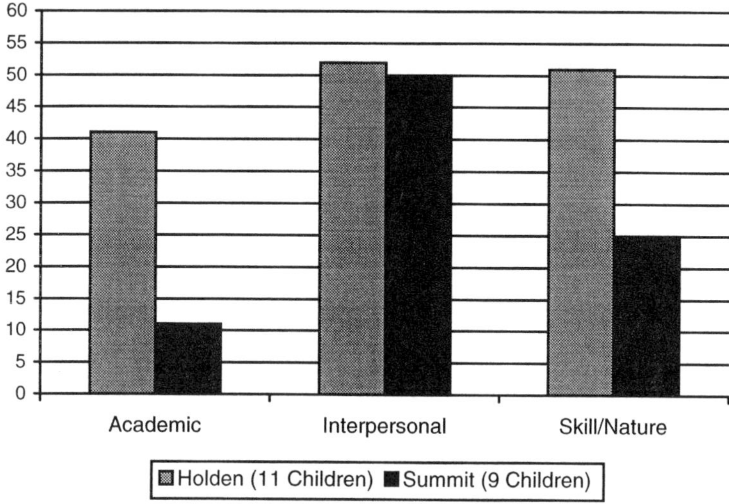


**Figure 9.1.** Types of lessons, by community.

Forty-five-month-old Mary (a pseudonym) lives in the Holden community. In this example, she is attending a party at her aunt's house. Mary's 15-year-old sister is entertaining Mary and two cousins, who are about Mary's age. They are sitting on the stairs, and Mary and her two cousins are drawing with markers on paper big sister is holding on her lap. Here, older sister initiates an academic lesson for the three young children.

*Sister*: Okay, I'll write. . . . Can you write your name?

*Mary*: I . . . I can write my name. I can do it. I want to give you an L.

*Sister*: Your name doesn't have an L in it. I'll show you. This is an M. This is an A. Then an R, and this is a Y. And you both have an A [points to the two cousins]. A for Amy and A for Andrew.

Thirty-four-month-old Eric (a pseudonym) lives in Summit. In this scene, Eric is playing Uno, a card game, with his mother. His father is sitting nearby, watching television. The academic lesson here occurs in the context of being able to count cards as part of playing the game.

*Eric*: You got to draw two cards.

*Father*: You got seven this time.

*Eric*: Nah-uh. I'm going to turn over another one.

*Mother*: Let's see how many you got. No. Lay 'em down one at a

time. Say, one.... Lay 'em down. You've got to count the same ones over again.
*Eric*: I got one, two, three, four ... [As he counts, Eric places cards on the ottoman that they are using as a card table. Sometimes he puts down one card, sometimes several cards as he counts.]
*Mother*: Count them right. Lay 'em down one at a time. One ... No, I didn't say slide it off. One, two, three, four, five ...
*Eric*: I did count 'em.
*Mother*: You weren't counting right.
*Father*: Eric, count the cards.
*Eric*: I did count 'em.
*Mother*: Lay 'em down.

The proportion of Summit boys and girls involved in lessons was as expected, given the greater proportion of observations of girls. In the Holden group, however, boys were proportionally and actually more likely to be involved in lessons than were girls. As Figure 9.2 shows, however, boys in both groups were more likely to be involved in academic lessons than were girls, whereas the opposite was true of interpersonal lessons.

These data indicate that children from the two communities were involved in rather strikingly different types of activities. Those from the Holden community were more likely to be exposed to lessons and conversation than were their Summit counterparts. Similarly, they were much more involved in these activities. The differences between the two groups were most striking in terms of academic lessons, skill/nature lessons, and academic play, with the Holden children more involved than the Summit children. By contrast, the greatest proportion of the lessons in which the Summit group was involved were interpersonal lessons – that is, lessons dealing with good behavior toward other people.

If Kohn's analysis is correct, parents who work in the professional sphere should value independence and self-initiative in their children more than parents who work in the nonprofessional sphere, whereas parents who work in the nonprofessional sphere should be more likely to value obedience and following rules. Although our data on the parents' values and beliefs about child rearing have yet to be fully analyzed, they appear to support Kohn's position (Hogan et al., 1996). Kohn left unexamined the issue of whether or not parents *actually* encourage or support their children's attempts to show these qualities in everyday life, although he was able to show that children

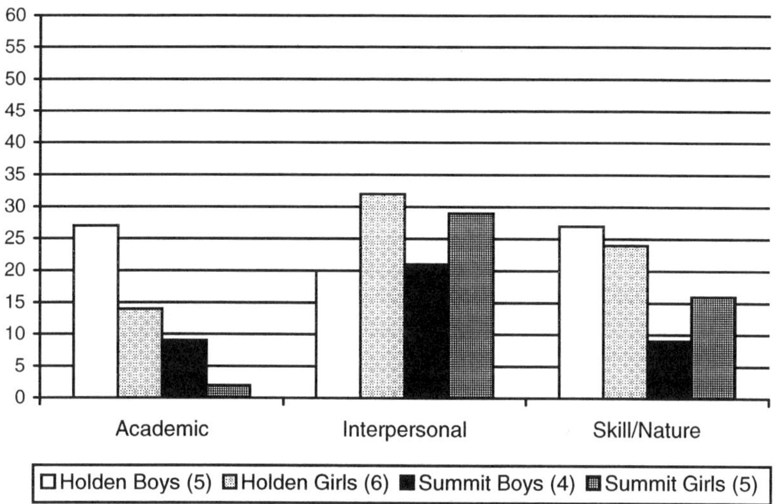


**Figure 9.2.** Lessons, by community and gender.

do subscribe to the same values (Kohn, Slomszynski, & Schoenbach, 1986). The children in our study were too young to allow a verbal assessment of their own values; instead, we were able to examine directly the extent to which children initiated activities and became involved in those activities under their own direction or following suggestion from someone else.

In general (as depicted in Figure 9.3), people other than the child were most likely to initiate lessons – but the Holden children were far more likely to initiate (to ask how something is done, how to spell a word, and so on) than those from the Summit community (26% vs. 10% of initiations, respectively). Differences between boys and girls were minimal.

More striking, however, was the fact that irrespective of who initiated the lesson, the Holden children were far more likely to initiate their own involvement in it than were the Summit children, as shown in Figure 9.4 (self-initiated involvement in 55% vs. 27% of the lessons, respectively). The Summit children were more likely to be involved because someone else had ensured that they would – providing unrequested information or telling the child how to behave. It is worth noting that, in both groups, girls were actually and proportionally more likely than boys to initiate their own involve-

Initiations

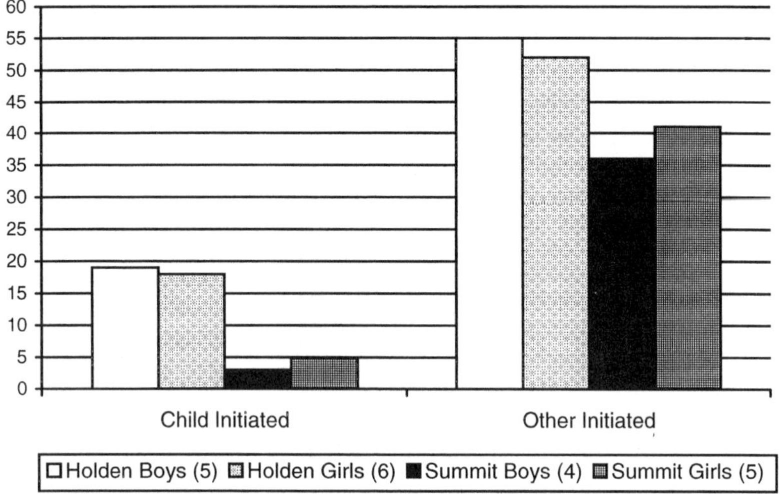


**Figure 9.3.** Initiation of lessons, by community and gender.

Initiations

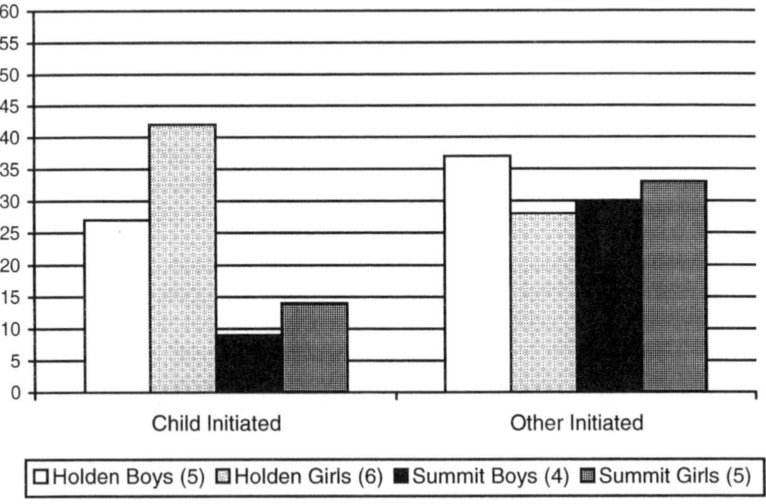


**Figure 9.4.** Initiation of involvement in lessons, by community and gender.

ment in lessons, though this was a good deal more apparent in the Holden than the Summit group. These data, which clearly suggest that these children are accustomed to some degree of self-direction before they are 4 years of age, appear to support Kohn's thesis that professional parents set goals for their children of independence and control over their environments.

By following these children over an extended period of time (20 hours, spread over 1 week, covering the equivalent of each child's entire waking day), we were able to get a reasonable sense of the different physical environments in which they were situated. Both groups of children spent about two-thirds of their time in or around the home and about 10% of their time in public spaces (parks, shops, church, etc.). The major difference was that the Holden children spent more of their time than the Summit children in formal preschool settings (20% vs. 14%, respectively) but less in other people's homes (5% vs. 9%), with much of this difference accounted for by the Summit children's greater time spent in less formal child care arrangements.

The two groups of children differed in that the types of lessons in which they engaged were either rather consistent across home and preschool setting (in the Holden group) or inconsistent (in the Summit group). For the Holden children, the proportions of academic, interpersonal, and skill/nature lessons were approximately the same in home as in school, although there were rather more academic lessons in preschool and rather more skill/nature lessons at home (proportions of 27:35:38 at home, 86 lessons in total; 37:40:22 in school, 40 lessons in total). For the Summit children, however, the proportions were strikingly different (proportions of 6:51:43 in the home, 51 lessons in total; 39:61:0 at school, 18 lessons total). Very few lessons occurred in homes other than their own (6 in each group of children), evenly divided by lesson type in the Holden group, 4 being interpersonal lessons in the Summit group.

Interesting differences were also found in the children's social partners in lessons. In both groups, the children's mothers served as the primary social partner in lessons – in 70% of all lessons in the Holden homes and in 61% in the Summit homes. However, although the fathers were only rarely involved in lessons with their children in Holden (6% of all lessons at home), they were much more likely to be involved in Summit, featuring as partner in almost 16% of the cases. This pattern actually reflects the situation more generally – even when taking into account the fact that fathers were somewhat more available to be partners in Summit (i.e., they were within the immediate setting for a greater proportion of observations than was true for the Holden fathers), they were still far more likely to serve as their child's partner in all activities.

## Conclusion

We have argued that social classes may be thought of as constituting different cultural groups within society, cultural groups that have different sets of values about child-rearing practices and different expectations for their children that are passed on from generation to generation. In that sense, the study reported here is a comparison of different cultural groups, defined not by national boundaries or racial category, but by the value systems that shape the contexts and processes that make up their life experiences. Holden and Summit children, engaging in their regular everyday activities with their typical social partners in their typical settings, are engaged simultaneously in the process of coming to understand their culture and in the process of constructing it anew, with the help of those more experienced in the ways of that culture.

If psychologists are to move away from considering cultures or social classes simply as "social addresses," or as ways of dividing up data for purposes of statistical analysis, it is necessary to examine the ways in which membership in these groups translates into different life experiences. By actively engaging in the life experiences available to them, these children are involved in processes of development that distinguish two groups in the same city, living only a few miles apart, sharing the same racial background, but nevertheless living different lives.

To understand these activities, we have drawn from psychological and ecological theoretical frameworks that emphasize the interrelatedness of individual development and sociocultural phenomena, and that stress the need to cut across different levels of analysis. We have examined what Bronfenbrenner has termed "developmentally instigative" characteristics at the individual level (gender and self-direction) and found that boys and girls are differentially involved in the activities that are available to them, and that the children in one group are much more likely than those in another to initiate activities and initiate their own involvement in activities once they have started. We have examined these activities as they formed, focusing on who started them and how, as well as who were the partners involved. However, without consideration of the broadest level, the macro level of culture (here instantiated as social class), it is difficult to understand why it is that the children and their partners in these two groups act as they do.

The distinct patterns of available lessons and of children's involvement in them suggests a structure, a system shared by the broader group on which the pattern is based. For a connection between the broader world and what is occurring in the lives of these children, we have relied on the insights of Kohn and his colleagues. Their data, collected in a very different way (using surveys and questionnaires, and drawing on a large number of respondents), strongly suggests that parental workplace experiences may in part account for the values and beliefs that parents have about how to raise their children so that they can become economically self-sufficient. If this is the case, we argued that these values and beliefs are likely to be reflected in the types of activities that parents make available to their children and the extent to which parents encourage children to exhibit either self-direction or conformity. This is, of course, what our data reveal.

Kohn's sociological account provided a link between parental workplace practices (the exosystem in Bronfenbrenner's terms) and child-rearing values and beliefs, which we extended to the everyday activities of young children and their social partners, using methods adapted from cultural anthropologists and cultural psychologists.

Bronfenbrenner's ecological (person–process–context) model required that we focus on developmentally instigative aspects of children. In this instance we have examined both gender and the degree to which children initiate (instigate) their involvement in activity. It also requires that we focus on developmentally instigative aspects of the surrounding context, cutting across two or more levels. Here we have chosen to examine social class as an exosystem factor (impacting children indirectly), the different settings in which children spend their time as a mesosystem factor, and partners in activity as a microsystem factor. The processes that are assumed to be operating and that serve to translate social class differences into different outcomes for the children growing up within different social classes are jointly constructed by the children themselves (their own active involvement in activities and their active initiation both of the activities themselves and of their participation in them) and by their social partners, who make different settings and activities available to their children and engage with them to different extents.

It is clear that individual communities, differentiated along a complex of factors (income, education, and occupation) that serve to mark social class, variously arrange activities considered important in this society. Their children, moreover, before the age of 4, have come to behave dissimilarly – at least to the extent of differing in the degree to which they are self-directed – and to engage differentially in these activities.

## References

Barker, R. G., & Wright, H. F. (1951). *One boy's day.* New York: Harper.

Bloch, M. N., & Pellegrini, A. D. (1989). *The ecological context of children's play.* Norwood, NJ: Ablex.

Bronfenbrenner, U. (1988). Interacting systems in human development. Research paradigms: present and future. In N. Bolger, A. Caspi, G. Downey, & M. Moorehouse (Eds.), *Persons in context: Developmental processes* (pp. 25–49). Cambridge University Press.

(1989). Ecological systems theory. In R. Vasta (Ed.), *Annals of child development* (vol. 6, pp. 187–249). Greenwich, CT: JAI Press.

(1993). The ecology of cognitive development: Research models and fugitive findings. In R. Wozniak & K. Fischer (Eds.), *Development in context: Acting and thinking in specific environments* (pp. 3–44). Hillsdale, NJ: Erlbaum.

Bronfenbrenner, U., & Ceci, S. (1994). Nature–nurture reconceptualized in developmental perspective: A bioecological model. *Psychological Review, 101*, 568–586.

Bronfenbrenner, U., & Crouter, A. C. (1983). The evolution of environmental models in developmental research. In P. H. Mussen (Ed.), *Handbook of child psychology: Vol. 1. History, theory, methods* (pp. 357–414). New York: Wiley.

Cairns, R. B. (1992). The making of a developmental science: The contributions and intellectual heritage of James Mark Baldwin. *Developmental Psychology, 28*, 17–24.

Carew, J. V. (1980). Experience and the development of intelligence in young children at home and in day care. *Monographs of the Society for Research in Child Development, 45*(6–7, Serial No. 187), 1–89.

Clarke-Stewart, K. A. (1973). Interactions between mothers and their young children: Characteristics and consequences. *Monographs of the Society for Research in Child Development, 38*(6–7, Serial No. 153), 1–109.

Cole, M. (1985). The zone of proximal development: Where culture and cognition create each other. In J. V. Wertsch (Ed.), *Culture, communication and cognition: Vygotskian perspectives* (pp. 146–161). Cambridge University Press.

Cole, M., & Cole, S. (1992). *The development of children*, 2nd ed. New York: Scientific American.

Corsaro, W. A. (1985). *Friendship and peer culture in the early years.* Norwood, NJ: Ablex.

(1992). Interpretive reproduction in children's peer cultures. *Social Psychology Quarterly*, *55*(2), 160–173.

Davydov, V. D., & Zinchenko, V. P. (1989). Vygotsky's contribution to the development of psychology. *Soviet Psychology*, *27*(2), 22–36.

Dumont, R., & Wax, M. (1976). Cherokee school society and the intercultural classroom. In J. Beck, C. Jenks, N. Keddie, & M. F. D. Young (Eds.), *Worlds apart* (pp. 334–345). London: Collier Macmillan.

Dunn, J. (1988). *The beginnings of social understanding.* Cambridge, MA: Harvard University Press.

Dunn, J., & Wooding, C. (1977). Play in the home and its implications for learning. In B. Tizard & D. Harvey (Eds.), *Biology of play* (pp. 45–58). London: Heinemann Medical.

Edwards, C., & Whiting, B. (1980). Differential socialization of girls and boys in light of cross-cultural research. In C. Super & S. Harkness (Eds.), *Anthropological perspectives on child development* (pp. 45–56). San Francisco: Jossey-Bass.

Ellis, S., Rogoff, B., & Cromer, C. (1981). Age segregation in children's social interactions. *Developmental Psychology*, *17*, 399–407.

Ember, C. R. (1973). Feminine task assignment and the social behavior of boys. *Ethos*, *1*, 424–439.

Erickson, F., & Mohatt, G. (1982). The cultural organization of participation structure in two classrooms of Indian students. In G. Spindler (Ed.), *Doing the ethnography of schooling* (pp. 132–174). New York: Holt, Rinehart, & Winston.

Fischer, J. L., & Fischer, A. (1966). *The New Englanders of Orchard Town USA*. New York: Wiley.

Glick, J. A. (1992). Werner's relevance for contemporary developmental psychology. *Developmental Psychology*, *28*, 558–565.

Goodnow, J. (1984). Parents' ideas about parenting and development: A review of issues and recent work. In M. E. Lamb, A. L. Brown, & B. Rogoff (Eds.), *Advances in developmental psychology, Vol. 3* (pp. 193–242). Hillsdale, NJ: Erlbaum.

Goodnow, J., & Collins, W. A. (1990). *Development according to parents: The nature, sources, and consequences of parents' ideas.* Hillsdale, NJ: Erlbaum.

Harkness, S., & Super, C. (1985). The cultural context of gender segregation in children's peer groups. *Child Development*, *56*, 219–224.

(1986). The developmental niche: A conceptualization at the interface of child and culture. *International Journal of Behavioral Development*, *9*, 545–569.

Heath, S. B. (1983). *Ways with words: Language, life, and work communities and classrooms.* Cambridge University Press.

Hogan, D. M., Tudge, J. R. H., Snezhkova, I. A., & Kulakova, N. N. (1996, February). *US and Russian parents' valuation of self-direction in their children: The role of social class.* Paper presented at the annual meetings of the Society for Cross-Cultural Research, Pittsburgh, PA.

Hood, L., McDermott, R. P., & Cole, M. (1980). "Let's *try* to make it a good day" – Some not so simple ways. *Discourse Processes*, *3*, 155–168.

Kohn, M. L. (1977). *Class and conformity: A study of values*, 2nd ed. Chicago: University of Chicago Press.

(1979). The effects of social class on parental values and practices. In D. Reiss & H. Hoffman (Eds.), *The American family: Dying or developing*? (pp. 45–68). New York: Plenum.

Kohn, M. L., & Schooler, C. (1983). *Work and personality.* Norwood, NJ: Ablex.

Kohn, M. L., & Slomszynski, K. M. (1990). *Social structure and self-direction: A comparative analysis of the United States and Poland.* Oxford: Basil Blackwell.

Kohn, M. L., Slomszynski, K. M., & Schoenbach, C. (1986). Social stratification and the transmission of values in the family: A cross-national assessment. *Sociological Forum*, *1*, 73–102.

Lave, J. (1988). *Cognition in practice.* Cambridge University Press.

Lee, S., & Tudge, J. (1995, February). *Young children's play in South Korea and the United States: Cross-cultural and sub-cultural comparisons.* Paper presented at the annual meetings of the Society for Cross-Cultural Research, Savannah, GA.

LeVine, R. A., & White, M. I. (1986). *Human conditions: The cultural basis of educational development.* New York: Routledge & Kegan Paul.

Lubeck, S. (1985). *Sandbox society: Early education in black and white America.* London: Falmer.

Luster, T., Rhoades, K., & Haas, B. (1989). The relation between parental values and parenting behavior: A test of the Kohn hypothesis. *Journal of Marriage and the Family*, *51*, 139–147.

McDermott, R. P., Gospodinoff, K., & Aron, J. (1978). Criteria for an ethnographically adequate description of concerted activities and their contexts. *Semiotica*, *24*(3–4), 245–275.

Mead, M. (1961). *Coming of age in Samoa.* New York: New American Library.

Morelli, G. A., & Tudge, J. R. H. (1989, February). *Bridging the gap: A new look at the ontogeny of gender differences in children from two cultures from a Vygotskian perspective.* Paper presented at the annual meetings of the Society for Cross-Cultural Research, New Haven, CT.

Munroe, R. H., & Munroe, R. L. (1971). Household density and infant care in an East African society. *Journal of Social Psychology, 83*, 3–13.

Nicolopolou, A. (1993). Play, cognitive development, and the social world: Piaget, Vygotsky, and beyond. *Human Development, 36*, 1–23.

Ochs, E., & Schieffelin, B. B. (1984). Language acquisition and socialization: Three developmental stories and their implications. In R. A. Shweder & R. A. LeVine (Eds.), *Culture theory: Essays on mind, self, and emotion* (pp. 276–320). Cambridge University Press.

Richards, M. P. M. (1977). An ecological study of infant development in an urban setting in Britain. In P. H. Leiderman, S. R. Tulkin, & A. Rosenfeld (Eds.), *Culture and infancy: Variations in the human experience* (pp. 469–493). New York: Academic Press.

Rogoff, B. (1978). Spot observation: An introduction and examination. *Quarterly Newsletter of the Laboratory of Comparative Human Cognition, 2*, 21–26.

(1981). Adults and peers as agents of socialization: A Highland Guatemalan profile. *Ethos, 9*, 18–36.

(1990). *Apprenticeship in thinking: Cognitive development in social context.* Oxford University Press.

Schwartzman, H. G. (1978). *Transformations: The anthropology of children's play.* New York: Plenum.

(1986). A cross-cultural perspective on child-structured play activities and materials. In A. W. Gottfried & A. C. Brown (Eds.), *The contribution of play materials and parental involvement to children's development* (pp. 13–29). Lexington, MA: Lexington Books.

Shweder, R. A. (1990). Cultural psychology – What is it? In J. W. Stigler, R. A. Shweder, & G. Herdt (Eds.), *Cultural psychology: Essays on comparative human development* (pp. 1–43). Cambridge University Press.

Smilansky, S. (1968). *The effects of sociodramatic play on disadvantaged preschool children.* New York: Wiley.

Tammeveski, P., Meltsas, M., & Tudge, J. R. H. (in press). Parenting in socio-cultural contexts: Teaching and learning in two groups of Estonian parents and their preschoolers. *Polish Quarterly of Developmental Psychology.*

Tudge, J. R. H. (1982). Lack of control and the development of incompetence. *Cornell Journal of Social Relations, 16*(2), 84–97.

Tudge, J. R. H. (in press). Internalization, externalization, and joint-carving: Comments from an ecological perspective. In B. Cox & C. Lighfoot

(Eds.), *Sociogenetic perspectives on internalization.* Hillsdale, NJ: Erlbaum.

Tudge, J. R. H., Kulakova, N. N., & Snezhkova, I. A. (in press). Culture and social stratification in Russia: Parents' child-rearing values and beliefs under conditions of rapid social change. *Etnograficheskoe Obozrenie* [*Ethnographical Review*].

Tudge, J. R. H., Lee, S., & Putnam, S. E. (in press). Young children's play in socio-cultural context: South Korea and the United States. In M. C. Duncan, G. Chick, & A. Aycock (Eds.), *Playing fields: Excursions in research and theory on play.* Champaign, IL: The Association for the Study of Play Press.

Tudge, J. R. H., Putnam, S. E., & Sidden, J. (1993). Preschoolers' activities in socio-cultural context. *Quarterly Newsletter of the Laboratory of Comparative Human Cognition, 15*(2), 71–84.

(1994). The everyday activities of American preschoolers: Lessons and work in two socio-cultural contexts. In A. Alvarez & P. Del Rio (Eds.), *Perspectives in socio-cultural research: Vol. 4. Education as cultural construction* (pp. 109–121). Madrid: Fundacion Infancia i Aprendizaje.

Tudge, J. R. H., Putnam, S. E., & Valsiner, J. (in press). Culture and cognition in developmental perspective: Reading as a co-constructive process. In B. Cairns & G. H. Elder Jr. (Eds.), *Developmental science.* Cambridge University Press.

Tudge, J. R. H., Sidden, J. A., & Putnam, S. E. (1990). *The cultural ecology of young children: Coding manual.* Unpublished manuscript. University of North Carolina at Greensboro.

Tudge, J. R. H., & Winterhoff, P. A. (1993). Vygotsky, Piaget, and Bandura: Perspectives on the relations between the social world and cognitive development. *Human Development, 36*, 61–81.

Tulviste, P. (1991). *Cultural-historical development of verbal thinking: A psychological study.* Commack, NY: Nova.

Valsiner, J. (1987). *Culture and the development of children's action.* New York: Wiley.

(1989). *Human development and culture: The social nature of personality and its study.* Lexington, MA: Lexington Books.

van der Veer, R., & Valsiner, J. (1988). Lev Vygotsky and Pierre Janet: On the origin of sociogenesis. *Developmental Review, 8*, 52–65.

(1991). *Understanding Vygotsky: A quest for synthesis.* Oxford: Blackwell.

(1994). *The Vygotsky reader.* Oxford: Basil Blackwell.

Vygotsky, L. S. (1978). *Mind in society.* Cambridge, MA: Harvard University Press.

(1987). *The collected works of L. S. Vygotsky: Vol. 1. Problems of general psychology.* New York: Plenum.

Wertsch, J. V. (1985). *Vygotsky and the social formation of mind.* Cambridge, MA: Harvard University Press.

(1991). *Voices of the mind: A sociocultural approach to mediated action.* Cambridge, MA: Harvard University Press.

Whiting, B. B. (1976). The problem of the packaged variable. In K. F. Riegel & J. A. Meacham (Eds.), *The developing individual in a changing world: Vol. 1. Historical and cultural issues* (pp. 310–321). Chicago: Aldine.

Whiting, B. B., & Edwards, C. P. (1988). *Children of different worlds: The formation of social behavior.* Cambridge, MA: Harvard University Press.

Willis, P. (1977). *Learning to labour: How working class kids get working class jobs.* New York: Columbia University Press.

PART FOUR

# Commentaries

# 10 Developmental Science: A Case of the Bird Flapping Its Wings or the Wings Flapping the Bird?

*Jeanette A. Lawrence*

In Chapter 1, Terry Winegar urges developmental scientists to reflect on their scientific practices. Reflection, including self-reflection about the researcher's own scientific aims and assumptions, should result in explicit clarification of goals and theoretical commitments, and their methodological derivations. Effective work on the central questions of the field is dependent on a clear understanding of the multiple levels involved in research and the appropriateness of the links made between these levels. Winegar identifies the levels of research as metatheory, theory, methodology, method, data, and phenomenon, interconnected in a linear progression with feedback loops of implications. Inappropriate dominance by any level will involve problems of level autonomy or fusion and, therefore, unproductive research efforts and obfuscation of the central questions of developmental science. Winegar argues for clearer articulation of research activities at each level and warns about the dangers of substituting work at one level for careful attention to another level. In particular, he is concerned about substituting mindless methods and frenetic data collection for methodology, theory, and metatheory.

In similar vein, Joachim Wohlwill (1991) discussed relations between method and theory in developmental psychology, in what became his final word to the field. There are some striking convergences in the two approaches, and the title of my commentary focuses on the discussion of Winegar's claims within a nice piece of imagery suggested by Wohlwill.

Like Wohlwill, Winegar is concerned that contemporary developmental research is in danger of "the wings flapping the bird" (Wohlwill, 1991, p. 127), that is, being in a situation where methods

This commentary was supported by a grant from the Australian Research Council.

and data-analytic models unduly direct the theoretical component of research. While Wohlwill was specifically commenting on structural-equation models, his identification of the dangers incurred when methods drive theory coincides with one of Winegar's central concerns. According to Wohwill (1991):

> The further development of these models may well influence the ways in which future researchers will formulate their questions concerning the dynamics of development, and of transactional relationships between the environment and the developing individual. (p. 127)

Powerful statistical models and data-analytic techniques such as structural-equation modeling carry with them great potential for actually generating research questions and, by implication, research programs, precisely because of the novel and extensive facilities they offer. Possibilities for grubbing through data seem to be endless. Winegar adds to this the dangers associated with restricting the conceptualization of developmental "research" to empirical investigation and, consequently, to the problems incurred by defining, as well as driving, research by activities at its empirical investigative levels. The problems associated with gross and unreflective empiricism are real for contemporary developmental psychology.

Once developmentalists try to investigate complexities of the socially rich contexts in which development occurs, they are putting themselves in methodological danger, as Wohwill understood. Because contextualism and co-constructivism have gained ground in the past few decades, a parallel heightened demand has been created for methods that can examine and describe situational complexities. But the methods involved can take over the enterprise. As Winegar points out, questions about the processes and organization of development and the emergence of novel phenomena demand multifaceted investigative procedures. Winegar rightly suggests that we have made ground in widening the focus of our research to include context in analyses of personal development. If the connected activities of more than one person and social institutions over time are of interest, then contemporary developmentalists need to use investigative methods that will handle multiple inputs from mulitiple sources over multiple occasions.

A new and powerful tool can generate its own fascination, but so can a comfortable, well-accepted method that introduces no problems for journal reviewers. Once a technique has been proposed as a way of dealing with some of the problems in a research question, and its facility has been demonstrated by a respected researcher, then use of the method can become the driving force for numerous studies by other researchers. Endless rounds of studies can show how the technique applies to various samples, ages, and contexts. Segall, Dasen, Berry, and Poortinga (1990, p. 349) criticize popular "safari-style research" in which favorite tests are taken to exotic cultures and results are compared across cultural samples. Similarly, there can be a developmental "technique gravy train" that facilitates reception of a study. For example, meta-analysis seemed to enjoy that position for some time. Closer to home, the much revered longitudinal method can generate its own rhythm and research questions. Data-collection impetus can be sustained for a long time, with vague connections to theoretical perspectives and questions so that the annual or semiannual collection of data becomes its own driving force. With changes in emphasis in the discipline, such data may become less fashionable and raise issues of the relevance of the project. An immense pit of data is available for mining in different ways. With a new method of analysis in hand, one or more researchers can go back and back to the same data set to ask the kinds of questions the method dictates. Thus, it is possible for new and powerful methods of data collection or analysis to drive research projects and research programs.

Nevertheless, neither Winegar nor I is simply criticizing the use of the tools and methods of contemporary developmental science. What is at issue is the relationship of empirical data collection and analytic methods to the theory and purposes of developmental research. Further, Winegar pushes for greater explication of assumptions, basic principles of the researcher's metatheory about how humans develop and what that means.

I see four burdens in Winegar's account of doing developmental science: the identification of what can be called research in developmental science; the need to be reflective, especially about directions of influence in research activities; problems related to the concurrent connectedness and differentiation of different contributions to a research program; and specification of proper metatheoretical issues (processes, organizational change, and the emergence of novelty).

While agreeing strongly with Winegar's position about the dangers of crass empiricism, I wish to point out another danger that could arise from a surface reading of his argument. This is the danger of assuming that there is an automatic bird–wing connection in which only one metatheory will be suitable for driving the wings (methods) of a particular research program, and that it will automatically flap those wings if employed. This interpretation may involve too simple a reading of Winegar's case. However, because his case against method-driven research is timely and significant, it should be taken seriously, and this means reexamining some of his points about fusion and autonomy as he lays out those problems. Could I therefore stretch the aerodynamic analogy a little further?

We can liken the development of a research enterprise as laid out by Winegar to early human efforts to fly. In his treatise on aeronautics in classical times, Clive Hart (1972, p. 30) tells how early enthusiasts like Daedalus worked on beating wings attached to their arms. Humans imitated the methodology of birds. Methods came from empirical observation and were thought about in what could be considered a theory of flying methods or a flying methodology. However, metatheories were not strictly related to method, but rather to the spiritual and psychological importance given to the human desire to fly. Early enthusiasts were motivated by visions of overcoming the Fall, becoming attuned to nature, or engaging in hazardous departures from the established order that would test their powers and liberate them. It was possible to work from these and other metaphysical assumptions and still search for methods of imitating birds when it came to the business of actually trying to fly. A single set of metatheoretical assumptions and principles will not inevitably lead a developmental researcher to adopt a particular methodological approach.

A researcher's metatheory may not be as bound to the kind of linear progression through the other levels of the research as Winegar's case seems to imply. Basic assumptions and organizing principles may differ, especially when these assumptions are related to the processes of change. For instance, attachment to a co-constructivist position does not automatically entail adoption of a common set of assumptions about the processes involved in microgenetic or ontogentic change (see Valsiner & Lawrence, in press, for several accounts of person–culture interactions). The individual researcher may need to proceed cautiously without a thorough set of propositions about basic change mechanisms, because the field is in some confusion about what those mechanisms might be.

There seem to be at least two problems with Winegar's hierarchical account of research. In rejecting the tendency to equate research with the empirical investigative phase, Winegar fails to specify whether he is talking about an individual research project or a connected research program, and that may cause some confusion. In the case of an integrated, sequenced attack on a set of issues, it would seem that his partially linear movement would be more appropriately seen as a cyclically related set of activities in which individual pieces of research inform the total system in bidirectional feedback loops (see Branco & Valsiner, in press). In programmatic research, there may be a goal of feeding back into the total enterprise from different places. It is in such a situation that developmentalists should be able to work at the different levels of the connected program, by engaging in theoretical or theory of method work focused on the same research questions as the investigative activity.

Winegar also seems not to distinguish the practice of developmental science as a science from the sociology of scientific work within the discipline. Does this matter? I think so, because it may be in this distinction that much of the problem of method-driven theorizing – or rather nontheorizing, in Winegar's terms – occurs. Further, it would seem to be the social and institutional constraints on "doing research" that make the multilevel enterprise unpalatable. To examine how the scientific and social aspects of the conduct of developmental science may confuse the issue, let us take the case of a developmental researcher, R.

R graduated with a doctorate in a recognized school of psychology and did a postdoc working with a professor who had a developmental research program. R is appointed to an assistant professorship, say in the North American system, where R is obliged to publish a certain (undefined) amount within a definable time if R aspires to tenure and promotion. Major grants are not readily accessible, unless R continues to be tied to previous supervisors' projects. Let us further attribute to R a fairly independent spirit and reasonable ambition to get on in developmental psychology or, at least, to survive beyond tenure. R can either begin within the past supervisor's research program or branch out independently to develop a personal research program on an R-generated question. We will leave aside the issue of accepted paradigms and assume that the work can be embedded in an established paradigm.

If we take Winegar seriously, what is R to do? The goals of R's developmental science are multiple and can cover intellectual curiosity, metatheoretical commitments to a particular view of the world, and development, including, one would hope, the premise that developmental research is properly concerned with questions to do with the processes and organization of development and is interested in the emergence of novelty. If R follows Winegar's account of the most productive route for developmental science, R will need to work carefully at each level of the Winegar hierarchy. Metatheoretical assumptions will be clarified. This is the scientific practice of developmental science, and Winegar asks us to be explicit as well as reflective about these issues. When pursued with skill, knowledge, and care, it should lead to a progressive research program that exhibits some degree of coherence and to the discovery of novel phenomena by expanding coverage of the phenomena as the program proceeds (Chalmers, 1976; Lakatos, 1974).

Meanwhile, there are the social dimensions of R's science, and these include being productive, looking productive to R's senior colleagues, getting the research program going, writing grant applications, going to conferences, teaching, and engaging in all the other activities that fill an assistant professor's days and nights. How does R practice developmental science and also fulfill professorship requirements at the same time? Can R afford to engage in the type of research that Winegar suggests? Can R's work be multileveled? Can R put in the effort and time required by scientific practice? What form of scientific work is open to R? It has to be labeled "research," and here Winegar's reservations are potent. How will R's tenure committee evaluate R's research if R engages in theory building or metatheoretical analysis (especially if the criteria are aesthetic)? Will literature reviews count as research, especially if they are not published in *Psychological Bulletin?* In short, how does R do developmental science and survive in the developmental science system?

Most psychologists have experienced something of R's situation themselves or observed it secondhand. As someone from the Antipodes, I have watched many promising researchers face this type of dilemma, especially in North America. Of course, the tenured and mature researcher is not free of the need to keep producing. Surely one of the remedies offered to all researchers is the very kind of method- and data-driven research that in Winegar's and Wohlwill's terms is most likely to lead to degenerative research programs. These do not reveal new phenomena and are not coherent, in Lakatos's (1974) terms, and do not involve the type of theoretical and metatheoretical work that Winegar requires. So the problems are not simply those of the individual developmental researcher, but of the discipline itself. The problems are not scientific in nature as much as they are problems of the sociology of science (Chalmers, 1990) and the psychology of the professional development of the developmentalist. A co-constructivist account of R's plight suggests that the discipline provides the tools and the semiotic signs that create R-type dilemmas and method-driven research. It is quicker and easier, it generates papers, and it fits within what passes for a Kuhnian-type normal science in psychology. But does it, and indeed can it, advance developmental science?

Surely the need for self-reflection belongs to the whole discipline and not simply to individual Rs. As a discipline, no matter how much we call ourselves a developmental *science*, we will not encourage the development of progressive research programs unless we heed warnings by Winegar and Wohlwill. Are there some benchmark issues that will aid this self-reflection?

Winegar's plea for an enlightened view of what can be called "research" offers one way forward. Method and data-collection dominance would be relieved for many researchers, and not simply novice professors like R, if there were greater recognition of theoretical and metatheoretical work, as well as extended (not relaxed) evaluative criteria for contributions to developmental science.

The Lakatosian (1974) criteria of coherence and the revelation of new phenomena can be extended to include Chalmer's less relativistic philosophy of science, although his criteria were developed specifically for the natural sciences. Chalmers (1990, p. 115) argues that the practice of science can be judged in relation to its known and statable aims. For him, such aims are "to extend and improve our general knowledge of the workings of the natural world." The methods and standards of science can be judged by the extent to which they serve practically realizable versions of that aim (p. 24).

Heuristically, we can ask how well research questions and goals can be framed around process, change, and novelty in human activities if thorough work is not done at each level of research activity with roughly approximate effort and enthusiam. As Chalmers points out for the natural sciences, there is a genuine place for the researcher who works on the analytic dimensions of the whole scheme of activity. Similarly, Winegar gives developmentalists one way forward, precisely as a widening of research to cover such metatheoretical and theoretical work. Another way is to apply autonomy and fusion tests in personal and social reflection on research. Let us be careful about labeling as theory generalizations from findings, about using paradigmatic and measurement constructs as if they were concepts, and about giving investigative procedures autonomy in our work. This will go some way toward stopping the wings from flapping the bird. In dealing with the bird's flapping, let us be clear about our assumptions and goals, as well as explicit about how we seen them driving particular studies and sets of studies with the purpose of finding and explaining new phenomena. Being sure of the nature of the bird may go some way to allowing the bird to direct the process. But none of this can build a developmental science without simultaneous attention to what the practice of that science should be and how its social dimensions can assist its progressive development.

## References

Branco, A., & Valsiner, J. (in press). Changing methodologies: A co-constructionist study of goal orientations in social interactions. To appear in G. Misra (Ed.), *Cultural construction of social cognition.* Cambridge University Press.

Chalmers, A. F. (1976). *What is this thing called science.* Brisbane: University of Queensland Press.

(1990). *The fabrication of science.* Minneapolis: University of Minnesota Press.

Hart, C. (1972). *The dream of flight: Aeronautics from classical times to the Renaissance.* London: Faber & Faber.

Lakatos, I. (1974). Falsification and the methodology of scientific research programmes. In I. Lakatos & A. Musgrave (Eds.), *Criticism and the growth of knowledge* (pp. 91–196). Cambridge University Press.

Segall, M. H., Dasen, P. R., Berry, J. W., & Poortinga, Y. H. (1990). *Human behavior in a global perspective.* New York: Pergamon.

Valsiner, J., & Lawrence, J. A. (in press). Human development across the life-span. To appear in J. W. Berry, P. R. Dasen, & T. S. Saraswathi (Eds.), *Handbook of cross-cultural psychology: Vol. 2, Basic processes and developmental psychology.* 2nd edition. Boston: Allyn & Bacon.

Wohlwill, J. F. (1991). Relations between method and theory in developmental research: A partial-isomorphism view. In P. Van Geert & L. P. Mos (Eds.), *Annals of theoretical psychology*, (vol. 7, pp. 91–138). New York: Plenum.

# 11 Conceptual Transposition, Parallelism, and Interdisciplinary Communication

*Jeanette A. Lawrence and Agnes E. Dodds*

In Chapter 2, Michael Shanahan, Jaan Valsiner, and Gilbert Gottlieb address the usefulness of common concepts for describing human development and discuss their transposition across psychobiology, psychology, and sociology. The concepts are identified as theoretical principles of human development that arise out of "an epigenetic characterization of development as an emergent coactional hierarchical system" (Gottleib 1991a, p. 7). We interpret their statements as proposing that development should be viewed in terms of a systemic structure with bidirectional relationships between vertical and horizontal levels, occurring in social and personal time, and changing probabilistically, where changes are manifested in coactional coordinated patterns across levels of human functioning. Further, we see their final principle as a different kind of statement, not defining development as such, but rather identifying developmentalists' studies of change as activities located within a disciplinary domain and influenced by intellectual and social criteria.

Shanahan et al. are interested in establishing a foundation for interdisciplinary communication and multidisciplinary research in developmental science. Their analysis of the across-discipline parallelism and transposability of developmentally significant concepts is a timely piece of metatheoretical research. Wielding the analytic tool of examining the underlying structure of theories, the authors demonstrate that the developmental principles can be employed as heuristic definitions to identify commonalities of use in the three disciplines. They apply the heuristic definitions to two developmental theories to demonstrate the usefulness of such heuristics for assessing theoretical coverage of basic developmental issues: Kurt Fischer's theory of cognitive development and Harry Stack

We acknowledge the support of the Australian Research Council.

Sullivan's interdisciplinary, developmental approach to interpersonal psychiatry.

Within this volume's concern with different approaches to developmental science, the chapter challenges developmental theorists to look beyond their comfortable conceptualizations to parallel uses of major developmental concepts in allied disciplines. The potential gains from a less myopic vision on the part of developmental psychologists include a more closely analyzed basis for the multidisciplinary research that Gottlieb (1991b) argues would facilitate attacking the same problem from different disciplinary angles. An additional possible gain is a way of approaching some issues about individual change that cannot be addressed if development is viewed as the exclusive domain of any one discipline. Such an approach involves researchers working in combinations that genuinely call upon discipline-specific strengths in defining and identifying different aspects of the same problem.

It is not simply the case that the development of the person occurs within biological and social structures. Personal development is constrained by biological and social forces in a bidirectional set of activities (Valsiner & Lawrence, in press) that require levels of analysis that transcend traditional discourse about the cognitive and affective manifestations of individualized growth and decline. Shanahan et al. take the discussion of developmental concepts into new territory by asking us to examine their uses in psychobiology and sociology, and by suggesting that these concepts may represent shared conceptual ground. We wish to take up their challenge and build on it, by reconsidering the issues of transposability and parallel use, in the context of interdisciplinary inquiry. We suggest that the transposition of concepts and explanations is not a simple task, and that it is important to deal with concepts as they are theoretically imbedded in disciplinary discourse. Disciplinary discourses may offer parallel explanations of the same phenomena, and therefore invite transposition of the type that Shanahan et al. propose. But they also can focus on different aspects of the same phenomena, such that interdisciplinary research can profit from differences as well as similarities.

## Transposing Concepts

The idea of transposition involves changing one thing into another or transforming it into another mode of expression. It is commonly used in music and mathematics. Musically, by transposing a melody, the arranger changes the pitch and key of a piece, while retaining its melodic structure and rhythm. The transposed melody is recognizable to the listener as having the same structure as the original piece, and it resembles the original composition, without being identical to it. Nevertheless, the copy will be colored by the change, for example, in key from major to minor, and in pitch from treble to bass. Generally, a piece is transposed in order to broaden its usefulness. For example, by transposing a popular song like "Home Sweet Home" the arranger allows it be sung by all ranges of voice, and therefore makes it accessible to a greater audience. While the purist criticizes the alteration as not being true to the composer's intentions, the listener gains the advantage of hearing something attractive and familiar sung by a favorite singer.

By analogy, the transposition of developmental concepts from one discipline to another provides a recognizable trace that allows researchers to resonate to a familiar idea. But subtle differences may be incurred in the bringing over, related to the theoretical embeddedness of the concept, and therefore to its semiotic meaning. When technical concepts are used within a given discourse, they generally carry with them accepted, in-group common meanings. Initiates can talk to each other and assume that they mean the same thing when they use the concept. But if the same concept is used by researchers from different technical discourses, there is great possibility that the same word will be used and understood differently. Indeed, as Lawrence and Valsiner (1993) have demonstrated concerning the sociogenetic concept of internalization, researchers in the same discipline (e.g., developmental psychology) can use the same concept in distinctly different ways (see Valinser & Lawrence, in press, for an extended analysis of internalization–externalization processes).

A practical parallel can be drawn from courtroom discourse in which a judge and lawyer discuss the appropriate length of a defendant's sentence. Heumann (1990) points out that both may discuss and mean something entirely different by a "long sentence" in terms of months or years in prison. Similarly, the varied uses of "structure" in each of the three disciplines, as outlined by Shanahan et al., aptly illustrates problems that can occur in within- and between-discipline discussions. In almost any serious analysis of structure, change, and temporality by psychologists and sociologists, it will become necessary to clarify the senses in which these and a host of other common concepts is being used. Winegar (Chapter 1, this volume) appropriately tries to avoid one such problem by talking about "organizational change," where the discussion can be clearly placed among considerations of structure.

Harry Stack Sullivan (1953, p. 7) met the technical terminology problem head-on with one strategy when presenting his psychiatric theory. Acknowledging what he called "a fringe of difference in meaning," he decided not to use trick words or create new words by "carpentry of Greek and Sanskrit roots." Instead, Sullivan opted to use a word in common usage and clarify just what he meant to convey by that word. While this strategy may avoid the creation of "psychiatric neologisms," it does not necessarily avoid semiotic confusion.

Obviously there are dangers in opting for commonly used words. It is possible to think that colleagues from another discipline understand and agree with what you say when actually they are interpreting your major concept from a different set of assumptions and explanatory system. It is equally possible to become impatient with their "misuse" (according to your lights) of a favorite concept. According to Sullivan, the alternative to common words is a Babel-like restriction to jargon that is accompanied by assumptions that speaker and listener automatically share the same semiotic meaning. Shanahan et al. argue for communication that relieves modern developmental science from that long-standing and erroneous in-group assumption that one's meanings are universal. They provide a way of beginning the discussion by working upward from a model of development that works on biological conceptualizations and shows their applicability in the other two disciplines.

Nevertheless, across-discipline communication cannot proceed without considerable work on within-discipline discourses and their inferred meanings. For example, Fishbein (1990) points out that the obscurity of biological language bears some of the responsibility for misunderstandings about its contribution by other paradigms. Therefore, transposition of concepts cannot function as an automatic facilitator of interdisciplinary communication; rather, it functions as a second-order activity, once careful conceptual exegesis is made of each discipline's conceptualizations, and then only when interpretive discussion is part of the communication. It is not productive to assume that the use of parallel concepts and explanations will automatically eliminate the confusion that can accompany across-discipline discourse.

## Parallelism of Explanation

In a little-referenced paper, Piaget (1968) anticipated some of Shanahan et al.'s interests in parallel explanations, but went further to argue that across-level isomorphisms can be made only between their abstract, systemic models. Although Piaget's discussion focused specifically on divergent explanations within the single discipline of psychology, it is pertinent because he examined the reduction of psychological explanations to social and other levels (e.g., physical, organicist, behavioral). Addressing diverse explanations of consciousness, a difficult area to conceptualize, Piaget argued that competing explanations stemmed from psychologists' needs to generate problem solutions that would be both theoretically acceptable and heuristically fertile or, at least, would fit different theoretical assumptions. Theorists' accounts of agreed-upon phenomena of consciousness are directed at different levels of human functioning that resemble Gottlieb's (1991a) hierarchical levels, working upward from the individual and physical to the behavioral and social. The problem of competing accounts does not lie in their existence, because parallel explanations are natural outcomes of different theoretical assumptions. Researchers choose their level of explanation (and their concepts) according to theoretical commitments. The danger related to the diversity of available models, different from transpositional equivalence, involves the likelihood of reductionist explanations. According to Piaget, reductions of psychological explanations usually involve moves from complex to simple, or from psychological to extrapsychological, accounts (psychosociological or physicalist transformations).

Concerning psychosociological reductionism, without denying the significance of the social, Piaget (1968, p. 168) claimed that interindividual or collective explanations of intraindividual intellectual development cannot ignore the reality of "internal experience." Of course, one may agree with Piaget's claim that an "internal constructive mechanism based on the coordination of the subject's actions and internalization in operations" cannot be omitted from accounts of intellect and consciousness, without necessarily buying his assumptions of its temporal and logical primacy over the social.

The essential point is that explanations mounted at different levels do not automatically contain all the same elements or cover the same relationships between elements. If some elements (e.g., the coordinating activity of internal mechanisms) are omitted from the semiotic meaning of the original explanation, then it becomes difficult to say how the movement from one level to another is effected. It would seem that transposition would be an inappropriate way of moving from one level of explanation to another. Along these lines, although in another area of development, Grusec and Goodnow (1994) argue that the diversity of individual reactions to parental discipline, and particularly some children's rejection of parental efforts, points to the need for an internalization mechanism to explain why some disciplinary activities work for some children and others do not. Explanations of social (parental) activities alone do not account for the range of individual (child) reactions that interactively determine the outcome of those disciplinary activities. In general, sociological reduction of psychological activities and concepts such as Piaget described requires metatheoretical analysis that gives either alternative accounts of the psychological element or a rationale for avoiding them. In such cases, transposition of concepts is not possible.

Unfortunately, Piaget does not discuss genetic reductions at the same depth as sociological ones, but he does make his underlying principle clear. Reductions are useful only insofar as the transformations are made at the metatheoretical level of the abstract models that generate each explanation. Metatheoretical work on interdisciplinary communication and collaboration should occur at a higher level of abstraction than transposition or substitution of central concepts.

In summary, researchers explain developmental phenomena mostly at their own disciplinary level, using their own familiar concepts and arguing vehemently for their legitimacy. Theorists' underlying assumptions are important for understanding the meaning they are seeking to convey by the concepts they use in discourse. A worst-case scenario is a scientific environment where disciplinary discourses float past each other. Perhaps equally problematic is the situation where a concept is brought over from one discipline to another, without acknowledging its theoretical embeddedness and assumed meaning. Less extreme is a willingness to engage in dialogue using common concepts, without doing the metatheoretical analysis of underlying abstract models that Piaget demanded. Given the social aspects of research (Gergen, 1992; Lawrence, Chapter 10, this volume) and Gottlieb's (1991a) plea for genuine interdisciplinary approaches to developmental studies, the chapter by Shanahan et al. challenges us to look for resolutions of the transposition and parallelism issues. To enter into genuine interdisciplinary communication certainly requires transposition and translation, but it also requires a determined effort to turn from conceptual imperialism and conceptual myopia.

## Toward Resolving Some Interdisciplinary Conceptual Problems

If we are to initiate productive transposition or translation and to engage in informed communication that acknowledges the strengths and weaknesses of parallel explanations, we need to know if such metatheoretical work is a possibility. The kind of argument mounted by Shanahan et al. encourages us to believe that it is possible for members of the three disciplines to talk to one another about human development. They have common concepts for describing developmental phenomena. The next step is to determine if there are enough parallels in the use of those central concepts to permit interdisciplinary talk or enough open-mindedness to engage in discussion that capitalizes on concepts that are distinct to a particular approach. When concepts are shared, discussion may involve using Shanahan et al.'s conceptual tools for translation and negotiation, rather than accepting that researchers are talking about the same thing when they discuss, for example, "structure" or the temporal location of a subject or target group. That work cannot be done as transposition into another discourse, unless prior theoretical and metatheoretical analysis ensures that the changes involved do not incur distortions of the fundamental meanings of concepts.

Working in an interdisciplinary fashion when concepts are not shared involves consciously exploiting disciplinary differences. Gottlieb (1991a) paves the way for this position by showing that some of the presumed problems of cognitive and social theorists may be unnecessary. He demonstrates that recent advances in molecular biology actually remove support from psychologists who wish to automatically reduce cognitive levels of functioning to genetics. Instead, Gottlieb (1991a) argues persuasively for recognizing the bidirectional influences that occur between all levels of human structure and function. For instance, genetic levels can be influenced by social and experiential factors, such that "genetic determination" becomes a verbalism that should be replaced by accounts of bidirectional canalization.

If we take seriously Gottlieb's (1991a, 1991b, 1991c) argument and evidence for a multievel system analysis of behavior and functioning, we find developmental enquiry to be even more complex, especially in terms of the many influences on change that need to be considered. If he is correct, then it is inappropriatc to look to simplc cxplanations of developmental trajectories in terms of genetic predisposition or social constraints. Rather, we must deal with the complexities of multilevel, bidirectional activities that demand complex conceptual description and explanation. For example, the development of criminal conduct in childhood and adolescence has engaged the attention of a range of researchers with different theoretical approaches: sociological (e.g., McCarthy & Hagan, 1992), developmental-psychological (e.g., Moffitt, 1990), and biological (e.g., Fishbein, 1990). Studies in each discipline have contributed their explanations and predictions of the emergence of criminal and antisocial behavior, each drawing on discipline-based concepts.

While some ground can be made by following an individual theoretical perspective, an interdisciplinary approach holds out promise of being able to focus on genetic predispositions, developmental trajectories, and social structures in combination. In fact, Fishbein (1990) builds a case for fresh examination of biological perspectives on criminality, by arguing that multidisciplinary investigations are dependent on the assumptions and paradigms of different researchers. Her position is in agreement with ours that substantial metatheoretical work is a necessary prelude to across-disciplinary efforts. In relation to the onset of juvenile criminality, Moffitt (1990) related juvenile delinquency to attention deficit disorder, while McCarthy and Hagan (1992) focused on adverse situations. Fishbein (1990) demonstrated the relevance of factors that are biochemical (e.g., the effect of serotonin in modulating aggression), psychophysiological (e.g., slower brain rate activity), or psychopharmacological (e.g., effects of cocaine). To engage in interdisciplinary research that capitalizes on all or any of these approaches means to decide which of their theoretical concepts is profitable under particular conditions and which may be suitable for transposition.

Common concepts (e.g., aggression, antisocial behavior) are often loosely and inconsistently defined, as Fishbein warns, and therefore may be hard to use when working with colleagues from the other disciplines. Transposition cannot proceed without focusing on underlying abstract models, so that, for instance, the meaning of antisocial behavior will be understood in relation to the organization of personal experience, familial patterns of interpersonal activities, and class conduct.

Concepts that are peculiar to a discipline will expand the total view of the situation as they are added to the set of potential predictors, and precisely because they are likely to be tightly defined to perform in within-discipline analyses (e.g., neuropsychological and biochemical variables related to antisocial behaviors). A comprehensive analysis of the emergence of criminal conduct, like Piaget's example of the analysis of consciousness, may benefit most from an approach that avoids reductionism and even transposition, but consciously exploits prior theoretical analyses of paradigm-based contributions. For example, the explanation of judicial sentences and penalties has defied simple explanation for over half a century. While the issue of explaining sentences was an attractive field for psychologists, sociologists, and criminologists, their individualized applications of theory and method had poor explanatory power. Some, but mostly little, of the variance in sentences could be explained by most approaches. Homel and Lawrence (1992) demonstrated that the complexity of the phenomena required a combination of sociology's strengths for analyzing archival material of case details and contextual factors related to court climate, in conjunction with cognitive psychology's ability to analyze the mediating effect of sentencers' decision processes. Their analyses of sentences for 678 drinking-driver offenders in one Australian city combined data from different perspectives in a multivariate linear data analysis, without trying to reduce one level of explanation to another. This combined approach was able to account for 94% of the variance in sentencing decisions, because social-structural factors (e.g., age, gender, employment status), enviromental factors (court), and cognitive dimensions of magistrates' sentencing orientations were considered in their interactions. Theoretical perspectives of each discipline were retained and used to define the focus of the analyses in interdisciplinary framing and execution of research that is in the spirit of Shanahan et al.'s thesis.

It should be noted that analyses of overlaps and peculiarities in metatheoretical frameworks promise to be difficult and costly in both economic and personal terms. It is easier to rely on in-group jargon, and to use common concepts in loose, ill-defined ways, in the hope that definitions will be supplied by co-researchers. It is simpler to try to colonize the field with statements of conceptual superiority than to give way to colleagues' alternative explanations of pet phenomena. Genuine interdisciplinary discussion requires a willingness to look again at cherished concepts (both our own and our colleagues'), then to decide where and at what level their application to a particular developmental issue will be most profitable. Shanahan et al. do developmental scientists a genuine service by showing that some of their major concepts are in frequent use in different disciplines, and that an appreciation of their parallels and suitability for transposition should become a natural part of interdisciplinary discussion. We have suggested that there are alternatives to conceptual imperialism or despair when transposition seems inappropriate. Interdisciplinary research not only is able to proceed, but will prosper when discipline-specific concepts and explanations are brought to bear on developmental issues within the interdisciplinary context of metatheoretical analysis of disciplinary discourse.

## References

Fishbein, D. H. (1990). Biological perspectives in criminology. *Criminology*, *28*(1), 27–72.

Gergen, K. J. (1992). Towards a postmodern psychology. In S. Kvale (Ed.), *Psychology and postmodernism* (pp. 17–30). London: Sage.

Gottlieb, G. (1991a). Experiential canalization of behavioral development: Theory. *Developmental Psychology*, *27*(1), 4–13.

(1991b). Epigenetic systems view of human development. *Developmental Psychology*, *27*(1), 33–34.

(1991c). Experiential canalization of behavioral development: Results. *Developmental Psychology*, *27*(1), 35–39.

Grusec, J. E., & Goodnow, J. J. (1994). Impact of parental discipline methods on the child's internalization of values: A reconceptualization of current points of view. *Developmental Psychology*, *30*(1), 4–19.

Heumann, M. (1990). Criminal sentencing. *Law & Social Inquiry*, *15*, 121–133.

Homel, R. J., & Lawrence, J. A. (1992). Sentencer orientation and case details: An interactive analysis. *Law and Human Behavior*, *16*(5), 509–537.

Lawrence, J. A., & Valsiner, J. (1993). Conceptual roots of internalization:

From transmission to transformation. *Human Development*, *36*, 150–167.

McCarthy, B., & Hagan, J. (1992). Mean streets: The theoretical significance of situational delinquency among homeless youths. *American Journal of Sociology*, *98*(3), 597–627.

Moffitt, T. E. (1990). Juvenile delinquency and attention deficit disorder: Boys' developmental trajectories. *Child Development*, *61*, 893–910.

Piaget, J. P. (1968). Explanation in psychology and psychophysiological parallelism. Chapter 3 in J. P. Piaget, P. Fraisse, & M. Reuchlin, *Experimental psychology: Its scope and method* (translated into English by Judith Chambers) (pp. 153–189). London: Routledge & Kegan Paul.

Sullivan, H. S. (1953). *The interpersonal theory of psychiatry*. New York: Norton.

Valsiner, J., & Lawrence, J. A. (in press). Human development in culture across the life span. To appear in J. W. Berry, P. R. Dasen, & T. S. Saraswathi (Eds.), *Handbook of cross-cultural psychology: Vol. 2, Basic processes and developmental psychology*. 2nd edition. Boston: Allyn & Bacon.

# 12 The "Ecological" Approach: When Labels Suggest Similarities beyond Shared Basic Concepts in Psychology

*Angela Branco*

Since human beings started to reflect on the nature of their own development and psychological functioning, they have conceived the relationship between the individual organism and his or her environment in diverse and multiple ways. From psychology's first systematic efforts to organize itself into a scientific domain, its focus of investigation has fluctuated from the organism to the environment and vice versa, with different emphases on the role played by specific aspects of either the individual or the environment in the configuration of the phenomena. As Jonathan Tudge, Jacquelyn Gray, and Diane Hogan point out in their inclusive historical account of ecological thought in Chapter 3, very early theoretical psychologists realized that a more adequate way to approach the complexities of psychological events would require the assumption of interdependent relationships linking the individual and the environment. Though from different theoretical perspectives, that is what can be found, for example, in Dewey (1896), Baldwin (1895, 1906), Mead (1912, 1913, 1934), Vygotsky (1929, 1978), and Lewin (1933, 1939). The point I propose to discuss here is that the sharing of some basic assumptions (or even concepts), as we can find in these authors, does not necessarily imply further theoretical similarities or complementarity, as Tudge et al. suggest when analyzing Gibson's and Bronfenbrenner's contributions to psychology.

The utilization of the same "umbrella" terminology (Valsiner, 1994a) and the fact that Gibson concentrates his analysis on the physical world, while Bronfenbrenner emphasizes the social dimensions of the environment, may constitute an appealing suggestion to complementarity. Nonetheless, the label *ecology* applied by both authors to their respective work does not grant any theoretical proximity in the cornerstones of their theories. The divergent metatheoretical assumptions undertaken by Gibson and Bronfenbrenner concerning the utility of a conceptual dichotomy – derived from Lewin's "geographical" versus "psychological" fields – make the integration of their theories an impossible task.

As Tudge et al. point out, Gibson and Bronfenbrenner share a conviction that the organism and the environment are inseparable components of a single whole or systemic unit, which certainly qualifies their ideas as ecological (see Tudge and colleagues' historical account of the term). Also, Gibson and Bronfenbrenner are more similar to each other than to some other theorists who stress individual–environment (I–E) interrelatedness, such as Vygotsky, Mead, and others in the sociogenetic tradition in psychology. While sociogenetic thinkers devote their attention to the mechanisms through which the structures of the social environment produce or generate higher psychological functions, with the participation of the constructive, active individual, Gibson and Bronfenbrenner seem to skip the stance of intrasubjective processes and address the I–E linkage more directly (Figure 12.1).

The contrast between Gibson and Bronfenbrenner and the sociointeractionists lies in the emphasis that the sociogenetic tradition (e.g., Baldwin, 1906; van der Veer, 1994; van der Veer & Valsiner, 1991) places on the elaboration of intrasubjective mediation processes, built on a dynamic experience of "internalization" of cultural messages (Lawrence & Valsiner, 1993). The contrast with other versions of sociogenetic thinking that prefer the term *appropriation* to *internalization* (e.g., Rogoff, 1990; Wertsch, 1985) still holds, basically due to the level of elaboration found in their study of the individual psychological processes. Gibson insists on direct, nonmediated perception of the environment by the individual. Bronfenbrenner, albeit stressing the importance of the phenomenological apprehension of reality ("The phenomenological conception of the environment . . . lies at the foundation of the ecological theory"; 1979, p. 23), does not pay specific attention to the analysis of individual psychological processes.

Along the same line, the extent of "sharing" suggested by Tudge et al. between the ecological perspectives of Gibson and Bronfenbrenner and a co-constructivist framework (Valsiner, 1987, 1994b; Wozniak, 1986) cannot be considered significant, due to fundamental metatheoretical and theoretical divergences between them.

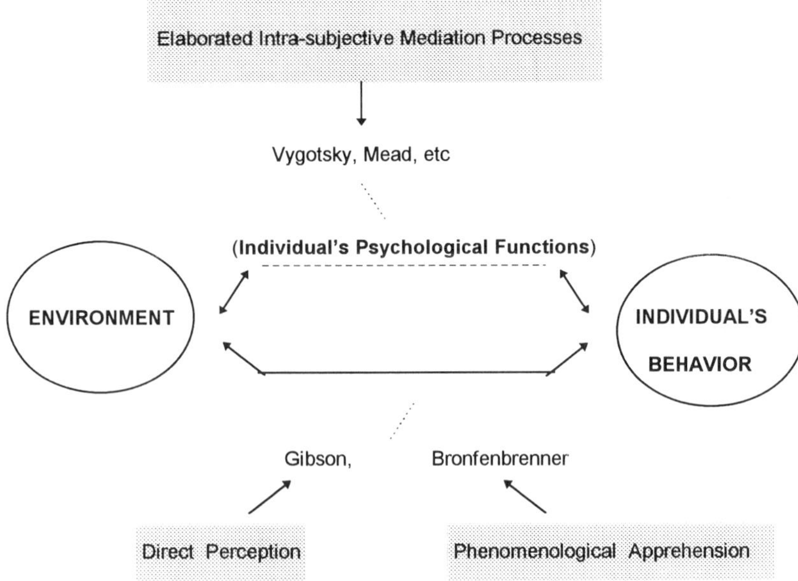


**Figure 12.1.** Alternative ways to conceptualize the relationship between the environment and the individual's behavior.

## The Metaphysical Argument

Gibson and his followers maintain the "direct" and nonconstructive character of psychological experience, arguing that the realm of psychological representation and higher cognitive processes are "metaphysical" inventions to be avoided (Gibson, 1979; Heft, 1989; Reed, 1988). Reed (1988) states:

> Modern psychology, sociology and anthropology have reached for the glittering ring of socially constructed meaningfulness, and have lost their footing on the ground. How can we achieve an ontology that points to meanings without determining them, that denies scientistic physicalism without adopting the sort of pseudo-scientific idealism that has always plagued the social sciences? (pp. 111–112)

He goes on to argue that "the animate environment is every bit as real as the physical world, and neither needs to be socially constructed, although both need to be perceived to be appreciated and used, and both can be appropriated for a whole host of social purposes" (p. 119).

Such statements, as well as arguments of a similar kind against what is designated as "mentalism" (Heft, 1989), abound in Gibsonian literature, suggesting between the lines a positivistic orientation that, according to Tudge et al., the ecological approach actively rejects. Concerning the notion of meaning, for instance, Gibson argues that the meaning of an object has to be found in direct perception, in the "affordance" of the object, with no participation by mediating processes. The incompatibility between this approach and the basic assumption of sociocultural and sociointeractionist thought – that is, the *social construction* of meaning (Gergen, 1994; Mead, 1912, 1913; Vygotsky, 1929) – is quite evident.

## Contrasting Assumptions and Object of Analysis

In their struggle against reductionism and the tradition of stimulus–response models in psychology, the theories of both Bronfenbrenner and Gibson bear on the ontological significance of relations (or interactions) between certain aspects of the environment and the organism. Conceptual compatibilities, however, do not seem to go beyond such basic assumptions, and many of the differences between their perspectives are mentioned by Tudge et al. Important differences discussed in the chapter include the key concepts on which each theory was constructed (perception vs. proximal processes of reciprocal interaction) and the focus given by each author in different levels of analysis. Concerning levels of analysis, a divergence can be found not only in relation to the specific dimension of the environment on which they concentrate their investigation (physical vs. social), but also in terms of the inclusiveness of their approach to the scientific study of I–E relationships. While Gibson constrains his work around the immediate experience of perception, linking together the organism and its environment at a microgenetic level, Bronfenbrenner takes a broader view of the intricate network of interdependencies among the multiple contexts embedding the individual, contributing a truly systemic framework to account for human development.

At first glance, such a microgenetic–macrogenetic contrast would invite a welcome complementarity between the theories. Nonetheless, this cannot be accomplished due to a fundamental friction at the methatheoretical level: Except for his early writings (1950, 1951, cited in Costall & Still, 1989), Gibson vigorously resisted any dichotomy in the scientific interpretation of human behavior, while Bronfenbrenner – following Lewin's (1933) propositions about the existence of "geographical" and "psychological" fields – explicitly refers to a phenomenological environment in coexistential relation with an objective, real world. In his seminal 1979 book, Bronfenbrenner attributed to this phenomenological domain a central role in the famous D = *f*(PE) equation. What is important to understand is the environment "as it is perceived rather than as it may exist in objective reality" (Bronfenbrenner, 1979, p. 4). In more recent publications, nevertheless, he reevaluated this excessive emphasis – in his words "the priority I accorded to the phenomenological imperative" (Bronfenbrenner, 1988, p. xiv) – acknowledging a special significance to "real" environmental conditions:

> As I have documented elsewhere (Bronfenbrenner, 1986a,c, in press [1988]; Bronfenbrenner & Crouter, 1983), findings to date . . . reveal that the most powerful environmental forces shaping human behavior and development emanate primarily from the objectively-measured, objective condition and events occurring in the life of the developing person. (p. xiv)

The perspective of integrating both "perceived" and "objective" realities, as Bronfenbrenner (1988) suggests, sounds absolutely alien to Gibson's radical propositions against "dualism" (Gibson, 1979). The concept of meaning, for example, is conceived in completely different ways: To Bronfenbrenner *meaning* is a cultural construct related to the phenomenological world, and it plays a central role in theory and applied issues concerning the development of programs and social policies. Gibson, however, reduces *meaning* to the concept of *affordance* (Costall & Still, 1989; Gibson, 1979, 1982; Hagen, 1985) in an attempt to suggest the "directness" of the experience and drive the concept away from the realm of representations or cognitive processes that he persistently avoids. He argues (1982) that "the meaning or value of anything consists of what it affords an observer, or species of observer. But what it affords the observer is determined by its material substance and its shape, size, rigidity, motion, etc" (p. 410).

Nevertheless, Gibson does not provide the concept of affordance with a clear definition (as Tudge et al. admit, and I later discuss), which implies that Gibson's notion of meaning does not help explain psychological phenomena in any particular way.

## Taking a Systemic Perspective on Dualism

The topic of dualism deserves special consideration. A seminal discussion about this subject within the context of the social sciences is presented in Dewey's article "The Reflex Arc Concept in Psychology" (1896), where he tries to banish the dualistic approach from the fields of psychological thought. The roots of Gibson's ideas can be found in his concept of a holistic coordination between aspects of environment and behavior, which represent a relevant contribution to a psychology used to reductionism and fragmentation. There we find a significant conceptual elaboration that works toward the construction of a systemic framework, which progressively – through numerous theoretical formulations (Fogel, 1993; Ford & Lerner, 1992) – aims to understand the complexities of psychological events.

Contemporary versions of a systemic theory, nevertheless, do not need to eliminate the existence of different realms or dimensions of reality in the study of behavior. Such diverse aspects, from a systemic approach, are considered "inclusive categories" (Valsiner & Cairns, 1992) that dialectically relate to each other as they integrate a single dynamic system. Discarding significant parts of human experience and labeling them as *metaphysical* or *insubstantial* is more deleterious to theoretical progress than trying to construct comprehensive models in tune with recent epistemological discussions taking place in the fields of modern science (Rosa, 1994). The issue of dualism in psychology should thus be overcome through the adoption of a multidimensional, systemic approach progressively elaborated to explain the intricacies of our object of study.

## Where Is Development?

Another aspect of Gibson's and Bronfenbrenner's theories that is difficult to reconcile is the subject of *development* itself. In his effort to contextualize human development, Bronfenbrenner's early writings (1977, 1979) give an almost exclusive importance to environmental factors, with little or no analysis of the developing person. However, he has since criticized this excessive emphasis – which ultimately resulted in the study of "context without development" (Bronfenbrenner, 1986, p. 288) – and began to develop theoretical constructs that account for the occurrence of development through the attributes of the individual and through characteristics of the environment. Such personal attributes and contextual characteristics, designated as "developmentally instigative," would promote or facilitate development of the individual in a variety of ways. The process through which they instigate development, however, remains a feature of the environment, and the role of the individual as a significant agency influencing his or her own development does not deserve special consideration.

Along a theoretical analysis of the interdependent network relating the components of his systemic model, Bronfenbrenner reveals a concern for patterns of behavioral consistency and change across time and contexts that are typical of a developmental approach (see Shanahan, Valsiner, & Gottlieb, Chapter 2, this volume). This concern can be found in Bronfenbrenner's theory at the microgenetic, ontogenetic, and macrogenetic levels of analysis.

Gibson, on the other hand, does not pay any special attention to developmental processes. His work is basically devoted to understanding, at a microgenetic level, the process of perception that coordinates the person and the object or event being perceived in the same immediate, direct experience. His references to patterns of change occurs when he proposes a "progressive differentiation" in the individual's ability to perceive the multiple affordances of an object (Gibson, 1953; Reed & Jones, 1982). Rather than conceptually approaching the notion of development, however, the concept of progressive differentiation better fits his description of learning processes (Gibson, 1953, 1979; Pick, 1979).

## Constructing a Systemic Theory

Bronfenbrenner's contribution is analyzed in Chapter 3 in a very comprehensive and critical way. Tudge et al. describe his systemic approach, highlighting the complex interdependence linking patterns of environmental influences and developmental events. Another important characteristic of his work is a constant concern for applied issues – like the development of social policies and the implementation of intervention programs – taking into account the systemic network embedding the developing individuals. This connection to the real world provides Bronfenbrenner with a rare opportunity to dynamically construct multiple aspects of his theory without losing track of psychology's scientific commitment to its object of study.

As Tudge et al. point out, Bronfenbrenner's theory is still being constructed and elaborated, yet the conceptual cornerstones and metatheoretical assumptions remain preserved as an integrating principle that provides the theory with consistency and coherence. The notions of structure and process typical of a systemic approach in developmental science (Ford & Lerner, 1992) are carefully intertwined as conceptual tools used to explain the complexities of contextualized developmental change. From micro- to macrosubsystems, a multiple causality model is constructed to account for human development over the life course, focusing particularly on ontogenetic processes. Albeit recognizing the importance of microgenetic processes (Bronfenbrenner, 1988, 1989), Bronfenbrenner does not elaborate further the dynamics of actual social interactions in promoting specific developmental changes. Such a lacuna, however, does not represent a failure to recognize the relevance of interactions, but may simply be an opportunity awaiting further theoretical development, especially when relevant empirical evidence become available.

## On Conceptual Uncertainties

Usually referred as the most original of Gibson's contributions to psychology, the concept of affordance creates rather than solves theoretical problems. Grounded in the Lewinian notion of "valence" (Lewin, 1933; Gibson, 1982), the concept of affordance really seems to represent a step forward concerning the idea that intrinsic structural characteristics of the environment play an important role in suggesting or inviting (or even "constraining"; Gibson, 1982, p. 411) certain types of conduct. That is particularly true when taking into account the productive boom of empirical research following Gibson's ideas demonstrating such relationship (see examples cited by Tudge et al.).

But what is an affordance? Gibson (1979) defines affordance as "a fact about the environment and a fact about behavior. It is both physical and psychical, yet neither. An affordance points both ways, to the environment and to the observer" (p. 129). Then he moves to affordances as "properties of things taken with reference to an observer" (p. 137). The emphasis on affordances as a property of the environment is pervasive in his theory (e.g., "The affordances of the environment are what it offers the animal, what it provides or furnishes"; p. 127), and the relative independence of the concept is clearly stated in total contradiction with the supposed relational character of the construct: "The affordance of something does not change as the need of the observer changes . . . the affordance, being invariant, is always there to be perceived" (Gibson, 1979, pp. 138–139); "The affordances of the environment are permanent, although they refer to animals and are species-specific" (Gibson, 1982, p. 410); "The affordances for an entire population do not change, even though people's knowledge, perception and skill differ within that population" (Reed, 1993, p. 54).

Gibson's insistence on the inseparability of perception and action (in fact, his inclusion of both in the same perceptual unit) and on the direct – instead of mediated – nature of perception, leads to an inevitable contradiction described by some as an "unresolved conflict in the heart of the theory" (Costall & Still, 1989, p. 438). Heft (1989) refers to this contradiction as a "tension" between two conflicting ideas: the fact that "properties of the perceived environment, including affordances, are considered to be *independent* of the perceiver" and the existence of a "relational approach to perception where *attributes of the perceiver contribute to* the specification of psychologically significant environmental properties" (p. 22; emphasis added).

The problem is that posing such directness in the perceptual experience and contrasting that with cognitive functioning is only possible if one takes a dichotomous perspective, something that Gibson refuses to do. Statements such as Reed's (1988) account of perception in contrast with cognitive processes sound particularly rooted in a supposedly rejected dichotomy: "We perceive independently of interpreting (and we often interpret independently of perceiving). No doubt we often interpret what we see. But we also see it" (p. 123).

Moreover, stressing the invariant nature of affordances and denying the cultural construction of objects' meanings (Costall & Still, 1989) may render Gibson's theory not applicable to the complexities of human phenomena. Heft (1989) asks, "Can the affordance concept be applied to cases of culturally derived meaning, or is it to be limited only to those meanings of a more transcultural or species-specific nature?" (p. 17). Attempting to find a broader applicability to Gibson's theory, Heft suggests the incorporation of individuals' "intentionality" in the analysis of the perceptual experience, but the results do not seem to preserve Gibson's main assumptions or clarify basic theoretical points. Some of his ideas induce curious reflections, like "one can adopt an intentional approach to perceiving, and with it acknowledge more fully the individual's participation in the perceiving process, without necessarily falling into the camp of mentalism" (pp. 23–24).

A persistent question comes to mind when we look at some attempts to extend Gibson's theory in similar ways (e.g., Guerin, 1990; Heft, 1989; Reed, 1988, 1993): If the linkage between the object and the organism really depends on past experience, intentionality, and so forth, what is the usefulness of a concept that brings with it the notion of invariance as its main characteristic? Prudently, Gibson himself and many researchers following his ideas (see examples given by Tudge et al.) constrained their work within the domains of the perception of less complex I–E relations involving inanimate objects. But even a simple object like a piece of paper (Cutting, 1982) can still represent a problem to the theory, for it doesn't constrain human behavior in any specific way.

The perception of a dog is a good example. Guerin (1990) argues that "we don't see a dog, but invariances we might label as a dog" (p. 44). Recently, while walking in my neighborhood, I had a very interesting "dog perception" that immediately triggered some cognitive processes in my mind, relating the experience to Gibson's ideas of direct perception or information pickup (Gibson, 1979). Passing by a house, I suddenly heard a dog barking dreadfully close to me. In previous walks, I had noticed an inconspicuous fence around the yard of that specific house, and the moment the dog barked I was not looking at the house (I had already passed by). When the dog announced its presence, however, instead of jumping, freezing, running away, or even looking at the dog (as I would probably have done if there were no fence representation in my mind), I simply walked normally, feeling protected by a fence I could not see but knew was there. If the action is put together with the perception of the object, even simple species-specific reactions like avoiding angry dogs may not exclude the existence of past experiences.

Further development of Gibson's theoretical ideas, according to Tudge et al., is particularly connected with the work of Eleanor Gibson and Ulric Neisser (E. Gibson, 1969, 1984, 1988; Neisser, 1988, 1992, in press, cited in Tudge et al., Chapter 3, this volume). Yet we do not find in the chapter specific information about the way

E. Gibson contributed "developmental concepts" to J. Gibson's theory, as Tudge et al. suggest. Neisser's theory, however, deserves special reference.

## Extension or Divergence?

Neisser's work is presented by the authors as a significant extension of Gibson's ideas and receives a special analysis in the text. The multiplicity of selves (ecological, interpersonal, extended, etc.) and Neisser's proposition of a second perception system – a recognition system – cannot be considered, however, a true extension of Gibson's ideas because they basically oppose fundamental assumptions underlying his theory. According to Tudge et al., "While the direct perception system specifies where one is situated in the environment with respect to the physical layout or to social interchanges, the recognition system allows for the acquisition of knowledge about what things are with respect to culturally specified meaning." As practically all human experience relates to things possessing "culturally specified meanings," Neisser's propositions actually reduces Gibson's theory to the domain of irrelevant issues, instead of "further distinguish[ing] Gibson's important contribution," or "ground(ing) other aspects of development in Gibson's ecological theory of perception," as Tudge et al. say. Moreover, referring to Neisser's propositions, the authors add that "These two systems are 'about different things'; use different kinds of information; and provide different kinds of certainty" (Neisser, 1992, p. 23, cited in Tudge et al.). Nothing could be more in open opposition to Gibson's struggle against the prevalence of dichotomous thought in psychology.

## Conclusion

In the context of theoretical psychology, the chapter by Tudge et al. represents a valuable opportunity to analyze the historical construction of ideas and to evaluate some of the contributions of the ecological approach, although the term *ecological* in reference to the authors discussed in the chapter would only apply to some basic characteristics already discussed. The fundamental similarity, as well as the main shared contribution, of Gibson and Bronfenbrenner lies in the emphasis on the role of environmental structures associated with a holistic approach, linking together the individual and the environment. That is a major contribution, taking into account psychology's persistent tendency to rely on analytic fragmentation. Such an approach, however, is translated by each author into specific grammars that seem to apply in different levels, thus rendering problematic an appropriate integration of their theories.

## References

Baldwin, J. (1895). *Mental development in the child and the race.* New York: Mcmillan.

(1906). *Thought and things: A study of the development and meaning of thought.* London: Swan Sonnenschein.

Bronfenbrenner, U. (1977). An experimental ecology of human development. *American Psychologist, 32*, 513–531.

(1979). *The ecology of human development: Experiments by nature and design.* Cambridge, MA: Harvard University Press.

(1986). Recent advances in research on human development. In R. K. Silbereisen, K. Eyferth, & G. Rudinger (Eds.), *Development as action in context: Problem behavior and normal youth development* (pp. 287–309). Heidelberg: Springer-Verlag.

(1988). Foreword. In A. R. Pence (Ed.), *Ecological research with children and families: From concepts to methodology* (pp. ix–xix). New York: Teacher's College Press.

(1989). Ecological systems theory. *Annals of Child Development, 6*, 185–246.

Costall, A., & Still, A. (1989). Gibson's theory of direct perception and the problem of cultural relativism. *Journal for the Theory of Social Behavior, 19*(4), 433–442.

Cutting, J. E. (1982). Two ecological perspectives: Gibson vs. Shaw and Turvey. *American Journal of Psychology, 95*(20), 199–222.

Dewey, J. (1896). The reflex arc concept in psychology. *Psychological Review, 3*(4), 357–370.

Fogel, A. (1993). *Developing through relationships: Origins of communication, self, and culture.* Chicago: University of Chicago Press.

Ford, D., & Lerner, R. (1992). *Developmental systems theory: An integrative approach.* London: Sage.

Gergen, K. J. (1994). *Realities and relationships.* Cambridge, MA: Harvard University Press.

Gibson, J. J. (1953). Social perception and the psychology of perceptual learning. In M. Sherif & M. O. Wilson (Eds.), *Group relations at the cross-roads.* New York: Harper & Brothers.

(1979). *The ecological approach to visual perception.* Boston: Houghton Mifflin.

(1982). Notes on affordances. In E. Reed & R. Jones (Eds.), *Reasons for realism: Selected essays of James J. Gibson* (pp. 401–418). New York: Earlbaum.

Guerin, B. (1990). Gibson, Skinner and perceptual responses. *Behavior and Philosophy*, *18*(1), 43–54.

Hagen, M. A. (1985). James J. Gibson's ecological approach to visual perception, In S. Koch & D. E. Leary (Eds.), *A century of psychology as science* (pp. 231–249). New York: McGraw-Hill.

Heft, H. (1989). Affordances and the body: An intentional analysis of Gibson's ecological approach to visual perception. *Journal for the Theory of Social Behavior*, *19*(1), 1–30.

Lawrence, J., & Valsiner, J. (1993). Conceptual roots of internalization: From transmission to transformation. *Human Development*, *36*, 150–167.

Lewin, K. (1933). Environmental forces. In C. Murchison (Ed.), *A handbook of child psychology*, 2nd ed (pp. 590–625). Worcester, MA: Clark University Press.

(1939). Field theory and experiment in social psychology: Concepts and methods. *American Journal of Sociology*, *44*, 868–896.

Mead, G. (1912). The mechanism of social consciousness. *Journal of Philosophy, Psychology and Scientific Methods*, *9*, 401–406.

(1913). The social self. *Journal of Philosophy, Psychology and Scientific Methods*, *10*, 374–380.

(1934). *Mind, self and society*. Chicago: University of Chicago Press.

Neisser, U. (1988). Five kinds of self-knowledge. *Philosophical Psychology*, *1*(1), 35–59.

Pick, A. D. (1979). *Perception and its development: A tribute to Eleanor J. Gibson*. New York: Erlbaum.

Reed, E. S. (1988). The affordance of the animate environment: Social science from the ecological point of view. In T. Ingold (Ed.), *What is an animal?* (pp. 110–126). London: Allen & Unwin.

(1993). The intention to use a specific affordance: A conceptual framework for psychology. In R. H. Wozniak & K. W. Fisher (Eds.), *Development in context: Acting and thinking in specific environments* (pp. 45–76). Hillsdale, NJ: Erlbaum.

Reed, E. S. & Jones, R. (1982). *Reasons for realism: Selected essays of James J. Gibson*. New York: Erlbaum.

Rogoff, B. (1990). *Apprenticeship in thinking: Cognitive development in social context*. Oxford University Press.

Rosa, A. (1994). History of psychology: A ground for reflexivity. In P. del Rio, A. Alvarez, & J. V. Wertsch (General Eds.), *Explorations in sociocultural studies: Vol. 1. Historical and theoretical discourse* (A. Rosa & J. Valsiner, Eds.; pp. 149–168). Madrid: Infancy and Learning Foundation.

Valsiner, J. (1987). *Culture and the development of children's action.* New York: Chichester.

(1994a). Reflexivity in context: Narratives, hero-myths and the making of histories in psychology. In P. del Rio, A. Alvarez, & J. V. Wertsch (General Eds.), *Explorations in socio-cultural studies: Vol. 1. Historical and theoretical discourse* (A. Rosa & J. Valsiner, Eds.; pp. 169–186). Madrid: Infancy and Learning Foundation.

(1994b). Culture and human development: Co-constructive perspective. In P. van Geert & L. Mos (Eds.), *Annals of theoretical psychology* (Vol. 10, pp. 247–298). New York: Plenum.

Valsiner, J., & Cairns, R. (1992). Theoretical perspectives on conflict and development. In C. V. Shantz & W. W. Hartup (Eds.), *Conflict in child and adolescent development* (pp. 15–35). Cambridge University Press.

van der Veer, R. (1994). Pierre Janet's relevance for a socio-cultural approach. In P. del Rio, A. Alvarez, & J. V. Wertsch (General Eds.), *Explorations in socio-cultural studies: Vol. 1. Historical and theoretical discourse* (A. Rosa & J. Valsiner, Eds.; pp. 205–209). Madrid: Infancy and Learning Foundation.

van der Veer, R., & Valsiner, J. (1991). *Understanding Vygotsky: A quest for synthesis.* Oxford: Blackwell.

Vygotsky, L. (1929). The problem of the cultural development of the child. *Pedagogical Seminary and Journal of Genetic Psychology, 36,* 415–434.

(1978). *Mind in society.* Cambridge, MA: Harvard University Press.

Wertsch, J. V. (1985). *Culture, communication and cognition: Vygotskian perspectives.* Cambridge Unviersity Press.

Wozniak, R. H. (1986). Notes towards a co-constructive theory of the emotion–cognition relationship. In D. J. Bearinson & H. Zimiles (Eds.), *Thought and emotion: Developmental perspectives* (pp. 39–64). Hillsdale, NJ: Erlbaum.

# 13 Problems of Comparison: Methodology, the Art of Storytelling, and Implicit Models

*Hideo Kojima*

The three chapters covered by this commentary deal with social and cultural change (either historical or by way of immigration) and individual adaptation. However, the chapters by Beth Kurtz-Costes and her colleagues (Chapter 6) and by Michael Shanahan and Glen Elder (Chapter 4) deal mainly with the methodology of comparisons, while the chapter by Dorothy Holland and Debra Skinner (Chapter 7) deals more directly with the interaction of the individual and changing, lived worlds. I shall begin with the methodology of comparisons and then move to the experiences of individuals in changing worlds. Finally I will discuss comparisons as storytelling.

## The Methodology of Comparisons

### *Chapter 6*

Kurtz-Costes, McCall, and Schneider begin their chapter by outlining five methodological and conceptual issues involved in cultural comparison. I can agree with all of their points if I accept their methodological framework. In my view, the authors' framework is based on a traditional research design that compares specific outcome variables that are to be explained by a small set of variables represented by two or more cultures. This position is apparent when the authors write about "confounding" variables. They seem not to be directly interested in the covariation pattern or configuration of cultural variables. Instead, their approach involves identifying each separate cultural variable as accurately as possible. In other words, their framework is a kind of multicausal model, and the research purpose is not directed to the cultural organization of variables related to human development, but rather to the causal processes that may be implicated in developmental outcomes.

The model of children's acculturation (Figure 6.1) exemplifies their framework. Age at migration is treated as one of the crucial variables in their model. The age variable, however, is not treated as a predictor in the causal model or like a variable in a nested comparison (as used by Shanahan & Elder). Instead, it is placed in a longitudinal developmental model. The critical issue becomes what psychological structures and functions are represented by this age variable.

**Competition between Cultures and Culture as Configuration.** Acculturation research has been conducted largely in a framework of sending and receiving cultures, presupposing that the individual or group migrates from one culture to the other. The chapter by Kurtz-Costes et al. is no exception. We can, however, think of another way in which two or more cultures interact: competition and interdependence between two nations or ethnic groups. The issue is apparently at the level of group, but it is also relevant at the level of the individual.

Let me begin at the group level. In their persuasive book meant for North American educators, parents, and policy makers, Stevenson and Stigler (1992) provide solid evidence that U.S. elementary school children fare poorly in mathematics when compared with their counterparts in East Asia (China, Japan, and Taiwan). They stated that "we have been accustomed to levels of performance that seemed satisfactory within the context of our own culture but which turn out to be anything but satisfactory compared with that of students from other countries" (p. 26). Contemporary North American and East Asian educational systems may function well domestically, but when these systems are placed in the context of a competitive and interdependent world, problems on each side become apparent. Generally speaking, when two systems (whether economic, social, political, religious, or cultural) interact with each other, a series of adaptation processes ensues in each system. Of course, the degree of change that is required as a result of interaction may not be the same for each system, as suggested by Kurtz-Costes and her colleagues.

An excellent example can be found in Japanese history. Since its centralized government was established in the sixth century (and continued well into the nineteenth century), Japan seems to have alternated between policies of openness and national seclusion in cultural, economic, and religious domains. After a period of active cultural and technological inception and active trading, which often required a great deal of domestic restructuring, there usually followed a period of relative inactivity with foreign cultures. However, it was during these periods of relative seclusion from foreign cultures that Japan assimilated foreign influences to develop its own characteristic culture.

I think the same process has occurred repeatedly in the history of other cultures, as well as in relations among subcultures. In the present era of global interdependence and competition, national, ethnic, or cultural seclusion and protectionism have become more difficult and unrealistic. Therefore, we are faced with competition between nations, cultures, or political-economic systems with regard to specific aspects of their systems – for example, production efficiency, educational achievement, and scientific progress.

Stevenson and Stigler's comparison of educational achievement was based on their belief that the observed differences in educational achievement are related to the societies' future functioning. However, it is appropriate to ask questions about the basic value presuppositions underlying cross-national or cross-cultural comparisons: Is a highly achieving society a good one? In what sense is it good? Doesn't the comparison at the specific aspects of achievement threaten the intrinsic values of the culture? After these value questions have been answered, we are in a position to learn from other cultures or societies by comparing our system and theirs.

Stevenson and Stigler claimed that U.S. and East Asian educational systems can be characterized and compared with each other using the same set of dimensions or categories. Some of the characteristics attributed by the authors to the United States (as contrasted with East Asian cultures) include the following. A higher priority is given to life adjustment and the enhancement of self-esteem than to academic learning. A greater emphasis is put on innate ability than on effort as the most important factor in academic achievement. American parents are more easily satisfied with lower levels of performance by their children. In addition, U.S. educators are more likely to address the needs of the individual child to the neglect of the level of achievement for all children.

This is a good example of a configurational view of cultural comparison; the target variable (educational achievement) is embedded in the total cultural and social configuration. The configuration within each society and culture reflects a functionally adapting and self-regulating system at a specific historical time. It is an open system, and interaction with other systems triggers the process of reorganization within the system.

This discussion at the group level may not be totally applicable to analysis at the individual level, for the individual is not simply a reflection of phenomena at the group level. Still the individual and group levels are mutually related, and the individual's acculturation process should be analyzed within the context of multilevel interrelations. I hope the ongoing research described by Kurtz-Costes and her colleagues reveals some aspects of these complex interrelationships. I turn now to the chapter by Shanahan and Elder, which characterizes the configuration as hierarchically nested sets of organizations.

## *Chapter 4*

The most crucial tasks for Shanahan and Elder are to vitalize the seemingly static nested comparisons of groups into a dynamic analysis of change processes at the individual and group levels, and to coordinate between these levels of change. Even though a longitudinal design is used, the changing processes of individuals and of interpersonal relationships cannot be directly observed, for the available data consist of differences between psychological states or developmental measures at more than two time points. Instead, these processes are constructed by researchers based on their theoretical model.

In this regard, the implicit assumption of invariance of processes across historical times is important, as Shanahan and Elder observe. Without that universal assumption, cycles of theoretical model building through insights and empirical tests become difficult. Still, as Elder's research from the Great Depression illustrates, the story of the Oakland and Berkeley children will not necessarily apply in full to children at the present time. Presumably both family and community functioned better then, as compared with the contemporary United States. Similarly, U.S. attitudes and policies toward returning soldiers after the World War II seemed to be quite different from those after the Vietnam War. Thus, it is conceivable, for example, that the positive effect of military service enjoyed by a subset of the children of the Great Depression is closely related to the historical and social conditions of the United States.

Evaluation of the characteristics of the cohort also reflects the values of the historical time. For example, the researcher's positive evaluation of daughters' participation in household work and their later family-oriented attitudes (Elder, 1974), together with their reversion to traditional women's roles witnessed after the World War II, are constrained by the values of the time. Therefore, a seemingly identical formal classification category does not necessarily hold across historical times and cultures. It is the researcher's task to go beyond the surface identity of the variables to look for functional equivalence of the relevant processes.

Let me discuss another issue raised by nested comparison. While a crossed classification generally presupposes no hierarchical ordering between the variables being cross-tabulated, a nested classification requires the selection and ordering of the variables. For some combination of the variables the hierarchical ordering between them is self-evident, but in others the way of nesting may not logically be so obvious. Shanahan and Elder state that the first nested comparison must involve a structural one that represents a family of processes that link social structure to individuals' functioning, and further nesting can be any of the other comparisons. In actuality, each of the nested variables may not stand for a single process but contain a set of component processes, and a process may be shared by more than two nested variables. For example, relational and reactive comparisons may not be completely independent of each other. It is conceivable that the availability of primary group resources to one person is partly determined by one's habitual adaptation strategy, and the latter is constrained by the former. Temporal comparisons may also be related to personal and relational comparisons, for an individual's timetable of life and development may be influenced partly by his or her personal and relational characteristics.

Therefore, an important research task involves a choice of the most appropriate ways to nest variables (or of the sequential choice of nested variables) for each specific research question. When the nesting from one study is generalized to another study undertaken in different times and places, model specification plays an especially central role in the arrangement of nesting.

This problem of nesting does not apply to the nested case studies that Shanahan and Elder describe, because no causal mechanism is modeled, and every possible combination of the variables is dealt with in the nested case studies. In essence, the proposed method is an attempt to make meaning of outliers that have been found in quantitative analyses of nested data. An example of qualitative comparative method applied to life histories of Terman's sample is indeed an interesting illustration. Shanahan and Elder focus on one outlier in the analysis and look for factors that led to it. They found, consistent with their expectations, ample evidence of the factors that gave meaning to the subject's life. The conclusion is plausible, but we still need verification by another case to make the argument more convincing. If a researcher with a specific framework searches for evidence to fit the model, he or she very often finds the sought evidence. I shall return to this problem in the section on storytelling.

## The Individual's Experiences in a Changing World: Chapter 7

"Songs change with the times, and the times change with songs." This is a common expression that the Japanese hear especially in connection with a TV show. It is a favorite subject of NHK, a Japanese public broadcasting system, which plays popular songs from the past several decades and often refers to the social conditions that prevailed when a particular song was popular. Listening to the song, TV viewers of various ages relive their own experiences at that time. Not only does this bring about cognitive reminiscences of one's experiences, but it also triggers a vivid recollection of one's physical, emotional, sentimental, and interpersonal experiences when one held a specific status in one's life course and also when specific historical events occurred.

The sequence of historical events for typical Japanese in their seventies may include 14 years of war between 1931 to 1945; relieved, but unstable and bitter lives after the war; rapid economic development, hard work, and improvement of life that began in the middle of the 1950s; social unrest and university upheaval in the late 1960s; and so on. Thus, in retrospect, many Japanese can understand the meaning of the expression, "Songs change with the times." In fact popular songs reflect the general social conditions of the times. In addition, though not broadcast through such conservative public media, voices of oppressed people can be heard through nursery songs (e.g., Matsunaga, 1964; Tamanoi, 1991) and folk songs. These songs often serve as outlets for inner feelings of resentment and resignation to the prevailing social conditions.

On the other hand, some Japanese can also appreciate the meaning of the expression "The times change with songs." They realize that popular songs not only foreshadow the next phase of the world, but may actually lead people to feel, think, and behave in a way that is expressed in songs. Thus, it is natural that before 1945 the Japanese police often became sensitive to the influence of popular songs and actually censored some that they suspected of making people grow war-weary or critical of the nationalistic and militaristic political systems.

During the 1950s and early 1960s, *Utagoe undo* (the singing voice movement) flourished in Japan. Young urban workers and students were especially involved in the movement. Songs were sung in groups at tearooms in towns and at political gatherings. Though the movement was connected with leftist associations, most popular songs were not revolutionary in sentiment. Instead, their overtones were largely realistic and progressive, and emphasized cooperation and social solidarity with peer workers and students. A typical song was as follows:

> Happiness, it's our hope.
> Though our daily work is very hard,
> It's very important to live insistently with our future in mind
> And beads of dripping sweat upon our foreheads.
> Comrades, let us sing together the song of happiness!
> Let us pursue together the echoing song!
>
> Happiness, it's our hope.
> Do not indulge in unrealistic hopes and dreams.
> It's very important to live beautifully and insistently,
> Focusing on the very present moment.
> Comrades, let us sing together the song of happiness!
> Let us pursue together the echoing song!

The postwar period was a time of rapid economic growth in Japan. The Japanese people hoped that hard work and social solidarity would bring about a better future. It was a time of positive social change. Thus, they sang together and tried to energize themselves.

This is in sharp contrast with more contemporary patterns in popular music. Consider karaoke bars, where people take turns singing to a recorded orchestral accompaniment. Generally they do not sing together but simply listen to, or even ignore, the others' songs. Nowadays most popular songs do not seem to lead people to think and behave in a particular way that is related to society. Instead, they simply elicit a personal memory that may be shared with others but is unrelated to social issues.

What Holland and Skinner have tried to demonstrate in their chapter is related to the basic theme "Songs change with the times, and the times change with songs" as applied in contemporary Nepalese society, especially from the woman's point of view. Holland and Skinner, however, have proceeded one step further. In Figure 7.3, especially by posing Point 4, they made a significant stride toward understanding the relation between lived worlds and the individual's subjective experiences.

At Point 4, the texts made public are incorporated into the lived culture, being brought into the everyday life of the individual who is situated in the world of interpersonal relationships. The lived culture in turn serves to produce new texts, thus contributing to the construction of new pathways. It is an open system that social conditions and individual's experience encounter at Points 1 and 3. All the processes comprising Points 1 through 4 represent microchange. Still, according to Holland and Skinner's example, the cycle moved fast enough to produce remarkable change in a few years.

In connection with Point 1, I would like to place the produced text in a wider context. According to Holland and Skinner, the produced text could be in any semiotic form. I quite agree with them because I thought the same way when I conceptualized the "ethnopsychological pool of ideas" on child rearing (Kojima, 1996). However, in Holland and Skinner's sense, the individual text is characterized as a rather short-lived one, while I think of a long-lasting pool of ideas or texts.

In my view, not only the form but also the content of the text is influenced by a large reservoir of shared texts; actually, many new texts are not completely new but are constructed out of the reservoir. Then some of the newly constructed texts are placed back into the cultural reservoir. The reservoir provides the individual and the group with source materials to construct new texts, especially when they are faced with new conditions that require the adaptation of current ideas and practices. In addition, it is difficult to appreciate the change of the individual and the society without comparing the present text with the past ones that are stored in the reservoir. I will return to this concept of reservoir, but here I wish to stress the importance of a rather stable structure that underlies changing texts and lived worlds.

## The Art of Storytelling about Change and Comparison

In this final section, I present a view that relates descriptions of change/continuity and similarity/difference to the metaphor of storytelling. The story is addressed to some potential audience, but its intrinsic process is self-discussion (i.e., internal dialogue). I begin with historical storytelling.

### *Historical Storytelling*

The Greek word *historia* is the etymological root of the English word *history*. It means true information obtained by means of objective inquiry and also the true story of the knowledge obtained in this way. Objectivism, as contrasted with constructivism, is *historia*'s basic characteristic. According to this position, free-standing phenomena certainly exist, and it is the historian's task to discover them and tell his or her true story to others. This position of objectivism may hold not only for natural phenomena, but also for human affairs. Many aspects of human affairs, and stories about them, intrinsically involve the dimension of time. But how can one obtain true information and tell a true story about human affairs? While I am not acquainted with historical works by the ancient Greeks, I believe that Greek historians were sophisticated enough not to take the informants' stories at their face value, cross-checking the information they were given.

However, a basic characteristic of history is that it is told and written only after a series of events is over. Historians can utilize records that have been taken almost simultaneously with the ongoing event, but they cannot tell an unfolding story by themselves. A running commentary on the spot is not history. Therefore, history is necessarily constructed after the fact and is necessarily influenced by the temporal framework. In this connection we may recall a historian's well-known remark: "History is a continuous process of interaction between the historian and his facts, an unending dialogue between the present and the past" (Carr, 1986, p. 24).

I believe that Carr's statement holds for any historical inquiry and history telling, including professional historians' work, sociological descriptions of social change, narratives of one's life history, and developmentalists' descriptions of human development. In these kinds of works, even though a history teller takes the position of objective *historia*, he or she still presupposes a certain philosophical explanatory framework, as well as the values held by the individual historian and the collective culture.

Take as an example research in the child study movement. In my view, though researchers tried their best to use objective methodology and get reliable data, many of their reports involved fitting the obtained results into a theoretical framework. The most popular framework of the time was recapitulation theory, and many researchers seemed to be satisfied only when they could fit their results into recapitulation theory. If they felt they had explained the results in terms of a popular theoretical frame – when they felt that they were able to give meaning to their own results – that was the end of their storytelling.

Contemporary developmental researchers do not believe in recapitulation theory. Still, it seems to me, we are doing the same kind of thing in our descriptions of ontogenetic change of individuals, as happens in case reporting by clinical psychologists, whether their position is behavioral or phenomenological. Generally speaking, neither developmental nor clinical psychologists are aware of the fact that they are telling historical stories. But in actuality they are doing just that. They can do piecemeal analyses of the obtained results without much storytelling. However, once they begin to synthesize the obtained results into a meaningful set of information, the storytelling begins. I am not arguing that telling a story is a bad thing. Instead, I would like to emphasize that we should be aware of the fact that we are telling a story, either our own or that of others.

A story cannot be constructed without a mental framework to organize information. I think that it is very hard to tell a story without some models of change or development, especially regarding its directionality. Depending on the historical storyteller and the theme that he or she deals with, the framework may have been or is being constructed through the process of telling history. In any case, the storyteller should be conscious of his or her latent working model, or constructed mental framework, for it constrains the products. In addition to the self-directed question of one's historical model, the question as to how that model has been constructed is crucial in comparative historical works.

What are the main contents of a historical model? If one views the elements of consciousness that relate to time, three components may be discerned (Figure 13.1): the constructed past, the present state, and a future perspective. Needless to say, the bound-

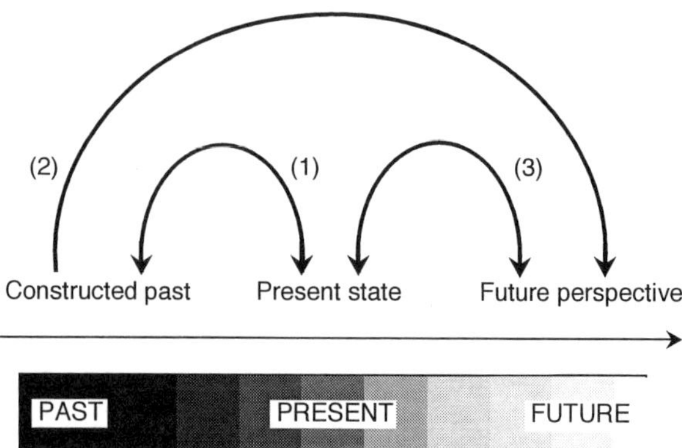


**Figure 13.1.** Interrelations among three components in history telling.

aries between these three times are not clear-cut but are fused. What are the relations among the three components in our consciousness of our own time? Shown in the figure are three arrows that describe the relations among the three components.

The figure describes the relations between components that appeared in the drawings and narratives of ones' own life, from birth to death. I developed the method, called LCS (life course study through drawing), to understand the individual's conceptualization of his or her own life course. However, the model can be applied to the more general issue of historical understanding and the construction of history.

The bidirectional arrow (1) connects the constructed past and the present state. It represents a view of history and historical storytelling as the narrator's internal discussion. Arrow (2) represents a view that one's future perspective is often constructed on the basis of one's constructed past. In a sense, our past works as a plot for our future. Finally, as the bidirectional arrow (3) shows, our future perspective influences the present state, and the former is accommodated to the latter.

I believe that the changing worlds of Renu, the Nepalese woman described by Holland and Skinner, can be represented by this scheme. For example, her songs that contain autobiographical references and commentaries on different phases of her own life represent her internal discussion between her past and present. She has also projected her constructed past onto her future, and her view of the anticipated future has cast a dark shadow on her life. However, all of these components in Renu's world are being changed through time, induced by sociopolitical changes as well as her activity as songwriter.

Some aspects of the psychological worlds of participants in research projects by Elder and colleagues and by Kurtz-Costes and colleagues may also be described by this scheme. Presumably these participants have their own history to tell. When they are faced with a new environment, their history of related aspects is to be invoked to guide their behavior. After a series of coping experiences, the history may be reconstructed to be stored in their memory system.

In addition, I suspect that this scheme may be used to understand researchers' implicit historical models of both social change and individuals' adaptation, which is explicated in the next subsection.

### *Hypothetical Dialogues between Historical Times*

Imagine what would happen if theorists on child rearing and development (naive ordinary people, expert advisors, and scientists) of more than two historical times were to exchange views. Would one expect responses such as "I know it" or "They knew it already!" very infrequently or rather frequently? When the latter is the case, I believe that it is not the theorists' belief in one specific position to the exclusion of any other but their awareness of the coexistence of contemporary divergent views that is an important condition for their recognition of similarity of thoughts across historical times. I think this argument also applies to intercultural discussion.

If I restrict my generalization to Japanese child rearing and health care theories during the past three and a half centuries, my view (Kojima, 1996) is that "they knew most of it already!" In Japanese writings from the mid-seventeenth to the mid-nineteenth centuries, we can see the awareness of infants' competence in sensory and cognitive domains and the importance of responsive caretaking of infants after 2 months of age. These writers also considered the need for the optimal balancing of the development of both intellectual abilities and wisdom in young children, even to the extent of restraining the development of the former in favor of the latter. It was also recognized that acquisition of certain kinds of knowledge and advanced skills, as well as freedom from errors, could not be possible before a person reached 40 or 50 years of age.

These theories occurred in print several times during the past two or three centuries, usually during periods in which the Japanese were trying to establish their cultural identity. Thus, it is probable that during the period when academic psychologists in Japan believed in the "incompetent infant" (a belief imported from the West) and thus neglected the importance of responsive caretaking from the early period of life and when (again under the influence of Western views) they believed there to be a rapid intellectual decline after middle adulthood, Japanese ethnopsychology may have maintained the opposing views, which were revived by academic psychologists only recently.

However, this newfound recognition is also the product of historical time. It was in 1976 that I came to know the existence of Japanese documents on child rearing and human development from the seventeenth century. In particular, I was amazed to find that, as early as 1703, a Japanese physician had given essentially the same advice to caretakers as present-day experts give. That is, he encouraged them to respond to an infant's smiling and vocalization contingently, as if talking to the infant at 60 days after birth. According to his theory, the caretaker's behavior induces the infant to smile and imitate the caretaker's vocalizations. If this sequence of caretaker–infant interaction is continued, the infant is expected to speak earlier, to be free from stranger anxiety, and never to develop mortal, convulsive illnesses. I was so amazed by this physician's insight that I continued to introduce his writings to developmentalists and to express my admiration of his keen observation and insight.

The child care book published in 1703 had been referred to by a Japanese promoter of the child study movement at the turn of the century and was printed in the early twentieth century, and again in 1976. Many physicians, educators, and some psychologists must have read it before me, but no one had ever noticed the value of the writing on the importance of the caretaker's responsiveness to the young infant. I was proud of my "discovery" of the value of this writing.

However, in the 10 years since then I have discovered that my appreciation of his insight was mere arrogance. My bitter awareness had two aspects. First, I realized that if I had read the physician's writings during my undergraduate training (which ended in 1959), it would have been very likely that I would have dismissed his insight as unscientific superstition and overinterpretation. New research by developmental scholars on the competence of the infant, on the dynamics of mother–child interaction, and on attachment had not been published yet. Therefore, it would have been very natural not to have understood the meaning of these writings. This is a good example of how our frameworks are influenced by the mainstream view of the discipline at a particular historical time.

My second reflection was more serious. It occurred to me that my amazement about the writings might be shared only by contemporary developmental researchers. They believe that they have discovered the developmental significance of mother–child interaction and relationships, and thus have contributed to the development of the discipline and also to the public good. However, I thought, the same kind of ideas must have appeared repeatedly in history. Is it at all conceivable that in the long history of humankind, no one has ever noticed the phenomenon that attracts the attention of present-day developmental researchers, and that no one has ever thought of a "theory" to explain the phenomenon? In addition, is it imaginable that contemporary psychological and psychiatric theories and research on infancy have developed completely independent of awareness and ideas by lay people and previous researchers? To me, this awareness was serious enough to rethink fundamentally our discipline.

One line of my rethinking has led me to develop a new concept in ethnopsychology. If we examine representative theories from each historical period and trace their changes, it appears as if whole societies' views on human development moved unidirectionally, with older views being replaced by new ones. On the contrary, I hypothesize, divergent views have always coexisted, and their components are not easily lost, but rather are preserved in the pool of ideas found in documents, in the symbolic expressions of rituals and practices, in memory traces in personal culture, and in other forms. This may be called the source-maintaining function of ethnopsychology.

A problem of my argument could be that the analyzer, in this case me, by knowing contemporary psychological theories, retrospectively searches past materials and analyzes the materials in terms of present-day conceptual and theoretical frameworks. But I am not maintaining that previous thinkers and present-day psychologists share an identical theory concerning child rearing and human development. What I propose is that there existed, in the ethnopsychological pool in early modern Japan, divergent components on the basis of which various schools of modern Western-oriented theories of child development and education could be constructed.

Finally, I suspect that diverse schools of modern Western theories of development and child rearing have also developed by uniquely selecting and combining some components out of their ethnopsychology in which diverse ideas had previously been generated, modified, and maintained. In the realm of child rearing, where humans' biological constraints make true innovation unlikely, the reconstruction (or in some cases simply the rediscovery and revival) of former theories and practices may not be unusual, but in fact quite common. Furthermore, it is probable that Japanese and Western ethnopsychological theories shared some basic components before the establishment of scientific psychology, as can be inferred from prevailing ideas on child rearing and human development shared by early modern Japanese ethnopsychology and by present-day Western scientific psychology.

It is not unlikely that ethnopsychological theories on child rearing and human development that have been developed and maintained by various cultures share some common set of concepts. This set of concepts, however, may contain heterogeneous, often mutually opposing views and related practices within itself. The critical point that I wish to raise with respect to comparison is that rather than comparing cultures and historical periods in terms of their modal characteristics of theories and practices, a common set of heterogeneous views can itself be used as a basic unit of comparison. That is what Stevenson and Stigler (1992) tried to demonstrate. Such a unit of comparison not only is useful for cultural research, but will also facilitate both historical and intercultural discussion at the individual level.

## References

Carr, E. H. (1986). *What is history?* (2nd ed., R. W. Davies, Ed.). London: Macmillan.

Elder, G. H., Jr. (1974). *Children of the Great Depression: Social change in life experience*. Chicago: University of Chicago Press.

Kojima, H. (1996). Japanese childrearing advice in its cultural, social, and economic contexts. *International Journal of Behavioral Development, 19*, 373–391.

Matsunaga, G. (1964). *Nippon no komori-uta* [Folk nursery songs in Japan]. Tokyo: Kinokuniya Shoten. (In Japanese)

Stevenson, H. W., & Stigler, J. W. (1992). *The learning gap*. New York: Summit.

Tamanoi, M. A. (1991). Songs as weapons: The culture and history of *komori* (nursemaids) in modern Japan. *Journal of Asian Studies*, *50*, 793–817.

# 14 The Promise of Comparative, Longitudinal Research for Studies of Productive-Reproductive Processes in Children's Lives

*William A. Corsaro*

In introducing this volume the editors argue for the need to focus directly on the processes or mechanisms of development and to document how and why these processes may vary across cultural, ethnic, racial, and socioeconomic groups. I feel these are laudable goals and would argue that we need new methodological practices to reach them. I have discussed elsewhere (Corsaro, 1993) the promise of comparative, longitudinal ethnography for studying productive-reproductive processes in children's lives. While I have relied on and see great potential in the use of ethnographic methods for studying socialization (or "interpretive reproduction," Corsaro, 1992), I believe a range of methods are appropriate for the study of developmental processes. However, whatever methods are employed are best placed in a general research program or agenda that is *longitudinal and ethnohistorical*, *multilevel*, and *cross-cultural*.

Longitudinal research, whether quantitative or qualitative, is important because it allows for a direct focus on the nature and results of changes in children's lives as they move through key developmental and transition periods. All three of the chapters I have been asked to comment on have at least some longitudinal features in their research designs.

The chapter by Beth Kurtz-Costes, Rona McCall, and Wolfgang Schneider on acculturation (Chapter 6) offers the most traditional and extensive longitudinal design of the three. As the authors note, it is surprising that there have been so few longitudinal studies of acculturation. Although Kurtz-Costes, McCall, and Schneider collected data on both parents and children, they have longitudinal data only for the children. The 9- to 10-year old children from four cultural or subcultural groups completed questionnaires assessing German fluency, attitudes toward school, school-related anxiety, beliefs about academic outcomes, and academic self-concepts three times separated by 4-month intervals during the first year of data collection. The authors imply that longitudinal data will be collected in subsequent years, but they provide no rationale for the three time periods or the 4-month intervals. Are these time periods simply a matter of sampling convenience or are they related to key events in the children's lives that occur in school or at home that might be captured by such spacing of data collection? The documentation of transitional events and their immediate and long-term effects is a key strength of longitudinal design. Such documentation is not offered in this case, nor do the authors discuss why parents were interviewed only once.

Kurtz-Costes, McCall, and Schneider are correct in their claim that the longitudinal design will allow them to test for bidirectionality operating among factors relating to acculturation and that it will enable them to document the rate of acculturation and adaptation for the immigrant children. However, their claim that "this project will allow us to observe directly the ways in which the immigrant children change as they adjust to life in West Germany" seems overstated. Although quantitative longitudinal research of this type is far superior to cross-sectional studies for predicting important individual outcomes, repeated quantitative measures of discrete variables at distanced points in time cannot identify what is actually occurring in family, peer group, school, and other settings where children spend their time. Quantitative longitudinal studies can document change and, in the case of acculturation, measure adjustment. However, qualitative longitudinal studies (intensive interviewing or ethnography) are often necessary to fill in the sketchy pictures that emerge from more large-scale quantitative studies.

Finally, the longitudinal and comparative research design in Kurtz-Costes, McCall, and Schneider's study of acculturation also allows for the possibility of historical grounding and comparison. A longitudinal study is historically grounded when it places the study of particular groups over some limited period (from one to several years) in a broader historical context (see Heath, 1983). Since the authors have longitudinal data on children from four groups in East and West Germany, they can place their findings on acculturation and other developmental changes in a broader historical context. Given their review of other studies of acculturation, it appears that the authors are in a unique position to make very important contributions to the literature on acculturation in this regard.

Although the chapters by Paul Winterhoff and by Jonathan Tudge and Sarah Putnam (Chapters 8 and 9, respectively) have longitudinal elements, the design and analysis are much more micro in focus than the study by Kurtz-Costes, McCall, and Schneider. In Tudge and Putnam's study families were asked to keep their daily routines unchanged as much as possible during an observation period of 20 hours over the course of a week with the aim of capturing "the equivalent of an entire waking day." Tudge and his colleagues observed continuously over 2- to 4-hour blocks, but activities were coded only during 30-second windows every 5½ minutes. Given this design we have at a minimum a longitudinal period of 30 seconds. Although this is an extremely limited time period, the design does allow for the researchers to place this 30 seconds into a wider socioecological and temporal context. The authors collected observations on several types of activities (lessons, work, play, conversation, and others) that were coded into a number of lower-level categories (e.g., four categories of lessons, five categories of work). Since the observations occurred over a week, any particular 30-second slice of behavior representing one of the activities could be grounded in a wider context. Thus, at least in theory, children's behaviors within and across categories could be examined longitudinally. That is, the authors could search for possible developmental changes as exhibited in children's behavior over the course of a 30-second interval or by comparing behaviors in activities such as lessons recorded at different points in time over the week period. The problem with this possibility, however, is Tudge and Putnam's decision to restrict observations of activities to 30-second periods in line with Whiting and Edwards's system of spot coding. As a result, the authors may, for example, arbitrarily cut off observation of an unfolding activity rather than continue to monitor and record it until it reaches its natural conclusion or evolves into another activity in line with their coding scheme. Nevertheless, Tudge and Putnam's data are very detailed and rich, and some type of longitudinal microanalysis as outlined earlier may still be possible.

Winterhoff presents two different types of analysis in his chapter. First, he argues that constraining subsystems are historically formed and can be viewed from a diachronic perspective. As a result Winterhoff undertakes a macrocomparative analysis of agrarian and technocratic sociocultural systems in terms of how particular societies within each of these systems constrain or promote children's activities. Winterhoff focuses specifically on variations in settings for social activity, limits on the pool of possible social partners, and those persons designated as appropriate overseers of children's activities in the two systems by examining secondary data from reports of other researchers in a range of agrarian and technocratic societies. Here longitudinal analysis at the micro level would need to be linked with careful examination of historical changes in the societies regarding how constraining or enabling subsystems were formed and how they affected individual development over time. Although Winterhoff's overall research design would allow for such analysis, the data presented in his chapter document only differences across the systems. We are not presented with information regarding how these differences arose historically, nor documentation of how they may affect individual development.

In a second analysis Winterhoff presents longitudinal data on friendship development in two kindergarten classrooms in U.S. society. His purpose is to demonstrate variability in friendship development within highly similar constraining circumstances. In this more microanalysis Winterhoff traces the friendship histories of specific children. Here his analysis is much like that of Rizzo (1989, 1992) and not only demonstrates the possibility of variability in similar systems, but captures the complexity of friendship as a cultural process (see Corsaro, 1994). Winterhoff's analysis documents the developmental fluidity of actual friendships and how these friendships are constituted through the children's participation in everyday practices in the local school and peer cultures and the more general adult culture or society. Here the analysis is clearly longitudinal. However, its processual and interpretive design is quite different than the outcome and positivist design that is much more common in traditional research in developmental psychology.

In addition to being longitudinal all three studies have, to various degrees, multilevel and comparative research designs. Although Kurtz-Costes, McCall, and Schneider collect individual-level recall, attitudinal, and self-report data from parents and children, they also surveyed respondents for a range of information regarding their own positions and participation in a wide range of cultural and institutional settings (occupational, school, family). Thus, the authors are in a position to ground the individual-level data in a broader cultural context. Furthermore, the sample design allows for cross-cultural comparison since data were collected from children and parents of four groups in East and West Germany. As Kurtz-Costes, McCall, and Schneider argue the selection of these four groups will allow theoretically informed comparisons regarding the acculturation process. Given this impressive research design the authors' forthcoming analyses of these data should lead to groundbreaking contributions to work on children's acculturation and to comparative research on human development more generally.

Although Tudge and Putnam refer to their study of U.S. preschoolers in two cultural communities as a cross-level analysis, the overwhelming majority of their data (even though extremely rich) is limited to observations of everyday activities within families. Tudge and Putnam have data on parental occupation, education, and income, but how these socioeconomic categories can be linked to the family interaction data is not clear. The authors see their work as a complement to the research of Kohn on class and conformity. While stressing the importance of parental beliefs and values (the mainstay of Kohn's research), Tudge and Putnam argue correctly that data on what parents actually do in interaction with their children is crucial and missing in Kohn's work. The authors mention data on parental beliefs, but for now their study is only multileveled in that they have background information on social class and can relate their findings to Kohn's earlier work. Nonetheless, given the wide attention that Kohn's work on class differences in socialization has received despite its lack of behavioral data, Tudge and Putnam's contention that their data complement Kohn's "rather well" is correct and important.

Tudge and Putnam's chapter is clearly comparative and has the potential of being cross-cultural as well. Their initial analysis of the range of differences across the two communities regarding the occurrence and nature of lessons in everyday activity is fascinating and highly insightful. However, it is difficult to estimate how these differences are related to cultural differences in the two communities because the version of the chapter I read provided no information on these two communities beyond the social class of the respondents as measured by occupation, education, and income. The analysis would be much more powerful (and truly cross-cultural) given the reference to cultural communities in the title if the authors could present more information on the (1) history of these communities, (2) ethnic background of the residents, (3) presence of religious and fraternal organizations, and (4) degree of stability of residences and patterns of migration in the communities.

As I discussed earlier, Winterhoff presents two types of analysis, a macrocomparative analysis of how children's activities are constrained or promoted across different sociocultural systems and a microanalysis of friendship development in kindergarten classrooms to demonstrate variability within highly similar constraining circumstances. In this sense Winterhoff's analysis is multileveled, but the two levels of analysis in this paper are not clearly connected.

Winterhoff presents an interesting and insightful cross-cultural analysis of agrarian and technocratic systems at a macro level that provides a broad outline of how constraining subsystems "guide but do not determine the development of social relationships." Although Winterhoff's cross-cultural analysis documents important sociocultural differences, his microanalysis of friendship development within two highly similar U.S. kindergartens demonstrates the high level of variability in children's social development and cautions against temptations to assume "homogeneity of action within cultural groups" or "absolute heterogeneity across sociocultural systems."

Overall, these three chapters present numerous provocative theoretical ideas, innovative research designs for the study of human development and interpretive reproduction, and initial, but highly promising, empirical results. I look forward to reading future reports based on these research studies.

## References

Corsaro, W. A. (1992). Interpretive reproduction in children's peer cultures. *Social Psychology Quarterly*, *55*, 160–177.

(1993, June). *Transitions in early childhood: The promise of comparative, longitudinal ethnography*. Paper presented at "Meaning and Context: A Conference on Ethnographic Approaches to the Study of Human Development," Berkeley, CA.

(1994). Discussion, debate, and friendship processes: Peer discourse in U.S. and Italian nursery schools. *Sociology of Education*, *67*, 1–26.

Heath, S. B. (1983). *Ways with words: Language, life, and work in communities and classrooms*. Cambridge University Press.

Rizzo, T. (1989). *Friendship development among children in school.* Norwood, NJ: Ablex.

(1992). The role of conflict in children's friendship development. In W. A. Corsaro & P. J. Miller (Eds.), *Interpretive approaches to children's socialization* (pp. 95–113). San Francisco: Jossey-Bass.

# 15 Integrating Psychology into Social Science

*James Youniss*

The discipline of academic psychology chose long ago to ally itself with the natural sciences and to ground itself in biology. In this regard, the discipline went a separate way from other social sciences such as sociology, which based itself on social and political history. As psychology grew after World War II, it interacted less and less with other social sciences, so that the cumulative effect has been a relative independence in the search for basic laws of human behavior. As long as it was believed that such laws were founded on eons of biological evolution, psychologists needed only to apply proper scientific methods to find and describe them. In recent years, however, this belief has weakened as many psychologists have come to recognize the limits of this view and to acknowledge that society and culture are every bit as fundamental as biology.

This realization has presented psychology with a new problem of trying to find gainful ways to study society and culture. After decades of neglect, psychologists need to develop sophisticated concepts for dealing with them. Two options are either to strive toward workable definitions or to tap into the rich scholarship that the other social sciences provide. The complexity of the task suggests the value of taking the latter path, and were it to be taken, psychologists could build forward from, rather than repeating, the debates that have already gone on within these disciplines. For example, there is a well-traversed debate on whether social reality should be parsed into exogenous independent variables or conceived as constituting forces that create persons. If social factors operate only as independent variables, they serve mainly as limiting conditions for the natural operation of biological laws. If, on the other hand, society is constitutive of individuals, then social factors are essential to the very makeup of psychological structure. Another case is whether society should be seen as large structures with deterministic force or as a series of microinteractions that re-create macrostructures via joint action. The former position minimizes the role of individual actors, while the latter makes individuals essential parts of the constituting process.

The complexity of these issues, with their important implications, suggests the wisdom of choosing to collaborate with the other social sciences. One could hardly find more exemplary chapters in this regard than Dorothy Holland and Debra Skinner's and Jonathan Tudge and Sarah Putnam's (Chapters 7 and 9, respectively). Both begin with core topics in developmental psychology – child rearing and identity – and address them through conceptual schemes that are grounded in social science traditions outside of psychology. Tudge and Putnam draw from sociological studies of social class and rearing, language socialization, and microanalytic approaches to society. The result is that children from different social classes are seen to acquire separate orientations to literacy through an embedded series of everyday interactions that begin in the home and extend throughout the community.

Holland and Skinner study identity processes in adult women by drawing from anthropological work on ritual, sociohistorical studies of women, and a refined reading of identity development that is mediated by narrative structures and political discussion. The usual treatment of identity emphasizes the private reflections of confused youth, but Holland and Skinner describe a process in which reflection occurs in public through a ritual that integrates personal interest with shared feminine concerns and political consciousness. Although the women in question live in contemporary Nepal, they resemble women in nineteenth-century America who developed networks of sisterhood to alter traditional roles regarding family, self, and society. By studying the ritual of Tij songs, Holland and Skinner show that an individual quest for identity is shared by a cohort of women and is embedded in political events in this cohort's life.

The present commentary on these two chapters will focus on the concepts used by the authors and connections to their sources in the social science literature. I hope to show the positive implications that follow from use of these concepts and to encourage their further exploration in psychological research.

## Chapter 9

The authors anchor their study in the literature of the 1950s on social class differences in child-rearing practices. They cite two investigators whose work helped establish the topic 40 years ago. Bronfenbrenner (1958, 1961), concerned with apparent changes in children of the 1950s, hypothesized that parents had adopted new rearing practices that essentially altered the experience and form of childhood. Bronfenbrenner (1958) reviewed published surveys of child-rearing orientations in U.S. parents from 1920 through the 1950s. These surveys contained data on duration of breast feeding, initiation of toilet training, styles of discipline, and the like. Bronfenbrenner concluded that, in fact, middle-class parents had changed their orientation from a strict outlook in the 1920s to a more liberal approach in the 1950s. For example, rather than using punishment for misdeeds, parents had begun to use "psychological methods" of reasoning and appeals to guilt. In addition, he noted that working-class parents, who were somewhat liberal in the 1920s, had become more restrictive and, thus, showed a different trend from their middle-class counterparts. For instance, middle-class parents had begun to treat male and female children alike, but working-class parents were treating sons and daughters differently (Bronfenbrenner, 1961).

Bronfenbrenner attributed these trends to a shift in parental roles; fathers were becoming less authoritarian and more affectionate, while mothers were taking greater control over family regimens. Bronfenbrenner also noted that child-rearing experts had simultaneously altered the advice they gave parents. John B. Watson (1928), for instance, advised parents to feed infants on schedules while Benjamin Spock (1968) advised parents to feed infants on demand. Watson encouraged parents to control children's behavior strictly, while Spock favored the use of psychological techniques that emphasized maintaining the parent–child relationship over exerting parental power.

Kohn's (1959, 1969) studies documented differences in the ways that middle- and working-class parents of the 1950s exercised parental authority. He attributed the differences to preparation for the societal roles that children were expected to play in adulthood. Kohn (1959) presented mothers with instances of everyday childhood misdeeds and asked them to say how they would respond. He observed that working-class mothers were more likely than middle-class mothers to punish children for wild play, fighting with siblings, or disobeying. Middle-class mothers, in contrast, were more apt to appeal to reason so that children would alter their own behavior.

Kohn (1969) studied fathers and sons to test the notion that the kind of work that fathers did transferred to ways in which they disciplined their sons. He observed that fathers who were entrepreneurs or held management positions promoted self-directedness in their sons, while fathers who were working operatives or held bureaucratic positions promoted conformity in their sons. This result was also reported by Miller and Swanson (1958), confirming the thesis that the former fathers promoted independence in anticipation that their sons would take positions like those they themselves had. Working-class fathers valued "getting along," which closely matched the trait that was adaptive in their work. Hence, Kohn's general contention that rearing was founded on one's class and work position in society received strong empirical confirmation.

It is worth asking why psychologists at the time did not pursue these interesting results. Why, given these clear demonstrations, did psychologists ignore social class differences to search instead for universal practices that produced the efficient acquisition and internalization of ideal behavior? One possibility is that learning theory, which was at the time the dominant theoretical paradigm, encouraged focus on the abstract form of parent–child exchange, and this took precedence over the persons or their motives. If the form of a rearing practice matched the natural criteria for learning, acquisition and internalization should follow, no matter what parents intended or children wanted. In this theoretical framework, parents served primarily as abstract parts within a natural process. Once effective procedures were found, it was believed they could be taught to any parent who would then want to use them, regardless of social class or other considerations.

This thinking held sway until the 1980s, when psychologists began to acknowledge that parents were cognitive agents who approached the child-rearing function with beliefs about children's capacities and preferences for outcomes (Goodnow, 1988; McGillicuddy-DeLisi, 1982). This awareness allowed parents to be brought back into the rearing process as agents instead of mere functionaries. The acknowledgment of parent beliefs and cognition in general, permitted child rearing to be situated in real time and space so that parents were seen as entering the process with desires, knowledge, and anticipations. After undue delay, then, psychologists in the past decade have been able to study the kind of parent Bronfenbrenner or Kohn envisioned in the 1950s. These parents come to the task of child rearing, not as disinterested scientists, but as interested parties who want their children to succeed at what they believe will give them access to society's resources, such as jobs, good family life, positive social relations, and healthy character (Youniss, 1995).

Tudge and Putnam build on these recent insights. They assume that in observing the daily routines of children in different social class settings, they are likely to find them engaged in variable kinds of interactions with other persons. This expectation would follow from the societal orientations that parents and others bring as beliefs about childhood and society. It is not that parents who are professional know "more" about child rearing than do nonprofessional parents. Rather, they view the child differently in light of the positions they are in, which leads to differential choices in rearing and, in turn, reproduces their different perspectives on society.

This work closely connects with two other literatures. One is language socialization, which studies the cultural learning that results from language acquisition. It assumes that patterns of interactions peculiar to a culture are acquired implicitly through participation in parent–child linguistic exchanges. Ward (1971), Ochs (1984), and Heath (1983) have illustrated the point clearly in their ethnographic observations of language socialization. Each has studied mother–child language routines in everyday settings and found that forms of exchange establish roles, hierarchy, and interests. Parents' ostensible aim is to get children to speak a particular language, but in the process parents communicate much more. They socialize manners, ways of showing respect, inhibition to certain signals, and attention to personal details. Through repeated linguistic interactions, children become members of a culture because they learn formal interaction patterns that define a culture (Youniss, 1992).

The second literature expands on this definition of culture as forms of interaction that groups of persons share. This definition is found in Collins (1979), who represents a genre of thinking called microsociology. He has described culture as "the symbolic reflections upon communications about the conditions of daily life, and the more abstract transformations and distortions of these experiences that can be symbolically created – that is, the medium for conversations and personal exchanges that groups are formed and various states of self-consciousness are generated" (p. 172). It follows that culture is a result of the actions of individuals who create, sustain, and modify it through their interactions. Culture is expressed through everyday actions such as conversations: "the negotiation of partners to talk with and topics to be given sway . . . talk containing larger proportions of discussion, ideological debate, entertainment, gossip, or personal topics [whose] distinguishing feature is the expression of utterances in shared symbols with reality-defining effects for the persons involved" (p. 58).

When carried a step further, this definition yields clear implications for Tudge and Putnam's interest in rearing practices and social class differences. As already intimated in the work on language socialization, children acquire culture as a by-product of participation in everyday interactions with others during which conversational rules are specified, permissible topics are designated, and ways to achieve mutual understanding are co-constructed. Corsaro and Eder (1990) propose that children enter a culture "by interacting with others, [so as to] establish understandings that become fundamental social knowledge on which they continually build" (p. 200). Hence, development of social understanding is not coming to see "reality" as adults do, but consists in acquiring interaction and communication patterns that allow children to construct mutual understandings with other persons. In this manner, the very material of interactions differentiates one from another culture and one social class from another. From these behavioral differences, consciousness of one's class or status can be constructed.

Collins (1985) proposes that class distinctions are mediated by "rituals [that] are weapons upholding and renegotiating the class structure. They not only create the self, but they rank selves into different social classes" (p. 157). Turning then to children and ways they become stratified, one can see the process occurring through styles of thinking, speaking, and dressing, as well as through tastes and manners (Bourdieu & Passeron, 1977). This approach nicely meshes with Kohn's earlier work, which shows that as mothers and fathers encourage certain interaction patterns that serve immediate interests – for example, stopping siblings from fighting – they instill interaction forms that differentiate classes. Interaction forms are the means by which individuals in classes come to know one another in distinction from outsiders.

This approach to society, class, and culture is essentially compatible with a theory of development that is based on construction, acknowledges social structure, but proposes that individuals are agents whose interactions are necessary to create and transform these structures (Tesson & Youniss, 1995). Society defined at the micro level readily links with a developmental psychology that gives agency to individuals through processes of construction that are social in nature. This brings up a key point that in coming out of its isolation to learn from other social disciplines, psychology need not give up insights it has previously gained. Individual agency and social construction are two such cases. Another advantage of Tudge and Putnam's work, therefore, is that its conceptual structure builds on other disciplines in such a way as to allow integration with a definite theory of psychological development. The psychological individual and society are integrated, not arbitrarily, but in the very interactive processes that comprise everyday life. Conversational styles, eating manners, forms of discipline, and expressions of humor serve as means for individuals to form identities and for identities to integrate persons into larger social organizations of family, class, and culture.

It is not incidental that several of the authors cited in this synthesis have noted, along with Tudge and Putnam, how participation in daily interactions can differentially prepare children for schooling. Heath (1983) and Ward (1971) showed how conversational patterns applicable to southern black rural areas run counter to communication patterns presumed by schools. Bourdieu and Passeron (1977) likewise argue that schools value kinds of thinking and communication that facilitate learning for some, but impede learning for other children. What Tudge and Putnam add is that already by 4 years of age, children from Holden and Summit have become adapted to separate cultures that are likely to benefit one, but not the other, when they enter another culturally reproductive institution of the school.

## Chapter 7

Holland and Skinner, who are anthropologists, approach identity in a different manner than usually found in the psychological literature. Rather than using the framework of stages, emphasizing an individualistic developmental process, and limiting focus to adolescence, the authors study women of mixed ages and demonstrate how identity formation is mediated by a public process that drives individual reflection. They chose to study an intriguing ritual in which individual women create songs to express personal feelings and reflect on normative roles in groups that provide empathic commentary. The group's feedback presumably provides input to the individual's self-reflection, which, in turn, leads to new articulation of feelings in recursive series. Hence, what is typically viewed as a private event is made into a public process in which individual identity is merged with social, cultural, and political considerations.

This approach to identity is conceptually related to the larger frames of *sisterhood*, or the shared psychological world of women, and *political consciousness* in which women view alterations of their marital roles as part of a political change that is taking place in Nepalese society. Because this approach is quite removed from the usual depiction of identity in terms of the lone adolescent musing over an uncertain future, it is worthwhile to elaborate on the literatures to which it is related. One link is to social-historical studies that have tried to uncover the bases of changing roles and relationships for women in Western societies. Another link is to the emerging literature on self through narrative. And a third link is to studies of public discussion in political socialization and identity. Concepts used by Holland and Skinner can be traced to these bases, and their empirical data illustrate how they can enrich a sociohistorical understanding of identity.

### *Women's History*

Over the past 20 years, an extensive literature has developed on the history of family life and women's roles as wives, mothers, and individuals. A portion of this literature has looked at women in the United States since the Revolution. Degler (1980) offers a perspective that meshes with the present study. His portrait begins with the 1820s and the dawning of the middle-class family with its emphasis on a division between women's domestic and men's societal orientations. By the middle of the nineteenth century, this division gave rise to the "doctrine of separate spheres" in which women were assigned the roles of devoted wife and mother and men were given society outside the home as their domain.

As the century progressed, women began to balk at their assignment and sought alternatives to it. Among other things, they reduced fertility by half from 1800 to 1900. Further, women increasingly chose to leave the confines of the home to engage in charitable and political activities that were directed to the moral improvement of society. They formed and joined organizations that were devoted to eliminating prostitution and sales of alcohol, on the one hand, and to obtaining voting and legal rights for women, on the other hand. By the century's end, these organizations had hundreds of thousands of members, as more and more middle-class women throughout the country saw themselves as potent moral-political agents.

A parallel between this shift in idealized women's roles in the nineteenth-century United States and in present-day Nepal is worth noting. The complaints of the Nepalese women, Renu and Kamala, are clearly aimed at the traditional family roles for women toward husbands, in-laws, and parents. These complaints are expressed through unhappiness with men's dominance and greater freedom and balanced by awareness that greater freedom for women may be possible under the coming democracy. The complaints of nineteenth-century U.S. middle-class women were also voiced against gender differences in traditional family roles that favored men and put women under continuous threat of pregnancy, loneliness, and hardship. As in Nepal, women in the United States placed hope in the political system, which promised individual freedom in principle. U.S. women took the principle seriously and sought legal reform that would grant them rights of property, child custody, and suffrage. The Tij songs are quite explicit about hopes that the political principle of democracy will help women achieve greater gender equality and personal autonomy.

Another parallel between Nepalese and U.S. women is seen in sisterhood, which serves as a major mediator for changing norms for women's identity. The Tij songs articulate individual feelings of unhappiness with the roles of wives, but the power of the expressions comes from their being shared by the other members of the group. The songs therefore provide opportunities for mutual validation among women who share similar life circumstances. By placing one's experiences in front of one's sisters, individual women gain support while they offer supporting validation in return. Degler (1980) and Cott (1977) have documented the importance of women-to-women relationships in the transformation of women's roles in nineteenth-century America. Women shared their private experiences through letters and visits in order to express their pain, get advice, and achieve mutual understanding. Subsequently, membership in organizations gave them further opportunities for sisterhood and the positive functions it served. Although the Tij ritual takes a different form from its U.S. counterparts, it is similar in function in that it gives women occasion to express their unhappiness with traditional roles and to explore alternatives that women can make real were they to act collaboratively as sisters.

There is a telling reality to these data that ought to inform the psychological literature on identity. Reflections on one's roles and relationships is first of all not a unique event, but usually occurs simultaneously in one's peers. Focus on the individual has blinded researchers to the common plight and joint reflection that actually shape the identity process. One can imagine that there are numerous equivalents to the Tij ritual that for youth include informal get-togethers at which peers share experiences and discuss ways to solve common problems with families, friends, and society. Failure to study the shared aspect of the identity process is a void in the literature that needs to be filled in order to counter the present surrealism that makes identity too abstract and individualistic.

### *Self and Narrative*

Grotevant (1993) has summarized potential gains from applying narrative concepts to the study of identity. Narrative is a genre of thinking in which individuals are viewed as organizing personal experience to construct thematic coherence in their concepts of self (Gergen & Gergen, 1983). Narratives are stories that denote who the self is, how the self got to be, and where the self is headed. A story is not an objective recounting or a disinterested depiction of the self that might be gotten, say, from a psychometric assessment. It is rather an individual's construction that justifies, thematizes, to provide the self with identifiable form, content, and meaning.

Consider the woman Renu from each of these perspectives. On a standard personality instrument, she might be categorized as "depressed," "lonely," "nurturant, but frustrated," and even "suicidal." From her Tij narratives, however, she is also seen as having woven her feelings into a story of hardship that bonds her feelings with those of other women. In addition, her narratives specify the sources of her pain: her parents, who failed to educate her; her husband, who does not respect her; and her in-laws, who treat her as a servant. Finally, her narratives achieve resolution with the prospect of a better future that would result if women joined together in a common effort to change the political structure in Nepal. This story does not eliminate the traits that an instrument might quantify, but it enriches them by adding meaning to a self that is situated in history, a framework of interpersonal relationships, and a political setting that deals with gender roles and justice.

There is more to learn from Tij songs than is at first evident from the parallel with self-narratives. The stories are composed for an audience of other women, as is noted in Kamala's greetings "Oh, dominated sisters of Nepal" and "Listen sisters, listen society." Obviously, their stories are not intended solely for private musing or to gain others' sympathy. They are designed to show solidarity with other women and to invite other women to join in critical reflection. To get this effect, the stories identify shared sources of problems and joint action as a means for resolution.

The stories command attention because they have historical validity and are politically grounded. As such, they uncover a process that goes beyond the Holden Caufield–esque private reflection of the confused U.S. adolescent. The stories are told to others to elicit public reaction that provides feedback to the narrator and encourages other women to listen to the author's point of view in order to engender unity among the participants. Although Holland and Skinner do not describe in their chapter the interactive component of the ritual, one can assume that songs generate exchanges that have effects on the group and the individuals. Hence, members of a group have their personal views validated, contradicted, and elaborated on, so that individuals no longer have to operate in private uncertainty but can function within a relationship of mutual feminine understanding.

In Grotevant's view, the narrative approach acknowledges that individuals continuously revise the stories by which they know themselves. This feature helps overcome some of the stiltedness associated with the stage approach to identity – for example, that identity must be resolved before individuals can proceed to the next stage of intimacy. One sees in the Tij songs that the intimate marital relationship is an occasion for revising identity with new input. The marital experience sharpens questions about the roles of dutiful daughter and wife and encourages women to think of themselves in a marital relationship of mutual respect with husbands. While confusion is evident in the songs, it is not due to a failure to resolve the prior stage. Confusion seems more likely due to current experiences of hardship that could not have been anticipated at a younger age. The experience of marriage stimulates women to construct new narratives that revalue their past lives and the traditional roles they accepted. The insight helps women imagine new roles and a political path to a more liberated future.

In sum, the narrative approach removes the restrictiveness of the stage model that gives identity an artificial and abstract air. It brings the identity process out of the private realm and makes it public so that the individual's reflections necessarily involve reciprocal feedback. This public aspect adds assurance that self-reflection will not be solipsistic by forcing the self to deal with a shared reality that has historical and political dimensions. Narratives are not just for self, but implicate others. In brief, "self narratives function much as histories . . . for such purposes as justification, criticism, and social solidification" (Gergen & Gergen, 1983, p. 256).

## *Political Talk*

Gamson (1992) has asked how people can form political ideas when the media continually bombards them with facts, opinions, and judgments. If they simply record what they were presented, they would have a jumbled array of the mixed messages that the media convey. A more likely prospect is that people interpret the input by constructing sense of the input. Gamson proposes that the process of making sense often takes the form of collective discussions in which individuals seek one another's interpretations through the free exchange of ideas. One person gives an opinion, another questions assumptions, a third offers an alternative framework, and so on, until the individuals have expressed multiple views that allow revision of initially held ideas.

Gamson's empirical data consist of 37 group discussions in which 188 adults exchanged ideas about current political issues, including Arab–Israeli relations and equal opportunity/affirmative action laws. Gamson proposed that discussions could be ordered around three components: (1) Most discussions dealt with a perceived injustice that came to be expressed in terms of moral indignation; (2) members of the group also discussed agency by assigning responsibility and suggesting ways that conditions could be altered to remove the injustice; and (3) in the course of most discussions, an identity component emerged as participants differentiated "we" from "they," or those who caused the problem versus those who would solve it.

Gamson's scheme can be readily applied to the Tij ritual, at least in principle. The songs deal with injustice and felt harm to individual wives, and to women in general. Agency is assigned to women as sisters who are asked to take remedial action while they work toward an imagined future. And solidaristic identity is created as husbands, parents, and in-laws are identified as sources of the problem (they), while women are defined as actors who will prevail (we). Although the songs refer to particular women as they publicly admit their problems, the songs encourage others to acknowledge that they share similar difficulties that should not be allowed to suppress women in the future.

The Tij ritual is a special case of political talk that affords women the opportunities to make sense of their lives. The process of talking allows women to see themselves as having been constituted through historical and political processes. Since we psychologists are so used to treating identity as the property of an individual self, it is worth elaborating on this point. Tij songs encourage women to think of themselves in terms of history, meaning both tradition and the opportunity their cohort has to redirect it. But more than contemplation is at stake since women are encouraged to make use of political change and take action by becoming involved in Nepal's political system. The self that emerges is clearly being embedded in history and politics so that self-definition is only incidently private, but very much public and cultural. In Gamson's (1992) terms, "Being a collective agent implies being part of a 'we' who can do something. The identity component of collective action frames is about the process of defining this 'we,' typically in opposition to some 'they' who have different interests or values" (p. 84).

## Conclusion

The authors of these two chapters promised to show how traditional topics in the field of development can be approached gainfully from the perspective of a culturally sensitive psychology. Both pairs of authors delivered on their promise with data that are interesting and novel, as well as interpretations that force one to take the cultural-historical approach seriously. My role has been to show how these efforts are related to approaches in other social sciences and to identify the conceptual groundings from which psychologists might draw in order to bring sociohistorical considerations into their thinking. By showing the usefulness of these conceptions as they bear on child-rearing and identity, I hope that more psychologists will look to these other disciplines as potential allies and be encouraged to cooperate with them in the future.

It may have been evident that the concepts I have used were selected so as to be compatible with two main premises about development. One is that individuals are agents who participate in the construction of society, culture, and history. This is one premise that has a strong basis in developmental psychology and should not be abandoned, say, in the face of deterministic models of social structure (Tesson & Youniss, 1995). The other is that personal agency actually works through collective action involving reciprocal exchange, interactive feedback, and mutual understanding. Society does not preexist to shape individuals, but individuals construct society, or else it could not have existence (Corsaro & Eder, 1990). In the same vein, individuals cannot construct society alone but need one another, because, outside of interpersonal relations, there could be no society. Some of the work cited by the authors of these two chapters goes back 40 years when researchers were trying to understand the place of social forces in psychological development. One can only imagine how advanced the field would be today had others built on this early work. More significantly, one can hope that work of the quality and freshness of these two chapters will encourage others now to take up the task of integrating what we know about the psychological individual with what we know about society, history, and culture.

## References

Bourdieu, P., & Passeron, J.-C. (1977). *Reproduction in education, society, and culture*. London: Sage.

Bronfenbrenner, U. (1958). Socialization and social class through time and space. In E. E. Maccoby, T. M. Newcomb, & E. L. Hartley (Eds.), *Readings in social psychology* (pp. 400–425). New York: Holt, Rinehart, & Winston.

(1961). The changing American child: A speculative analysis. *Journal of Social Issues*, *17*, 6–18.

Collins, R. (1979). *Credential society*. New York: Academic Press.

(1985). *Three sociological traditions*. New York: Oxford University Press.

Corsaro, W. A., & Eder, D. (1990). Children's peer cultures. *Annual Review of Sociology*, *16*, 197–220.

Cott, N. F. (1977). *The bonds of womanhood: "Woman's sphere" in New England, 1780–1835*. New Haven, CT: Yale University Press.

Degler, C. (1980). *At odds: Women and the family in America from the revolution to the present*. New York: Oxford University Press.

Gamson, W. A. (1992). *Talking politics*. Cambridge University Press.

Gergen, K. J., & Gergen, M. M. (1983). Narratives of the self. In T. R. Sarbin & K. E. Scheibe (Eds.), *Studies in social identity* (pp. 251–273). New York: Praeger.

Goodnow, J. J. (1988). Parents' ideas, actions, and feelings: Models and methods from developmental and social psychology. *Child Development, 59*, 286–320.

Grotevant, H. D. (1993). The integrative nature of identity: Bringing the soloists to the choir. In J. Kroger (Ed.), *Discussions on ego identity* (pp. 121–146). Hillsdale, NJ: Erlbaum.

Heath, S. B. (1983). *Ways with words*. Cambridge University Press.

Kohn, M. L. (1959). Social class and the exercise of parental authority. *American Sociological Review, 24*, 352–366.

(1969). *Class and conformity*. Homewood, IL: Dorsey.

McGillicuddy-DeLisi, A. V. (1982). Parental beliefs about developmental processes. *Human Development, 25*, 192–200.

Miller, D. R., & Swanson, G. E. (1958). *The changing American parent: A study in the Detroit area*. New York: Wiley.

Ochs, E. (1984). Clarification and culture. In D. Shiffrin (Ed.), *Georgetown University Roundtable on Language and Linguistics* (pp. 325–341). Washington, DC: Georgetown University Press.

Spock, B. (1968) *Baby and child care*. New York: Hawthorn.

Tesson, G., & Youniss, J. (1995). Micro sociology and psychological development: A sociological interpretation of Piaget's theory. In A. M. Ambert (Ed.), *Sociological studies of children* (pp. 101–126). Greenwich, CT: JAI Press.

Ward, M. C. (1971). *Them children: A study in language learning*. New York: Holt, Rinehart, & Winston.

Watson, J. B. (1928). *Psychological care of infant and child*. New York: Norton.

Youniss, J. (1992). Parent and peer relations in the emergence of cultural competence. In H. McGurk (Ed.), *Childhood social development* (pp. 131–147). Hove: Erlbaum.

(1995). Rearing children for society. In J. Smetana (Ed.), *Parent beliefs in context: New directions in developmental psychology* (pp. 37–55). San Francisco: Jossey-Bass.

# Author Index

Italic numbers indicate pages on which full citations appear.

# Subject Index